Contents

Preface

ALTHOUGH Ronsard holds an established position as the greatest French poet of any period prior to the nineteenth century, his reputation has a certain ambivalence. In recent years his poetry has been subjected more thoroughly than ever before to scholarly research, yet few critics discuss the fundamental character of his creative imagination, his specifically *poetic* powers, and many readers still find him, understandably enough, a 'difficult' poet. The more ambitious poems, in particular, may seem disconcerting at first sight, and even the love poetry is not always as accessible as the better-known 'anthology pieces' might lead one to expect.

If one sets aside the initial problem posed by the notorious frequency of Ronsard's erudite allusions (which the existence of a properly annotated edition has done much to alleviate), the difficulty arises in the first place from the fact that Ronsard demands from the modern reader flexibility of taste and of critical habit. Preoccupations of Romantic origin with 'originality' or with the sense of a direct communication of lived experience ('sincerity') have to be drastically modified if one is to appreciate a sixteenth-century poem; the influence of the traditional discipline of rhetoric – to isolate only one factor – predisposes the poet to present individual experience within the framework of established modes of expression, to the point at which a declaration of love in a mid-sixteenth-century poem

Ronsard the poet

may be almost indistinguishable from its equivalent in Petrarch or a classical Latin poet. Once such factors have been taken into account, a new kind of enjoyment may be released for the reader, not only in the full perception of Ronsard's brilliance in modulating a well-worn theme, but also in the search at a deeper level for those recurrent preoccupations and anxieties, absent from lesser poets, which give his work a fundamentally human centre. This leads us to the second major difficulty: Ronsard's poetry explores unfamiliar areas of experience in unfamiliar ways. 'Philosophical' and 'scientific' notions deriving from a contemporary world-view; religious and political argument; overt preoccupation with fame and financial backing; vatic inspiration, myths and lyres: such recurrent elements cannot be ignored by the reader, yet they may be hard to incorporate fully into a modern sensibility. Ronsard's education and environment were totally different from our own: he experienced the world differently. What is more, the focus is always changing, both within individual poems and from one poem or *recueil* to another: Ronsard is addicted to unexpected shifts of style, tone and subject matter, at times amounting to apparent self-contradiction. Hence his work does not respond easily to an attempt to grasp its meaning as a whole. Scève's *Délie*, although complex, can be seen as an enclosed and self-contained unit; d'Aubigné's expansive rhetoric is always related to a clear moral conviction. The centre of Ronsard's universe, by contrast, is much harder to establish: it is governed by a restless imaginative power which draws into itself an immense variety of contrasting elements, and which can therefore not be defined within a single frame of reference.

The object of this volume is to familiarize the reader with the features of Ronsard's world and with his recurrent preoccupations; to discuss some of his poetic aims and modes of expression as part of a living and developing whole; and, in particular, to study in a number of different contexts the operation of his poetic imagination: that is to say, the process by which the 'external' materials provided by contemporary culture and history are absorbed and transformed through the medium of

Preface

poetry. The volume does not attempt a systematic coverage of all the genres and themes treated by Ronsard, or of his biography or place in literary history: it takes for granted a good deal of factual material which can easily be obtained from standard studies of Ronsard and his milieu. The book has a different kind of comprehensiveness, proposing a range of modes of interpretation which should, between them, throw light on virtually any poem in the corpus. The special nature of Ronsard's cultural and historical environment is not neglected – indeed, it constitutes a central theme of five of the seven chapters – but the principal emphasis is placed on the *poetic* reactions which such factors provoke in Ronsard. In so far as the volume sets up a dialogue between his imaginative universe and the world in which he lived, it is the voice of poetry which predominates.

*

* *

*

Since the range of Ronsard's vision is so broad, and since it constantly escapes the limits of a single interpretation, it seemed natural to adopt the 'symposium' form, to invite several *seiziémistes* to bring their individual competence to the understanding of certain major centres of attention. Each of the contributors is personally acquainted with some at least of the others; as the project evolved, ideas were exchanged, interpretations discussed, the pattern adjusted somewhat in order to arrive at a better balance. At the same time, the contributors were encouraged to explore their material in the way they wanted, to formulate an individual view rather than to conform strictly to a predetermined programme: each chapter is an independent unit, adopting its own approach and style, selecting its own material. Yet at many points the paths meet, illuminating some central area from different but complementary angles. Sometimes, indeed, the main lines of an argument appear in two separate chapters, while a poem may be discussed in detail by more than one contributor. Such convergences

Ronsard the poet

have been allowed to stand, while some cross-reference has been provided to increase the sense of a connected whole.

The arrangement of the seven chapters, although not rigorous, is also not arbitrary. The first gives a broad, inclusive view of the principal features of Ronsard's poetic world; the last, while dealing with the later phases of his creativity, is also retrospective and demonstrates that many fundamental preoccupations remained constant to the very end. The intervening chapters consider Ronsard's materials and their transformation in five focal areas: the poetry of love, neo-platonism, myth, music and politics.

Chapter 1, then, surveys the shapes and processes, the landscapes, the mythical figures and personifications through which Ronsard's imagination customarily operates. It shows that he exploited a sixteenth-century world-view, but created from it a distinctive poetic vision, with its own priorities. Water, sunlight and sound constantly recur; the circle and the curve, clouds and dreams, movement, absorption, metamorphosis; and these imaginative preoccupations are inevitably linked with certain predominant values and concepts. Abundance, fertility and continuity are affirmed as against their opposite poles: emptiness, sterility, impermanence, dissolution and death. This balance between a positive poetic world and its negative counterpart often betrays an underlying uncertainty. The poet's need for communication and identification, his aspiration to extend his experience beyond the limits of finite personality, pervade his work from beginning to end; but the same factors suggest, too, a profound dissatisfaction with 'reality', with the world of everyday contingencies. Thus it is not surprising that among the most characteristic inhabitants of Ronsard's poetic landscape one finds figures embodying plenitude and deprivation, ambivalent personifications of fame, and, above all, a group of mythological deities representing poetry itself: poetry is here both the vehicle and the central theme.

The second and third chapters demonstrate Ronsard's transposition of two of the most powerful literary and intellectual traditions available to a sixteenth-century poet: petrarchism and neoplatonism. Chapter 2 analyses first the early Cassandre cycle of love poetry, in which the poet's desire to 'extend his experience' is embodied in a constant striving after beauty: a beauty compounded of both erotic and aesthetic pleasure, yet transcending both. This constant preoccupation draws upon the established attitudes of the petrarchan lover, transforming them without at any point seriously questioning their value. In the Hélène cycle, by contrast, the prevalent note is one of disillusionment: there is friction between the formal petrarchan situation, on the one hand, and the ironic portrayal of Hélène's individual temperament and of the poet's own advancing age on the other. The world of ideal beauty is no longer confidently affirmed; it has ceased to be the goal of an exuberant and dynamic quest, and where it appears, is now shown to be subject to temporal limitations, or even to be wholly illusory. Hence the antithesis between the two cycles illustrates, within a chronological schema (they are separated by a quarter of a century), the divided world of chapter 1, its energies and its uncertainties.

Chapter 3 shows how Ronsard exploited certain elements of a neoplatonist current of thought which was becoming popular in France in the middle third of the sixteenth century. The tendency towards poetic stylization makes the identification of committed philosophical positions in Ronsard difficult: his persona is inclined to shift, sometimes quite abruptly, between metaphysical idealism and an overwhelming preoccupation with sensuous experience. In the love poetry, neoplatonist notions and images have an essentially decorative function, or – as in the courtly *cartels* – are imposed by external demands. It seems that Ronsard, although interested in Ficino's claim for love (even physical love) as a means to perfection, never fully understood it and became increasingly sceptical of it. Elsewhere, he used a neoplatonist framework to buttress his claims for the poet's status: the belief that the poet is in some sense divinely inspired remained with him throughout his career, though his confidence in it was markedly in decline from the later 1550s onwards. It was perhaps above all in the hymns that

Ronsard the poet

Ronsard explored most deeply the religious nature of man and the cosmos: his poetic, mythopœic vision, transposing philosophical elements drawn mainly from neoplatonism, allowed him to probe central areas of man's experience – in particular, his ability to conceive of and aspire towards perfection – without falling into the quicksands of theological controversy.

The myths of Greece and Rome, perceived through a literary tradition as well as a philosophical one, provided Ronsard with his most wide-ranging and perhaps his most complex set of materials. Chapter 4 considers first his elaboration of a 'mythological style', analogous in many ways to contemporary modes in the visual arts: its central features are richness of surface texture, multiplicity, discontinuity and the creation of ambiguities at the borderline between 'reality' and 'myth'. The second part of the chapter attempts to assess the extent to which Ronsard's use of myth may be seen as allegorical. Reviewing some of the central areas of experience projected through his myths, it shows the conflict between the ideal of poetry as a quintessential form of truth, and the circumstances, internal and external, which prevented Ronsard from realizing that ideal. Myth as image prevails, in the end, over the systematization of mythological thought: the centre of Ronsard's universe is aesthetic rather than metaphysical; but – as chapter 3 had already shown – the elements of an intellectual structure remain none the less a fundamental part of his imaginative experience.

Within the world-view of the mid-sixteenth century, music held a privileged place. Echoing the divine proportion of the cosmos, it theoretically had the power, when properly composed, to re-establish order in man's soul, to calm his passions and hence, on a more ambitious scale, to bring peace to a nation in conflict with itself. In these respects its role was analogous to that of poetry, the harmonies of which are also based on numerical proportion. Elements of this belief are reflected in the musical practice of the period; at the same time, singing, playing and dancing formed an essential part of court life. Thus it is not surprising that Ronsard's poetry is steeped in musical reference of one kind and another. Chapter 5 discusses how far

[6]

Preface

Ronsard was involved in the musicmaking of his time, examines his theoretical writings on music, the presence of musical metaphor and myths in his poetry, and the ways in which he exploits aspects of contemporary musical entertainment for imaginative purposes. Here, as elsewhere, Ronsard gives absolute priority to his own medium, despite his nominal adherence to the theory that the best poetry, following what was thought to be the Greek practice, should be sung. Musical setting he leaves to others, making only minor concessions to their formal requirements; the whole spectrum of musical theory and practice is transposed into the poetic domain, where it becomes primarily a metaphor for the powers and diversity of poetry itself. Hence music, like myth, is for Ronsard a way of both illustrating and commenting on poetic creation; it, too, facilitates the transference between external reality and imaginative vision, conferring a special aesthetic status on the contexts in which it appears.

Among the circumstances which resisted the full realization of Ronsard's poetic ideal, political events and the debates they provoked are pre-eminent. Chapter 6 shows in detail how, at the end of the Italian wars and the beginning of the wars of religion (1558–63), Ronsard responded to the need to write poetry of a public nature, voicing the policy of the king and subsequently entering into a personal – though still public – debate with leading Calvinists. Throughout his career Ronsard's poetry had been and was to remain deeply bound up with a vision of the destiny of the nation, for which he attempted to provide a prescriptive model based largely, once again, on myth. In this context the central episode represented primarily by the *opuscules* of 1558–9 and the *Discours* of 1562–3 constitutes both a test case and a crisis. As the mouthpiece of official policy, Ronsard was forced to register bewildering shifts of political and moral position, at one moment advocating war, at the next celebrating peace and the virtues of the nation's former enemies: far from transcending temporal limitations, as he had once envisaged, his poetry was now subject to the contingencies of history. Moreover, such poetry

Ronsard the poet

had to adopt a style readily accessible to a wide audience, while Calvinist writers, unambiguously asserting the priority of truth over the medium, were not slow to attack Ronsard's notorious veneration of pagan sources, his use of myth and his moral equivocations. In replying to such charges, Ronsard in the end reasserted his belief in the freedom and superiority of the poetic imagination. There is little doubt, however, that the questioning which his view of poetry underwent at this stage had a lasting effect, emphasizing with greater clarity both the tensions within the poetic universe itself, and the cleavage between this universe and any other value system.

Chapter 6 is thus concerned with a watershed in the development of Ronsard's poetry. Although the lack of adequate patronage was already posing acute problems by the mid-1550s, and although the later part of Charles IX's reign represents in many respects a relatively stable and prosperous period in his career, it is nevertheless undeniable that the energies and ambitions represented by the early odes, *amours* and hymns were never to be fully recaptured. There is a continuing pre-occupation with certain themes and styles, the fabric of the universe has not changed substantially, and Ronsard's poetic powers as illustrated by much of his later poetry reach a new peak of refinement. But in the 1570s and 1580s his awareness of physical decay becomes increasingly apparent, pointing towards the personal experience of death in the *Derniers Vers*; the final collapse of the *Franciade* project removed the central focus of his aspiration towards a supreme poetic achievement; while events in the political and religious domains continued to provide a sinister and ironic commentary on his prophetic view of the nation's destiny.

Chapter 7 demonstrates the continuities: the coexistence of movement and solidity, of the dynamic and the stable, still provides a central axis of Ronsard's imagination and style; so, too, does the oscillation between 'nearness' and 'distance', concreteness and stylization, which suggests once again a poetry conscious of its own relationship with reality and of its power to transpose and transform. But inevitably a sense of

Preface

withdrawal makes itself felt; the vision has lost some of its amplitude, and a note of irony begins to predominate in the treatment of myth and – as chapter 2 had already shown – of love. Likewise, Ronsard continues to gather contemporary nobility and royalty into a poetic pantheon, distancing them from the fast-disintegrating world of political realities, and from time to time he himself joins them in his role of Orphic priest; but the disguise is not complete and the consciousness of mortality intrudes more and more insistently. The tension is prolonged to the last: in the *Derniers Vers* Ronsard struggles to impose on the reality of his own death – precariously yet triumphantly – the harmony of an aesthetic structure.

The function of the epilogue is twofold. In the first place, by probing in depth the structure and fabric of a single sonnet, it reveals Ronsard's command of his stylistic resources, his ability to reorganize the conventional patterns of language in terms of a higher poetic vision. Since the analysis takes into account the revisions to which this poem – like so many others in the corpus – was subjected, it illustrates also Ronsard's restless search for harmony of form and expressive precision. In the second place, the sonnet is chosen as a microcosm of Ronsard's imaginative world: many of the preoccupations and procedures considered in the preceding chapters are here seen emblematically woven together, constituting an eloquent restatement of Ronsard's view of the universe, of love, of himself, and – by implication – of poetry.

For if this volume has an overall thesis, it is that the exigencies of poetry itself dominate every aspect of Ronsard's work. 'Sur toutes choses tu auras les Muses en reverence, voire en singuliere veneration. . . . Tu seras laborieux à corriger et limer tes vers, et ne leur pardonneras non plus qu'un bon jardinier à son ante, quand il la voit chargée de branches inutiles.' (*L* XIV, 4, 6–7; *Pl* II, 996, 997) The preoccupation with poetic style and texture, and the incessant probing of the status and nature of poetry together form the central motive power of his whole output. Whether directly or obliquely, the creative imagination comments on itself in every poem. It comments,

[9]

too, on the external conditions in which it operates: literary traditions, philosophical and religious modes of thinking, the social milieu, the political and historical moment all become the materials of a poetry which goes beyond them but which also, in the process, evaluates them.

After fifty years or more of detailed research, the complexity of Ronsard's vision, his wide-ranging *intelligence* as a poet, need no further demonstration. What is still too often ignored, perhaps, is his extraordinary capacity for converting 'external' structures into 'internal' ones, and the degree of imaginative judgement which is implied by the ability to confer on them a new meaning. The world-view of his day was already, in many respects, a fragmented one: the medieval dream of an encyclopedia of knowledge reflecting a structured universe had been extended, by the mid-sixteenth century, to the point at which it began to disintegrate. This is already apparent in the work of Rabelais, whose *Tiers Livre* seems to belie the optimistic education programmes and utopias of the first two books; Montaigne illustrates the same process at a later stage. All three writers were fundamentally in search of a reliable inward criterion, in the light of which the moral, aesthetic, and intellectual domains (and the relationship between them) might be confidently assessed. The search, amid the immense fabric of the Renaissance universe, could not but remain exploratory, unresolved, itself fragmentary, but it provided an imaginative impetus which – like Rabelais's Diogenic barrel – proved virtually inexhaustible. Furthermore, Rabelais and Montaigne, no less than Ronsard, were deeply preoccupied with the act of writing itself: their work constantly examines itself, judges itself, questions its own status. For Ronsard, this inquiry was, in the end, predominantly an aesthetic one: his ambition to establish the autonomy of poetry, its independent seriousness, is not paralleled in Rabelais or Montaigne. Perhaps equally important is the fact that his claim for the 'prophetic' nature of the poetic vision failed, in one sense at least: his role as mentor of the nation was not realized, and his notion of poetry as an oblique expression of supernatural truths did in fact rapidly

Preface

become outdated (to be revived, in a different form, some 300 years later). For the failure liberated, precisely, his poetic imagination, allowing it to create its own structure: not the rigid, imprisoning system of ideas rejected by both Rabelais and Montaigne, but an organic structure, capable of evolving and shifting its focus, of embracing fertile antitheses without needing to resolve them.

Many of Ronsard's poems have long since acquired for themselves an immortality close to that which he himself dreamed of: their appeal is direct, and they seem to require little or no commentary. The reading even of these, however, can gain in depth if they are related as fully as possible to the *œuvre* seen both as a totality and as an evolving process: the exploration of this organic structure may restore to all of its individual parts their special colour and richness.

*

* *

*

Without the impetus provided by the insights of three critics in particular – Marcel Raymond, Henri Weber and Gilbert Gadoffre – this volume could hardly have existed in anything like its present form. Their influence is acknowledged again and again in the individual chapters, and it is to them, first of all, that I should like to pay homage here.

Professor Gadoffre deserves the further thanks of all the contributors for making available to them in two successive years his hospitality, as well as his understanding of Ronsard and his times, at the Institut Collégial Européen at Loches. On the second of these occasions (July 1972), the contents of the volume were discussed in detail by a distinguished international group of scholars, to whom my colleagues and I are deeply indebted: we regret only that no record of the proceedings could be included in the volume.

I am personally most grateful to Professor D. G. Charlton and to Dr M. Jeanneret, both of whom, in the early stages of the project, gave advice that was to prove decisive to its

Ronsard the poet

evolution. And, now that the volume is all but complete, I wish above all to thank the contributors themselves: for their co-operation and patience in the face of editorial coercion and other difficulties; and for the very great pleasure which it has given me to work with such stimulating colleagues and friends.

I am grateful also to my wife for her help with the indexes.

Terence Cave

*

*   *

*

Unless otherwise indicated, all quotations from Ronsard are given according to the first published text of the work in question, as reproduced in P. Laumonier's complete edition in the *Société des textes français modernes* series (L). A parallel reference to the edition by G. Cohen in the *Bibliothèque de la Pléiade* (*Pl*) is added in each case. L is the essential scholarly edition; *Pl* is the only complete edition which is easily handled and accessibly priced. Further details of these and other editions are provided in the first section of the bibliography. Where there are discrepancies between the first published text and the 1584 text, a note is often – though not always – provided by the author of the chapter. The use of two editions brings up the whole question of Ronsard's successive revisions of his work, and the reader is invited to make his own comparisons wherever possible, taking into account the intervening variants as provided by Laumonier.

It is assumed throughout that a complete edition will be used. No anthology is adequate for an interpretation which attempts to be in any way comprehensive. However, a skeleton 'anthology' for the volume is in effect provided by the chronological list of texts cited.

Aspects of Ronsard's poetic vision

I. D. McFARLANE

WHEN the modern reader first makes contact with the poetry of a Renaissance humanist, he will probably be struck forcibly by two points: the poet is writing within the framework of a cosmology which, in spite of local differences of stress and viewpoint, is accepted in its general outlines by the members of the sixteenth-century world; and in the second place the poet does not appear to be seeking 'originality'. He is glad to be associated with a recognized tradition, he will happily fish in the common pool of *topoi* and consecrated themes and he is likely to view with suspicion the activities of the imagination which only the Romantic revolution has placed in a privileged position. He would regard it as his task to reproduce with the greatest fidelity what was to be found in the universe around him: he might wish to represent as accurately as possible something close at hand – and the *blason* techniques were readily available – or he might follow the medieval view in interpreting phenomena at an allegorical level, or yet he might, especially after the spread of neoplatonic theories, consider such phenomena in the light of man's progress towards a higher spirituality. But, whatever view he took, one may be sure that, at a conscious level, he was content to tread a well-worn path and to walk in the footsteps of established authorities; he was writing for a recognizable public whose training, taste and

Ronsard the poet

literary and philosophical framework of reference were similar to his. It is this cluster of circumstances that often makes it difficult for the new reader to come to terms with Renaissance poetry: the frequency of hackneyed commonplace, the interminable variations on a petrarchan theme, the exploitation of recurrent images – all these features give an impression of *déjà vu* which may rapidly pall. How then can we differentiate between these poets of whom only a handful appear sufficiently gifted to rise above the conventions in which they work? What is it, for instance, that makes Ronsard tower head and shoulders above his contemporaries? What criteria should we apply in order to sort out the wheat from the tares in the field of Renaissance poetry? In this chapter I shall try to describe some aspects of Ronsard's poetic world, aspects which are 'constants' in spite of changing perspectives, shifting stresses and contradictory attitudes and which, in the pattern they form, do separate Ronsard from his contemporaries. They, I hope, may help to explain why his poetry transcends its time and makes him a writer of major stature.

The inspiration of Ronsard's poetry depends greatly on the Renaissance world picture, and unless we are aware of this foundation, much of his writing will remain a closed book, not only because specific references to current attitudes will pass unrecognized but, more important, because Ronsard is always trying to reach beyond himself, and this search for transcendence will inevitably be expressed in concepts, images and allusions that belong to his time.[1] In addition Ronsard makes phenomena, as it were, reverberate in a much finer *caisse de résonance* than do his contemporaries; he creates an imaginatively coherent world in which phenomena are closely associated, but it is also one that bears many likenesses to the world picture

---

[1] On the Renaissance world picture, see A. C. Lovejoy, *The Great Chain of Being* (Cambridge, Mass., Harvard University Press, 1936); Herschel Baker, *The Dignity of Man* (Cambridge, Mass., Harvard University Press, 1947); E. M. W. Tillyard, *The Elizabethan World Picture* (London, Chatto and Windus, 1943); A. K. Varga, 'Poésie et cosmologie au XVIe siècle', in *Lumières de la Pléiade* (Paris, Vrin, 1966), pp. 135–55.

Aspects of Ronsard's poetic vision

accepted by the humanists of his time. There is no need to offer a detailed portrait of that Renaissance *vision du monde* here: a bare outline will suffice. Man enjoys a privileged position in the chain of being, standing between the divine reason and the animal world. Beyond the sublunar world, there is the supreme being, radiant, perfect, eternal, immutable; and on this side of the moon, there is the flawed world, since the Fall a prey to passions and motion, compounded of the four elements in an uneasy equilibrium often disturbed by discord, and controlled by destiny and the stars within the limits permitted by the divine will. Man's efforts will be directed towards his spiritual ascension and final reunion with the divine principle. Within this cosmological framework there were many areas where religions and philosophies might differ – and these divergences are prominent features in the Renaissance landscape: the problems concerning the soul, the degree of human liberty, the theological implications of psychological theory, all these and many others exercised the humanist mind in a period of civil disturbance and ideological polarization. Humanists often shifted their attitudes on vital points, and critics have detected such variations in Ronsard.[1] From a literary standpoint, however, what is more important is the manner in which Ronsard's imagination apprehends the universe. That he should be aware of the movement that characterizes the sublunar world is hardly surprising in a Renaissance humanist; but the degree to which that awareness is developed and the ways in which it is expressed and linked with other concepts will tell us much about his poetic originality. The presence of the sun in his verse is similarly to be expected in a writer who had more than a smattering of neoplatonic learning and was familiar with the petrarchan tradition – one thinks for instance of Britonio's sequence the *Gelosia del Sole*; but he treats solar themes differently from Pontus de Tyard and he allows more space to them than does another poet of high talent in the petrarchan

[1] See, for instance, I. Silver, 'Ronsard's reflections on cosmogony and nature', *Publications of the Modern Language Association of America,* 79 (1964), pp. 219–33.

Ronsard the poet

tradition, Maurice Scève. Indeed, Ronsard's imaginative grasp of the world around him seems to be more powerful, more ranging, more coherent than that of other members of the Pléiade.

There are indications that Ronsard himself was aware of the role imagination should play in poetry and of the value that could be given to the poetic world in its relation to human existence. In recent years critical attention has turned to this problem,[1] and there are grounds for thinking that Ronsard was feeling his way towards a more positive, more favourable understanding of the imagination whose role had been viewed with suspicion by classical theorists and medieval thinkers. Ronsard has often pronounced on the functions of poetry, and perhaps not always consistently. He offers us a vatic conception of neoplatonic origin, he sees in poetry the means of conquering time only to reject it in moments of dejection, he stresses variously the social function of praising famous men and he throws out the suggestion that poetry may act as a lightning conductor for love, as a device for dissipating passions, in order to 'soulager [son] cœur'. He accepts the traditional distinction between history, which makes it its business to describe the real, and poetry, which allows its maker to work in the field of the *vraisemblable*, but at the same time he has reservations about Ariosto whom he condemns for being 'fantastique' and straying beyond the bounds of the poetically valid. And yet he has on more than one occasion mentioned that his temperament was affected by the accident of his birth under Saturn: in the *Epistre au lecteur* that introduces the *Trois Livres du recueil des nouvelles poësies* (1564), he describes himself as 'un poëte melancholique et fantastique' (*L* XII, 16; *Pl* II, 991); a similar definition occurs later when he sees himself as 'Melancholique et plein d'imagination' (*L* XVII, 162; *Pl* I, 203). Undoubtedly he takes delight and satisfaction in the world of the imagination, which for some critics makes up for the frus-

[1] See Grahame Castor, *Pléiade Poetics* (Cambridge University Press, 1964).

Aspects of Ronsard's poetic vision

trations and inadequacies of his real life.[1] We shall therefore try to explore, even if only partially in both senses of the word, this imaginary world of Ronsard's poetry, which became a reality for him from an early age; however, its complexity, its coherent relationship to its parts and the polyvalency of the imagery Ronsard uses to express it make it difficult to choose the ideal point of entry. We shall first look at some of its recurrent features and shapes, then examine the registers in which relationships between phenomena are apprehended; and after taking a look at the changing and ambiguous nature of his intuitions, we shall consider the setting and denizens of his world, and the way in which poetry is not only means of expression and exploration but also theme in this universe of his making.

*
* *
*

What must strike any reader of Ronsard is the instant delight he takes in certain fundamental aspects of nature, not merely for the further associations they may possess, but in themselves. He draws much inspiration from some of the elements:

> pour tes mesdisances le Soleil ne laisse de me luire, ny la terre de me porter, les vents de me recréer, et l'eau de me donner plaisir . . . (L XII, 22; Pl II, 994)

Elsewhere he speaks sympathetically of the continuity that can exist between the elements, even though he is fully aware of their discordant relationships (L XVI, 284; Pl I, 757). When he is not describing the elements in a poetic form of philosophic discourse, his preferences go towards water and fire (usually as light):

[1] 'Tout se passe comme si Ronsard avait transposé dans son univers poétique cette union de l'esprit et des sens qui lui a été refusée, et dont il chante l'épithalame dans son œuvre, avec la gravité heureuse d'un clerc qui célèbre un culte au nom d'une communauté', G. Gadoffre, *Ronsard par lui-même* (Paris, Éditions du Seuil, 1960), p. 65.

Ronsard the poet

L'onde et le feu, ce sont de la Machine
Les deux seigneurs que je sen pleinement

(L IV, 69; Pl I, 37)

and of these two, water seems to play the greater part in his writing. He recognizes that without water everything will die (*L* VIII, 93 ff.; *Pl* II, 204, modified), but water attracts him in a more vital way and also for its richness as an image. He dallies in order to reproduce the movement of water, as for instance in the *Hymne de Calaïs et de Zetes*, when the vessel sets out for the open sea:

Adonque la galere egalement tirée
Aloit à dos rompu dessus l'onde azurée,
Et de longs plis courbés s'entrecoupant le dos
Se trainoit tortement sur les bosses des flots,
Ainsi qu'une chenille à dos courbé s'efforce
De ramper de ses pieds sur le ply d'une escorce.
Chascun d'un ordre egal tire son aviron,
La vague en tournoiant escume à l'environ,
Le rivage s'en fuit, et rien n'est manifeste
A leurs yeux, que la Mer, et la voute Celeste.

(L VIII, 291; Pl II, 141)

As so often in Ronsard, comparison is introduced to portray something over which the poet wishes to linger, and the picture becomes a study in watery movement, rich in curves and undulation. On more than one occasion he has described the pleasures of swimming: he may associate it with the washing away of ennui, or see in it a means of purification, but he loves the physical activity of moving in water—elsewhere he wishes he could be transformed into a fish – and he is fascinated by the temptation to be absorbed by water, a theme which occurs in the poem on Hylas (*L* XV, 246–7; *Pl* II, 387–8), though the youth resists more than Goethe's *Fischer*.

The sea plays an important part in Ronsard's poetry:[1] it is

---

[1] W. B. Cornelia, *The Classical Sources of the Nature References in Ronsard's Poetry* (New York, Columbia University, 1934), chapter 5.

Aspects of Ronsard's poetic vision

accepted as the 'semence de toutes choses'; it must feature in the poems of voyage, such as the *Franciade*; it is the birthplace of Venus, and therefore is rich in images for the expression of love. Ronsard may also indulge in a fine description of a storm at sea, as in the *Hymne de Pollux et de Castor* (*L* VIII, 296; *Pl* II, 214), but the sea is not his favourite manifestation of water; and at the mythological level, Neptune tends to appear chiefly as a troublemaker and as the enemy of Pallas or Venus. What Ronsard admires in water is not its destructive power, but its expression of continuity and undulating pattern; this is one reason perhaps why ponds and lakes rarely attract him, for they are too stagnant. He enjoys the waves of the sea when they are restrained, plashing gently against the coast:

C'est plaisir que . . .d'oyr contre les bords
Les flots de la grand mer quand les vents ne sont forts
(*L* XII, 162; *Pl* I, 990)

and he is frightened of the wild sea that could engulf and destroy him:

Je sçay chanter l'honneur d'une Riviere,
    Mais quand je suis sur le bord de la Mer,
    Pour la louer, la voyant escumer
    En sa grandeur si profonde et si fiere,
Du cœur s'enfuit mon audace premiere,
    Prés de tant d'eau, qui me peut abysmer.
(*L* XIII, 194; *Pl* II, 527-8)

Elsewhere we detect in Ronsard the 'horreur du gouffre', and for him the waters of a river are not only restful, but symbolize valuable aspects of experience. In forms that avoid stasis as much as violence, water by its continuity and perpetual transformation reflects the variety of existence; it is associated with countless themes in Ronsard's poetry: purification, the Muses, memory, fecundity, love, but also oblivion, fickleness, illusion. It is the ideal symbol of the presence of both permanence and the impermanent in human life.

This ambiguity is not present in Ronsard's treatment of light which, unless linked with the excessive heat of high summer, is always treated in the major key. Beauty for him is often conceived in terms of radiance (beauty 'luisoit', *L* VIII, 258; *Pl* II, 126), but there is a primitive delight in the presence of the sun:

> il n'est rien si beau que de voir la lumiere
> Du Soleil . . .   (*L* VIII, 171; *Pl* II, 285)

And the poet takes pleasure in the play of sunlight on objects. There is a striking example of this in a passage where the sun, as a term of comparison, assumes almost more importance than the thoughts of Cupid that form the starting point of the simile:

> Son penser vole et jamais ne s'arreste
> Decà delà virant et tournoyant
> Comme l'esclair du soleil flamboyant
> Sortant de l'eau nagueres respandue
> Dans un chaudron à la panse estandue:
> Ce pront esclair, ores bas ores haut
> Par la maison sautelle de meint saut
> Et bond sur bond aux soliveaux ondoye
> Pirouetant d'une incertaine voye,
> Et fait courir ses longs rayons espars
> De place en place errant de toutes pars.
>   (*L* XVI, 211; *Pl* I, 723, substantially modified)

The theme of sunlight is linked here with water, itself seen as content of a vessel, as reflection and especially as movement; and the kinetic quality of the scene is conveyed by a succession of verbs, the careful choice of epithets – 'espars' is often used by Ronsard with dynamic meaning, particularly with reference to hair – and the adverbial phrases of place which help to impart a vertical as well as a horizontal movement to the play of light.

Though Ronsard is not averse to portraying the moon and the stars as vehicles of light, they pale into insignificance compared with the sun, which is often described in considerable detail;[1] and though he justifies the use of extended periphrasis

---

[1] 'Ronsard's poetic world is almost wholly sunlit', A. W. Satterthwaite, *Spenser, Ronsard and Du Bellay* (Princeton University Press, 1960), p. 131.

to describe sunrise and sunset on grounds of poetic practice sanctioned by earlier writers, this is rather a theoretical support for his own imaginative preference. The sun has also its normal role in the cosmology of the times: it is 'l'âme, l'œil et la Vye' of the universe; it sustains and nourishes 'cette grande Machine'; but Ronsard's references often carry a warmth and intensity that the recognition of the sun's role in the scheme of things does not strictly compel:

> Soleil, source de feu, haute merveille ronde,
> Soleil, l'Ame, l'Esprit, l'œil, la beauté du monde . . .
> $\qquad$ (*L* XIII, 110; *Pl* I, 920, altered)

It is connected with life, immortality, absence of fear, peace, love; its thematic resonance is further enriched when it appears in the mythological guise of Apollo. Ronsard's fascination with this source of light shows itself in a variety of ways: for instance in a heightened linguistic intensity, as in an early sonnet on Cassandre:

> Pareil j'egalle au soleil que j'adore
> $\quad$ L'autre soleil. Cestuy là de ses yeulx
> $\quad$ Enlustre, enflamme, enlumine les cieulx,
> Et cestuy ci toute la terre honore
> $\qquad$ (*L* IV, 9–10; *Pl* I, 4)

and line 3 is the line which was not altered when Ronsard revised the first quatrain substantially. Then, when he describes the heliotrope, the focus on the sun though justified by the context is more lovingly presented than is necessary:

> Quand le Soleil, ton amoureux, s'abaisse
> Dedans le sein de Tethys son hostesse,
> Allant revoir le Pere de la Mer,
> On voit ton chef se clorre et se fermer,
> Palle, deffait; mais quand sa tresse blonde
> A grands bouquetz s'esparpille sur l'onde

[21]

Ronsard the poet

> Se resveillant, tu t'esveilles joyeux,
> Et pour le voir tu dessilles tes yeux,
> Et sa clarté est seule ton envie,
> Un seul Soleil te donnant mort et vie.
>
> (*L* XV, 175; *Pl* II, 365–6)

The heliotrope's dependence upon the sun is expressed not only directly, but in the echo of the words 'se resveillant', 'tu t'esveilles'.

Light, chiefly the sun, is used as a symbol for a wide range of values cherished by Ronsard: poetry, virtue, fame. It is also associated with the colour of gold: this link occurs often, as one might expect, in the love poems to Cassandre, one of whose most sung features is her hair, but this symbol of youth and beauty is also applied to men – their beard is 'un petit crespe d'or' – and in the *Hymne de l'eternité*, Jeunesse is portrayed in similar terms:

> Jeunesse, au chef crespu, dont la tresse luy vient
> Flottant jusqu'aux talons par ondes non tondue,
> Qui luy frappe le doz en filz d'or estendue.
>
> (*L* VIII, 249; *Pl* II, 123)

and this is also found in descriptions of the sun:

> Le Soleil en crespa sa chevelure blonde
> Et en dora son char, qui donne jour au monde.
>
> (*L* VIII, 192; *Pl* II, 266)

The only occasions on which Ronsard speaks unfavourably of gold are those which refer to the gold mines and money, considered anti-natural and sources of unhappiness; otherwise golden light, often represented in terms of movement, is a symbol of vitality, of youth and of happiness.

A word may be said here of Ronsard's continuing pleasure in the play of light on glass and crystal. There is a remarkable *Elegie du verre*, to which we shall return later (pp. 54–5), as it goes well beyond the present context; but it reveals the delight of the poet in the way glass not only multiplies the vitality of light

Aspects of Ronsard's poetic vision

and yields a rich iridescence, like the rainbow he sometimes describes, but also acts as a mirror. The nightingale is found singing to its own reflection (*L* II, 165 ff.; *Pl* II, 729 ff.) in a poem that is a study of reflection, reverberation and illusion; elsewhere Ronsard compares himself to a mirror (*L* XVII, 247; *Pl* I, 242), and of course he explores the Narcissus theme. The topic deserves a more detailed treatment, but glass and reflection in the mirror (or water) are important themes because they bring together the central preoccupations of life and illusion that are so marked a feature of Ronsard's poetry.

Finally, among the elemental features I have chosen to single out in Ronsard's poetic world, there is sound. There is no need perhaps to develop the point by means of numerous quotations; but notice how he so often describes water not simply by its shapes and movements, but by its sound: he loves

les rides creuses
De l'eau qui bruit profondément

(L III, 123; Pl I, 388)

and indeed exhorts the Muses not to be afraid of the water. In his descriptions of nature, birds sing, and his characters speak. Is this love of sound the stronger for Ronsard's increasing deafness? Perhaps, but however that may be, for him the world is in great measure *parole*, and one of the ways in which he describes hell and death is to conceive them as soundless. Ronsard once asserted that a man who was unable to appreciate music was, to all intents and purposes, incapable of spiritual betterment; and, when he portrays Cassandre, he will sometimes draw our attention to her voice, which is capable of influencing nature around her. For Ronsard the *néant* is essentially silent and he will fill his world with sound, word and song.[1]

In Ronsard's world, then, we have the stressed presence of water, light and sound; these elemental features afford a vital delight often shorn of any symbolism; but they also form the point of departure for a rich imagery that casts much light on

---

[1] See below, chapter 5, on the presence of music in Ronsard's poetry.

his values. These features often occur in certain registers or
through certain shapes and patterns, and it is time for us to
look briefly at some of these.

*
*   *
*

A prominent shape that recurs with impressive frequency in
Ronsard's poetry is the circle (and the curve) which may be
apprehended in terms of concavity or plenitude. The poet, of
course, follows current symbolism in seeing in the circle the
symbol of perfection:

> en la forme ronde
> Gist la perfection qui toute en soy abonde . . .
>
> (L VIII, 142; Pl II, 191)

God's perfection is conceived in circular terms; and some of
the sophisticated developments in the sonnet of the egg
(L XVII, 334; Pl I, 324) stem from this general principle.
Ronsard had orchestrated the motif early on in the *Ode de la paix*:

> Elle courba le large tour
> De l'air, qui cerne tout autour
> Le rond du grand parc où nous sommes,
> Peuplant sa grande rondeur d'hommes
> D'un mutuel acroissement:
> Car partout où voloit la belle,
> Les amours volloient avecq'elle
> Chatouillant les cueurs doucement.
>
> (L III, 7; Pl I, 359)

And when he wishes to express the ideas of harmony, perfection, immutability and eternity, we shall not be surprised to find
him employing the circle or referring to the concept of *rondeur*.

The curve, the uncompleted circle, is, however, found with
perhaps more insistence. We shall note its association with
movement, but in more static form it occurs when Ronsard
wishes to conjure up the idea of abundance, *joie de vivre* and

fertility. It is not unusual for a scene to be described with particular stress on a pattern of curves, to the exclusion of the metaphorical associations:

> Les autres, deus soufflets entonnent
> Lesquels en leurs ventres enflés,
> Prennent le vent, et le redonnent
> Par compas aus charbons soufflés. . . .
> Un peu plus haut parmi les nues
> Enflées d'un vague ondoiant,
> Le Pere ses fleches connues
> Darde aval d'un bras foudroiant. . . .
> Entre l'oraige, et la nuit pleine
> De gresle martelant souvent,
> Le pilote cale à grand peine
> La voile trop serve du vent,
>> La mer le tance et les flots irés baignent
>> De monts bossus leurs rampars qui se plaignent.
>>> (*L* I, 261; *Pl* II, 705)

There is in Ronsard a poetry of the wind and 'enflure' to which we must return later, as it ties up with some of his key concerns; here it is the formal quality of the curves that has caught his eye. Equally frequent though is the association of these curves with the concepts I have mentioned. Ronsard is very fond of describing goblets and vessels made out of choice metal. This is partly because they give him the opportunity to reproduce the exciting and intricate motifs fashioned on their outer surface; but he is also fascinated by these vessels because by their shape and content they symbolize plenitude. Nymphs, we are told, have their 'cruches profondes' (*L* XII, 61; *Pl* II, 247) and at a more exalted level, Ronsard sees the seeds of all things contained within innumerable vessels:

> Là, sont divinement encloses
>> Au fond de cent mille Vaisseaux,
>> Les semences de toutes choses,
>> Eternelles filles des eaux . . .
>>> (*L* III, 126; *Pl* I, 389)

[25]

Ronsard the poet

He may also refer to his friend's learning as 'ton vase abondant'; he would be less attracted by Rabelais' description, 'un abysme de science', for he has a deep fear of the abyss, which comes out in a number of passages over the years. Ronsard prefers the circumscribed hollow, which so often becomes the sign of fertility: it may be a symbol of poetic or artistic abundance, as when he describes the richly decorated, but also richly hollow lyre. More commonly it is a symbol of natural richness, of a fecundity whose maternal overtones he may underline. The countryside is portrayed in such terms: nature 'commence de s'engrossir en sa semence', is likened to a mother 'en gésine' and is characterized by her 'champs plantureux'; Ronsard may use the epithet 'tétineux' to describe her surface, and he recalls 'les ventres des campaignes . . . fertiles . . . ou brehaignes'. He seems to elaborate on what, at the point of departure, is a well-known commonplace; but he will take the metaphor further: he talks of the 'ventre large du grand Tout', and he often likens the sea or the hollowed-out ship to a mother: the *Argo* is called the 'mère' of the sailors, and the ship will move through 'le plus creux ventre de la mer'. The theme of fecundity will of course attract its own cluster of associations – fruit, manna, dew, honey, milk and so forth – but from our present angle it is a major illustration of Ronsard's imaginative desire to link the curve with the idea of plenty, both natural and artistic. In this context, one can see why the cave of the Muses acquires special significance.

The poetic uses to which Ronsard puts the curve rarely involve a static description: we saw that the idea of productivity and abundance was nearly always present, and so is another quality: movement. We mentioned this apropos of his interest in water, but his preoccupation with motion goes much further. At a philosophical level, Ronsard has referred to the traditional view that motion is an inevitable characteristic of our sublunar universe, whereas God lives in an eternal mode of stillness and serenity. Occasionally he expresses a yearning for the peace that the world cannot give, but more normally movement, the immediate manifestation of life as we know it,

Aspects of Ronsard's poetic vision

is a source of continual fascination in his eyes; it is associated with the various things that give value and enjoyment to existence: the passions, fertility, youth, love, warmth. Ronsard is attracted by phenomena in which motion is very evident, and there are passages where it is studied for its own delight: one thinks for instance of the departure of Calaïs and Zetes in pursuit of the Harpies (L VIII, 275; Pl II, 133–4).

The same undulating, swirling movement attracts him in smoke:

> (quand un pasteur qui garde
> Ses brebis dans un bois, laissant choir par mesgarde
> Au tronq d'un arbre creux quelque tison de feu,
> Des le commencement il prand vigueur un peu,
> Se nourrissant au pied, puis tout le feste allume,
> Puis toute la forest il embraze et consume)
> Un reply de fumée entresuivy de pres,
> Puis un aultre, et un aultre, et puis un aultre apres
> Se courbe en ondoyant . . .
>
> (L VIII, 289; Pl II, 140)

This passage forms part of a comparison introduced to describe a serpent, which, like the caterpillar, is often sharply observed by Ronsard. The serpent, for various reasons, possesses in his poetry a wider role than the merely descriptive. There is the traditional theme of the serpent symbolizing perfection as the circle, with its tail in its mouth, and Ronsard does refer once to this interpretation. In a love poem he associates the serpent with the cycle of the year; it also signifies renewal, because it sheds its skin at regular intervals, and therefore Ronsard connects it with spring and the rejuvenation of the earth. In the *Franciade* the snake is linked with Hyante in two ways: first, it is a symbol of jealousy, which enters her heart in this guise, and second it forms part of a decoration she wears, and here Ronsard's choice of motif is determined partly by the mythological flashback in the picture, partly because of his delight in movement for its own sake:

Ronsard the poet

Son col d'ivoire honora d'un carquan
Fait en serpent, ouvrage de Vulcan:
D'or et d'email merveille élabourée,
Qu'il fit jadis pour la deesse Rhée,
Et Rhée à Nede en present le bailla:
De ce serpent tout le dos escailla
D'aspres replis: si bien que la facture
De l'artisan surmontoit la nature.

(*L* XVI, 251; *Pl* I, 742)

In the same book, the serpent is given as an example of life upon this globe (ibid., 285; 757). So often, Ronsard's predilections are revealed in the choice of element for his more extended comparisons, and it is of a snake he thinks when he sets out to describe Francus' ship reaching harbour:

la navire poussée
Ayant la prouë et la poupe froissée
Rouloit à peine: ainsi que le serpent
Qui sur le ventre à peine va rampant
Par le chemin, quand d'un coup de houssine
Quelcun luy rompt l'entre-deux de l'eschine.
Plis de sus plis en cent ondes retors
Sifle, retraine, et retourne son corps,
Se releschant son venin il remâche,
Et renouër ensemble se retâche.

(ibid., 184; 713)

The serpent, for all its important associations, appeals to the poet for its special expression of movement: there are other animals which come into the picture because they embody some vital energy – this is one of the reasons why Ronsard has a special feeling for the horse, which recurs as a motif over the years – but Ronsard is most fascinated not by violent, sudden gesture or motion, though he can represent the angry movement, the flash of lightning or the stormy wind with an impressive sense of immediacy, but rather by the slower movement that manifests itself in a twisting, wavy pattern, and this

Aspects of Ronsard's poetic vision

is a pattern that expresses not only vitality but continuity and duration; Ronsard's constant preoccupation with this type of motion is reflected also in his theoretical writings, for when he treats of 'suitable' epithets to be employed in composition, he gives as examples not only the 'ciel voûté' but the 'onde coulante' (*Abbregé*). A closer study of his poetic diction would reveal a high proportion of verbs denoting action and flow, the liking for epithets and present participles to evoke the idea of undulation, the use also of the abstract noun, rather than the epithet, to bring out the quality of the thing described, often in this context motion, fluctuation, 'enflure'; three examples come to mind:

> le branle d'une onde
>
> (*L* III, 46; *Pl* I, 591)

> Le feu, l'air et la terre, et l'enflure de l'onde
>
> (*L* IX, 107; *Pl* II, 442)

> Voir bondir par les prez l'enflure des ballons
>
> (*L* XVIII, 8; *Pl* I, 790)

Here we see Ronsard using a device which we often associate with the post-Flaubertian period but of whose poetic value he is clearly aware. The nuance of duration is often introduced by words connected with the idea of length, and this appears for instance in three well-known lines that describe Ronsard's love of rivers:

> J'aimois le cours suivy d'une longue riviere,
> Et voir onde sur onde allonger sa carriere,
> Et flot à l'autre flot en roulant s'attacher . . .
>
> (*L* XVIII, 34; *Pl* I, 276)

These lines also illustrate a feature we have come across elsewhere, the portrayal of undulating succession by means of repetition ('onde sur onde', 'flot . . . flot'); this helps to give a certain swaying movement to the verse, and it is a device that recurs throughout Ronsard's writing, from the *Amours* down to the last poems.[1]

All the examples so far given have expressed the idea of movement that is more or less horizontal; but Ronsard also is attracted by the vertical presentation, and here, though he may describe the Muses plunging into the waters (*L* III, 124; *Pl* I, 389) or the falling flight of the lark (*L* VII, 290; *Pl* I, 330), he seems to prefer the ascending, spiralling movement of objects. In some cases this may be associated with the idea of apotheosis or spiritual elevation; it is also present when Ronsard portrays the dissolution of clouds evaporating in the higher air; but whether the movement represents a climb towards higher things or simply to vanishing point, he remains enchanted by the whirl of persons or objects, so that he lingers in his picture of a dance,[2] or of smoke, or even of a flaming brand:

> Francus qui tient une torche fumeuse
> Boute le feu: la flammeche gommeuse
> D'un pié tortu rampant à petit saut
> En se suivant s'envole jusqu'au haut:
> Le bois craquete, et la pile alumée
> Tomba soubs elle en cendres consommée,
> Le vent souflant du soir jusqu'au matin.
>
> (*L* XVI, 207; *Pl* I, 722)

Descriptions of this kind may give an impression of 'realism' in Ronsard's nature poetry, but he is often less interested in the appearance of the thing than in its essential quality, whether it be light or shape or movement. Moreover this awareness of fundamental qualities such as movement reappears in contexts where we might, at first, expect other elements to be stressed. Thus the famous poem on Mary Queen of Scots' departure, so admirably analysed by Marcel Raymond, is among other things

[1] See below, chapter 7, pp. 288–302, for a complementary discussion of Ronsard's preoccupation with movement.
[2] See comments on this theme in the sonnet from the Hélène sequence in chapter 2, below, pp. 114–15; also chapter 5, pp. 234–7, and 7, pp. 291–3.

Aspects of Ronsard's poetic vision

a study in movement;[1] and this is true of certain love poems as well, but one must add that this elemental imagery is so frequently associated in Ronsard's mind with key concerns that we are always being taken beyond a simple apprehension of movement or light. A pertinent example occurs in the *Amours de Cassandre*:

> Soit que son or se crespe lentement
>> Ou soit qu'il vague en deux glissantes ondes,
>> Qui çà qui là par le sein vagabondes,
>> Et sur le col nagent follastrement:
> Ou soit qu'un noud diapré tortement
>> De maintz rubis, et maintes perles rondes,
>> Serre les flotz de ses deux tresses blondes,
>> Je me contente en mon contentement.
> Quel plaisir est-ce, ainçoys quelle merveille
>> Quand ses cheveux troussez dessus l'oreille
>> D'une Venus imitent la façon?
> Quand d'un bonet son chef ell'adonize,
>> Et qu'on ne sçait (tant bien elle desguise
>> Son chef doubteux) s'elle est fille ou garçon?
>
>> (*L* IV, 77–8; *Pl* I, 40)

This sonnet is remarkable not only for the way in which the initial image is developed to include various points of reference, but for the verbal mastery with which the poet makes the words carry, in their rhythms and pattern as well as in overt meaning, the burden of the sonnet. Cassandre's hair is immediately apprehended as movement, in this case rather slow, but also as gold, with the associations on which we have already touched. From the first line onwards the movement is expressed in terms of water and wave: 'se crespe', 'vague' (almost a play on words), 'ondes', 'vagabondes' (brought into the orbit by the ambiguity of 'vague'), 'nagent', and so forth. The second quatrain restricts movement, but still without excluding reference to it ('tortement', 'flotz'), and it serves to extend the impression of richness and variety. For the present the poet's delight appears to be

[1] Marcel Raymond, *Baroque et Renaissance poétique* (Paris, Corti, 1955), pp. 140 ff.; see also below, chapter 7, p. 294.

almost entirely aesthetic. The water reference is maintained in the first tercet, since Venus rose from the sea, but this also introduces delicately a hint of love. However, the switch to the overt theme of ambiguity comes more especially in the second tercet, and crucially with the striking 'adonize' – all the more so as it appears to be a word invented by Ronsard. Yet the sense of ambiguity had already been prepared for by the language of the quatrains: words such as 'vague', 'glissantes', 'nagent', on first reading give the sense of idle play, but the shift from indeterminateness to ambiguity is an easy one, especially as in Ronsard water symbolism with its undulation and instability often has connotations of ambiguity. There is the *berceuse*, rocking rhythm of the quatrains with their 'Soit que . . . soit que', alternatives that imply uncertainty, and the repeated word roots: 'vague', 'vagabondes'; 'contente', 'contentement'; and of course the tempo of the whole sonnet is determined in some measure by the four adverbs in *-ment* occurring at the rhyme in the quatrains. Rightly the poem ends on a note of interrogation; even the use of the indefinite article (especially 'une Venus') strengthens this uncertain atmosphere, in which the subtle use of enjambment also plays its indispensable part.

Another sonnet from the same sequence illustrates the way in which Ronsard introduces movement, fluctuation and curve to such an extent that these qualities seem to assume almost more importance than the ostensible object of the poem: sonnet CLX is, as Laumonier remarks, a 'blason du tétin', but the *topos* is transformed by the way in which Ronsard creates a pattern of shape and movement:

> Ces flotz jumeaulx de laict bien espoissi,
>   Vont et revont par leur blanche valée,
>   Comme à son bord la marine salée,
>   Qui lente va, lente revient aussi.
> Une distance entre eulx se fait, ainsi
>   Qu'entre deux montz une sente esgalée,
>   En toutz endroictz de neige devalée,
>   Soubz un hyver doulcement adoulci.

Aspects of Ronsard's poetic vision

Là deux rubiz hault eslevez rougissent,
  Dont les rayons cest ivoyre finissent
  De toutes partz unyment arondis:
Là tout honneur, là toute grâce abonde:
  Et la beauté, si quelqu'une est au monde,
  Vole au sejour de ce beau paradis.

(L IV, 152–3; Pl I, 83)

The poem depends in great part on its binary movement, because of its subject – incidentally Ronsard has a marked predilection for the twin theme, especially in his mythological poems – but also because of certain repetitions (first quatrain and tercets) and the to-and-fro movement he describes. The curves and circles are set in a framework of reference that, enriched by jewels, colour, light and platonic terms, is essentially mobile – the geographic features, mention of distance, the moving sea, the pathway, the melted snow and the final upward direction, all these move the poem away from such sensual charm as the subject might possess to a sensuous awareness of motion and plenitude. This approach figures in many poems; there is an interesting image in a slightly later *Amours* poem (*L* V, 109; *Pl* I, 18), where a similar theme is introduced:

Ha, seigneur dieu, que de graces écloses
  Dans le jardin de ce sein verdelet,
  Enflent le rond de deus gazons de lait

and in the *Elegie à Janet peintre du Roy*, the imaginary portrait of his mistress is dominated by these motifs: her hair is 'ondelez', her forehead is 'en bosse revoûté', her cheek is 'fosselu' and 'pommelu', her stomach 'en miroir arrondi', her knees are compared to 'deux monts'. This way of apprehending objects will be found in a great many poems by Ronsard, either to describe one or two details or to give a portrait on a larger scale. This preoccupation with certain shapes and movements is

Ronsard the poet

a constant, indeed a main characteristic of Ronsard's imagination.

*

*   *

*

This essential concern with movement is closely allied to other dominant themes that run through Ronsard's work, and to these we must now turn our attention. I would single out three leitmotives for closer inspection: a preoccupation with phenomena that involve absorption, assimilation or some sort of osmotic process; the well-known interest in metamorphosis; and thirdly a less easily definable area in which change appears to entail a hesitation on the frontiers between reality and dream, plenitude and void, *être* and *néant,* frontiers that are quickly reached when the poet tries to go beyond the confines of his 'normal' but separate identity.

Ronsard willingly uses imagery of distillation, flow and melting to describe phenomena that have a positive value for him, whereas those that are associated with separation, and indeed death, are presented in terms of fixation, freezing and solidity. The individual images are not in themselves 'original'; many belong to the petrarchan tradition, but what is more noteworthy is their frequency and range of relevance. Images of melting recur time and again: they are, obviously enough, a sign of rebirth or of coming to life, and thus they appear in the love poems or those that describe the arrival of spring. But at the same time, they are suggestive of greater receptivity, for life is not only vitality and movement, it is also communication and fusion. It is therefore quite normal for love to be felt as a breaking down of barriers, as a process of melting and blending. Ronsard, early in his love poetry, talks of passion melting like ice (see, for example, *L* IV, 119–20; *Pl* I, 67).

He admires the inamorata's voice that makes 'sucre couler'; elsewhere the lover expresses the desire to '[se] fondre en langueur', and there are several instances of wax being used as an image to express the feelings of love. In the Sinope series of

Aspects of Ronsard's poetic vision

sonnets, No. VIII is interesting in this context because it opens
on a sequence of wishful metamorphoses, but also because the
variants of 1560–72 introduce precisely the type of imagery I
have mentioned, the sense of melting accompanied by the
theme of water infiltrating (here in the form of dew, often
associated with love and naturally the rebirth of morning):

> Tout ainsi que la nege au chaut soleil se fond,
>   Je me fondrois en vous d'une douce rousée.
>
> $(L$ X, 93; Pl I, 150$)$

Conversely a passion like jealousy will penetrate his veins in a
very different manner:

> D'un sang froid, noir, et lent, je sens glacer mon cœur.
>
> $(L$ X, 90; Pl II, 878$)$

The fact that Ronsard is often writing in a tradition in which
the inamorata remains cold and unreceptive and that he
expresses himself optatively rather than in terms of experience
does not alter the fact that for Ronsard love is seen in terms of
infiltration.

The last example points at the same time to another vein of
imagery often explored by Ronsard, especially in the love
poems; when he is smitten by passion he feels as if it were penetrating his body, and the description of the 'moment' is more
often than not couched in physical terms. The petrarchan gaze
of his beloved is pressed into service, but even more common
is the description of his blood and veins invaded by this outside
force that possesses him and identifies itself with him. Alternatively he may hope to be absorbed totally in the being of his
inamorata: this is a theme that is predominant, for instance, in
the *Continuation des amours*. This feeling of being absorbed or
enveloped, though naturally expressed in the love poems, is
also found elsewhere; we have seen it in connection with the
pleasure of swimming, and it also forms a motif in the treatment
of old age and death: in *De l'élection de son sepulcre*, the theme of
embrace and envelopment occurs at various levels: the river
Loir is described as 'autour coulant', and its sister river the

Braie is referred to in terms of 'giron', a word constantly associated with water; and then the poet would gladly be shaded by a tree, 'embrassé' by the ivy and have his tomb decorated by a 'vigne tortisse' which would cast its shade all about: and he sums up his dream thus:

> Tout alentour l'emmure
> L'herbe, et l'eau qui murmure,
> L'un d'eus i verdoiant,
> L'autre ondoiant.
>
> (*L* II, 101; *Pl* I, 537)

Both symbols of continuity, the grass and the water, will surround him in death. Yet, as in so many cases of Ronsard's fundamental imagery, the margin between enveloping and engulfing and therefore destroying is a very thin one: when he writes

> le long reply des âges
> En roulant engloutist nos œuvres,
>
> (*L* XVIII, 247; *Pl* II, 647)

undulation, so often associated with life, is here combined with the verb *engloutir* to suggest oblivion and the denial of duration.

This ambiguity in the field of imagery is to be found also in another cluster of terms used by Ronsard to suggest the interpenetrability of phenomena and drawn from the vocabulary of hunger, eating and digestion. These terms commonly occur in his love poetry and, up to a point, they reflect fidelity to a certain stylistic tradition. They are serviceable because they can express both the destructive and the more attractive qualities of passion. When the poet uses words like *ronger* or *dévorer*, clearly love is being portrayed as corrosive or rapacious; and similar terms describe the ravages of time ('le Temps mangeard'), or the sea nibbling away at the coastline. Reference is made to Pluto and 'son enfer glouton' (*L* II, 109; *Pl* I, 539), and Ronsard thinks of life being 'englouti[e] à la vieillesse'(*L* I, 101; *Pl* I, 383); similar tones will be heard when he introduces the Prometheus theme. Equally frequent, perhaps more so, are the occasions on which the poet uses such alimentary imagery to suggest vital communication and assimilation. There is of course a lover of food and wine in Ronsard, for whom one sign of death is that we shall cease to drink and be merry, and one recalls more than one poem in which such pleasures are described with extended gusto. These experiences are also carried over into the metaphoric field: eternity is painted as ever feeding upon itself (*L* VIII, 251; *Pl* II, 124); death even is conceived as nourishing nature. In the love poems the poet wishes to 'se repaistre' on his passion, he sees himself as 'goulu', and though the imagery does not always serve to express undiluted happiness or satisfaction, it may constitute a fundamental factor in the texture of a sonnet (*L* IV, 121–2; *Pl* I, 68). Significant too, perhaps, is that two of the neologisms in the *Amours* belong to this same field of reference:

> Se desoyfver d'une amere liqueur,
> S'aviander d'une amertume estresme . . .
> > (*L* IV, 25; *Pl* I, 11).

In 1567, Ronsard struck out these words and replaced them by the more conventional 'boire' and 'manger'; but this hardly reduces the interest of his earlier urge to linguistic creation. He will use certain verbs which combine a sense of assimilation and identification with one of continuity or prolongation: the two that appear very frequently are 'sucer' and 'humer', and a striking example may be found in the *Adonis* when Venus, by kissing the dead youth, hopes to absorb and prolong, through total assimilation, the experience of her love with him:

> O trois fois bien aymé, eslieve un peu tes yeux,
> Chasse un peu de ton chef le somme oblivieux,
> A fin que ma douleur à ton oreille vienne,
> Et que je mette encor ma levre sur la tienne,
> T'embrassant en mon sein pour la derniere fois:
> Car là bas aux Enfers, Adonis, tu t'en vois!
> Pour le dernier adieu baise moy, je te prie:
> Autant que ton baiser encores a de vie

Ronsard the poet

Baise moy pour adieu: ton haleine viendra
Dans ma bouche et de là dans le cœur descendra,
Puis jusqu'au fons de l'ame, à fin que d'age en age
Je garde dans mon sein cest amoureux bruvage,
Qu'en tes levres baisant d'un long traict je boiray.
Humant je le boyray, et puis je l'envoiray
Pour le mettre en ta place au fond de ma poitrine,
Car desormais de toy joüira Proserpine.
    Ainsi disoit Venus, qui, sa levre approchant
Sur les levres du mort, pleurant alloit cherchant
Les reliques de l'Ame, et les humoit en elle,
A fin de leur servir d'une tombe eternelle . . .

(L XII, 124–5; Pl II, 33)

And in this passage, the wish to draw out the experience in long
memory is expressed partly by the repetition of various words
that confer a lingering quality upon the text.

These images of assimilation may be developed in conjunction with others from neighbouring areas of meaning: even in
this passage, Venus is developing the idea of suffusion through
her being. Ronsard likes to develop a description where some
element spreads, as here, like love coursing through the veins
'de conduis en conduis' or like the flame of a heath fire that
gathers momentum, or like some chain reaction. Ronsard also
favours the image of distillation: it is often used to describe the
process of sleep approaching:

Vien donc sommeil, et distille
Dans mes yeus ton onde utile . . .

(L II, 124; Pl I, 543)

There is in Ronsard a poetry of the clear drop distilled and
communicating some rich essence; but the image is understandably introduced most commonly when the poet is
describing the process of rejuvenation and fertilization, as for
instance in the appearance of spring; the theme also recurs in a
later variant to the text of the *Hymne du ciel*:

Aspects of Ronsard's poetic vision

Du grand et large tour de ta celeste voute
Une ame, une vertu, une vigueur degoute
Tousjours dessur la terre, en l'air et dans la mer,
Pour fertiles les rendre et les faire germer:
Car sans ta douce humeur qui distille sans cesse,
La terre par le temps deviendroit en vieillesse . . .

(L VIII, 147; not in Pl)

Distillation serves to evoke the continuity of a world whose
permanence seems otherwise threatened. And within the orbit
of the images we have been considering in this section, the
theme of fertility and 'enflure' is inevitably developed in rich
and varied manner. Some of Ronsard's early love poetry is
indeed remarkable for the frankness with which he treats this
motif; one may attribute this in part to the *bouillonnement* of
youth, but it would be a distortion of the truth to see nothing
more than the satyr in these effusions. These images of fertility
are in fact one aspect of a cluster of associations that are very
deepseated in Ronsard's psychological make-up. They express,
of course, a rich awareness of life, but they also reflect the
poet's preoccupation with continuity and, equally important,
with communication and identification, and as I have hinted
earlier, these patterns of imagery seem to reveal a profound
desire to go beyond the limits of the individual self. Indeed, is
it not likely that such essential concerns also lie behind his
fascination with the phenomenon of metamorphosis which
plays so large a part in his poetry?

*
*   *
*

In his awareness of the underlying continuity of matter,
Ronsard also recognizes its inability to maintain one particular
form for any length of time:

la forme se change en une autre nouvelle

(L VIII, 178; Pl II, 289)

Ronsard the poet

rien ne peut estre
Longuement durable en son estre
Sans se changer incontinent

(*L* I, 209; *Pl* II, 695)

unless of course it has become inert, 'pesant' and insensitive.
Ronsard draws the line between the animate and the inanimate
at different levels. When he wishes to liken the hardness of the
inamorata to some object, he may choose a rock or an oak; yet
elsewhere he sees in the trees the outward forms of dryads.
However that may be, life means change and variety; and a
quickening of activity may constitute a prelude to transformation. Such transformation, adumbrated in Ronsard's images of
transubstantiation (stripped of theological harmonics of
course), is also a sign of the interpenetrability of phenomena;
and there are variations on the theme, such as the possibility of
metamorphosis after death (*L* VII, 121; *Pl* I, 122) or the
question of metempsychosis, a doctrine with which Ronsard
flirts in more than one passage, though his conscious attitudes
will bring him down on the orthodox side of the metaphysical
fence. All this implies that his concern with metamorphosis
cannot be explained solely in terms of certain literary traditions
that were vigorous in his time, such as the petrarchan canon or
the Ovidian developments which were particularly fashionable
in the middle third of the sixteenth century. Moreover the
frequency with which the motif recurs in Ronsard's poetry
points once again to something closely connected with his
vision du monde.

There are several areas in which Ronsard treats this theme of
metamorphosis. He is naturally entranced by the classical
legends of the transformations of the gods; and here there are
two categories. On the one hand we have tales of the gods who
are capable of assuming divers shapes, and this is no doubt one
of the reasons for Ronsard's interest in Jupiter; and on the
the other stand the heroes, the nymphs and other demi-gods
whose fate it was to be converted into a plant, a star or something else. These destinies may have various allegorical mean-

Aspects of Ronsard's poetic vision

ings likely to attract the Renaissance humanist, but Ronsard is equally caught up by the metamorphotic process. The demons who so fascinate the poet have the faculty of assuming different forms, and one of their qualities is to act as intermediaries between gods and humans in Ronsard's world. In their being, metamorphosis and communication are significantly combined. Moreover, in those poems where mythology and court encomium overlap substantially, the theme of apotheosis and metamorphosis can play a useful role, but, as I have already said, the whole question must be understood at a deeper level.

The theme also occurs in the love poetry where the mythological associations, though present, are not as central as in our first category. One of the powers possessed by the inamorata is the gift of transforming the lover or nature: the *topoi* of the 'cent metamorphoses' and the Medusa image recur regularly, as one would expect in love poetry strongly coloured by the petrarchan tradition. There is however another situation that is very commonly exploited by Ronsard, so much so indeed that it cannot be explained away as part of a conventional pattern: under the force of love, the poet expresses the desire to be changed into something or someone else. Love, since it is also hope and *songe*, introduces a gap between reality and wish, and therefore Ronsard often treats it in the context of the dream: several of the poems that deal with metamorphoses associated with love are very interesting precisely on account of the directions taken by Ronsard's imagination. In the early *Fantaisie à sa dame* (L I, 35; *Pl* II, 690) he imagines himself transformed into a cloud, and the qualities he associates with the cloud are revealing: 'amour', 'perseverance', 'loyauté', 'attente', 'esperance'. Then he would like to be changed into a rock, then a fountain, a swan, a heliotrope ('soucy'), an 'umbre vaine' and finally a boat. In the Cassandre cycle the motif is very common and may form the kernel of some poems: in XVI Ronsard would wish the transformation of his being into fire, rock, tree trunk and of his thoughts and sighs into birds and zephyrs respectively; in CXVIII, the wishful metamorphoses are essentially a sophisticated form of *adynata*; but the motif can be treated at greater length outside the sonnets, as for instance in the *Elegie* to L'Huillier concerning the departure of Mary Queen of Scots: the poet wishes that he were a rock, a fountain, a bird, a star, for in his mind desire and transformation are akin to one another: and he talks elsewhere of

> mon desir
> Qui en vivant en cent formes me muë.

> (*L* XV, 198; *Pl* II, 908)

A striking example will also be found in the *Voyage de Tours*, where, having made his invocation to the boat carrying away his Marion, Ronsard wishes he were the water that supported and transported it:

> On dit au temps passé que quelques uns changerent
> En riviere leur forme, et eus mesmes nagerent
> En l'eau qui de leur sang et de leurs yeux sailloit,
> Quand leur corps ondoyant peu à peu defailloit:
> Que ne puis-je muer ma resamblance humaine
> En la forme de l'eau qui cette barque emmeine!
> J'irois en murmurant sous le fond du vaisseau,
> J'irois tout alentour, et mon amoureuse eau
> Bais'roit ore sa main, ore sa bouche franche,
> La suivant jusqu'au port de la Chapelle blanche . . .

> (*L* X, 224–5; *Pl* I, 144–5)

In isolation this passage can be seen as a means of giving greater resonance to the love theme by introducing the nature motif; but it is also characteristic of more permanent elements in Ronsard's imaginative make-up. Apart from the general search for metamorphosis, there is the identification with water, with its harmonies of life, love, continuity, and here the theme of envelopment which we saw was a feature of his apprehension of life. In the context of love we have a good example of the poet trying to go beyond his own personality which is by definition ephemeral, and hoping thereby to realize hopes that, in the *actuel,* can be nothing more. Metamorphosis suggests therefore a certain dissatisfaction with present reality which is

not lasting and not necessarily the only *valid* one; it is therefore not surprising that the motif of metamorphosis is one of
the ways in which we enter into Ronsard's imaginative world,
on which more will be said later. It is, as is evident from the
passage just quoted, a means possibly of deceiving the present.
This suggestion occurs again in a chanson of the Marie cycle,
where the poet, in a dream, tries a series of *feintes* to allay his
passion, but recognizes that in the last analysis such tactics
are in vain (*L* VII, 277 ff.; *Pl* I, 120 ff.).[1]

Nevertheless, the subject of metamorphosis does bring us to
the threshold of another essential preoccupation – the problem
of the relation between reality and illusion or dream. For a poet
in whose eyes form is always changing, and for whom life
could not be without hope, so often characterized as 'faulse',
the line of demarcation between *paraître* and *être* must be a very
thin one:

> Bref, sans l'Espoir le Monde periroit.
>
> (*L* XV, 92; *Pl* II, 354)

Moreover one sees Ronsard often trying to go beyond the
limits of normal human apprehension: witness his interest in
dreams, in the 'supernatural', in drink as a means of release, in
phenomena that appear to exist on the threshold between fact
and fiction, such as clouds or perhaps glass. This important
area in Ronsard's imaginative life deserves further investigation.

$$*$$
$$*\qquad*$$
$$*$$

Ronsard tends to develop the theme of unreality, *paraître* or
dream along certain lines. To begin with, there is the well-
known statement that life is a dream, that we cannot grasp its
essence, because it is for ever in a state of flux – in this context

[1] See below, chapter 2, pp. 90–1, for an analysis of a 'metamorphosis'
sonnet from the 1552 *Amours*.

Ronsard the poet

the wishful metamorphoses can be understood as the desire to accept change but in a manner most favourable to one's own condition. Happiness passes away; everything on earth is *songe* and *fumée*; and sometimes Ronsard allows himself the comparison of man as an actor on the stage of the world. To the recognition of change as the dominant feature of existence, there are several possible reactions. Ronsard may resign himself to the fact that only the present is meaningfully real; this tune may be harmonized with well-established anacreontic commonplaces, and this is indeed an important aspect of Ronsard's traditional reputation. He may, secondly, resort to conventional attempts to confer continuity upon existence: it is here that the theme of glory and of the poet's role comes into its own, and Ronsard uses it, both for his private musings and in his ceremonial verse, to counter the onslaughts of time and oblivion; but this is not a conviction that is unshakable in his mind. Ronsard has also given fresh expression to an older idea whereby humanity ensures its permanence through love and 'semences'. There is, however, a fourth reaction, like many other of Ronsard's attitudes ambivalent, but significant: the power of man to create illusion in order to solace himself; his imagination, in dream or perhaps in poetry, will shape a world in which the buffetings and frustrations of real life will be softened and blurred out of the picture. Of course there is another aspect to Ronsard's interest in dreams: he is well aware of current views on their validity as communicators of truth, but his attitude, at this level, must be limited to some extent by the consequences of the use of dream-interpretation for the discussion of determinism and God's will. His continuing preoccupation with the problems of dreams, prophecies and astrology is none the less an illuminating feature of his thought.

However, the role of illusion, indeed of self-deception, is one that recurs and, though Ronsard's attitude in this context is variable, it does underline the useful presence of unreality as part of life. There may be more fanciful play than serious purpose in his poem about the imaginary horse feeding on air,

Aspects of Ronsard's poetic vision

fumée, wind and dream,[1] but his ironic conclusion about the themes of imagination and illusion does not remove one's awareness of the attraction which they continue to have for the poet. The mirage theme often appears in the love poems, when the lady has shown herself to be intractable and indeed hostile. Ronsard is interested in the effect of love in absence: he notes that love is stronger in dreams, absence, memory (*L* XII, 291; *Pl* II, 37); a fit of pique perhaps or does such an attitude jar all that much with other references to the imaginative life? Alternatively, the poet may try to fashion an illusion as a surrogate for reality:

> Car feindre d'estre aymé (puis que mieux on ne peut)
> Allege bien souvent l'amoureux qui se veult
> Soymesmes se tromper, se garissant la playe
> Aussi bien par le faux que par la chose vraye.
>
> (L X, 290; Pl I, 996)

In the Cassandre cycle he had already referred to himself as 'heureusement de moymesmes trompeur', and the theme recurs in later poems, especially in the Hélène cycle, where he is ready to accept an attitude 'pour me faire plaisir' and where he senses that happiness is more likely to be gained in dream:

> Embrassant pour le vray l'idole du mensonge . . .
> Quand tout mon reconfort ne dépend que du songe.
>
> (L XVII, 244; Pl I, 240)

He will also develop the countertheme that 'l'homme est malheureux qui se repaist d'un songe' (*L* XVII, 293; *Pl* I, 275). What is surely significant is not that Ronsard affirms or denies the theme of illusion's worth or that he 'laughs off' the poems in which he indulges his fancy about clouds or dreams, but that his mind is continually moving along the axis of this problem of reality and mirage. Is there not some imaginative existence

---

[1] On Ronsard's love of horses, see H. Naïs, *Les Animaux dans la poésie française de la Renaissance* (Paris, Didier, 1961), pp. 407 ff.

which goes beyond everyday 'reality' and is both more real
and more worthwhile?[1]

It is in this context that a word may be said about Ronsard's
fascination with clouds; the cloud, as phenomenon or image,
enters his poetry with a certain frequency:

> Ne plus ne moins qu'on voit l'exercite des nües,
> En un temps orageux egalement pendües
> D'un juste poix en l'air, marcher ainsi qu'il faut,
> Ny descendant trop bas, ny s'eslevant trop haut:
> Et tout ainsi qu'on voit qu'elles mesmes se forment
> En cent diversitez, dont les vents les transforment
> En Centaures, Serpens, Oiseaux, Hommes, Poissons,
> Et d'une forme en l'autre errent en cent façons . . .
>
> (L VIII, 120; Pl II, 168)

The clouds here form the term of comparison for the demons;
he is attracted by their intermediate state between sky and earth,
their movement and their continual transformations. The most
uninhibited presentation of the cloud motif is no doubt
Folastrie VIII, Le Nuage ou l'ivrogne, and the context is significant,
because it is developed by a man taken beyond his normal self,
by drink, into a fantastic world, where truth and illusion are
blended into one another (L V, 47 ff.; Pl II, 761 ff.). As in the
previous quotation, one can see that Ronsard is struck by their
round shapes, their constantly billowing, changing contours,
but also by their evaporation; and in various poems these
features acquire a heightened, metaphoric value. They are
usually associated with dissimulation, and the theme of *enflure*
may, as in the case of the Titans, move from the purely physical
and verge on *hubris*; more normally, however, the clouds are
seen on the borders between truth and illusion. In *Les Nues ou
nouvelles,* they are represented at first as a natural phenomenon:

[1] See also Grahame Castor, 'The theme of illusion in Ronsard's *Sonets pour
Helene* and in the variants of the 1552 *Amours*', *Forum for Modern Language
Studies,* 7 (1971), pp. 361–73; and below, chapter 2, *passim.*

Aspects of Ronsard's poetic vision

L'air cependant qui s'imprime des nues
Forme en son sein des chimeres cornues,
Et comme il plaist aux grans vens de souffler,
On voit la nuë estrangement s'enfler,
Representant en cent divers images
Cent vains portraicts de differens visages. . . .
Car dedans l'air telles feinctes tracées
Des cœurs humains estonnent les pensées:
L'une en saultant et courant en avant,
Vuide, sans poix, sert d'une basle au vent,
L'autre chargée est constante en sa place,
L'une est de rien, l'autre est pleine de glace,
L'autre de neige, et l'autre ayant le teinct
Noir, azuré, blanc et rouge, s'espreinct
Comme une esponge aux sommets des montagnes:
L'autre s'avalle aux plus basses campagnes,
Et se rompant en sifflemens trenchans
Verse la pluye et arrose les champs.

(L XIII, 268–9; Pl II, 925–6)

Another shorter passage in the *Franciade* (*L* XVI, 101; *Pl* I, 679) indulges in a similarly kinetic picture of clouds; but often Ronsard goes on to suggest their metaphorical value: in *Les Nues* he writes, when comparing the *nouvelles* to them, that:

[Le bruit . . .] tantost en l'oreille,
Tantost bien hault il raconte merveille,
Triste tantost, tantost joyeux et gay
Mesle si bien le faux avec le vray,
Que des propos racontez à la troupe
Chacun en parle, et en disne, et en soupe.

(L XIII, 275; Pl II, 929)

Thus the clouds appeal to Ronsard not only by their fluctuating shapes, but by their ambivalent meanings that take us to the confines of reality and illusion: illusion perhaps, but as the *nouvelles* indicate, a force that can affect the lives of people.

Ronsard the poet

Clouds, too, may vanish into thin air, but they also produce rain, so that they are equally at the limit of physical reality.

With this uncertainty about the identity of the clouds, we touch upon something that is fundamental to Ronsard's poetry and indeed to his outlook upon life: a persistent ambivalence about certain aspects of existence which is revealed not only in what one might call his intellectual statements about them, but also in a number of the themes he explores because of their indefinite nature, and finally in his imagery which, reflecting his *vision du monde*, often serves to embrace contradictory, ambiguous aspects of or attitudes towards some phenomenon. Critics have pointed to variants that show a shift in Ronsard's view of fundamental matters: his interest in metempsychosis, his cogitation on demons, astrology and free will, statements that suggest a Lucretian outlook about the permanence of matter beneath changing exterior form, or a pantheistic view of the universe ('Dieu est partout, partout se mesle Dieu'), and perhaps also varying ideas on death and the hereafter.[1] On less exalted matters, yet ones that continued to haunt him, a similar fluctuation can be found: the importance of fame, especially posthumous fame, the doubts about what poetry can or cannot achieve in this context, the merits and failures of poetic activity, sometimes sublime in its vatic role, at others disrupted by the 'intermittence' of inspiration. On a broader front, there is a persistent ambivalence towards life itself, with its imperfections and inadequacies, but also with its *moments privilégiés* and its ever-changing variety and abundance. Nor can Ronsard make up his mind at what level of reality, aided and abetted sometimes by illusion, life is most successfully lived. This existential uncertainty is closely linked with the desire to go beyond the limits of the self; and the excursions into activities that might expand the horizon of consciousness can be readily understood

[1] H. Busson, 'Sur la philosophie de Ronsard', *Revue des cours et conférences,* I (1929–30), pp. 32–48, 172–85. We await Isidore Silver's *magnum opus* of which the first volume appeared in 1969: *The Intellectual Evolution of Ronsard,* volume I: *The Formative Influences* (St Louis, Washington University Press) (three volumes to follow).

Aspects of Ronsard's poetic vision

in this context. One of the high qualities of Ronsard's poetry is precisely that it gives utterance to these feelings and attitudes in all their complexity and does not seek to resolve them by some artificial cutting of the Gordian knot; and some of his richness stems from the combination of a deep intuition of nature and of the creation of a pattern of imagery, based on that intuition and capable of expressing these complex emotions.

This *vision du monde* comes through to the reader not only in the so-called philosophical hymns (where sometimes the presence of imagery is reduced), but also in the more personal elegies, in the court poems and in the love cycles. No doubt the poet has drawn, as in other contexts, on contemporary, traditional elements for his explicit statements about love: it makes the world go round, it helped to bring order out of chaos, it is essential for the continuation of the human species; there are many other strands one could add to the inventory. In the moods Ronsard evokes on love's journey, he moves from one end of the spectrum to the other, singing earthly love, petrarchan frustrations, spiritual ecstasy, but also doubts on the validity or even reality of his passion. To see in him a neoplatonic disciple or a satyr *tout court* is oversimple; for Ronsard love is a cardinal illustration of all that is involved in life. He senses the ephemeral quality of experience in human existence, and yet to what extent does he yearn after the *repos* of eternity? His imagination is far more involved when it apprehends what our sublunar destiny has to offer: life with the vitality of its passions, however flawed they may be, by which man gains awareness of his being. And this is perhaps a reason why Ronsard's portrayal of love – as well as of other feelings – is so often undertaken with the help of images which have what one might call a turntable quality. If his definition of Cupid as 'Ensemble Dieu profitable et nuisant' (*L* XVI, 143; not in *Pl*) can at one level be taken as the rephrasing of a commonplace, it nevertheless reflects at the same time the poet's refusal to apprehend life from one angle only.

This complex attitude to life is often expressed by

[49]

means of images relating to water. We have already had occasion to note how water symbolized for Ronsard the continuity and the fluctuating shape of life; but he also accepts its traditional association with oblivion and death (the waters of Lethe). It is fickle and changeable because it is flux, and because it reflects it is also the symbol of illusion. The insubstantial character of human existence can therefore be compared to 'une onde qui suit l'onde'. To express the vanity of this world, Ronsard also uses images that introduce the wind and sometimes smoke. Sometimes he draws a sympathetic picture of the zephyr, which is traditionally associated with love; elsewhere he takes delight in the wind as the expression of movement and speed, and in the *Franciade* – an overall failure no doubt, but a splendid storehouse of material illustrating Ronsard's *vision du monde* – the first book concludes with studies in the effects of wind and water where kinetic pleasure is paramount. When the wind is linked with human values or qualities, the associations tend to be unfavourable: it becomes the companion of winter, or enters as one term of a comparison with anger or the misfortunes of war. Most frequently, however, it makes its appearance with water, and it is often the force that shapes a river or stream into the undulating motion so dear to Ronsard's heart. It is here, surely, that the ambivalence of the wind begins to be revealed: at this end of the spectrum it has an invigorating role, breathing ('insuffle') vitality into the water that otherwise might well be dormant; but at the other end, it becomes the force that dissipates, that leads to evaporation. The moment of dissolution can be suggested by Ronsard in unforgettable lines by the use of such images:

> mes liesses sont un songe devenues,
> Lequel s'evanouist, et sans effet se perd,
> Aussi tost que nostre œil par le jour est ouvert,
> Ou comme l'onde coule, ou comme la fumée
> Se perd du vent soufflé en replis consumée.
>
> (*L* XII, 122; *Pl* II, 32; last two lines added in 1584)

Aspects of Ronsard's poetic vision

We saw earlier how Ronsard linked together the curve and *enflure* to express the sense of plenitude, of fecundity and happiness. It takes very little for the inflated curve of plenitude to be transformed either into so much wind, as in the passage just quoted, when the loss of shape is tantamount to the loss of existence; or into overinflation, so that imagery in this area comes to express the seamier side of life. The reference may be so conventional as to be almost trite, as when Ronsard uses the phrase 'enflé d'ambition'; *enflure* will also be associated with *hubris*, sometimes at a descriptive level:

> Maintenant que l'Hyver de vagues empoullees
> Orgueillist les Torrens . . .
>
> *(L* XVII, 317; *Pl* I, 257)*

or at other times at a moral level, as in the Hélène cycle, where illusory love, pride and the cloud are brought together in the Ixion fable. When *enflure* is associated with death and putrefaction, Ronsard may also use epithets such as 'bouffi' to stimulate the mind's eye, but outside this context, they would not automatically carry such depressing overtones: when Ronsard describes the ghosts of the drowned sailors in book II of the *Franciade*, this is how he presents the picture:

> voicy les fantaumes de ceux
> Dont la grand mer en vagues departie
> Avoit les corps et la vie engloutie,
> Enflez, bouffis, écumeux, et ondeux,
> Aus nez mangez, au visage hideux,
> Qui . . . De Francion environnoient le chef.
>
> *(L* XVI, 125; *Pl* I, 690)*

And a similar combination of *enflure* and putrefaction will be employed in an anti-aulic context.

What is surely more interesting are those cases where the imagery of *enflure* is exploited to express Ronsard's attitudes to things that inspire complex reactions in him; moreover the fact that these concepts are expressed in allegorical portraits that have much in common is particularly revealing. First of all there is his description of Promesse, envisaged in terms of inflation and bubble:

> Sa robbe estoit enflée à grans plis ondoyans

and Ronsard brings in the imagery of wind, 'fumée' and 'ondes ampoullées'; later when she addresses the poet at his bedside, she says:

> Je fay ce que je veux, tout tremble dessous moy,
> Et ma seule parole est plus forte qu'un Roy . . .
> je sçay
> Mesler bien à propos le faux avec le vray . . .
> Car tousjours la parolle est maistresse du cœur.
>
> (L XIII, 8 ff.; Pl II, 98 ff.)

Her ability to mix truth and falsehood echoes the line in the Les Nues cited earlier. The poem is in great measure anti-aulic, and Ronsard rejects Promesse's blandishment by appealing to his 'sainct Apollon', so that he establishes a distinction between the false word, Promesse's medium of expression and way of life, and Apollo's legitimate inspiration in poetry. Nevertheless, in view of what we have already said and also of some other utterances of Ronsard, one must recognize that the place of the *parole* in the no-man's-land of truth-illusion is an ambiguous one.

Ronsard's portrait of Renommée betrays the same unease since his attitude to glory is so shifting.[1] He accepts her traditional presentation with the trumpet: 'Le vent à joüe enflée au creux d'une trompette' (L X, 307, Pl II, 425). She is associated with poetry, fame and light (L I, 92; Pl I, 378), and elsewhere with Mercury (L XVIII, 113; Pl I, 1035); but when he gives the reader a picture of her, he stresses her plumage, her iridescence and her voice, often without obvious approval or disapproval, but the portrait suggests both variety, attractiveness and *paraître* (L XIII, 66; Pl I, 840–1). In the *Franciade* she is presented as 'pronte . . ./Au front de vierge, à l'echine

[1] See F. Joukovsky, *La Gloire dans la poésie française et néolatine du* xvie *siècle* (Geneva, Droz, 1969).

Aspects of Ronsard's poetic vision

emplumée,/A la grand' bouche', and a few lines later, the portrait is resumed in similar terms: 'Cette Déesse à bouche bien ouverte,/D'oreilles, d'yeux et de plumes couverte' (*L* XVI, 52–3; *Pl* I, 659). She must, however, be rather closely related to Victory, though Ronsard defines the latter as the sister of Fortune; in this portrait, Victory is given the same attribute of beautiful raiment, but is also thought of as totally fickle:

> Royne du monde, invincible Victoire,
> Dont les habits sont pourfillez de gloire,
> D'honeur, de pompe, et dont le front guerrier
> Est honoré de palme et de laurier:
>   Royne qui sœur de Fortune te nommes . . .
>   Tu es douteuse, incertaine et sans foy,
> Tu fais, defais, comme il te plaist, un Roy,
> Puis le refais, et les citez, tenuës
> Sous Tyrannie, esleves dans les nuës.
>   (*L* XVI, 195; *Pl* I, 719, substantially modified)

A few lines on, Fame is brought into the picture, and the theme of the *songe* pressed into service: Victory accompanied by hope, and then by fear, is bruited abroad:

> . . . Quand le Renom aux ailes emplumées
> Seme partout l'effroy de tes armées.
>   Aucunefois tu flates les humains,
> Aucunefois tu coules de leurs mains
> Un songe vain, faute de te poursuivre,
> Et le veincu veinqueur tu laisses vivre:
> Et le veinqueur qui te pense souvent
> Tenir chez luy ne tient rien que du vent.

A further harmonic is added by the presence of 'l'arrogance': the theme of *hubris* is one that occurs more frequently in the later poems, where it is introduced hand in hand with 'ne sçay quelle impudante esperance'. In all these passages, if we take them together, there is a fairly clear association of several themes: reputation, the word, dream, mutability, *paraître*, but in the individual context, Ronsard may often come down in favour of one attitude by means of an explicit statement. Nevertheless the underlying ambiguity of these concepts is never far off, and the association of poetry and fame, seen from this angle, is more complex than it first appears.

The theme of what I have called, for the sake of brevity, the 'inflated curve or hollow' recurs, furthermore, in certain passages where Ronsard is concerned with the act of poetic or artistic creation. There are some significant lines in the *Elegie du verre* which reveal not only the reasons for Ronsard's attraction to glass, but also its associations with important themes in his poetry, such as Bacchus:

> Aussi, vraiement, c'estoit bien la raison
> Qu'un feu, venant de si bonne maison
> Comme est le ciel, fust la cause premiere,
> Verre joly, de te mettre en lumiere,
> Toi retenant comme celestial
> Le rond, le creux, et la couleur du ciel . . . .
> Toi compagnon de Venus la joyeuse,
> Toi qui garis la tristesse epineuse,
> Toi de Bacus et des Graces le soin,
> Toi qui l'ami ne laisses au besoin,
> Toi qui dans l'œil nous fais couler le somme,
> Toi qui fais naistre à la teste de l'homme
> Un front cornu, toi qui nous changes, toi
> Qui fais au soir d'un crocheteur un Roy. . . .
> C'est un plesir que de voir renfrongné
> Un grand Cyclope à l'œuvre enbesongné,
> Qui te parfait des cendres de fougere,
> Et du seul vent de son aleine ouvriere.
> Come l'esprit enclos dans l'univers
> Engendre seul mile genres divers,
> Et seul en tout mile especes diverses,
> Au ciel, en terre, et dans les ondes perses
> Ainsi le vent duquel tu es formé,

Aspects of Ronsard's poetic vision

De l'artizan en la bouche enfermé,
Large, petit, creux, ou grand, te façonne
Selon l'esprit et le feu qu'il te donne.

(*L* VI, 167–8, 170; *Pl* I, 887–9)

At one level glass becomes almost a synonym for wine in a passage which incidentally develops the theme of going beyond oneself, even if only in dream. Equally attractive to Ronsard is the way in which glass is blown creatively into shapes that remind him of the perfection of the universe and suggest its great diversity. The relation of wind and form that constitutes so important an aspect of Ronsard's imagination reappears here in the significant context of artistic creation. Something of this lies behind Ronsard's description of the bagpipes in the *Chant pastoral* to Marguerite de France, and his evocation of Syrinx in her original form (*L* IX, 177–8; *Pl* I, 967–8); another example is the lyre, whose ornamentation the poet often takes great pains to describe but which also delights him by its 'ventre orgueilleux' and the sounds it brings forth:

Ce fut Toy [Mercure] qui premier effondras la Tortue,
Faisant de chaque trippe une corde menue
Qui sonnoit sous le poulce, et le dedans osté,
De son doz escaillé tu fis ton Luth voûté
Large, creux et ventru, où comprimé s'entonne
L'air qui sortant dehors par les cordes resonne.

(*L* XVIII, 272; *Pl* II, 656–7)

These phenomena of sound and form are portrayed with loving care and evident satisfaction; and yet are we so very far from Renommée and her trumpet, about whose lasting worth Ronsard had on more than one occasion expressed his misgivings?

Once again we find ourselves back in the area of Ronsard's central concerns. We have detected in his poetry a predilection for certain forms and patterns, as well as for several elemental phenomena; and all these, in addition to their formal and kinetic pleasure, come to be associated in his mind with deep-seated preoccupations: continuity, change, diversity, but also

Ronsard the poet

an awareness of the complexity and ambiguity of our existence. Ronsard's imagination is fired by the 'ondoyant et divers' character of life, and though he realizes its imperfections in the face of eternity, it is this life rather than the next which engages his artistic attention. He seeks to capture in his poetry the instant, with its variety and its iridescence; and yet his poetry also suggests hesitation and perhaps dissatisfaction. His imagery reveals a desire for identification, for fulfilment by going beyond himself, and this is surely one reason why Ronsard so often turns his gaze towards those areas of experience where the individual *conscience* might be widened, transcended: the dream, astrology, absorption in another, admiration for Bacchus, and so forth. The sense of exclusion and frustration may account in part for his interest in the Cybele-Atys myth: Cybele of course is mythologically connected with Saturn in the eyes of the Romans for whom she is Ops; she is the goddess of plenty and identified with Terra. She becomes associated in Ronsard's mind with *abondance* – hence no doubt why Catherine de Médicis, *mère plantureuse*, is linked in his verse with the goddess. The pine tree, an essential element in the worship of Cybele, is often introduced by Ronsard in comparisons concerning Paris, Calliope or philosophy. Here the reference to Atys (as in *Le Pin*) is crucial: whatever Ronsard's dislike of the myth's brutality, does he not see in it a symbol of the poet's mission, his need for solitude, and the dissociation between experience and the creative process? The theme of solitude recurs in his writings: not merely in the love cycles but also in his conception of the Muses' cave, which is set apart and far from the madding crowd. The contrast between Cybele and Atys is reflected in the contrast of *abondance* with privation and solitude. How far these thoughts reached Ronsard's 'concience claire' is another matter; but they might well confirm the impression that, for the poet, poetry often serves to 'meubler sa solitude', to bring together in meaningful form the bits and pieces of an unsatisfied existence and to suspend in a poetic world the feelings and intuitions that did not remain free from doubt at the levels of everyday reality and metaphysical speculation. In projecting his poetic world into words, Ronsard is also able to transcend the limitations of his own identity, though he knows full well how narrow a margin seems to distinguish *être* from *néant*. He has created an imaginary world, and peopled it with denizens who, among other things, represent certain values he cherished; at the same time, he has given us glimpses of what one might call an antiworld, which expresses his fears and anguish. Before we enter the other poetic world, let us briefly examine his web of negative values.

*
* *
*

Though we usually associate Ronsard with a sunlit and abundant presentation of nature, there are passages where he expresses very different intuitions, and one might tentatively range these under three main headings. First, Ronsard's awareness of forces in nature that appear to him in a sinister light: his evocation of ghosts, cats and darkness is usually in the key of fear and unease. There is also the picture of France rent by the wars of religion, and though I do not detect in Ronsard that acute sense of the *monde cassé* that one associates with certain poets of the Counter-Reformation period, he is nevertheless extremely sensitive to the presence of death and putrefaction, and there are passages in which one notices a heralding of Agrippa d'Aubigné. Finally there occur in his poems, here and there, moments of awareness that plenitude has vanished and that the sun has gone out of his sky, moments too when even poetry is seen to be discontinuous in its activity. In short, he is conscious of a *revers de la médaille* in a life by whose variety and vitality his imagination is for ever thrilled.

Ronsard has a very patent fear of dissolution, evaporation, dissipation; images of flight, of vanishing, of draining or ebbing may be recruited to express this emotion. Like d'Aubigné Ronsard uses the epithets 'palle' and 'blesme' with affective overtones to describe those whose vitality has fallen to the minimum; one of the most impressive illustrations of this

Ronsard the poet

motif is the portrait of the giant in the *Franciade* killed by the opening of his veins and whose blood drains away. Ronsard's attitudes to death are many, and not to be defined in a few, swift words; nevertheless the fear of dying is a recurrent motif, and Ronsard often sees death as the end of feeling. He has a horror of *engourdissement* as well as of dissolution; the body is by its very nature sluggish, and only the mind that activates it can prevent it from relapsing into torpor (*L* X, 102; *Pl* II, 466–7). The theme is developed variously; in the love poetry Ronsard may consider himself as dead, under the influence of the inamorata, and he will describe himself as 'terre', 'escorce', 'immobile'; on the other hand a man who is incapable of love is equally characterized as 'leaden'. The image of rusting is often introduced to signify ebbing vitality and in one poem Ronsard suggests that poetry and philosophy serve among other things to prevent man rusting in sleep (*L* VIII, 96; *Pl* II, 205). Life is therefore seen as steering a middle course between evaporation and inertia.

Night, understandably, tends to be associated with the forces that work against life: in *L'Hymne de l'hyver* Ronsard paints with evident relish the victory of light over night, the *ténèbres* and the Titans. Nevertheless, the poet's attitude to night is a mixed one, and what he says of sleep is true in some measure of night, evoking

> Tous les songes et les formes
> Où la nuit tu te transformes
> Pour nos espris contenter
> Ou pour les espovanter.
>
> (*L* II, 123; *Pl* I, 543)

In so far as night is 'la bonne mère commune' and envelops the human being in peace and safety, she is welcome; she may also be thought of as an accomplice furthering the designs of love. Nevertheless, she is the opposite of light; she is associated with the presence of ghosts and therefore of fear. In an early poem darkness and 'paresse' are associated (*L* I, 24; *Pl* II, 685); death is defined as 'la fille de la Nuit'. This ambivalent attitude to

Aspects of Ronsard's poetic vision

the dark is manifested in Ronsard's descriptions of caves. In so far as the *antre* forms part of a pastoral, idyllic setting, it affords him pleasure:

> Plus me plaisoit un rocher bien pointu,
> Un antre creux de mousse revestu.
>
> *(L* IX, 175; *Pl* I, 966)*

Caves help one avoid the extremes of hot and cold (*L* XII, 106; *Pl* I, 953); they are the pleasant 'maisons solitaires' for nymphs, and of course they are essential for the Muses who require solitude in which to carry out their functions. Yet Ronsard admits to a certain fear of caves from his youth (in the same *Chant pastoral* from which I have just quoted); and there seem to be two main reasons for this phobia. On the one hand, 'l'horreur d'un antre' stems from the absence of the light of day. Hence also Ronsard, more often than not, takes great pains to describe caves or grottoes that are inhabited by witches or giants: a significant passage occurs in the *Hymne de l'autonne,* concerning the cave of Auton, a wind for whom he has little liking:

> Son Antre s'estuvoit d'une chaleur croupie,
> Moite, lache, pesante, ocieuse, asoupie,
> Ainsi qu'on voit sortir de la gueulle d'un four
> Une lente chaleur qui estuve le jour.
>
> *(L* XII, 55; *Pl* II, 243)*

This quotation brings together a number of Ronsard's *bêtes noires*: inertia, weight, passive dampness and a lack of tension ('lache')—remember, in passing, Ronsard's description of the brains of dead men as a 'fromage mol'; and in the passage on Maladie following Auton's cave, we shall find, naturally, epithets to denote 'enflure', but also several features already brought out in the description of the cave. On the other hand, the cave is shunned by Ronsard because he associates it with the *abysme* and the *gouffre*; we have seen elsewhere the poet's dislike of the void, and on one occasion he admitted that he had dismissed the idea of suicide because of his fear of the *néant*. In so far as the cave is seen as the opening onto the abyss, it becomes a 'vray soupirail d'Enfer'. In this context the difference between the rounded hollow, symbolizing plenitude or sometimes artistic activity, and the bottomless *creux* is very great; abhorrence of the pit is expressed graphically in the *Franciade*:

> Pres le bocage une fosse cavée,
> A grande gueule en abysme crevée,
> Beoit au ciel ouverte d'un grand tour,
> Qui corrompoit la lumiere du jour
> D'une vapeur noire grasse et puante . . .

(*L* XVI, 273; *Pl* I, 752)

This fear of the viscous and the void is amplified a page or so later when Francus, offering the sacrificial victim to Hecate, adds a prayer:

> priant à haute voix
> La royne Hecate et toutes les familles
> Du noir Enfer qui de la Nuit sont filles:
> Le froid Abysme, et l'ardent Phlegeton,
> Styx et Cocyt, Proserpine et Pluton,
> L'Horreur, l'Enfer [misprint for la Peur,
>   1573–84], les Ombres, le Silence,
> Et le Chaos qui fait sa demeurance
> Dessous la terre en la profonde Nuit,
> Voisin d'Erebe, où le soleil ne luit.

(ibid., 275; 753)

Elsewhere Tartarus is portrayed as 'ce gouffre beant' (*L* III, 130; *Pl* I, 391). What is striking in these passages is the manner in which the same associations and indeed similar parts of speech and vocabulary recur to bring out Ronsard's fears of the anti-world.

There is, however, another important feature that must be mentioned: the silence, included in Ronsard's catalogue. We have seen already the importance that sound has for the structure of Ronsard's world, and that for instance the wideranging symbol of water was apprehended in terms of sound as well as of

movement and continuity. There are several bravura passages
where the poet describes sound – as for instance in the extended
comparison between the bulls and the furnaces (*L* VIII, 286;
Pl II, 139) or in the battle of the Cyclops; and in the love
poetry, it is not only Cassandre's eye, but her voice that counts,
in one sonnet to such an extent that it induces movements and
transformations in nature. Above all hell is linked with silence;
in *L'Orphée*, it is described as 'ce silence coy' (*L* XII, 137;
Pl II, 70). In another context mention is made of 'silences
sombres', a striking image which associates absence of sound
with absence of light. The death of a poet, his friend Du Bellay,
inspires a most moving passage, the portrait of a ghost:

> L'autre jour en dormant (comme une vaine idole
> Qui deça que delà au gré du vent s'en volle)
> M'aparut Du Bellay, non pas tel qu'il estoit
> Quand son vers doucereux les Princes arrestoit,
> Et qu'il faisoit courir la France apres sa lyre,
> Qui encore sur tous le pleint et le desire:
> Mais have et descharné, planté sur de grands os.
> Ses costes, sa carcasse, et l'espine du dos
> Estoyent veufves de chair, et sa diserte bouche,
> Où jadiz se logeoit la mielliere mouche,
> Les Graces et Pithon, fut sans langue et sans dens,
> Et ses yeux, qui estoyent si promps et si ardans
> A voir dancer le bal des neuf doctes pucelles,
> Estoyent sans blanc, sans noir, sans clarté ny prunelles,
> Et sa teste, qui fut le Caballin coupeau,
> Avoit le nez retraict, sans cheveux, et sans peau,
> Point de forme d'oreille, et la creuse ouverture
> De son ventre n'estoit que vers et pourriture.
>
> (*L* X, 366–7; *Pl* II, 571–2)

Ronsard's attitude to death, as to so many other central problems of the human condition, remains complex.[1] In the *Hymne*

---

[1] See also below, chapter 7, pp. 315–18; and E. Dubruck, *The Theme of
Death in French Poetry of the Middle Ages and the Renaissance* (The Hague,
Mouton, 1964).

de la mort, the general tone is undoubtedly Christian; the poet sees death as the leveller, the world as something ephemeral and mutable, and the soul as the essential part of a being that finds its way to its eternal home. Elsewhere too Ronsard stresses the differences between the pagan and the Christian views of death (e.g. *L* XII, 271; *Pl* II, 21), and in a late poem death 'n'est plus rien qu'un passage' (*L* XVII, 384; *Pl* II, 480). But the dead are also seen as 'un peuple gresle, le visage plombé, les yeux mornes et creux' and death is presented as 'un dormir de fer' (*L* VII, 94; *Pl* II, 528), for man is nothing when he sleeps and feeling has forsaken him. Since the 'spirit' is apparently unable to manifest itself properly without the body, one sometimes wonders whether Ronsard's consciously religious acceptance of the afterworld is felt, at an imaginative level, as deeply as the life on this planet or indeed as intensely as his apprehension of the antiworld. He paints more readily the dissolution of death than its resolution in the next world. It is therefore no surprise that in his poetry Ronsard has created, perhaps not with premeditated intent or in any schematic manner, a world in which he can hold eternity in the palm of his hand and can capture in the web of words those values he prizes: a world that has a spatial existence and also is peopled by representatives of these values.

Ronsard's poetic universe tends to acquire form and substance in the more extended compositions – eclogues, hymns and so forth – but it does not clash with the world in which the *Amours de Cassandre* have their being. Indeed one of the notable features of this universe is the way in which it makes its appearance in so many different poetic genres: in the stylized eclogue, but also in the *Franciade,* whatever its temporal and geographic distance in theory, in the ode and the more exalted forms of court poetry. It is sometimes conjured up in prophecy (often in poems with some political reference), but it also resembles

Aspects of Ronsard's poetic vision

very closely a sort of paradise lost that figures in Ronsard's
poetry. It is remarkable how frequently the theme of the
golden age recurs: it may well have entered his poetry as a
useful *topos* at hand, and it is certainly serviceable when Ronsard wants to flatter a reigning monarch or to evoke a happier
world when humanity was not plagued by religious wars. Yet
there is more to the theme than that: the frequency of allusion,
the details of conception which make Ronsard's age of gold
rather distinct from that of his contemporaries or indeed his
predecessors.[1] And when he expresses yearning for some
finer existence, he conjures up, not the spiritual home of
heaven that one finds, say, in the writings of Marguerite de
Navarre, but a certain idyllic way of life from which the world
has progressively fallen away. Of the various descriptions
offered by Ronsard, Navarrin's (in the *Bergerie*, L XIII, 101 ff.;
Pl I, 930–1) is interesting for the way in which the distinctions
between gods, humans and animals are blurred, the seasons are
made to disappear and death is viewed as a peaceful melting
into a *songe*. Ronsard's world, in so far as he gives it a recognizable personality, is essentially pastoral.

Ronsard, as one would expect, has views on nature in the
universe that owe a great deal to contemporary attitudes –
natura naturans and *naturata*, the relationship between nature,
destiny and God; and there is a rather different sense when the
poet speaks of the need to follow nature, though he may in so
doing express his conviction that man and nature form part of a
whole pattern.[2] But I am not here concerned with Ronsard's
view of nature in the everyday world or its part in the cosmological scheme, but with poetic nature as he creates it as an indispensable element of his imaginary world. There are of course
a number of features that link that world with 'reality', for it
seems to stand between everyday existence and pure mythology
or the fantasy of Ariosto's universe, to quote an example

[1] See E. Armstrong, *Ronsard and the Age of Gold* (Cambridge University
Press, 1968).
[2] See D. B. Wilson, *Ronsard, Poet of Nature* (Manchester University Press,
1961).

Ronsard the poet

mentioned by Ronsard himself. Nature is portrayed as forming a continuum, in contrast to man's own ephemeral span of life ('Nous, le songe d'une vie', *L* VI, 191; *Pl* I, 629); more emotionally, she is welcomed as the 'bonne mère', and the theme of sympathetic bonds between man and nature is a well-worked one, whether it be in the realm of love poetry, where the rejected lover seeks solace and solitude in the woods or the open spaces, whether he sees his love reflected in all natural phenomena, or whether he imagines in such phenomena the results of metamorphosis, which poetically blurs the distinction between animate and inanimate. Above all, for Ronsard, the sensible world is the means whereby the intelligible world can find expression. In these circumstances, it is to be expected that the poet will introduce many nature scenes into his verse; nature is one of the obvious sources for those 'ecstatiques descriptions' he admired in Virgil and hoped other poets would emulate. She is often the imaginative correlative of Ronsard's own attitudes and emotions; she is also admirable because of her variety and ability to delight:

> Aussi sa [i.e. God's] saincte pensée
> Deseignant ce monde beau,
> A sa forme commencée
> Sus le deseing d'un tableau,
> Le variant en la sorte
> D'un protraict ingenieux
> Où maint beau traict se rapporte
> Pour mieux decevoir les yeulx . . .
>
> (*L* III, 180; *Pl* I, 618, with interesting variant)

In this passage, three themes are intertwined: nature seen as painting, nature as 'deception' at the artistic level and finally nature's variety, a feature that Ronsard will stress throughout his career.

When Ronsard describes nature, much depends on the tone and style of the genre in which he is writing. The relatively sober description he gives in a late *Elegie* to Hélène (*L* XVIII, 34; *Pl* I, 276) seems closer to everyday life than is often the

Aspects of Ronsard's poetic vision

case, though the picture has its own form of stylization. The poet wanders alone in the forests

> Sur les bords enjonchez des peinturez rivages;

he follows the 'cours suivy d'une riviere', where the complexity of the moving water is admirably expressed; he refers to fishing and hunting; then he contemplates nature, especially the sky, as a source of knowledge; and finally in the countryside he cultivates the muse as a solace against the refusal of life, and in particular Hélène's love. But in many of his more highflown compositions, by the very nature of the genres in which he is working – the eclogue, the epic, the hymn, the court poem – we shall find a greater degree of stylization that gives aesthetic distance to the phenomena of nature (see below chapter 7, pp. 302 ff.). Nevertheless the various ingredients contribute to an essentially homogeneous world, pastoral in atmosphere and able to accommodate denizens whose own origins are equally varied. In a sense, the recommendations given by Ronsard (though perhaps in the words of his biographer Claude Binet) for the writing of epic poetry in the preface to the *Franciade* give us a very good idea of this ideal world, in which nature and art combine to create its special atmosphere (*L* XVI, 340–3; *Pl* II, 1024 ff.; quoted in part below, chapter 4, p. 178). It is a world characterized by richness and variety, but not confined to the epic dimension, for Ronsard often goes beyond a normal contact with 'reality' to enter this fairytale universe. Margot's description of France as she might be without the curse of the religious wars is illuminating:

> Soleil source de feu, haute merveille ronde,
> Soleil, l'Ame, l'Esprit, l'œil, la beauté du monde,
> Tu as beau t'eveiller de bon matin, et choir
> Bien tard dedans la mer, tu ne sçaurois rien voir
> Plus grand que nostre France. . . .
>   Il ne faut point vanter cette vieille Arcadie,
> Ses rochers, ny ses pins, encore qu'elle die
> Que ses pasteurs sont naiz avant que le Croissant
> Fust au Ciel, comme il est, de nuit apparoissant.

Ronsard the poet

> La France la surpasse en desers plus sauvages,
> En plus hautes forests, en plus fleuriz rivages,
> En rochers plus amis des Dieux, qui sont contens
> De se montrer à nous et nous voir en tout temps.
>   O bienheureuse France abondante et fertille!
> Si l'encent, si le basme en tes champs ne distille,
> Si l'amome Asien sur tes rives ne croist,
> Si l'ambre sur les bords de ta mer n'aparoist:
> Aussi le chaut extreme et la poignante glace
> Ne corrompt point ton air . . .
>
> (*L* XIII, 110–11; *Pl* I, 935)

Ronsard then goes on to describe in more detail the wealth of the provinces, the multiplicity of rivers that bathe the feet of the towns. In this tableau not only do we find examples of features of nature that have caught our attention earlier in this chapter, but the pattern of the whole corresponds very closely to the poet's ideal *locus amœnus*; and even in this passage there comes a moment when patriotism melts into memories from the world of romance:

> Elle a produit Renault, et Rolland, et encore
> Un Ogier, un Yvon . . .
>
> (ibid., 112–13; 936, expanded)

In his descriptions of landscape – the *blasons* are a different matter by the nature of their genre – Ronsard tends to single out the same features: caves, rocks, woods, rivers, fountains, the more general aspects which however, as we have seen, are strongly associated with various moral and imaginative constants. By the use of *copia* he may amplify these details to produce a fairytale atmosphere, rich, abundant, but in no way strident, possessed rather of a *mezzoforte* in the major key, conjuring up a sense of *épanouissement*, harmony and unity in diversity. In other words, Ronsard's descriptions tend to move towards a world that may start partly in reality, but soon acquires a certain stylization and autonomy.

Furthermore, this is a world in which people will live; Ronsard is not really a solitary by nature, and with his keen

Aspects of Ronsard's poetic vision

sensitivity to movement and vital forces, it comes as no surprise that he should personify and animate his world. The inhabitants seem at first a motley crew; they come from divers sources, and sometimes they or the events they undergo are invented by the poet, but they harmonize without difficulty with their background. The first category one might mention are figures we loosely call allegorical; in the older, medieval context such figures form part of an interpretation of poetry that Ronsard knew well, but used only limitedly. He does from time to time introduce straight allegory into his work, as in the poem about the king and the boar or the tale of the Milesian wife, but his creations normally have rather more flexibility. They help to animate his universe because they both represent values and concepts integral to his *vision du monde* and preserve a family air with the other inhabitants. These characters appear in relatively isolated fashion, but they have their attendants and processions just like the more recognizably classical figures (such as Bacchus). The ones that stick in one's memory tend to be expressions of elements that belong to Ronsard's antiworld: Fortune, Jealousy, Maladie. Let us take as an example the portrait of Jealousy in the *Franciade*:

> Elle estoit lousche et avoit le regard
> Parlant à vous tourné d'une autre part.
> De fiel estoit sa poitrine empoulée,
> Son col plombé, sa dent toute rouillée,
> De froid venin sa langue noircissoit,
> Comme saffran son teint se jaunissoit,
> Boufie, enflée, inconstante, et farouche,
> A qui le ris ne pendoit à la bouche.
>   Jamais ses yeux ne prenoient le sommeil
> Soit au coucher ou lever du soleil,
> Veillant sans fin, toujours pensive et blesme,
> Et se rongeoit de sa lime elle mesme
> Se tourmentant de travail et d'ennuy
> Quand le bonheur favorisoit autruy . . .
>   (*L* XVI, 233–4; *Pl* I, 734–5)

Ronsard the poet

Here are most of the elements we have already associated with Ronsard's antiworld: gangrenous inflation, leaden black, inconstancy, erosion, to which is added yellow, the traditional symbol for jealousy. These characteristics are repeated in the attendants, rapidly sketched though they are: Melancolie, Desespoir, Folie, Rage and Trespas. Jealousy is also associated with serpents: she feeds on them, and when she visits Clymene she breathes into her

> Un long serpent qui en glissant luy perse
> Foye et poumons.

Curiously enough, when Ronsard comes to describe the attendants of Fortune, a number of those that accompanied Jealousy are found again in her train: 'despit qui se ronge le cœur', 'maladie', 'deconfort', 'fureur', 'desespoir' (L X, 26; Pl II, 404), and of course others. Renommée and Victoire, as we saw before, also have a number of traits in common; and these points suggest that the figures, whatever they owe to an allegorical tradition, denote, in descriptions that recall Ronsard's imagery elsewhere, forces and feelings that are constantly present to him, and they embody in a negative manner the counterpart to values underpinning his universe. These positive values tend to be expressed through other classes of inhabitants.

The first of these categories comprises the nymphs, satyrs, *fées* and dryads; also the heroes who rank as demi-gods and who, in the encomiastic poetry, are royalty and members of the court; and the *daimons*. These distinctions are to some extent arbitrary, in that, for instance, the nymphs and satyrs are described in one poem as demons, whereas elsewhere the nymphs are seen as the companions of the Muses. In Ronsard's world the figures that represent positive values tend in many contexts to lose the marks that distinguish them from their neighbours. Though many of them have classical origins, it is worth remembering that from the age of twelve, so the poet tells us, Ronsard was imagining the presence of satyrs in his world, and indeed from the even tenderer age of six he was

[68]

Aspects of Ronsard's poetic vision

populating the countryside with nymphs and other fairy figures. Of course, the various categories may acquire considerable importance: this is certainly the case of the *daimons*, with whom Bacchus is identified in *Dithyrambes*. One could say that they are essentially vessels of communication: thus they appear in the process of inspiration, when poets sleep and dream; they presided at Ronsard's birth; they act as intermediaries between gods and men; and they stand in an intermediate position between the angels and the heroes. Since they were affected by the Fall they are themselves subject to human passions; they can be influenced by magicians and they are able to assume all shapes, feeding on vapours and wind.[1]

More substantial, partly because of their weighty roles, but also because they are differentiated more precisely as individuals, are the gods. In recent years, a good deal of attention has been paid to the presence and roles of these gods in Renaissance literature and thought, and Ronsard naturally figures in these monographs on Prometheus, Orpheus, Narcissus and others; nevertheless, the part played by the gods in Ronsard's poetic world has yet to receive an *étude d'ensemble*.[2] From time to time Ronsard gives us lists of classical gods; it becomes apparent that the same names tend to recur, so that we must presume that these are more important than others. In the *Elegie* to Chastillon (*L* X, 13; *Pl* II, 428) he wrote:

> Luy . . . Fait honneur à Ceres, à Palles, et à Pan,
> A Bacchus, au Soleil qui nous ramene l'an,
> Aux Muses, à Phœbus, aux Faunes, et aux Fées

[1] See A-M. Schmidt, *La Poésie scientifique en France au* xvie *siècle* (Paris, Albin Michel, 1938); also his edition of the *Hymne des daimons* (Paris, Albin Michel, [1939]); and below, chapters 3 and 4, pp. 151–2, 195–6.
[2] Recent monographs include: R. Trousson, *Le Thème de Prométhée dans la littérature européenne* (Geneva, Droz, 1964); M-R. Jung, *Hercule dans la littérature française du* xvie *siècle* (Geneva, Droz, 1966); Y. F-A. Giraud, *La Fable de Daphné* (Geneva, Droz, 1968); F. Joukovsky, *Orphée et ses disciples dans la poésie française et néolatine du* xvie *siècle* (Geneva, Droz, 1970); G. Demerson, *La Mythologie classique dans l'œuvre lyrique de la 'Pléiade'* (Geneva, Droz, 1972). See also below, chapter 4.

Ronsard the poet

– a passage which incidentally shows how Ronsard can blur
the various categories. In the epistle to Robert Dudley, subsequently offered to Elizabeth of England, Merlin the magician,
for all his medieval origins, speaks as a classical scholar and
mentions the following gods and attendants bearing gifts after
Jupiter: Love, Mars, Pallas, Juno, Phœbus, Prometheus,
Mercury and Peitho (Persuasion, who appears from time to
time elsewhere). All these figures have fairly important roles in
Ronsard's scheme of things, except perhaps Juno who rarely
rises above her classical functions; but there are others to
claim our attention: Neptune, Venus, Saturn, Orpheus,
Hercules, Narcissus, Castor and Pollux, and some persons
connected with the Argonauts whose fortunes exert a fascination on the poet. Faithful to his age, Ronsard is aware of the
values attached to these gods by the classical tradition, by the
neoplatonists and by Christian syncretists, but it is more useful
to see them as a collective presence in his poetic world. Even
in this fairly short list, certain gods have only a sporadic or
minor rule: Neptune, for instance, is only modestly present
outside those tales that unfold at sea or involve his conflict
with Venus. Jupiter, of course, has a part as it were, *hors série*,
as the father of the gods: equated with God, he is also seen as
the creator, but he will be pressed into service in Ronsard's
court poems, and he doubtless attracts him as a god susceptible
to love and capable of many transformations.

There is however a group of gods who do seem to have a
weightier presence and whose functions overlap in some
measure: these gods are all connected with the Muses and the
world of speech and poetry. Thus Ronsard gives space willingly to Bacchus, Apollo, Orpheus and also Mercury; and the
Muses have their privileged place. Ronsard has devoted two
substantial poems to Bacchus, quite apart from numerous
scattered references elsewhere. Bacchus who, in one poem,
stands with Pallas at the door of the Muses' abode at Meudon,
appears in *Dithyrambes* and the *Hinne de Bacus* as a most wide-
ranging symbol, involving laws, polity, Ceres, vitality, government of waters, youth, love, knowledge and especially recon-

Aspects of Ronsard's poetic vision

dite knowledge. He becomes the embodiment of many of Ronsard's cherished values, and the poet seems eager, particularly in the *Hinne*, to reduce the features that might diminish the god's stature – namely his drunkenness and his effeminacy. Orpheus' role is no less broadly based: he is associated frequently with adventure (the Argosy), but also with the arts, especially music and poetry, and he prolongs the Orphic tradition of initiatory knowledge of the universe; moreover his amatory life is, if anything, played down, and in one poem art is seen as a means of compensating for, even of forgetting, the failure in his 'real' life. Apollo, whose symbolism in classical legend was very rich, is endowed with many meanings in Ronsard too, including the sun and light, medicine, poetry and the pastoral world. Mercury, on whom the older Ronsard wrote an important hymn, is another god who plays a polyvalent role: among other features are noted his friendship with Apollo, his interest in alchemy and portents. He is the giver of sleep and the interpreter of Jupiter; and it is Mercury's lyre that Ronsard describes in such elaborate detail. Two things strike one in particular about this quartet of mythical figures: their functions overlap in some degree, and they resemble one another by the fact that Ronsard stresses their artistic, creative significance and reduces the amatory part of their legend; indeed they often give the impression of being apart, and Ronsard does refer to Bacchus as 'solitere'. Their presence helps thus to reinforce the role of the Muses: they are in addition linked with Apollo, Mercury and Pallas in the *Abbregé* when Ronsard is discussing 'theologie allegoricque'. One should add that Pallas plays a supporting role here, as does also Peitho, whom Ronsard personifies for the purpose. The Muses are furthermore seen as solitary in the *antres*. In short, one of the striking features of Ronsard's poetic world is the impressive presence of the representatives of poetry. Ronsard is not the only French poet for whom poetry is its own subject, and the world he conjures up before us is one created both for and by poetry.

Before we leave this world, a few words would not be out of

Ronsard the poet

place on the way in which Ronsard conveys to the reader its richness and idyllic vitality. Its atmosphere is determined in some measure by the literary and other sources on which Ronsard has drawn. He selects elements from the classical world, from medieval romance, from the *rhétoriqueurs*, especially Jean Lemaire de Belges; but there are sources closer to him as well: something of the *paraître* of court life has found its way into his universe, he is sensitive to the visual arts and he has been an assiduous reader of Ariosto, who seems to attract him more than his derogatory remarks on him would suggest, and also of the *Amadis* sequence, which contains elements of stylization, diversity and *copia* that are related to those of Ronsard. The rock of virtue may have its source in Hesiod, but it also looks very much like a property from the *rhétoriqueur* stage scenery. This world manifests itself not only in the largescale, more sophisticated genres like the epic and court eclogues; we can find it in the *Amours de Cassandre*, where sonnet CXIII, of petrarchan inspiration, offers us a landscape that is just like what we see in the broader frescoes. We are in a fairy world, 'éloigné du vulgaire', in which fundamental feelings, urges and attitudes find their rightful expression.

What strikes us immediately, as we have noticed before, is the blend of vitality and abundance. Ronsard conveys the sense of this richness in part by the use of *copia* and by the organizing of imagery that is elemental in origin. He stresses the variety and diversity of his world. He also employs rather different techniques which allow us to apprehend his patterns in depth and resonance. One of these methods is the skilful use of time-shifts. Such a device of course is a *sine qua non* in the epic framework, such as Ronsard is trying to establish in the *Franciade*, but it occurs elsewhere too. Prophetic utterance, naturally expressed in various tones of feeling, reflects Ronsard's concern to present his material in non-rectilinear fashion and to enrich the present with harmonics from the past and the future. A useful example, though it does not show Ronsard at his poetic best, will be found in the hymn to Henri II, where he describes the king's birth attended by a number of familiar faces:

Aspects of Ronsard's poetic vision

Si tost qu'elle se veit voisine d'acoucher
Et que ja la douleur son cœur venoit toucher,
El' vint à sainct Germain, où la bonne Lucine
Luy osta la douleur que lon sent en gezine:
Adonq' toy, Fils semblable à ton Père, naquis,
Et, sans armes naissant, un royaume conquis.
Lors les Nymphes des bois, des taillis et des prées,
Des pleines, et des montz, et des foretz sacrées,
Les Naiades de Sene, et le pere Germain,
Te couchant au berceau te branloient dans leur main,
Et disoient: Crois Enfant, Enfant, pren' acroissance,
Pour l'ornement de nous et de toute la France,
Jamais tant Jupiter sa Crete n'honora,
Hercule jamais tant Thebes ne decora,
Appollon sa Delos, comme toy par ta guerre
Honoreras un jour cette Françoise terre . . .

                                    (*L* VIII, 23–4; *Pl* II, 148)

In the invocation, past and future are intertwined, and the mythological figures, including saint Germain, surround the infant monarch not only by their swarming presence, but also through various levels of reference introduced by the names of Hercules, Apollo and Jupiter, whose polyvalent symbolism becomes apparent as we read more and more of the poet's works.

More striking, because more frequent and perhaps more personal, is Ronsard's predilection for introducing into his verse material at one remove from reality, that is from the primary reality he is portraying. We have noticed a tendency for Ronsard's descriptions to move without fuss into a more stylized idiom, so that we have soon left 'everyday' things. There is a classic example of this in the poem to the Cardinal de Lorraine when Ronsard is describing the 'grotte de Meudon' (see below, chapter 4, pp. 176–8). As we advance from the entrance, we are caught up in what is a very different world; the process reminds us of Balzac's technique in *La Peau de chagrin*, when Valentin enters the antique dealer's shop and soon finds himself in a world that makes one think of the

Ronsard the poet

Arabian Nights rather than of Paris. A more common device is Ronsard's practice of describing in great detail events, usually of legendary origin, depicted in elaborate works of art, or paintings within a castle or motifs on armour. Ronsard refers with satisfaction to 'grands vaisseaux d'histoires honorez'; goblets are also finely 'ciselez de fables poétiques'; there are the 'fabuleux manteaux' worn by denizens of his world, and one cannot forget the famous example of the lyre elaborately wrought and decorated on both sides (see below, chapter 4, pp. 190–2). These descriptions within a description often involve a temporal as well as a spatial shift, and from this point of view the numerous descriptions of the golden age acquire an additional aesthetic value, over and above their thematic role. The *rhétoriqueur* temple is also utilized as a framework for similar evocations of the past, though presented at the same time through the poet's prophetic vision, so that, as in the earlier case cited of Henri II, Ronsard is playing with a wide time reference (*L* VIII, 76; *Pl* II, 834). Sometimes the perspectives may be further multiplied: in the hymn to Chastillon, the poet tells us that in the temple he will place a portrait of his own protector near that of the Connétable; he describes the way in which he is attired, and this apparel includes 'l'esclat cramoisy d'une robe pourprée / De mainte belle histoire en cent lieux diaprée'. Among the objects and persons represented on this cloak we shall find some old friends:

> Là, d'un art bien subtil j'ourdiray tout au tour
> La Vérité, La Foy, l'Esperance et l'Amour,
> Et toutes les Vertuz qui regnerent à l'heure
> Que Saturne faisoit au monde sa demeure.
> Sur ceste robe apres sera portraict le front
> De Pinde, et d'Helicon, et de Cirrhe le mont,
> Les antres Thespiens, et les sacrez rivages
> De Pimple, et de Parnasse, et les divins bocages
> D'Ascre, et de Libetrie, et de Heme le val,
> Et Phebus, qui conduit des neuf Muses le bal . . .

> (*L* VIII, 77–8; *Pl* II, 835)

[74]

Aspects of Ronsard's poetic vision

This passage, not as rich as some, is a useful example of Ronsard's poetic habits; and it also shows how very thin indeed can be the margin between encomiastic poetry and the world of his poetic vision. There is a sensuous delight in the description of these scenes at one or more removes from reality, and the arabesques Ronsard weaves at this level are an important factor in his poetic impact; sometimes the language acquires a momentum of its own which reminds one of Coleridge. At the same time, the poet, by this varied level of presentation, gives us the impression of a multidimensional reality; Ronsard seems to achieve a sort of kaleidoscopic effect, in which the poetic process grows organically rather than architecturally.

In his more extended poems he does not always trouble to compose his material so as to satisfy the Cartesian mind, and the 'logical' links between the different tableaux of a diptych or triptych may not always be immediately clear; these 'ecstatiques descriptions' have a vitality of their own, but they often bring us back to Ronsard's central concerns, familiar themes like the golden age, the round of the Muses and others. What Ronsard has said about philosophy may surely be applied, *mutatis mutandis,* to the roving of his imagination:

> Elle [i.e. Philosophie], voyant qu'à l'homme estoit nyé
> D'aller au Ciel, disposte, a delié
> Loing, hors du corps, nostre Ame emprisonnée,
> Et par esprit aux astres l'a menée,
> Car en dressant de nostre Ame les yeux,
> Haute, s'attache aux merveilles des Cieux,
> Vaguant par tout, et sans estre lassée
> Tout l'Univers discourt en sa pensée,
> Et seulle peut des astres s'alïer
> Osant de Dieu la nature espïer.
>
> (*L* VIII, 86–7; *Pl* II, 201–2)

Some of these apparently 'gratuitous' descriptions are employed, not merely to ensure mobility in the reader's imaginative response, but to introduce themes that add important

Ronsard the poet

harmonics to the situation and are often key themes in Ronsard's scheme of values and interests. When for instance, in the *Franciade*, Venus is about to visit Hyante, she first transforms herself into a 'vieille' – her nature ('trois-testue') can show itself in the form of Hecate, goddess of the night; then she approaches Hyante sleeping and lays her belt on the bed. This belt is possessed of great magic force, but Ronsard also recounts its origin, which allows him moreover to evoke love as the power that informs the world. Then we are given an idea of what was portrayed on the belt (which must have been rather large): the two Cupids, whose traits are listed in some detail, Jeunesse and her attendants. Associations have taken us quite a long way from the point of departure; Ronsard's imagination, 'vaguant' and 'disposte' – two epithets often recurring with favourable meaning – is like a piece of seaweed, floating to and fro, yet anchored to its main subject.

The 'Chinese-box' technique is sometimes used to present a personage at two levels; thus Neptune wears a cloak on which is embroidered a motif referring to an event in his own life (*L* II, 134–6; *Pl* I, 546–8); and in the *Hymne de Calaïs et de Zetes*, the twins Castor and Pollux, who were already mentioned by Orpheus singing to the Argonauts at rest, are presented in their own right ('fleur de chevalerie'). They are wearing a 'robe de pourpre' (a *chlamys* surely) which their mother had presented them with before their departure; on the cloak are portrayed various scenes which in part concern themselves (*L* VIII, 263–4; *Pl* II, 128). The lives of the twins are presented, as Gide would say, *en abysme,* as in a Dutch painting (see below, chapter 4, pp. 160, 172).

There is another method of presentation: sometimes the poet gives us a portrait of himself, but seen through the eyes of the inamorata, and therefore in unflattering terms; and he has also introduced into his poetry the theme of Narcissus looking at himself in the water. But these devices occur less frequently, and in the case of Narcissus raise issues that bear on the problem of illusion and reality, and therefore do not come under the same rubric as the devices with which we have just been concerned. Nevertheless, in so far as they are techniques for providing a multiplicity of angles and for increasing the iridescent diversity of Ronsard's world, they must be mentioned.

*
*　　*
*

In considering certain aspects of Ronsard's world, I have tried to show how they form a pattern at the imaginative level and constitute permanent elements in his *vision du monde*. His intellectual attitudes often shifted on important points, and of course there is an undeniable evolution in his poetic production; apart from such important questions as the variants and the search for different stylistic effects, especially in the later editions, one does notice as Ronsard grows older a deepening of response to reality and yet at the same time an increased power of detachment. Nevertheless the 'constants' in his imaginative apprehension of life are genuine: certain themes, certain ambiguities, certain images tend to recur. He has an undoubted cosmic vision, which comes through even in the so-called minor genres. His range of imagery has an elemental, archetypal character; his ways of apprehending reality are similar even in contexts where one could theoretically have expected a greater local divergence. He has moreover created a poetic world characterized by a very great variety (his images of the *prées diaprées* or of the rainbow come readily to mind); by a sense of ever-deepening layers of awareness; by a powerful stylization that gives form and control to the world of sensations, feelings and structures he is trying to communicate; but above all by an immense vitality. This vitality is seen in the phenomena of life that attract him, in the choice of imagery, in his poems of exuberance (*Bacchanales, Les Nues*, etc.) however much he tried to play down their importance, in his admiration of Pindar for his 'superbes inconstances', in his delight in fashioning arabesques and allowing language its own momentum. At the same time, he is the poet of expanding consciousness, who tends to situate his intuitions in those areas where

Ronsard the poet

our responses to experience are endowed with a rich ambivalence: change/permanence; life/death; fusion/solitude; plenitude/void; *être/néant*, but also *paraître*. For him life is change, diversity, discontinuity too, *épanouissement*, going beyond oneself, seeking identification beyond, sunlight, dream, but especially the stuff of poetry – Ronsard would surely have admired the *Après-midi d'un faune*. And by his own *sorcellerie évocatoire* he has fashioned a world lying somewhere between 'reality' around us and on the one hand a metaphysical world and on the other a universe of sheer fantasy, such as he fought shy of in Ariosto. This world he could not have built for himself without a mastery of language possessed by no French poet before him and few since, an imagery rich in reference and fundamental in character, and a sense of verbal music that informs his innumerable metrical patterns and helps to confer upon Ronsard's poetry that impression of 'resonance' that sets him apart from most of his contemporaries. An English critic not so long ago referred to

> a quality without which no poet ever wrote great poetry. I mean simply an energetic consciousness and an appetite for life, a zest that displays itself in verbal fluency and intensity, a readiness for experiment, a capacity for intellectual excitement, and a lively observation of the varied form of nature and humanity.

This was in fact L. C. Knights writing about Shakespeare; but the definition is also one that fits Ronsard. However, Ronsard's greatness would not be borne in on us today solely because of his verbal mastery, or his immense capacity for absorbing and assimilating divers aspects of the classical world, though I would not wish to underplay these gifts; he reaches us because he is so close to the sources of fruitful consciousness and gives shape to attitudes and intuitions from which any proper response to life must start.

Petrarchism and the quest for beauty in the *Amours* of Cassandre and the *Sonets pour Helene*

GRAHAME CASTOR

ALL Ronsard's collections of love sonnets are marked to a greater or lesser degree by the conventions of petrarchism. This is not at all unexpected, of course, for in the period between the publication of Scève's *Délie* and, say, the repeated re-editions of the *Premieres Œuvres* and the *Œuvres* of Desportes in the 1580s and 1590s, petrarchism, whether of the spiritualized, neoplatonic kind or in its *précieux*, 'witty' form, was the dominant idiom for any love poetry which had serious literary pretensions.[1] Ronsard was by no means the first French poet to

[1] This remains true despite a temporary reaction against petrarchism, of which the best-known manifestation is perhaps Du Bellay's ode *A une dame,* first published in the second edition of his *Recueil de poësie,* 1553, and later, in the *Divers jeux rustiques* of 1558, retitled *Contre les petrarquistes.* For a detailed survey of French petrarchism in this period, see J. Vianey, *Le Pétrarquisme en France au* XVIe *siècle* (Montpellier, Coulet, 1909; Geneva, Slatkine, 1969). A useful introduction to the topic in general is provided by the first two sections in L. Forster, *The Icy Fire: five studies in European petrarchism* (Cambridge University Press, 1969). On Ronsard's love poetry the following should be consulted: F. Desonay, *Ronsard poète de l'amour,* 3 volumes (Brussels, Gembloux J. Duculot, 1952–9); D. Stone, *Ronsard's Sonnet Cycles: a study in tone and vision* (New Haven and London, Yale University Press, 1966); A. Gendre, *Ronsard poète de la conquête amoureuse* (Neuchâtel, La Baconnière, 1970); and H. Weber, *La Création poétique au* XVIe *siècle en France* (Paris, Nizet, 1956), volume I, chapter 5, 'La poésie amoureuse de la Pléiade (étude de thèmes)'.

produce a collection of love poems written in the petrarchan manner; Scève with his *Délie* (1544), Du Bellay in *L'Olive* (1549 and 1550), and Pontus de Tyard with the *Erreurs amoureuses* (1549) and the *Continuation des erreurs amoureuses* (1551) all preceded him. Nevertheless Ronsard's *Amours* of 1552 and 1553 were a major contributing factor to the 'naturalization' of petrarchism in France, to the extent that Ronsard came to be thought of by admirers as the French Petrarch, '[le] Petrarque Vandomois', as Olivier de Magny was to call him.[1] A few years later Ronsard would move away from Petrarch to some extent and would look towards rather different models:

> les amours ne se souspirent pas
> D'un vers hautement grave, ains d'un beau stille bas,
> Populaire et plaisant, ainsi qu'a fait Tibulle,
> L'ingenieux Ovide, et le docte Catulle.
>
> (*L* VII, 324; *Pl* I, 115)[2]

Petrarchan echoes persist in Ronsard's love sonnets, however, and are still to be found, discreetly mingled with the other influences, not only in the *Continuation des amours* and the *Nouvelle continuation des amours* but also in the Sinope and Astrée poems and in the poems 'Sur la Mort de Marie'. Finally, with the *Sonets pour Helene* – where we may suppose that Ronsard is both responding to the current literary taste at court and also aiming to outshine Desportes, his younger rival for court attention – there is (on the surface, at least) a fullscale return to the petrarchan manner. Yet here, as in the collection addressed to Cassandre twenty-five years earlier, Ronsard is not simply a passive imitator of his models. For although he seems to have drawn rather more heavily on the poems of Petrarch himself than on those of his imitators, it is clear from even a

[1] *Les Gayetez* (1554), ed. A. R. MacKay (Geneva, Droz, 1968), p. 84.
[2] The poem *A son livre*, from which these lines are taken, originally appeared as an epilogue to the *Nouvelle Continuation des amours* (1556). From the first collected edition (1560) onwards it became the prologue to the *Second Livre des amours*.

Petrarchism and the quest for beauty

casual reading that neither the *Amours* nor the *Sonets pour Helene* are particularly close in spirit to the poems to Laura. As is the case with most Renaissance poets who adopted the petrarchan style in love poetry, Ronsard's petrarchism lies above all in the motifs and the diction which he employs. In both collections he freely uses formulas, themes, image patterns, *concetti*, which are to be found in Petrarch, but the overall significance and implications of these two *recueils* differ very perceptibly (and in each case in a very different way) from those of the *Rime*. As always, Ronsard exploits for his own independent purposes the conventions which he is adopting.

In broad outline Petrarch's *Rime* may be said to be an account of the overpowering and deeply disturbing effect which the poet's love for Laura has had upon him. While she is alive he experiences an agonized oscillation between hope that his love will at some time be fulfilled, and pain and despair at its non-fulfilment, while at the same time continually striving to achieve a kind of moral and spiritual purification through love. After Laura's death the poet is first overcome by desperate grief, and then gradually he begins to move towards some resolution of the conflicting tensions within him. The sequence ends with the poet seeking the peace of resignation and repentance through prayer to the Virgin Mary. The poems form both a narrative and an exploration of the poet's inner life, an emotional, psychological and spiritual progress from the 'giovenile errore' referred to in the opening sonnet, through what he calls in the same poem 'le vane speranze e 'l van dolore', to the longed-for eternal peace envisaged in the final appeal to the Virgin. It is a narrative dominated by the precariously poised conflict in the poet between antithetical feelings and aspirations, and by the all-pervading melancholy which both colours and is coloured by the paradoxical *dolendi voluptas* of his love for Laura.

The first line of the first sonnet of Ronsard's *Amours*, 'Qui voudra voyr comme un Dieu me surmonte' (*L* IV, 5; *Pl* I, 3) is an adaptation of a much-imitated formula from one of

Ronsard the poet

Petrarch's sonnets.[1] The rest of the collection, too, is scattered with a host of direct and indirect allusions to Petrarch's *Rime* and to poems by later Italian writers imitating Petrarch. But the *Amours* have no clear narrative structure, no coherent progression in a moral or spiritual dimension of the kind which can be traced in the *Rime*. Nor is the characteristic petrarchan combination of anguished introspection and melancholy a feature of Ronsard's collection. What overall use, then, does Ronsard make of the petrarchan associations which he so clearly advertises in the *Amours*? A fully detailed answer to this question would inevitably be both lengthy and complex. However, an approximate answer of a general nature may be possible within the present compass, and an initial clue to it may emerge from an examination of Ronsard's treatment of the *dolendi voluptas* motif.

Although the general emotional colouring of the *Amours* is considerably lighter than that of Petrarch's *Rime,* the theme of the poet's sufferings in love is by no means neglected in the French collection.[2] Indeed, occasionally it is expressed with the

[1] Sonnet CCXLVIII, lines 1–2:

> Chi vuol veder quantunque po natura
> e 'l ciel tra noi, venga a mirar costei . . .

('He who wishes to see how much nature and the heavens can achieve among us should come to gaze upon her'), Francesco Petrarca, *Rime, Trionfi e Poesie Latine,* ed. F. Neri, G. Martellotti, E. Bianchi, N. Sapegno (Milan–Naples, Ricciardi, 1951), p. 322. (The plain prose renderings of Petrarch into English are my own.) Ronsard uses this formula again in sonnet LIII of the *Amours* (*L* IV, 55; *Pl* I, 28):

> Qui vouldra voyr dedans une jeunesse,
> La beauté jointe avec la chasteté . . .

(In the following discussion of the *Amours* all my examples happen to come from the 1552 edition; the points could equally well be illustrated from the sonnets which were added for the 1553 edition.)

[2] Throughout, I am concerned with the relationship between the poet and Cassandre and that between the poet and Hélène as they are represented within the respective collections of poetry, not as they may or may not have existed in real life. In what follows, therefore, 'Ronsard' will refer to the historical Ronsard, and 'the poet' (or 'the lover') to the *je* of the poems.

Petrarchism and the quest for beauty

kind of fierce power which one usually associates only with d'Aubigné's *Le Printemps*:

> Franc de raison, esclave de fureur,
>> Je voys chassant une Fére sauvage,
>> Or sur un mont, or le long d'un rivage,
>> Or dans le boys de jeunesse et d'erreur.
> J'ay pour ma lesse un cordeau de malheur.
>> J'ay pour limier un trop ardent courage,
>> J'ay pour mes chiens, et le soing, et la rage,
>> La cruaulté, la peine, et la douleur.
> Mais eulx voyant que plus elle est chassée,
>> Loing loing devant plus s'enfuit eslancée,
>> Tournant sur moy la dent de leur effort,
> Comme mastins affamez de repaistre,
>> A longz morceaux se paissent de leur maistre,
>> Et sans mercy me traisnent à la mort.
>>> (*L* IV, 89–90; *Pl* I, 50)

There are echoes here of the allegorical *chasse d'amours*,[1] but also of a passage from the end of Petrarch's canzone XXIII, 'Nel dolce tempo de la prima etade':

> I' segui' tanto avanti il mio desire
> ch'un dì, cacciando sì com'io solea,
> mi mossi, e quella fera bella e cruda
> in una fonte ignuda
> si stava, quando 'l sol più forte ardea.
> Io, perché d'altra vista non m'appago,
> stetti a mirarla, ond'ella ebbe vergogna,
> e per farne vendetta o per celarse,
> l'acqua nel viso co le man mi sparse.
> Vero dirò, forse e' parrà menzogna,
> ch'i' senti' trarmi de la propria imago,
> et in un cervo solitario e vago

---

[1] As presented, for instance, by the *rhétoriqueur* Octovien de Saint-Gelais in *La Chasse et départ d'amours*, published at Paris in 1509.

Ronsard the poet

di selva in selva ratto mi trasformo,
et ancor de' miei can fuggo lo stormo.[1]

Behind the obvious similarities between the two passages,
the differences are equally apparent. Both allude to the myth of
Acteon, transformed into a stag and killed by his own hounds
as punishment for having chanced to see Diana bathing in a
woodland pool.[2] The poet in Petrarch's poem comes upon his
lady, 'quella fera bella e cruda', in a disarmingly provocative
situation: 'in una fonte ignuda / si stava'. Disarming, too, is
the irritated gesture with which she dismisses him and transforms him into a stag, forever fleeing from his own hounds.
Since Petrarch stops well short of Ovid's gruesome death-
scene, his is a calm and unmelodramatic presentation of the
incident, with only slight, understated hints of menace.
Ronsard's poem, on the other hand, is considerably more
harsh in tone, and immeasurably more violent in outcome. All
the emphasis here is upon the destructive power of the passion
which the poet feels and of the suffering which he undergoes
in the pursuit of his lady. Ronsard's lover never actually
catches up with his 'Fére sauvage', and thus does not even have
the momentary delight of watching her as she bathes. He is
destroyed long before that can happen, consumed by the
consequences of his own 'fureur' in a paroxysm of cruelty and
horror; the insistent, nightmarishly inescapable alliteration of
the last tercet seems to intensify the agony quite merci-
lessly.

The marked violence of tone in this poem is not often

---

[1] *Rime,* ed. cit., pp. 31–2. ('I followed my desire so far that one day I was
out hunting, as was my wont, and that beautiful, harsh beast was standing
naked in a fountain when the sun was burning most strongly. I, since
other sights bring me no pleasure, stopped to gaze upon her, at which
she felt shame, and to revenge herself or to conceal herself, with her hands
she splashed water into my face. I will speak truly – perhaps it will seem a
lie: I felt myself torn away from my own outer form and I am transformed into a lonely, beautiful stag, swiftly running from wood to wood;
and still I flee from my own pack of dogs.')
[2] See Ovid, *Metamorphoses,* book III.

[84]

Petrarchism and the quest for beauty

matched in the Cassandre volume.[1] More usually in recounting
the sufferings of the lover Ronsard adopts a much gentler
manner. A case in point is sonnet LI, 'Dedans des Prez je vis
une Dryade' (L IV, 53–4; Pl I, 27), where the poet portrays the
effect which his first sight of Cassandre has had upon him:

> Des ce jour là ma raison fut malade,
> > Mon cuœur pensif, mes yeux chargez de pleurs,
> > Moy triste et lent: tel amas de douleurs
> > En ma franchise imprima son œillade.
> Là je senty dedans mes yeux voller
> > Un doulx venin, qui se vint escouler
> > Au fond de l'ame: et depuis cest oultrage
> Comme un beau lis, au moys de Juin blessé
> > D'un ray trop chault, languist à chef baissé,
> > Je me consume au plus verd de mon age.

There are no extremes of suffering here. Even the poison
which seeps, insidiously, into the depths of the poet's soul is
'Un doulx venin';[2] and the word 'oultrage', with its associations of violence (whether moral or physical), seems almost to
take on an air of mock exaggeration as it is gradually sub-
merged in the atmosphere of wilting exhaustion created by the
image of the lily which immediately follows.

A similar lack of harshness in the evocation of suffering
characterizes sonnet CXXVII, 'Or que Juppin epoint de sa
semence' (L IV, 123–4; Pl I, 69–70), which in its overall
structure – the contrast between the joyous beauty of spring
(traditionally the season most closely associated with love) and

[1] But see also sonnet XIII (L IV, 17; Pl I, 8) on the Prometheus theme;
sonnet XXXV (L IV, 38; Pl I, 16–17), which likens 'ce penser qui devore
mon cuœur' to a 'Lion affamé' (line 13); sonnet LXXXI (L IV, 82; Pl I,
46), where similar images are developed further in the direction of
horror; and sonnet LXXXV (L IV, 85–6; Pl I, 50), a bitter attack on
'Meschante esperance', that 'Harpye, et salle oyseau' (line 12).
[2] Cf. Petrarch, sonnet CLII (Rime, ed. cit., p. 218), lines 7–8: 'per quel
ch'io sento al cor gir fra le vene / dolce veneno, Amor, mia vita è corsa'
('because of that sweet poison which I feel in my body, swirling within
my veins, o Love, my life is over').

the deep sadness of the poet – has clear affinities with Petrarch's sonnet CCCX, 'Zefiro torna, e 'l bel tempo rimena' (*Rime*, ed. cit., p. 396). The quatrains and the first tercet of Ronsard's poem are taken up with the coming of spring, which is presented both at the celestial level of the gods and at the terrestrial level of the seasons and the winds and the earth. It is only in the final tercet that Ronsard turns (with an echo of another of Petrarch's sonnets)[1] to the lover's state of mind:

> Seul, et pensif, aux rochers plus segretz,
> > D'un cuœur muét je conte mes regretz,
> > Et par les boys je voys celant ma playe.

At the end of Petrarch's 'Zefiro torna . . .' the lover had described how, in his wretchedness, all pleasures become torments:

> > e cantar augelletti e fiorir piagge
> > e 'n belle donne oneste atti soavi
> > sono un deserto e fere aspre e selvagge.[2]

The plight of Ronsard's lover seems less extreme, however, and only the final word of the poem hints at a deeper agony.

Indeed, in poems which nominally deal with the sufferings of the lover Ronsard often underplays the negative, painful aspects of the experience, and instead emphasizes very firmly its pleasurable aspects. The two poems just examined show clear signs of this tendency, as will have been apparent already. The very proportions of sonnet CXXVII, for instance, are significant in this respect. Eleven out of the fourteen lines are devoted to the splendidly exuberant portrayal of spring: Jupiter, at one end of the cosmic scale, 'epoint de sa semence/ . . . /L'humide sein de Junon ensemence', while at the other, the fields and the flowers 'De mille et mille et de mille couleurs, / Peignent le sein de la terre si gaye'. Although these eleven lines build up, through the repeated subordinate clauses, to the

---

[1] Sonnet XXXV, 'Solo e pensoso i più deserti campi' (*Rime*, ed. cit., p. 51).
[2] 'The singing of little birds and the flowering of the slopes and the gentle deeds of fair ladies are to me a desert and harsh, savage beasts.'

climax of the final tercet expressing the melancholy of the poet
as he wanders 'Seul, et pensif' amid rocks and woods, yet much
of the emotional power of the poem still seems to remain with
the vibrantly beautiful evocation of spring. Beside this (and
despite the disturbing undertones of the veiled allusion at the
end of the second quatrain to the story of Tereus and Philo-
mela) the poet's sadness seems to lose significance; in effect, it
is the representation of the surging vigour of spring (enriched
in the first quatrain by echoes of Virgil's splendidly sonorous
account in the *Georgics* of the coming of spring, and in the
second, perhaps, by distant echoes of the *Aeneid*)[1] which
predominates in this poem.

A somewhat similar overall effect is achieved by sonnet LI.
The comparison at the end of the poem between the drooping
lily and the poet '[qui] me consume au plus verd de mon age'
inevitably recalls the beautiful flower image of the first quatrain:

> Dedans des Prez je vis une Dryade,
> > Qui comme fleur s'assisoyt par les fleurs,
> > Et mignotoyt un chappeau de couleurs,
> Eschevelée en simple verdugade.

In part this echoes lines from one of Petrarch's most attractive
sonnets on the beauty of Laura (CLX, 'Amor e io sì pien di
meraviglia'):

> Qual miracolo è quel, quando tra l'erba
> quasi un fior siede! ovver quand' ella preme
> col suo candido seno un verde cespo![2]

But there is an even greater immediacy and vividness in
Ronsard's evocation of his 'Dryade'. Her own flowerlike
beauty is further enhanced by the actual flowers which surround her and which she is fashioning into a chaplet for her

---

[1] See *Georgics*, book II, lines 325 ff., and *Aeneid*, book III, lines 69 ff.
[2] *Rime*, ed. cit., p. 226. ('How wondrous it is when she sits amidst the
grass like a flower! or when she presses with her white breast a tuft of
green!')

hair, and also by the suggestion of 'sweet disorder' in her dress. The beauty of the nymph and of the idyllic pastoral setting in which the poet sees her is conveyed so vividly in this quatrain that it is never completely overshadowed by the account of the 'amas de douleurs' which follows: the poet's delight in her beauty seems to persist, as a delicate but insistent memory, right through to the 'beau lis' at the end of the poem.

The implication that the poet's enslavement to his *dame* brings him pleasure and delight rather than pain, in that it enables him to experience beauty in a particularly intense way, in fact appears very early in the *Amours*. The theme is partially broached in the opening sonnet, where the poet announces that anyone who considers the effects which the god of love has had upon him (the poet) will realize, first, that reason is powerless against the onslaught of Cupid, but also that the poet himself is 'trop heureux, / D'avoir au flanc l'aiguillon amoureux'. It is treated more fully, however, in the third sonnet of the collection. This, too, is a poem on the theme of Cupid the archer, who in this case not only strikes his fiery arrow into the poet's heart, but also entangles him in the golden net formed by his lady's hair:

> Dans le serain de sa jumelle flamme
> Je vis Amour, qui son arc desbandoit,
> Et sus mon cuœur le brandon éspandoit,
> Qui des plus froids les moëlles enflamme.
> Puis çà puis là pres les yeulx de ma dame
> Entre cent fleurs un retz d'or me tendoit,
> Qui tout crespu blondement descendoit
> A flotz ondez pour enlasser mon ame.
> Qu'eussay-je faict? l'Archer estoit si doulx,
> Si doulx son feu, si doulx l'or de ses noudz,
> Qu'en leurs filetz encore je m'oublie:
> Mais cest oubli ne me tourmente point,
> Tant doulcement le doulx Archer me poingt,
> Le feu me brusle, et l'or crespe me lie.

> (*L* IV, 7–8; *Pl* I, 4)

Petrarchism and the quest for beauty

The whole sonnet conveys a kind of gratified acceptance, a welcoming even, of the pain of love. The opening line, itself another echo of a phrase from Petrarch's sonnet CLX, establishes through the associations of the word 'serain' and the music of 'sa jumelle flamme' – *m* and *l* delicately poised in a chiasmus on each side of the mute *e* – an atmosphere of peace and relaxation which momentarily holds the reader back before he topples headlong into the sudden surprise of seeing 'Amour, qui son arc desbandoit, / Et sus mon cuœur le brandon éspandoit'. The quatrains build up, through the details of the Cupid motif, to the evocation of Cassandre's hair, whose full, wavelike movement completely envelops the poet in its languor. This atmosphere of intense, overpowering beauty is sustained in the tercets through the insistent, almost hypnotic repetition of 'doulx' (and 'doulcement'), and also through the repetition of other words and sounds which intertwine with the dominant 'doulx . . . doulx . . . doulx . . . doulcement . . . doulx' pattern and pick up some of the earlier motifs. The rhyme words 'flamme' and 'enflamme' in the first quatrain, for instance, are echoed by the initial consonants of 'fleurs' and 'flotz' in the second; meanwhile, 'fleurs' and 'flotz' are themselves echoed in the *l* of 'blondement' and 'enlasser', and these words in turn form an intricate pattern of sound with 'descendoit' and 'ondez', thus weaving the second quatrain into a richly complex texture which seems to embody in the very 'forme sensible' of the words the particular quality both of the beauty of the woman's hair and of the poet's response to that beauty. The patterns set up here are then elaborated and resolved in the tercets in the peace of 'Si doulx son feu, si doulx l'or de ses noudz, / Qu'en leurs filetz encore je m'oublie'. Similarly, the word 'or', with all its associations of magnificence and splendour, provides another (but more straightforward) cumulative echo which links the tercets with what has gone before and emphasizes the luxurious physicality of the experience which the poem is evoking. Significantly, it is with gold that the poem ends, in a specific reminder of the most sensuously beautiful part of the sonnet. The implication seems clear: it is not the lover's possible pain which is paramount, but rather the extreme beauty of Cassandre's hair, experienced by the poet as a *douceur* even more intense than that caused by the prick of Cupid's arrow or the burning of love's fire.[1]

Yet the poet/lover does not merely yield, passively, to the pull which beauty exerts upon him; he also actively reaches out after it, stimulated by what Henri and Catherine Weber have called 'l'élan imaginatif, l'impatience qui l'emporte vers la beauté'.[2] This 'élan imaginatif' is particularly apparent in sonnet XX:

> Je vouldroy bien richement jaunissant
> En pluye d'or goute à goute descendre
> Dans le beau sein de ma belle Cassandre,
> Lors qu'en ses yeulx le somme va glissant.
> Je vouldroy bien en toreau blandissant
> Me transformer pour finement la prendre,
> Quand elle va par l'herbe la plus tendre
> Seule à l'escart mille fleurs ravissant.
> Je vouldroy bien afin d'aiser ma peine
> Estre un Narcisse, et elle une fontaine
> Pour m'y plonger une nuict à sejour:
> Et vouldroy bien que ceste nuict encore
> Durast tousjours sans que jamais l'Aurore
> D'un front nouveau nous r'allumast le jour.
>
> (L IV, 23–4; *Pl* I, 10–11)

At one level the poet's desire to make love to Cassandre is expressed very directly and straightforwardly, for the basic structure of the sonnet consists of the insistent repetition of the simple formula '(Je) vouldroy bien . . .' at the beginning of each quatrain and tercet. But it is the mythological allusions –

---

[1] This luxurious intensity of response to the beauty of Cassandre's hair is also to be found in sonnet XXXIX, 'Quand au matin ma Deesse s'abille' (L IV, 42; *Pl* I, 19) and sonnet LXXVI, 'Soit que son or se crespe lente-ment' (L IV, 77–8; *Pl* I, 40): see above, chapter 1, pp. 31–2.

[2] Pierre de Ronsard, *Les Amours,* ed. H. and C. Weber (Paris, Garnier, 1963), p. xii.

the indirect expression of his amorous feelings – which determine the predominant atmosphere of the sonnet. The voluptuous, lascivious associations of the Jupiterian metamorphoses in the quatrains are, if anything, intensified by the image of Narcissus and his pool. Indeed, the episodes of the lover's transformations are presented with such sensuous detail, and the rhythm and the patterns of sound are so persuasive, that it is easy to half forget that the poem expresses merely a wish, and that the acts of seduction evoked there are in reality only acts of the poet's imagination. It is as though the poet's longing for Cassandre – the fulfilment of which, at the straightforward 'biographical' level, is impossible within the conventions of the petrarchan narrative – can nevertheless be fully realized through the *sorcellerie évocatoire* of poetry. In his sonnet Ronsard has brought into being a world where the ideal and the unattainable have become totally real, and can be securely and confidently enjoyed. For the space of this poem the poet *is* Jupiter making love to Danaë in a shower of gold, enticing Europa to him and carrying her off on his back; he *is* Narcissus, plunging in ecstasy deep into the pool; and for the space of this poem the lover *is* uninterrupted by any dawn. Equally, Cassandre *is* Danaë, poised in a dream-like languor between waking and sleeping; she *is* Europa, gathering flowers and herself about to be gathered, like a flower, by Jupiter; and she *is* the 'fontaine', ready to enfold Narcissus in her depths. The sonnet expresses both the poet's longing and his exultant delight at the realization of his longing; but more importantly, it also embodies within itself precisely that quality of luxuriously sensuous beauty which is the object of the poet's longing.

The same phenomenon can sometimes be seen in the poems on the theme of the *songe amoureux*, where the lover dreams that his desire for his lady, unfulfilled in waking reality, is nevertheless fulfilled for one brief and delightful moment in his dream. In sonnet XXIX (*L* IV, 32–3; *Pl* I, 14), for instance, the quatrains evoke the experience which the poet enjoys as a result of his dream. The beauty and intensity of this experience are very powerfully conveyed in the first four lines, where the sinuous movement of the verse is the exact rhythmical equivalent of the poet's ardent, vinelike embrace of the myriads of beautiful flowers:

> Si mille œilletz, si mille liz j'embrasse,
>> Entortillant mes bras tout alentour,
>> Plus fort qu'un cep, qui d'un amoureux tour
>> La branche aymée impatient enlasse . . .[1]

In the second quatrain the rhythm takes on an expansive, almost soaring quality, as the poet evokes his delight in more generalized terms:

> Si le souci ne jaunist plus ma face,
>> Si le plaisir fonde en moy son sejour,
>> Si j'ayme mieulx les ombres que le jour,
>> Songe divin, cela vient de ta grace.

Only in the tercets is his pleasure lessened, as he indicates his disappointment at the inevitable disappearance of the illusion:

> tu me fuis au meillieu de mon bien,
> Comme l'esclair qui se finist en rien,
> Ou comme au vent s'esvanouit la nuë.

Yet even here, the air of gentle languor which surrounds these final images of disappointment suggests that the joy and exhilaration created by the dream have not been completely invalidated.

An even more powerful experience of delight in beauty, and a markedly more permanent-seeming one, is evoked by sonnet CI. From the very first line the dream experience is accepted totally by the poet, and it remains unthreatened by any awakening into cold reality; throughout, the only kind of reality to be presented is that of the poet's dream:

---

[1] These lines are further enriched by their literary associations. The opening line both alludes to and transcends the familiar petrarchist likening of the loved woman's complexion to beautiful flowers; and the image of the vine was well-established in erotic poetry, both classical, neolatin and vernacular.

Petrarchism and the quest for beauty

Quand en songeant ma follastre j'acolle,
  Laissant mes flancz sus les siens s'allonger,
  Et que d'un bransle habillement leger,
  En sa moytié ma moytié je recolle:
Amour adonq si follement m'affolle,
  Qu'un tel abus je ne vouldroy changer,
  Non au butin d'un rivage estranger,
  Non au sablon qui jaunoye en Pactole.
Mon dieu, quel heur, et quel contentement,
  M'a fait sentir ce faux recollement,
  Changeant ma vie en cent metamorphoses:
Combien de fois doulcement irrité,
  Suis-je ore mort, ore resuscité,
  Parmy l'odeur de mile et mile roses?

                              (*L* IV, 100; *Pl* II, 748)

Very rapidly the sonnet establishes a mood in which languorous
ease is mingled, inextricably, with exuberant delight. The
atmosphere of extreme relaxation suggested by the second line,
which extends and particularizes the implications of 'j'acolle',
serves to set off, by contrast, the poet's intense delight in making love to his lady, which is conveyed both in the playful
endearment 'ma follastre' and also in his lingering (in lines 3–4)
over the pleasurable memory of his own skill as a lover. The
whole first quatrain leads up syntactically and emotionally to
the climax of line 5, whose intricate pattern of repeated sounds,
each echoing an earlier sound, seems to intensify and prolong
the mood evoked in the preceding lines. This is sustained
throughout the remainder of the quatrain by the paralipsis in
which the poet rejects all imaginable material wealth in favour
of his dream. To mention such things – plunder brought back
from distant lands, the gold gleaming in the bed of the river
Pactolus – is surreptitiously to use their associations to enhance
the sumptuous aura of the dream itself. But the lines also echo a
passage in one of Horace's odes, where the poet presumes that
Maecenas – to whom the poem is addressed – would not accept

Ronsard the poet

all the treasures of Araby as an adequate exchange for the riches
of his mistress's hair and of her embraces:

> num tu quae tenuit dives Achaemenes
> aut pinguis Phrygiae Mygdonias opes
> permutare velis crine Licymniae,
>   plenas aut Arabum domos,

> cum flagrantia detorquet ad oscula
> cervicem aut facili saevitia negat,
> quae poscente magis gaudeat eripi,
>   interdum rapere occupet?[1]

We may take it for granted, presumably, that Ronsard intended
the voluptuous associations of this passage to be drawn into
his own poem.

It is an illusory embrace which the poet has experienced (line
10), but the exclamation of extreme pleasure in the preceding
line suggests that this is felt to be the cause of no pain, nor even
regret. Indeed, the poet's sensations seem to be enhanced, not
invalidated, by being dreamed, as he hovers, uncertainly but
delightfully, between activity and relaxation, between opposed
and alternating states which are finally reconciled in the culmin-
ating ecstasy of the last line.

Clearly, Ronsard is drawing on the traditional symbolism of
roses to express the ideal beauty of woman. But the roses are
presented only through their scent, perhaps the most vividly
sensuous manifestation of their physical presence, and one
which both epitomizes and heightens the experience which the
poet has been evoking. Here the roses are not just symbols of
beauty, nor simply visual images of beauty; more than this,
their presence in the poem seems to create a very immediate

---

[1] *Odes,* II, xii, lines 21–8. ('Would you exchange a lock of Licymnia's
tresses for all that rich Achaemenes once owned, or for the Mygdonian
wealth of fertile Phrygia, or the well-stocked homes of the Arabians, as
she bends her neck toward your eager kisses, or in teasing playfulness
refuses to give them (yea, refuses, since, more than he who asks them, she
delights to have them snatched), or at times is first herself to snatch
them?' Loeb edition, p. 137.)

and direct sensation of beauty. The poem seems now to move beyond the particular physical world of lovers' embraces and languorous dreams, into an infinitely expanding world of intensely experienced beauty, 'Parmy l'odeur de mile et mile roses'.

This tendency of the poet to transcend the immediate circumstances of his love for his lady is also manifested in sonnet C, 'Le pensement, qui me fait devenir' (*L* IV, 99–100; *Pl* II, 748), where anticipation of delight alone, unaided by the freedom which dreams grant to the imaginative powers, and without (on this occasion) the immediate impulse of urgently felt desire, is sufficient to enable the poet to reach out towards, and to enter, the ideal world of directly experienced beauty. The sonnet begins with the poet noting the overpowering effect which the mere thought of '[le] bien qui me doibt avenir' has upon him: 'mon ame / Desja desja impuissante, se pasme'. Indeed, he wonders in the second quatrain whether he will be able to withstand 'Sans mourir . . . / Le doulx combat, que me garde Madame'. The effects achieved by these opening lines depend partly on their gently hypnotic rhythm, which quietly overrides the metre (two successive enjambments lead directly into the eager, yet swooning reduplication of 'Desja desja impuissante . . .'); and partly on the allusion to the richly evocative Ovidian *topos* of the combat of love and the sweetness of dying therein:

> felix, quem Veneris certamina mutua perdunt!
> di faciant, leti causa sit ista mei!
> Induat adversis contraria pectora telis
> miles et aeternum sanguine nomen emat . . .
> at mihi contingat Veneris languescere motu,
> cum moriar, medium solvar et inter opus.[1]

[1] *Amores,* II, x, lines 29–32, 35–6. ('Happy he whom the mutual strife of Love lays low! Ye gods, let my end come from such a cause! Let the soldier give his breast to cover with hostile darts, and buy eternal glory with his blood. . . . But for me – may it be my lot when I die to languish in Venus's embrace, and be dissolved in the midst of its delight.' Loeb edition, pp. 413 and 415.)

[95]

Ronsard the poet

Ronsard's poet then turns to Venus herself, 'que l'escume féconde, / Non loing de Cypre, enfanta dessus l'onde', and appeals to her to receive him into her care:

> Si de fortune en ce combat je meurs,
> Reçoy ma vie, o deesse, et la guide
> Parmy l'odeur de tes plus belles fleurs,
> Dans les vergers du Paradis de Gnide.

This is the moment of the poet's apotheosis, as, bathed in the pleasure afforded by the scent of '[les] plus belles fleurs', he is finally led into the paradise of Venus, the wooded garden of amorous peace, whose air of wondrous enchantment seems to be summed up in its strange, mysterious-sounding name, 'Gnide', placed right at the end of the poem, so that its echoes linger hauntingly in the reader's mind after the music of the rest of the poem has died away.

Occasionally Ronsard clothes these aspirations towards beauty in neoplatonic colours:

> Comme on souloit si plus on ne me blasme
> D'estre tousjours lentement otieux,
> Je t'en ren grace, heureux trait de ces yeulx,
> Qui m'ont parfait l'imparfait de mon ame.
> Ore l'esclair de leur divine flamme,
> Dressant en l'air mon vol audacieux
> Pour voir le Tout, m'esleve jusqu'aux cieux,
> Dont ici bas la partie m'enflamme.
> Par le moins beau, qui mon penser aisla,
> Au sein du beau mon penser s'en vola,
> Epoinçonné d'une manie extreme:
> Là, du vray beau j'adore le parfait,
> Là, d'otieux actif je me suis fait,
> Là, je cogneu ma maistresse et moy-mesme.
>
> (L IV, 164–5; Pl I, 88)[1]

---

[1] There had been a certain neoplatonic colouring to the *Vœu* with which Ronsard prefaced the *Amours,* for he referred there to Cassandre as 'UNE

Petrarchism and the quest for beauty

It is appropriate, no doubt, to remember that for Pontus de Tyard's 'Solitaire' the final stage of the soul's reascent, fired by 'fureur divine', to 'la source de son souverain bien et felicité derniere', is achieved by means of love:

> En fin, quand tout ce qui est en l'essence, et en la nature de l'Ame, est fait un, il faut (pour revenir à la source de son origine) que soudain elle se revoque en ce souverain *un*, qui est sur toute essence, Chose, que la grande et celeste Venus accomplit par Amour, c'est à dire, par un fervent, et incomparable desir, que l'Ame ainsi eslevée a de jouir de la divine et eternelle beauté.[1]

Ronsard's expression of this 'fervent et incomparable desir' is characteristically urgent and impassioned:

> O sainct brazier, ô feu chastement beau,
>   Las, brusle moy d'un si chaste flambeau
>   Qu'abandonant ma despouille cognue,
> Nét, libre, et nud, je vole d'un plein sault,
>   Oultre le ciel, pour adorer là hault
>   L'aultre beauté dont la tienne est venue.
>
> (*L* IV, 135; *Pl* I, 75)

However, it is to the paradisiac world embodied in the image of 'les vergers . . . de Gnide' that the poet most insistently aspires, a world which brings fulfilment to his physical longings and also to his aesthetic emotions. To this extent, the *Amours* are an account not so much of the poet's pleasures and pains in love, as of his continual striving to experience as intensely and

---

BEAUTÉ QUI SAGEMENT AFFOLE' (line 11); however, this expression disappeared completely in the revision for the 1578 and subsequent editions (*L* IV, 4; *Pl* I, 2). For a study of 'les points de contact et les interférences' between platonism and sensuality in the love poetry of the Pléiade, see H. Weber's contribution to *Lumières de la Pléiade* (Paris, Vrin, 1966), pp. 157–94; see also below, chapter 3, pp. 128–37.

[1] Pontus de Tyard, *Solitaire Premier*, ed. S. F. Baridon (Geneva, Droz; Lille Giard, 1950), p. 20.

directly as possible a world of total beauty. The love which the
poet is portrayed as feeling is less love for a particular woman –
indeed, the reader has little impression, after completing the
Amours, of Cassandre as an individual person – than love for
the poetic ideal of beauty to which she gives access and which
she embodies. From this point of view, the poet's worship of
Cassandre and his yearning for her may be regarded as a kind
of allegory of the artist's eternal obsession with and pursuit of
'le Beau'. This eager reaching-out after total beauty and the
exultant embodiment of it in poetry constitutes a major part
of the overall meaning of the *Amours*. For while at the surface
level of the petrarchan conventions Cassandre is presented as a
paragon compounded of all perfections, and the poet, equally
in accordance with the conventions, as her ardently yearning
lover, the ardour and the yearning seem not infrequently to
outgrow those conventions. When this happens, in the very
expression of his passionate longing for and delight in beauty,
the poet makes real and embodies within the verse precisely
those sensuous, almost palpable qualities of beauty after which
he strives.

This beauty, the beauty which is achievable only in and
through poetry, is manifested in the Cassandre *Amours* with
great power and great immediacy. But what seems at least
equally striking in this collection is the air of exuberant self-
confidence which the poet so often displays in his pursuit of
beauty. Sonnets such as 'Franc de raison, esclave de fureur'
seem to represent relatively isolated moments of frustration
and tormented anguish, while only occasionally does the poet
experience periods of self-doubt.[1] Nor are the materials which

---

[1] To the earlier references (see p. 85, note 1) may perhaps be added the
following: sonnet XIX (*L* IV, 22–3; *Pl* I, 10), which contains a series of
grim prophecies from Cassandre ('De tes souspirs tes nepveux se riront. /
Tu seras faict d'un vulgaire la fable'), and to which the sensuous exuberance of the succeeding sonnet ('Je vouldroy bien richement jaunissant')
forms a complete contrast; sonnet XXVIII (*L* IV, 31–2; *Pl* I, 14), where
Cassandre appears disturbingly in the poet's dreams 'Ores en forme, ou
d'un foudre enflammé, / Ou d'une nef, ou d'un Tigre affamé' (this poem,

Petrarchism and the quest for beauty

Ronsard brings together in this collection – the petrarchan conventions on the one hand, and the personae of the poet and his lady on the other – made to resist the processes of poetic transformation to which they are subjected. Cassandre is fully assimilated into the range of the conventions; at no time does she appear as a woman whose individual personality and attributes cannot be totally accounted for within those conventions. Thus she never threatens to disturb the poet's aesthetic vision, still less to prevent it from being realized. The poet, too, is able to accept his role as petrarchan lover willingly and without question. His ability to create, through the magic of words, a self-sustaining world of total beauty thus remains fundamentally unchallenged, either from outside himself or from within.

$$*$$
$$*\qquad*$$
$$*$$

With the *Sonets pour Helene*, however, the use which Ronsard makes of the petrarchan conventions and the attitudes which his poetry evinces seem to have shifted quite markedly and to have become altogether more complex and more ambivalent than they were in the *Amours*. Not surprisingly the passage of twenty-five years has brought with it a considerable change both in the kinds of theme which Ronsard chooses to stress and in the overall mood and atmosphere which he chooses to create.

The *Sonets pour Helene* place themselves very squarely and very clearly within the petrarchan tradition; for, like the *Amours*, they contain many motifs and images for which parallels can readily be found in Petrarch's *Rime* and in the

---

too, is immediately followed by one much more positive in tone: 'Si mille œilletz, si mille liz j'embrasse'); and sonnet CL (*L* IV, 144–5; *Pl* I, 79), where in the final tercet a centaur suddenly snatches Cassandre away and destroys the poet's slowly growing feeling of confidence in himself: 'un centaure envieux sur ma vie / L'ayant en crope au galop l'a ravie, / Me laissant seul, et mes criz imparfaitz.'

works of his Italian imitators. But it is also suggested in the very first sonnet of the *Sonets pour Helene* that to some extent, at least, this will be an 'anti-petrarchan' collection – or rather that there will be clear variations from the standard petrarchan patterns.[1] Having sworn by Castor and Pollux, and by various features of nature which lovers might be expected to hold dear, that he seeks no other love than Hélène, the poet then goes on: 'Vous seule me plaisez: j'ay par election, / Et non à la volée aimé vostre jeunesse'. This is a quite striking assertion, for more usually it is fate (often acting through the agency of Cupid) which is held to be responsible for the petrarchan lover's enslavement to his lady. Ronsard's poet, on the other hand, claims here that he has of his own volition chosen to love Hélène. Moreover, in doing so, he seems to reverse one of Petrarch's own expressions, used in an analogous context: 'Amor la spinge e tira, / non per elezion ma per destino'.[2] Not only this, however: it may perhaps be that the phrase 'à la volée' ('casually', 'without thinking') is also intended as an ironic, deflating antithesis to the petrarchan 'destino'. For a certain tendency to irony appears throughout the poem. In insisting on his faithfulness to Hélène, for example, the poet had sworn that 'autre part je ne veux chercher autre avanture'

[1] The anti-petrarchan aspects of the *Sonets pour Helene* are also stressed by Mary Morrison in her article 'Ronsard and Desportes', in *Bibliothèque d'humanisme et Renaissance,* 28 (1966), pp. 303 ff.

[2] 'Love drives and draws it on, not by choice but because of fate' (sonnet CCXLVII, 'Parrà forse ad alcun che'n lodar quella', *Rime,* ed. cit., p. 321). 'La' / 'it' here is the poet's 'mortal tongue', stimulated by love to attempt the impossible task of adequately singing the praises of the divine Laura. Ronsard's assertion in this sonnet does not prevent him from sometimes ascribing the cause of his love to fate; see the opening lines of the eighth sonnet in book I (*L* XVII, 203; *Pl* I, 219): 'Tu ne dois en ton cœur superbe devenir / Pour me tenir captif: cela vient de Fortune'; or lines 5–7 of sonnet XXII in the same book: 'L'Amour et la Raison, comme deux combatans, / Se sont escarmouchez l'espace de quatre ans: / A la fin j'ay perdu, veincu par destinee' (*L* XVII, 214; *Pl* I, 228). Such discrepancies suggest that Ronsard is more concerned to adapt given motifs to the particular 'message' of an individual poem than to achieve complete consistency between one poem and another.

(line 8). But 'avanture' seems an unexpectedly worldly term for the petrarchan lover to use of his relationship with his lady. And the poem ends in a similarly anticlimactic fashion:

> Je suis de ma fortune autheur, je le confesse:
> La vertu m'a conduit en telle affection:
> Si la vertu me trompe, adieu belle Maistresse.

To envisage in the very first sonnet of the collection that the relationship might end, and virtually to threaten his 'belle Maistresse' with this possibility, makes a sharp contrast with the usual attitudes towards his lady which the conventions lead one to expect of the yearning and languishing lover.[1] Indeed, on reading further in the *Sonets pour Helene* one realizes that Ronsard is both accepting the petrarchan conventions and simultaneously rejecting them. It is as though he uses the conventions as a kind of melody against which he can set the continually intrusive counterpoint of a set of attitudes which completely undermine – and indeed make impossible – the conventional petrarchan relationship between the poet and his lady.

Like Cassandre in the *Amours*, Hélène is presented from the beginning as a paragon of beauty and virtue:

> Tout ce qui est de sainct, d'honneur et de vertu,
> Tout le bien qu'aux mortels la Nature peut faire,
> Tout ce que l'artifice icy peut contrefaire,
> Ma maistresse, en naissant, dans l'esprit l'avoit eu.

[1] Cf. the poet's aggressively anti-petrarchan reactions in the poem *A son livre* of 1556. There, having doubted whether Petrarch really persisted in loving Laura for thirty years if she did not respond to him ('Ou bien il jouissoit de sa Laurette, ou bien / Il estoit un grand fat d'aymer sans avoir rien'), he announced that he had broken off his relationship with Cassandre precisely because she had been so unresponsive, and that he would do the same again if it should turn out that his present love had similar shortcomings: 'Laquelle tout soudain je quitteray, si elle / M'est, comme fut Cassandre, orgueilleuse et rebelle, / Pour en chercher une autre' (lines 163–5; *L* VII, 315–25; *Pl* I, 111–15). The piquancy of the situation in the *Sonets pour Helene,* of course, is that anti-petrarchan attitudes should be flaunted in a setting so strongly coloured by petrarchism.

Ronsard the poet

> Du juste et de l'honneste à l'envy debatu
> Aux escoles des Grecs: de ce qui peut attraire
> A l'amour du vray bien, à fuyr le contraire,
> Ainsi que d'un habit son corps fut revestu.
>
> (*L* XVII, 197; *Pl* I, 216)[1]

In a later poem, the poet urges the god of love to contemplate Hélène's perfections as she strolls through a garden:

> Amour, qui as ton regne en ce monde si ample,
> Voy ta gloire et la mienne errer en ce jardin:
> Voy comme son bel œil, mon bel astre divin,
> Reluist comme une lampe ardente dans un Temple:
> Voy son corps, des beautez le portrait et l'exemple,
> Qui ressemble une Aurore au plus beau d'un matin:
> Voy son esprit, seigneur du Sort et du Destin,
> Qui passe la Nature, en qui Dieu se contemple. . . .
> Voy sortir un Printemps des rayons de ses yeux:
> Et voy comme à l'envy ses flames amoureuses
> Embellissent la terre, et serenent les Cieux.
>
> (*L* XVII, 249; *Pl* I, 244)

Yet on occasion the poet's praise and admiration of Hélène are expressed in distinctly equivocal terms. In sonnet XVIII of book II, for example, the final two lines seem to go some considerable way towards overriding the apparently unambiguous praise contained in the main body of the poem:

> Toute vertu divine acquise et naturelle
> Se loge en ton esprit. La Nature et les Cieux
> Ont versé dessus toy leurs dons à qui mieux mieux:
> Puis pour n'en faire plus ont rompu le modelle.

---

[1] Cf. the *Amours,* sonnet II, second quatrain:

> Tout ce qu'Amour rarement couvoyt,
> De beau, de chaste, et d'honneur soubz ses ailles,
> Emmiella les graces immortelles
> De son bel œil qui les dieux emouvoyt.
>
> (*L* IV, 6–7; *Pl* I, 3)

Petrarchism and the quest for beauty

> Icy à ta beauté se joint la Chasteté,
> Icy l'honneur de Dieu, icy la Pieté,
> La crainte de mal-faire, et la peur d'infamie:
>   Icy un cœur constant, qu'on ne peut esbranler.
> Pource en lieu de mon cœur, d'Helene, et de ma vie,
> Je te veux desormais ma Pandore appeller.
>
>   (*L* XVII, 261; *Pl* I, 258)

The reader may pause, perhaps, at the mention of 'La crainte de mal-faire, et la peur d'infamie', which seem somewhat limited, negative virtues when set against her possession of 'Toute vertu divine', asserted with such assurance in the preceding quatrain. But to insist on calling Hélène 'ma Pandore' seems very much of a two-edged compliment here. Pandora was indeed the perfect woman, thanks to all the gifts bestowed upon her by the gods; but by opening the box entrusted to her and releasing all the evils it contained, she also became the scourge of mankind. It is in favour of the ambivalent associations of this name that the poet dismisses other possible appellations for Hélène: not only the conventional hyperboles of 'mon cœur', 'ma vie', but even her actual name, Hélène, with all its rich echoes and associations.[1]

Ambivalent, too, is the ending of sonnet XLIX in book II:

> Tu as pour tes vertuz en mes vers un honneur,
> Qui malgré le tombeau suivra ta renommee.
>   Les Dames de ce temps n'envient ta beauté,
> Mais ton nom tant de fois par les Muses chanté,
> Qui languiroit d'oubly, si je ne t'eusse aimee.
>
>   (*L* XVII, 285; *Pl* I, 271)

---

[1] We may contrast this use of the Pandora theme with that in sonnet XXXII of the *Amours* (*L* IV, 35–6; *Pl* I, 15), where the negative implications are not developed at all. Interestingly enough, 'ma Pandore' in the present poem was replaced for the 1584 edition by the less harsh 'mon destin'. Perhaps the most striking use of the Pandora theme in the sixteenth century is at the end of the second *dizain* in Scève's *Délie*: Délie inspired love in the poet at his first sight of her, 'Comme de tous la delectation, / Et de moy seul fatale Pandora'.

The first line of the last tercet could be understood to mean: your contemporaries do not envy your beauty – enviable though it is – but rather your fame. On the other hand it could be read as: they do not envy your beauty (for it is not great enough to be envied), but your fame. It is not a question here of deciding which of these readings is 'correct'. Both are possible, and the ambivalence must therefore be taken as part of the poet's intention, which is clearly both to emphasize that he is conferring immortality upon Hélène, and also, slyly, to suggest doubts about the perfection of her beauty.[1]

Doubts of a similar kind are raised in sonnet XXXII in the same book. The first quatrain evokes in lively detail the rich beauty of Hélène's hair:

> Ces cheveux, ces liens, dont mon cœur tu enlasses,
> Gresles, primes, subtils, qui coulent aux talons,
> Entre noirs et chastains, bruns, deliez et longs,
> Tels que Venus les porte, et ses trois belles Graces . . .
>
> (L XVII, 272; Pl I, 263)

With rather elaborate preciosity the poet then develops the petrarchan conceit of the first line ('ces liens . . . Me tiennent si estrains, Amour'), before returning in the first tercet to the praise of her hair. But this time his manner seems a little less straightforward than before:

> Cheveux non achetez, empruntez ny fardez,
> Qui vostre naturel sans feintise gardez,
> Que vous me semblez beaux!

In sonnet CI of the *Amours* the figure of paralipsis had been used to intensify the luxurious atmosphere of the poet's dream (see p. 93 above); here, the same figure is made to operate in

[1] Cf. sonnet XXIV of the *Amours diverses*, lines 10–11 (L XVII, 307; Pl I, 225): 'Vous n'estes si superbe, ou si riche en beauté, / Qu'il faille desdaigner un bon cœur qui vous aime.' In 1584 this sonnet was incorporated, along with a number of others, into the *Sonets pour Helene*; for a discussion of the significance of the 'traffic' (in both directions) between the *Amours diverses* and the *Sonets pour Helene,* see D. Stone, *Ronsard's Sonnet Cycles,* pp. 227–44.

the reverse direction. The mere mention of false or dyed hair –
even though the poet is only asserting that Hélène has no need
of such aids to beauty – is enough to bring the poem very
firmly down to earth again after the grandeur of the reference
to 'Venus . . . et ses trois belles Graces' in the first quatrain.

It is not only in her physical attributes, however, that Hélène
seems to fit with less than complete precision into the petrarchan norm. The lady's aloofness, the absence on her part of any
positive response or encouragement to the lover was obligatory in the petrarchan tradition. But in Hélène's case the aloofness is presented almost as a fault in her individual temperament,
rather than as something inevitable within the conventional
situation. The poet notes in one sonnet, for instance, that when
Hélène talks to him her voice is 'De desdain, de froideur et
d'orgueil toute pleine' (L XVII, 281; Pl I, 268). Indeed, he
complains elsewhere, she seems to dislike pleasing people,

> ayant le desdain si joint à la beauté,
> Que de plaire à quelcun semble qu'il vous desplaise.
> (L XVII, 226; Pl I, 234)

The poet had already warned her in a distinctly moralizing,
even patronizing tone of the dangers of pride:

> Amour, comme estant Dieu, n'aime pas les superbes.
> Sois douce à qui te prie, imitant le Lion:
> La foudre abat les monts, non les petites herbes.
> (L XVII, 221; Pl I, 231)

Furthermore, she is hypocritical in her dealings with the
poet. She claims to enjoy 'les plaints des chetifs amoureux, /
Toute voix lamentable, et pleine de tristesse', but

> Voz propos sont trompeurs. Si vous aviez soucy
> De ceux qui ont un cœur larmoyant et transy,
> Je vous ferois pitié par une sympathie:

Ronsard the poet

> Mais vostre œil cauteleux, trop finement subtil,
> Pleure en chantant mes vers, comme le Crocodil,
> Pour mieux me desrober par feintise la vie.
>
> (L XVII, 216–17; Pl I, 229)[1]

The thinly veiled bluntness of tone in which this accusation is made is particularly striking, as is the fierce scorn with which on another occasion he accuses her of intellectual dishonesty and deliberate self-deception in pleading that her honour would be compromised if she were to respond to his wooing:

> Cest honneur, ceste loy sont noms pleins d'imposture,
> Que vous alleguez tant, faussement inventez
> De noz peres resveurs, par lesquels vous ostez
> Et forcez les presens les meilleurs de Nature.
>
> Vous trompez vostre sexe, et luy faites injure:
> La coustume vous pipe, et du faux vous domtez
> Voz plaisirs, voz desirs, vous et voz voluptez,
> Sous l'ombre d'une sotte et vaine couverture. . . .
>
> Vostre esprit est trop bon pour ne le sçavoir pas:
> Vous prendrez, s'il vous plaist, les sots à tels apas:
> Je ne veux pour le faux tromper la chose vraye.
>
> (L XVII, 266–7; Pl I, 296)[2]

As we have seen, even the compliments which the poet pays Hélène seem sometimes to have a sharp edge of irony about them. He portrays himself puffing and panting up the stairs to Hélène's apartment 'au sommet du palais de noz Rois' only to receive a cool and scornful brush-off when he gets there (L XVII, 280–1; Pl I, 268–9). 'Tu es vrayment Deesse', he adds, 'assise en si haut lieu'; but the snag is that even though I climb so high, I'm no god (lines 9–10). The compliment to Hélène could be taken at its face value, as sincere; or it could equally

[1] 'Suivant les anciens auteurs, le crocodile pleurait en apercevant les passants, sans doute pour les attirer et les dévorer ensuite, de là l'expression: larmes de crocodile' (Ronsard, Les Amours, ed. H. and C. Weber, p. 733).
[2] In the 1584 collected edition, this poem is removed from the Sonets pour Helene and placed in the Amours diverses.

well be taken as a piece of tongue-in-cheek irony ('You really are a goddess, aren't you – I hadn't believed it before – living right up here!') which means the reverse of what it says. Similarly, the opening quatrain of sonnet XII in book I reads at first as an entirely charming compliment to Hélène:

Deux Venus en Avril (puissante Deité)
Nasquirent, l'une en Cypre, et l'autre en la Saintonge:
La Venus Cyprienne est des Grecs la mensonge,
La chaste Saintongeoise est une verité.

(L XVII, 206; Pl I, 221)

By being contrasted with 'La Venus Cyprienne', the goddess of terrestrial, sensual love, Hélène is implicitly identified with the celestial Venus, goddess of divine love. But we know, with the hindsight gained from later poems, that Hélène's 'chasteté' is not always a quality which the poet feels able to praise whole-heartedly.[1] Moreover, the present sonnet follows immediately after one in which Hélène has been seen flippantly turning away from the poet to flirt with someone else: 'Arrivant un mortel de plus fresche jeunesse / . . . / Tu me laissas tout seul pour luy faire caresse' (L XVII, 206; Pl I, 220). Does the poet's compliment, then, carry with it the muted hint that, whereas the Cyprian Venus was, sadly, merely a delightful fiction, the chastity of the Venus of the Saintonge is, equally sadly, very much a reality? As with sonnet XLIX of book II (see pp. 103–4 above), it seems that the two meanings coexist, with the result that the ambiguity serves tentatively to undermine the conventions by suggesting the poet's impatience with them. For no matter how much, on one level, he tries to assimilate Hélène to the conventional norm, on another he cannot ignore the reality of her individual temperament.

Nor, it is clear, can the poet of the *Sonets pour Helene* ignore what he is himself. As often as not we see him very much ill at ease in the role of the yearning, languishing lover which the

[1] See especially the famous anti-platonist sonnets: 'Bien que l'esprit humain s'enfle par la doctrine' (L XVII, 229; Pl I, 236) and 'En choisissant l'esprit vous estes mal-apprise' (L XVII, 230; Pl II, 919). (The latter sonnet did not appear at all in the 1584 collected edition.)

conventions impose upon him. In marked contrast to the
Amours of Cassandre, the Hélène collection contains only one
poem – sonnet LII in book I – which takes as its whole theme
the delight derived by the poet from his sufferings:

> Je sens une douceur à conter impossible,
> Dont ravy je jouys par le bien du penser,
> Qu'homme ne peut escrire, ou langue prononcer,
> Quand je baise ta main contre Amour invincible.
>
> Contemplant tes beaux rais, ma pauvre ame passible
> En se pasmant se perd: lors je sens amasser
> Un sang froid sur mon cœur, qui garde de passer
> Mes esprits, et je reste une image insensible.
>
> Voila que peut ta main et ton œil, où les trais
> D'Amour sont si ferrez, si chauds et si espais
> Au regard Medusin, qui en rocher me mue.
>
> Mais bien que mon malheur procede de les voir,
> Je voudrois mille mains, et autant d'yeux avoir,
> Pour voir et pour toucher leur beauté qui me tue.
>
> > (*L* XVII, 242–3; *Pl* I, 239–40)

And even this poem has its ambivalences, as the inhibiting,
negative aspects of the experience ('Un sang froid . . . [le]
regard Medusin') almost succeed in stifling the 'douceur à
conter impossible', only for it to be firmly reasserted in the
final tercet.

For the rest, the poet seems to emphasize very clearly the
misery of his situation: 'La douleur me consomme: ayez de
moy pitié,' he urges Hélène early in the second book; 'Vous
n'aurez de ma mort ny profit ny louange' (*L* XVII, 251; *Pl* I,
245). But perhaps the poet's most acute and most immediate
source of discomfort in his relationship with Hélène is his
awareness of his own rapidly advancing years:

> Trois ans sont ja passez que ton œil me tient pris.
> Je ne suis pas marry de me voir en servage:
> Seulement je me deuls des ailes de mon âge,
> Qui me laissent le chef semé de cheveux gris.
>
> > (*L* XVII, 208; *Pl* I, 221)

Petrarchism and the quest for beauty

Repeatedly he returns to this theme, and to his clear realization of the inappropriateness of his situation – that of an old man trying to play a young man's game:

> Maintenant en Automne encore malheureux,
> Je vy comme au Printemps de nature amoureux,
> Afin que tout mon âge aille au gré de la peine:
>   Et ores que je deusse estre exempt du harnois,
> Mon Colonnel m'envoye à grands coups de carquois
> R'assieger Ilion pour conquerir Heleine.
>
> (L XVII, 255; Pl I, 247)[1]

The self-mocking irony of this passage is underlined, of course, by the implied contrast between the poet's all too mundane predicament, and the grandiose associations of the story of Helen of Troy. There are echoes, too, of Ovid's *Amores*, which serve to sharpen the irony still further:

> Militat omnis amans, et habet sua castra Cupido . . .
> quae bello est habilis, Veneri quoque convenit aetas.
>   turpe senex miles, turpe senilis amor. . . .
> Fessus in acceptos miles deducitur agros . . .
> me quoque, qui totiens merui sub amore puellae,
>   defunctum placide vivere tempus erat.[2]

Ronsard's poet is both ashamed at the indignity of the position in which he finds himself, and annoyed at not being able to

---

[1] Cf. also, for example, the sonnet 'Comme un vieil combatant, qui ne veut plus s'armer' (L XVII, 263; Pl I, 258–9), or the first quatrain of 'Je m'enfuy du combat, ma bataille est desfaite' (L XVII, 294; Pl I, 277–8). The *topos* of the poet's 'chef grison' is a favourite one with Ronsard, which appears in his love poetry as early as 1553, in one of the sonnets included in the second edition of the *Amours* (L V, 140; Pl I, 49). But only in the *Sonets pour Helene* does it become an insistent motif.

[2] *Amores* I, ix, lines 1, 3–4 ('Every lover is a soldier, and Cupid has a camp of his own…. The age that is meet for the wars is also suited to Venus. 'Tis unseemly for the old man to soldier, unseemly for the old man to love'), and II, ix, lines 19, 23–4 ('The tired-out soldier is let retire to the acres he received…. I, too, who have served so oft in the wars of woman's love – 'twere time, my labours o'er, I lived in peace'). Loeb edition, pp. 355 and 409.

resolve it satisfactorily. In a sonnet from book I which is based on the familiar petrarchan metaphor of the lover's relationship with his lady as a perilous, storm-tossed sea voyage, the development of the metaphor at the end leads to no grand emotional gesture, no elegant, harmoniously pointed 'conceit' – but merely to a wry, half-punning, half-resentful statement of frustration, presented in a flat, unemphatic rhythm which is in total contrast to the vigour and panache of the *Amours*:

> Je suis seul, me noyant, de ma vie homicide,
> Choisissant un enfant, un aveugle pour guide,
> Dont il me faut de honte et pleurer et rougir.
> Je ne crain point la mort . . .
> . . . seulement je me fasche
> De voir un si beau port, et n'y pouvoir surgir.
>
> (*L* XVII, 199–200; *Pl* I, 217)[1]

Yet the resentment which the poet feels is directed as much at himself as it is at Hélène. He resents above all the ease with which his reason yielded to love's attacks – an act of treachery which has brought about ceaseless hostilities between different parts of his being. In the following sonnet the poet begins by using the petrarchan formula 'Bienheureux fut le jour . . .' to express his pleasure in remembering the moment of his soul's submission to Hélène's 'douce rigueur';[2] but very rapidly after the first quatrain the mood darkens, and the poem ends with tormented images of war and betrayal:

> La Raison pour neant au chef fit sa retraite,
> Et se mit au dongeon, comme au lieu le plus seur:
> D'esperance assaillie, et prise de douceur,
> Rendit ma liberté, qu'en vain je re-souhaite.

[1] In Petrarch see, for example, sestina LXXX, 'Chi è fermato di menar sua vita' (*Rime,* ed. cit. pp. 118–19), or sonnet CLXXXIX, 'Passa la nave mia colma d'oblio' (ibid., p. 255).

[2] Cf. Petrarch, sonnet LXI, 'Benedetto sia 'l giorno e 'l mese e l'anno' (*Rime,* ed. cit., p. 88).

Petrarchism and the quest for beauty

Le Ciel le veult ainsi, qui pour mieux offenser
Mon cœur, le baille en garde à la foy du Penser:
Lequel trahit mon camp, desloyal sentinelle,
  Ouvrant l'huis du rempart aux soudars des Amours.
J'auray tousjours en l'ame une guerre eternelle:
Mes pensers et mon cœur me trahissent tousjours.

  (L XVII, 234–5; Pl I, 237–8)[1]

The poet also, of course, resents the great discrepancy which
exists between the nature of his own feelings for Hélène and
her minimal response:

Ma fievre croist tousjours, la vostre diminue:
Vous le voyez, Helene, et si ne vous en chaut. . . .
La vostre est à plaisir, la mienne est continue.

  (L XVII, 242; Pl I, 239)

In fact, the inequality between the poet's feelings and Hélène's
is such that eventually he decides to put an end to the relationship. Foreseen as a possibility in the opening sonnet of the
collection, and specifically wished for in sonnet XXXIII of
book II ('je veux de mon col les liens destacher', L XVII, 273;
Pl I, 294), the break becomes definitive some twenty sonnets
later:

Adieu, cruelle, adieu, je te suis ennuyeux:
C'est trop chanté d'Amour sans nulle recompense.
Te serve qui voudra, je m'en vay . . .

Reason is recalling him, the poet claims, and he resolves to
nurture Cupid no longer, 'cest Enfant qui me ronge, / Qui les
credules prend comme un poisson à l'hain' (L XVII, 293;
Pl I, 275). I'm giving up, he continues in the following sonnet,

[1] Similar images are used on a number of occasions in the *Sonets pour
Helene*: cf., for example, the upbraiding of Reason, 'qui mon fort aban-
donnes', in the sonnet 'Maistresse, quand je pense aux traverses d'Amour'
(L XVII, 233; Pl I, 296), or the poet's blaming of his 'ame' ('la sotte
qu'elle est') in 'Mon ame mille fois m'a predit mon dommage' (L XVII,
281; Pl I, 269). Cf. Petrarch, sonnet CCLXXIV, 'Datemi pace, o duri
miei pensieri' (*Rime*, ed. cit., p. 360).

it is time to acknowledge defeat and go home; it is not that I am being unfaithful to you – merely that old age has caught up with me:

> Je m'enfuy du combat, ma bataille est desfaite . . .
> Ja dix lustres passez, et ja mon poil grison
> M'appellent au logis, et sonnent la retraite. . . .
> Je ne suis ny Pâris, ny desloyal Jason:
> J'obeis à la loy que la Nature a faite.

(L XVII, 294; Pl I, 277–8)

His grounds for complaint, he acknowledges, lie within himself – but also in Hélène's aloof pride. She will repent of it, he supposes – 'si tu as un bon cœur' (and the 'si' is clearly less than complimentary) – but by then it will be too late. And the sonnet ends with a wearily bitter *sententia*: 'le tard repentir ne guarist le dommage'.

As we have already seen, such attacks, in which the poet's resentment is turned upon Hélène herself, are by no means uncommon in the *Sonets pour Helene*. Some, indeed, are particularly fierce and virulent. In sonnet LVI of book I, for instance, the poet appeals to love to avenge his misery by turning Hélène's hair white and making her old:

> Je ne veux point la mort de celle qui arreste
> Mon cœur en sa prison: mais, Amour, pour venger
> Mes larmes de six ans, fay ses cheveux changer,
> Et seme bien espais des neiges sur sa teste.
>
> Si tu veux, la vengeance est desja toute preste:
> Tu accourcis les ans, tu les peux allonger:
> Ne souffres en ton camp ton soudart outrager:
> Que vieille elle devienne, ottroyant ma requeste.
>
> Elle se glorifie en ses cheveux frisez,
> En sa verde jeunesse, en ses yeux aiguisez,
> Qui tirent dans les cœurs mille poinctes encloses.
>
> Pourquoy te braves-tu de cela qui n'est rien?
> La beauté n'est que vent, la beauté n'est pas bien:
> Les beautez en un jour s'en-vont comme les Roses.

(L XVII, 245–6; Pl I, 241)

Petrarchism and the quest for beauty

The icy hostility of the quatrains is unmistakable, as is the dismissive scorn (particularly in line 9) for what the poet sees as Hélène's unjustifiable self-satisfaction; only in the last line, with its inevitable echoes of 'Mignonne, allon voir si la rose . . .', does the tone become more gentle again. Elsewhere, the poet plays on the etymology of Hélène's name, and accentuates the violence suggested by the Greek word ἑλεῖν:

> Ny la douce pitié, ny le pleur lamentable
> Ne t'ont baillé ton nom: Helene vient d'oster,
> De ravir, de tuer, de piller, d'emporter
> Mon esprit et mon cœur, ta proye miserable.
>
> (*L* XVII, 254; *Pl* I, 246)

In a later poem, he even tells her brusquely that she is not worthy of her name, and should change it. The sun, he points out, enters the sign of the Gemini (her brothers) in May:

> Mais ton corps nonchalant, revesche et rigoureux,
> Qui jamais nulle flame amoureuse n'assemble,
> En ce beau mois de May malgré tes ans ressemble,
> O perte de jeunesse! à l'Hyver froidureux.
>   Tu n'es digne d'avoir les deux Jumeaux pour freres:
> A leur gentille humeur les tiennes sont contraires,
> Venus t'est desplaisante, et son fils odieux.
>   Au contraire, par eux la terre est toute pleine
> De Graces et d'Amour: change ce nom d'Heleine:
> Un autre plus cruel te convient beaucoup mieux.
>
> (*L* XVII, 283–4; *Pl* I, 270)

The laconic, matter-of-fact tone, edged with bitterness, of this last line and a half and the puncturing of the petrarchan ideal which is undertaken both explicitly and implicitly throughout the poem are evident in a strikingly large number of the *Sonets pour Helene*. It is significant that a trace of these characteristics can be detected even in the one sonnet which seems to concentrate exclusively on realizing beauty in the way that it had so successfully been realized in a number of poems in the Cassandre *Amours*. This is the famous 'ballet d'Amour' sonnet of book II:

> Le soir qu'Amour vous fist en la salle descendre
> Pour danser d'artifice un beau ballet d'Amour,
> Voz yeux, bien qu'il fust nuict, ramenerent le jour,
> Tant ils sceurent d'esclairs par la place respandre.
>   Le ballet fut divin, qui se souloit reprendre,
> Se rompre, se refaire, et tour dessus retour
> Se mesler, s'escarter, se tourner à l'entour,
> Contre-imitant le cours du fleuve de Meandre.
>   Ores il estoit rond, ores long, or' estroit,
> Or' en poincte, en triangle, en la façon qu'on voit
> L'escadron de la Gruë evitant la froidure.
>   Je faux, tu ne dansois, mais ton pied voletoit
> Sur le haut de la terre: aussi ton corps s'estoit
> Transformé pour ce soir en divine nature.
>
> (L XVII, 270–1; Pl I, 262)

What is conspicuous above all in this poem is the way in which the movement of the dancers is mirrored perfectly in the movement of the verse. The smooth, graceful entry of the first line is soon followed by the rapid steps of the repeated *s* and *d* sounds in 'en la salle descendre / Pour danser d'artifice', which stitch their two lines together, before the easy, onward flow is resumed with the phrase 'un beau ballet d'Amour'. With the commencement of the main clause in line 3 the movement quickens and also becomes more elaborate, as the verb is held back by an interposed concessive clause, before relaxing once more into the elegant, sweeping gesture of Hélène's eyes, which is suggested by line 4. This moment seems to be held, suspended, at the end of the quatrain in the word 'respandre', each of whose sounds echoes and brings to rest the earlier parts of the line. After this brief pause the dance begins again, moving more swiftly now, with shorter and more rapidly varied phrases which nevertheless remain closely related to each other in sound and in syntactical form, as the pattern of movement grows increasingly intricate and complex. In the tercets, the movement is at first staccato; there is no longer a rapid succession of verbs to provide continuity of movement. Instead, for a line and a half the dance seems almost to consist of separate tableaux. But the smoothly flowing movement is quickly resumed, taking on now the relaxed, soaring quality of birds' flight; and Hélène herself seems no longer earthbound, but able to fly, free of physical weight, her body 'Transformé . . . en divine nature'. She achieves (because the poet has created for her) the ease and freedom of movement which ordinary human beings experience only when dreaming. But there is one phrase at the end which reminds the reader that Hélène *is* only earthly after all: her body was transformed '*pour ce soir* en divine nature'. In the *Amours*, one may feel, the 'pour ce soir' would not have been there; the world of ideal beauty achieved by the poet would have been self-sufficient, self-contained and invulnerable to erosion by the ordinary, everyday world. Here, however, even at the moment when the poet is experiencing beauty most intensely, he is aware that it is an experience of limited duration; only momentarily did Hélène (and the poet) achieve perfection. The phrase 'pour ce soir' remains unemphasized in Ronsard's line: the main weight clearly falls upon 'Transformé' and 'divine nature'. But the encroachment which it represents of the ordinary world upon the poetic is a very important part of the meaning of the poem.[1]

Perhaps the clearest instance in the *Sonets pour Helene* of this seemingly inevitable encroachment is provided by Ronsard's treatment of the *songe amoureux* theme. In the *Amours*, as we have seen, the amorous dream had often constituted for the poet the occasion for a particularly intense and richly delightful experience of beauty, one which transcended (with varying degrees of permanence) the limitations of the everyday human world. The theme occurs only twice in the *Sonets pour Helene*, the first time in sonnet LIV of book I (*L* XVII, 244; *Pl* I, 240).

[1] This sonnet is further discussed below, chapter 7, pp. 293–4. Chapter 7 also considers other sonnets from this cycle in a manner relevant to the present context (pp. 300–2, 309, 314).

Ronsard the poet

Here, echoing an epigram from the *Greek Anthology*,[1] the poet hopes that the petals of the flowers which he has hung over Hélène's door, and which were 'arrosez' with his tears, will fall upon her as she leaves her room next day, 'de telle sorte / Que son chef soit mouillé de l'humeur de mes pleurs' (lines 7–8). The tercets, however, develop a very different idea from this graceful gesture of the languishing lover:

> Je reviendray demain. Mais si la nuict, qui ronge
> Mon cœur, me la donnoit par songe entre mes bras,
> Embrassant pour le vray l'idole du mensonge,
> Soulé d'un faux plaisir je ne reviendrois pas.

The illusion and self-deception involved in the dream experience are heavily stressed in this passage, and the irony of the poet's situation is fully brought out by the deliberate ambiguity of the two lines which close the poem:

> Voyez combien ma vie est pleine de trespas,
> Quand tout mon reconfort ne depend que du songe.

On one level the poet's life is full of pain and wretchedness, since his only solace is the illusory one provided by dreams. Yet on another level it is full of delight, since the satisfaction of his feelings towards Hélène depends not on reality, but on complaisant illusion. The final rhyme, however, inevitably recalls the harsher, more unequivocal 'idole du mensonge' of line 11, reinforcing, even in the moment of asserting the value of the dream, its inescapably deceptive nature.

The fullest development of the theme, however, is to be found in book II, sonnet XXIII:

> Ces longues nuicts d'Hyver, où la Lune ocieuse
> Tourne si lentement son char tout à l'entour,
> Où le Coq si tardif nous annonce le jour,
> Où la nuict semble un an à l'ame soucieuse:

[1] See book V, epigram 145. For a discussion of Ronsard's use of the *Greek Anthology* in the *Sonets pour Helene,* see J. Hutton, *The Greek Anthology in France and in the Latin writers of the Netherlands up to the year 1800* (Ithaca, Cornell University Press, 1946), pp. 363–74.

Petrarchism and the quest for beauty

Je fusse mort d'ennuy sans ta forme douteuse,
Qui vient par une feinte alleger mon amour,
Et faisant, toute nue, entre mes bras sejour,
Me pipe doucement d'une joye menteuse.
    Vraye tu es farouche, et fiere en cruauté:
De toy fausse on jouyst en toute privauté.
Pres ton mort je m'endors, pres de luy je repose:
    Rien ne m'est refusé. Le bon sommeil ainsi
Abuse par le faux mon amoureux souci.
S'abuser en amour n'est pas mauvaise chose.

                    (*L* XVII, 264–5; *Pl* I, 259)

Most noticeable here is the extent to which the account of the sensuous delight afforded by the dream (line 7) is hedged about by elements which underline very firmly the negative aspects of the experience. First the opening quatrain describes with great vividness the oppressiveness and seeming interminability of winter nights to the insomniac lover: the moon in her movement across the sky is wearisomely sluggish; even the cock is slow to crow. Not only is the winter setting here the very antithesis of the expected norm in love poetry – since spring is traditionally the season associated with love – but also the lover's complaint at the almost unbearable length of the nights is the reverse of the wish often expressed by poets evoking a night spent (whether in reality or in imagination) with their mistress: namely, that it might last for ever. In addition, even when evoking Hélène lying with him, 'toute nue, entre mes bras', the poet recognizes from the beginning that it is merely an illusion. All the positive notations ('alleger', 'doucement', 'joye') are sharply offset by negative ones ('par une feinte', 'Me pipe', 'menteuse'), with the result that the pleasure and peace which the poet experiences in making love to Hélène are greatly diminished by his continual awareness that they are illusory feelings. The full irony of his situation is made apparent in the final tercet. The extent of his delight is summed up in an understated, matter-of-fact hemistich ('Rien ne m'est refusé'), and then the rest of the tercet offers contrasting reflections on his experience. On the one hand benevolent sleep, whose benevolence lay precisely in bringing the poet's lady to his bed, is acknowledged to be but a deceiver in fact. Yet from another point of view there are compensations even in this: since reality offers the poet no satisfaction, his dream, deceptive illusion though it is, is better than nothing.[1]

All this, with its rueful air of making do with the second-best, is a far cry from the exuberance and enthusiasm of the *Amours*. Indeed, the richly sensuous world of beauty to which the poet could so confidently attain in company with Cassandre seems to be glimpsed only rarely in the *Sonets pour Helene*. The resistance which Ronsard's materials now offer to the process of poetic transformation seems to be considerable. There had apparently been little or no difficulty in placing upon Cassandre's shoulders a mantle of beauty woven out of the petrarchan conventions and classical mythology, and enriched by all the resources of Ronsard's verbal skills. Hélène, on the other hand, cannot be idealized so readily: despite the *éblouissement* which he experiences, the poet cannot forget that Hélène is less than totally beautiful, that she can be standoffish almost to the point of unsociability, that she prefers intellectual to physical pleasures – indeed, scorns the physical – or that she is coldly indifferent to his feelings towards her. There are clear limitations on the poet's side also: he is old, he is waspishly impatient and resentful of the frustrations he experiences, and the effort involved in pursuing Hélène is finally too much for him. Both Hélène and the poet, in fact, are presented not so much in terms of the idealized petrarchan stereotypes of the lady and her lover, but rather as two individual human beings, with recognizably human faults and limitations. The atmosphere and mood of the *Sonets pour Helene* are at many points those of the ordinary, everyday world, as is the diction, with its throwaway phrases and semi-colloquialisms. In the *Amours*, of

[1] These two *songe amoureux* poems are treated slightly more fully in my article 'The theme of illusion in Ronsard's *Sonets pour Helene* and in the variants of the 1552 *Amours*', *Forum for Modern Language Studies*, 7 (1971), pp. 361–73.

course, it had not been part of Ronsard's intention to create such an impression; there the poetic had predominated, not the everyday. Perhaps it is significant in this connection that Hélène is so often addressed directly.[1] Her individual presence is felt by the poet (and by the reader) in a particularly vivid way, for as well as being admired and worshipped as the embodiment of perfection, she is also a person to whom the poet talks, whom he argues with and berates. The humanness of the situation is underlined again and again, for an ironical awareness of the limitations imposed by this aspect of their relationship seems to haunt the poet constantly.

In the end, wounded, irritable and thoroughly aggrieved, he simply gives up the struggle.[2] Ronsard seems to be overwhelmed now by a sense of the apparent impossibility of embodying ideal beauty in poetry in any but a fragmented, intermittent fashion; it is as though he is suggesting that his poetic stamina cannot be sustained in the way that it once could, and that his earlier confidence and appetite for the pursuit of beauty are much diminished. Read in this light, the *Sonets pour Helene* become, most movingly, a collection of poems about the pains and anguish of middle age, with all its desperate awareness of fading powers and rapidly passing time.[3] Beauty, which strikingly often in the *Amours* had been experienced in a way which enabled the poet to transcend and to ignore the imperfections of the everyday world, is for the most part felt to be frustratingly out of reach in the *Sonets pour*

[1] In the *Amours* only about one in eight of the poems addresses Cassandre directly, whereas in the *Sonets pour Helene* only about one in four does *not* address Hélène directly.

[2] We may contrast this reaction with that implied towards the end of the *Amours,* where the poet seems merely to be making a temporary pause in his endeavours: 'Je congnoy bien qu'encor' je ne suis pas, / Pour trop aymer, à la fin de ma rime' (L IV, 171; *Pl* I, 97).

[3] I do not mean to suggest, of course, that this theme appears in Ronsard's work for the first time with the *Sonets pour Helene.* One of its most striking and most extended treatments occurs as early as 1560 in the *Elegie au seigneur l'Huillier* (L X, 292–8; *Pl* I, 885–6). But in the *Sonets pour Helene* it becomes a major theme of the whole collection. See also below, chapter 4, p. 206; chapter 7, p. 314.

Helene, and in any case of all too brief duration. There is an almost irreducible discrepancy now between the poet's desire and its object. Whereas the *Amours* had expressed Ronsard's exultant confidence in his own poetic abilities and in the full validity of the aesthetic and emotional experience of love, in the *Sonets pour Helene* the petrarchan love-sonnet sequence has become the vehicle for feelings of disillusionment and irritation at the inescapable limitations of human existence.

The role of neoplatonism in Ronsard's poetic imagination

A. H. T. LEVI

Est deus in nobis, agitante calescimus illo. OVID

THE inner coherence of the work of a poet is not philosophical but imaginative. Whereas a philosopher may produce a logically consistent and articulate account of the world, or of some aspect of human activity or experience, the poet may attempt to explain, explore, or more often just tentatively probe the meaning of his experience in a series of images or metaphors which are unconnected with each other and even, on a conceptual level, logically incompatible. When in 1912 Apollinaire wrote the famous second line of *Zone*,

Bergère ô tour Eiffel le troupeau des ponts bêle ce matin,

he was using language in such a way as to be unintelligible at the level of ordinary prose discourse, although the poetic image of the Eiffel Tower watching over the Seine bridges in the early morning as a shepherdess watches over her flock of bleating lambs presents the townscape to us in such a way as, at least potentially, to enable us to see it in a new light.

The poet's understanding of his experience in the world, his poetic 'vision', is often communicated through images or metaphors. Sometimes, as often in Ronsard, it is communicated through allusions to myths or with the aid of a philosophical scaffolding. Ronsard found certain neoplatonist ideas particularly useful in his endeavour to communicate his own poetic vision of the world, but this does not mean that he was committed to them on the philosophic, conceptual level. He may have been. But even if he was, the adequacy or consistency of his philosophic scaffolding is no guide to the power of the poetic vision which it supports, or to the imaginative power of the poetry which uses it.

Ronsard's use of a philosophical substructure, like his use of myths, makes his poetry difficult of access to those who, like ourselves, have to make conscious efforts to penetrate them. But these are difficulties which derive from remoteness in time and cultural experience. There are other difficulties of access too often overlooked which only partly derive from Ronsard's period and which he to some extent shares with more modern poets. Some of Ronsard's verse is precious, stilted or affected at one level while being totally serious at another. To understand it requires not only some familiarity with the myths and philosophies on which he drew to communicate his poetic vision, but also some sensitivity to the different registers of discourse available in the sixteenth century. Ronsard could court, flatter, condemn or solicit patronage. He could treat his own experience lightheartedly, ironically, intensely or with deliberate exaggeration. The Cassandre, Marie and Hélène cycles of love poetry were obviously written in different poetic registers. In some poems, Ronsard changed the lady's name as he republished a poem written for someone else. The last poems for Marie were almost certainly a disguised tribute to Henri III who had deeply mourned the death in childbirth of Marie de Clèves, certainly not the Marie of the earlier Marie poems. Ronsard could write a *profession de foi* in one tone, compose a mere frivolity in another and indulge in a meaningful *jeu d'esprit* in a third. Only the most careful literary analysis can establish what the poet meant to be instinctively conveyed, what experience he is writing about, with what significance he endows it and on what level of commitment or diffidence he is communicating.

The role of neoplatonism

in Ronsard's generation, was first to diminish and finally, during the wars of religion, to be destroyed. The humanists were to become conservative and defensive. Montaigne was to laugh at Ficino on love, to turn his back on pagan virtue, to scoff at women who wrote theology, and once more to separate faith from reason and grace from nature. Plutarch, Seneca and Epictetus were to become more fashionable sources than Plato. While the pastoral took root in the rest of Europe, France was to transpose a neoplatonist framework into a neostoicism concerned to explore the virtues of moderation, self-knowledge and constancy in adversity.

Ronsard spans the period from the high optimism of the years before 1550 to the gloomy outlook of the humanists during the wars to which no resolution seemed possible. He published his first four books of odes in 1550 (new style). He died in 1585, a year after the bitterness of the wars had been exacerbated by the death of the Duc d'Anjou, which left the Protestant Henri de Navarre as legitimate heir to the French throne. The evolution of Ronsard's imaginative attempts to understand his own experience and to communicate to his contemporaries his understanding of the world in which he lived had necessarily, by force of historical circumstance, to mirror the successive crises of confidence undergone by his age. They are mirrored in his changing utilization of the neoplatonist framework, and in his changing commitment to the philosophical scaffolding on which he was to draw enthusiastically, defensively, even cynically, in some moods but not in others, and in order to probe some sorts of experience but not others. An examination of Ronsard's relationship to the neoplatonist tradition, at the heart of the imaginative universe of some of his precursors, should reveal his crises of confidence and commitment and show, in its exploitation or neglect, something of what Ronsard was trying to understand and communicate.[1]

[1] On the subject of Ronsard's utilization of the neoplatonist tradition, there is a considerable body of literature. See especially: H. Hornik, 'More on Ronsard's philosophy', *Bibliothèque d'humanisme et Renaissance*, 27 (1965), pp. 435–43; I. Silver, 'Ronsard's early philosophy', *Studies in*

Ronsard the poet

RONSARD'S LOVE POETRY AND THE
NEOPLATONIST TRADITION

It is possible to find in Petrarch's *Canzoniere* the suggestion that human love is connected with the quest for the supreme good. The petrarchan tradition developed, however, in such a way as to become characterized by a series of conceits, images and formal attitudes which distinguished it clearly from the Ficinian tradition, relying on instinctive human love as a guide to moral fulfilment. Du Bellay's early love poetry is in some ways neoplatonist. That of Ronsard is not. From the beginning Ronsard's view of love is limited to its sensuous perspectives (see above, chapter 2, *passim*). It becomes more earthy as Ronsard turns away from the debilitating preciosity of the petrarchan tradition, as exemplified in the Italian poets Tebaldeo and Serafino, towards Anacreon and the poets of the *Greek Anthology* for his inspiration. Ronsard's poetic enthusiasms are a function of his own development. When he discovered a Greek author with whom he felt a real kinship, he could be bowled over even to the detriment of his own poetry. From the beginning, however, his love poetry avoids serious neoplatonist perspectives. The 1552 *Amours*, with their frequently petrarchan imagery and stylized postures, can juxtapose spiritual and sensuous images, but Ronsard is careful not to relate physical to moral experience, and he does not explore the possibility that the experience he analyses leads to moral enrichment.

Some of Ronsard's early allusions to the neoplatonist tradition in the love poetry cannot be regarded as much more than *jeux d'esprit*. A sonnet in the 1552 *Amours* for instance argues against Plato, whom Ronsard mentions (as well as

---

Philology, 45 (1948), pp. 119–33; *Ronsard's Reflections on the Heavens and Time, Publications of the Modern Language Association of America*, 80 (1965), pp. 344–64; H. Weber, *La Création poétique au XVIe siècle en France* (Paris, Nizet, 1956); 'Platonisme et sensualité dans la poésie amoureuse de la Pléiade' in *Lumières de la Pléiade* (Paris, Vrin, 1966), pp. 157–94; R. V. Merill and R. J. Clements, *Platonism in French Renaissance Poetry* (New York University Press, 1957).

The role of neoplatonism

against Aristotle and Empedocles, whom he does not), that there has to be a vacuum in the cosmos in order to accommodate the copious tears of his 'deuil Amour'.[1] In similarly light vein the ode to Denys Lambin from the third (1550) book attacks the platonist doctrine of reminiscence on the grounds that, if Ronsard had been able to 'remember' Homer's poetry, he would have been indistinguishable from Homer himself. When Ronsard states that the mind is like a 'tableau tout neuf' (L II, 15–17; Pl I, 499), he is not committing himself to an Aristotelian epistemological theory in any philosophical sense, but contriving a poetic conceit.

The Cassandre cycle contains several references to the atomism of Epicurus and Lucretius, but they are always poetic, as when Ronsard compares the atoms which 'hurtez ensemble, ont composé le monde' to the cares and pains which compose his own 'amoureux univers' (L IV, 40; Pl I, 17). In this sonnet Ronsard goes on to use another philosophical idea – the resolution of physical matter into earth, air, fire and water. If Ronsard dies of love, he will be resolved into voice. In another famous line, he compares the light from his lady's eye to his 'Endelechie', alluding to an important sixteenth-century quarrel about spelling and meaning without seriously taking sides (L IV, 58–9; Pl I, 30).[2] References to Plato are not infrequent, but even in these early poems Ronsard does not commit himself to any philosophical system or doctrine.[3] Indeed, when he

[1] L IV, 62; Pl I, 35. Muret rather heavily points out that Ronsard is merely affecting to take sides in an ancient philosophical dispute 'usant du privilege des Poëtes'.

[2] On the sixteenth-century quarrel, see Henri Busson, 'Ronsard et l'Entéléchie' in Mélanges Chamard (Paris, Nizet, 1951), pp. 91–5. Ronsard changed his mind about the spelling. See Les Amours, ed. H. Weber (Paris, Garnier, 1963), pp. 535–6.

[3] Among the allusions to platonic doctrines may be cited the 'bal des astres' (L IV, 29; Pl I, 13), the 'cheval noir' (L IV, 24; Pl I, 11), the reference to the realm of ideas and to love as the source of virtue (L IV, 63; Pl I, 32), purification by love (L IV, 134–5; Pl I, 75), love as a source of knowledge and virtue (L IV, 140–1; Pl I, 77–8), the erotic frenzy (L IV, 142; Pl I, 82) and divine beauty as a source of earthly beauty (L IV, 164–5; Pl I, 88).

alludes to the Androgyne legend, he deprives the theme of all
transcendental significance. The theme is treated so sensuously
that both the sonnets LXVII and CI of the the 1552 collection
were later to be suppressed (*L* IV, 68 and 100; *Pl* I, 287 and II,
748). Ronsard was later to turn even more firmly against the
neoplatonist perspectives of Ficino.

The first of the *Folastries* of 1553, elaborating a medieval
form under the influence of Ovid and Catullus, already tilts in a
lighthearted manner at the ideal of fidelity in love. In the epi-
graph of the *Nouvelle Continuation des amours* of 1556, Ronsard
defends his desertion of Cassandre in the poem *A son livre*. The
same poem scoffs at Petrarch's thirty years of fidelity to Laura:

> Ou bien il jouissoit de sa Laurette, ou bien
> Il estoit un grand fat d'aymer sans avoir rien.
>
> (*L* VII, 317; *Pl* I, 112)

The lover's ardour should remain attached to its object only so
long as it is requited. In the same poem, parodying a medieval
attitude, Ronsard states his readiness to leave Marie, too,

> si elle
> M'est, comme fut Cassandre, orgueilleuse et rebelle.

It is true that Ronsard complains when, in his turn, he is
deserted by Sinope, although he has only himself to blame for
presenting his rival to her.[1] But the fact that Ronsard puts no
premium on fidelity shows both how stylized his attitudes
could be and how inappropriate the neoplatonist tradition
seemed to him to serve as a scaffolding for his love lyrics.

Beneath the variations of tone and the different levels of
seriousness, an increasingly clear tendency in Ronsard can be
discerned. Love's meaning and significance is increasingly
explored in the realms of sensuous gratification. Even the long
and formal pastoral poem of 1559, the *Chant pastoral* to celebrate
the marriage of the Duc de Lorraine to the second daughter of
Henri II, with all its reminiscences of Theocritus, emphasizes
the merely ritual nature of the elaborately neoplatonist prepara-

[1] *L* X, 90 (1559); *Pl* II, 878. Ronsard suppressed this sonnet in 1578.

The role of neoplatonism

tions for entering the sacred grotto (see below, chapter 4, pp. 176–8) and the sensuous nature of the pleasure to which the mutual love of the spouses should lead them (*L* IX, 78; *Pl* I, 955). The joys of 1559 did, however, prompt Ronsard to some of his most optimistic verse. Earlier that year the peace of Cateau-Cambrésis had been signed, and the marriages fixed by the treaty were to be celebrated with magnificent pomp. In *La Paix au Roy* of that year, written before the king's tragic accident on 30 June, Ronsard alludes to love as the binding force of the universe, the neoplatonist *vinculum mundi*, in an unusually enthusiastic way (*L* IX, 112; *Pl* II, 444). But the 1560 first collected edition of the *Œuvres* again allows a defensive note to creep in. The wars of religion and economic crisis seemed already inevitable and, in *La Vertu amoureuse* from the fifth book of *Poëmes*, Ronsard presents a portrait of the perfect lover taken not from Ficino but from Horace and the stoic sages. The perfect lover conforms to the ideals of Epictetus, despising fortuitous events, fortune and seasonal changes (*L* X, 346; *Pl* I, 907). Love's effect is now to conquer passion, to foster self-knowledge, to dispel ignorance and to lead to virtue. These were to be the effects to be ascribed by the moralists during the wars of religion to moderation and constancy, which contrast with the sensuousness particularly characteristic of the Marie cycle, as shown for instance by the *concours de baisers* of the *Elegie à Marie* added to the 1560 *Œuvres* (*L* X, 241–2; *Pl* I, 177). There is no hint that passionate impulse could contribute to the attainment of spiritual fulfilment or cosmic insight, as it did for Ficino.

Such neoplatonist allusions as remain in the love poetry are fully attuned to the popular neostoicism of the wars of religion. Ronsard was embittered by the polemic of the *Discours*, and he prefaced the 1563 *Recueil des nouvelles poësies* with a long *Epistre au lecteur* in prose attacking his 'calomniateurs'. In the first book of the new collection, and the first of the four hymns to the seasons to be composed, nature is contemptuous about the institution of marriage, so contributing to a poetic statement in which fidelity is not seen as important, and which therefore

goes against the neoplatonist tradition by limiting the significance of love to its sensuous elements:

> Quand à moy je suis franche, et Deesse j'estime
> Autant un fils bastard, comme un fils legitime.
>
> (*L* XII, 38; *Pl* II, 235)

In the same collection Ronsard, having absented himself from
Genèvre, has recourse to the view popularized in France by
Castiglione's theory – a reactionary adaptation of Ficino – that
love flourishes best in the absence of the beloved:

> certes je sçay bien
> Que j'ayme mieux absent qu'estant pres de mon bien.
>
> (*L* XII, 291; *Pl* II, 27)

This somewhat factitious resort to a very attenuated neoplatonist doctrine illustrates well how Ronsard could embrace
and exploit whatever popular doctrine served his particular
purpose, in this case when he writes a love poem to an absent
mistress.

In 1565 Ronsard refers again to the Androgyne myth in
what appears to be a love poem. The poem starts:

> Pour vous montrer que j'ay parfaitte envie
> De vous servir tout le temps de ma vie

and the poet goes on to affirm that his 'foy'

> tellement vit en vostre amitié
> Qu'autre que vous n'y a part ny moitié.
>
> (*L* XIII, 170–1; *Pl* II, 889 ff.)

It is only later that we learn that this is a poem of love addressed
by one woman to another, a warning that we can never be sure
how far the poet's *je* can be identified with Ronsard himself.
However warm his direct spontaneity may sometimes seem,
none of Ronsard's verse escapes stylization. Whatever premium
the *Deffense et illustration* put on authenticity of emotion, it
would never have occurred to Ronsard not to present his feelings in stylized form even in his most intimate lyrics. It is

therefore often difficult to determine the exact emotional register of any given poem. The *Elegie* just mentioned written from one lady to another contains the line

Ce n'est qu'un cœur, qu'une ame et qu'une foy.
(*L* XIII, 175; *Pl* II, 892)

A commonplace of vaguely platonist derivation such as this can yet be used to convey real emotion. But the same line occurs in a court piece about love from the same collection, where the level of seriousness is certainly low (*L* XIII, 198; *Pl* I, 997). Ronsard had become a very accomplished poet indeed; the level of personal commitment is scarcely higher in the *Cartels* of 1569, in which he exploits the full panoply of Ficinian neoplatonism.

Ronsard had been ill intermittently during the preceding years, and there are signs that he was finding his stays at court and his obligation to produce pieces for court occasions increasingly distasteful in spite of his friendship with the young Charles IX. He spent what time he could at Saint-Cosme, the priory given him in 1565, and the sixth book of *Poëmes* in 1569 reflects his new interest in gardening and his dislike of court life. The court poetry of the late 1560s, almost all of it in the decasyllables preferred by Charles IX, was sometimes perfunctory (on this poetry, see also below, chapter 6, pp. 275–85).

The *cartel* as a literary form is an attack on an imaginary opponent in dialogue form, which it is not always easy to distinguish from the *mascarades* during which it might have been declaimed. The interest centred on the music, dancing, costumes and performers. We are left with the bare text, written to order for a court entertainment, intended to be declaimed by someone else, and necessarily stylized. It is in such pieces as this that Ronsard has recourse to Ficino. In the *Discours d'un amoureux desesperé et de son compagnon qui le console, et d'Amour qui le reprend* of 1569, which is in fact a *cartel* in dialogue form, Ronsard's Amour claims that love leads to virtue and reproves the 'amoureux':

> Mais ta raison par les sens depravée
> A la beauté corporelle aprouvée,
> Non la cœleste.
>
> (*L* XV, 100; *Pl* II, 360)

Love is here conventionally the *vinculum mundi*, the source of immortality, the intermediary between men and the gods and above all the transcendent force which links the soul to God in its quest for the source of the beauty of the beloved. Even here, however, Ronsard clearly regards the two loves as opposed to one another. The 'beauté du corps' provokes an

> Amour furieuse,
> Brutale Amour, charnelle, vitieuse,

while, as Amour tells l'amoureux,

> Debvois hausser tes yeux outre la nue
> Pour voir le Beau dont ta belle est venue.
>
> (*L* XV, 102; *Pl* II, 361)

The contrast between the two loves, commonly accepted as neoplatonist although debasing Ficino's own view, is even more pronounced in the pair of *cartels* in the same collection and probably written for the festivities of July 1567 when Claude de France and her husband, the Duc de Lorraine, visited the court. It is clear, too, in the *Elegie* for Genèvre published in the 1571 *Œuvres*, reviewing in decasyllables a past relationship from present disenchantment. The only possible relationship between the two loves is opposition:

> La difference est grande et merveilleuse
> D'entre l'amour et la rage amoureuse.
>
> (*L* XV, 335; *Pl* II, 93)

In 1578 Ronsard published in a new volume of his *Œuvres* his *Sonets pour Helene.* In 1574 Charles IX had died and Henri III had acceded to the throne. But Ronsard's dislike of court life dated from the mid-1560s, and it was not so much the death of Charles IX as the outbreak of the wars of religion in 1562, with the bitter polemic into which Ronsard was drawn, which marks the collapse of Ronsard's enthusiastic optimism. The court poetry of the late 1560s lacked personal commitment. Even the *Franciade* was in the end a *pièce de circonstance*. Like so many sixteenth-century authors Ronsard found his confidence permanently shattered by the outbreak of the wars of religion.

The Hélène cycle shows Ronsard's sheer technical mastery of the alexandrine love sonnet, but it was not merely composed to demonstrate Ronsard's superior technique, threatened though he was by the ascendancy of the somewhat precious poetry of Desportes. In this finest of all the cycles of love poems, Ronsard affects courtly postures and remains carefully silent about the physical attributes of the court lady whose praises he sang. But he shows real emotional power and complete technical mastery. This was court poetry into which Ronsard distilled his most deeply personal concerns, which did not necessarily include any authentic passion for Hélène. It befitted the *gloire* of France's Homer that he should sing the praises of someone whose name was so suitable. The increased element of stylization in Ronsard's portrayal of the relationship confirms the collapse of an earlier optimism, while Ronsard's commitment to his own destiny and craftsmanship endows the cycle with its remarkable emotional tension. In the course of the Hélène cycle, Ronsard incidentally rejects the whole heritage of Ficino, increasing the sense that his finest cycle of love poems is a work of disillusion.

Desportes had sung the praises of a love whose origins were no longer instinctive. The spiritual union of souls which he idealized in fact emasculated the power of the Florentine neoplatonist vision by opposing the two loves as Ronsard had come to oppose them.[1] But whereas Desportes idealized the spiritual love, Ronsard had already in 1575, in an *Estrenne* accompanying a gift to Charles IX of Leone Ebreo's dialogues on love, made the other choice:

[1] On Desportes and neoplatonism, see Robert M. Burgess, *Platonism in Desportes* (Chapel Hill, University of North Carolina Press, 1954).

Ronsard the poet

Mais s'il vous plaist de choisir mieux,
Prenez celuy qui est en terre,
Et laissez l'autre pour les dieux.

(*L* XVII, 61–2; *Pl* I, 611)

Desportes had sung vicariously the love of his patrons for their ladies. Ronsard's failure to publish the Hélène cycle separately suggests the decreasing importance he attached to his 'elegies, epigrammes et sonnets'. His obvious concern throughout the whole Hélène cycle with his own reputation suggests that, while the formal genre of a love cycle had ceased to interest him, he was none the less willing to take up a challenge. What he put into the poems was a strong, perhaps even desperate, affirmation of his own poetic mission.

The Hélène sonnets do however show how strongly Ronsard was by now reacting against the whole neoplatonist tradition. The challenge to Desportes becomes a challenge to the Florentine tradition as Desportes misunderstood it:

l'esprit ne sent rien que par l'ayde du corps.

(*L* XVII, 213; *Pl* I, 227)

Ronsard, like Montaigne, now insists against Plato on the union between body and soul. He exploits it to reproach Hélène:

Or' vous aimez l'esprit, et sans discretion
Vous dites que des corps les amours sont pollues.

(*L* XVII, 229; *Pl* I, 236)

The following sonnet, suppressed in 1584, is even stronger:

En choisissant l'esprit vous estes mal-apprise,
Qui refusez le corps, à mon gré le meilleur . . .
Aimer l'esprit, Madame, est aimer la sottise.

(*L* XVII, 230; *Pl* II, 919)

The final attack comes in a posthumous sonnet added to the Hélène cycle in 1609 which attacks Leone Ebreo for his platonism with astonishing violence (*L* XVIII, 313–14; *Pl* II, 674). Ebreo's *Dialoghi d'Amore* published in 1535 and twice translated into French (Denis Sauvage, 1551; Pontus de Tyard, about 1552) had popularized Ficino. The sonnet starts unpromisingly enough

> Je n'ayme point les Juifs . . .

and it finishes with three lines addressed to Leone,

> Faux trompeur, mensonger, plein de fraude et d'astuce
> Je croy qu'en luy coupant la peau de son prepuce
> On luy coupa le cœur et toute affection.

(L XVIII, 313–14; Pl II, 674)

The examination of the relationship of Ronsard's love poetry to the neoplatonist tradition throws considerable light on his poetic development and originality, if only because it compels us to examine the poetic register in which he is writing, his stylized relation to the *je* of the poems, and his commitment to the views he is exploiting, or to their denial when he rejects them. Neither Desportes nor Ronsard really understood Ficino, but they chose the opposite horns of the dilemma occasioned by their common misunderstanding. The merely conventional, and more than debased, reactionary neoplatonism of the court pieces must be discounted, and something of Ronsard's position in the Hélène cycle must be ascribed to his desire to contradict Desportes. But the development of Ronsard's love poetry none the less shows a movement away from neoplatonist optimism about human instinct as a guide to virtue, thereby revealing a great deal about Ronsard's poetic virtuosity and achievement. It is in the other realms of poetic activity that Ronsard's philosophy, perhaps not more committed than in the love poetry, is more closely integrated into the poetry itself.

RONSARD'S OTHER POETRY

Ronsard's later attitude towards his love poetry is summed up in two remarks. In a letter of uncertain date, referring to the *Sonets pour Helene*, Ronsard refers to the 'petits et menus fatras come elegies, epigrames et sonnetz' (L XVIII, 499–500; Pl II,

1047). In the posthumous preface to the *Franciade* published in
1587 (*L* XVI, 345–6; *Pl* II, 1025), Ronsard contrasts the true
poet with the 'versificateur, composeur d'Epigrammes,
Sonnets, Satyres, Elegies et autres tels menus fatras, où
l'artifice ne se peut estendre'.

It was in the other spheres of poetic activity, to which he
anyway attached more importance, that Ronsard more consistently exploited the neoplatonist tradition, especially to
expound his theory of poetic inspiration. Perhaps more
importantly still, Ronsard used the neoplatonist tradition to
establish and populate a spiritual universe situated between
man and God. Man's aspirations to self-transcendence could be
examined for their possible satisfaction in this quasi-divine
realm, and human activities and emotions could be implicitly
evaluated by asserting that they were caused by God through
the medium of the 'spiritual realm' and its inhabitants, which
in various poems included nymphs, gods, angels, philosophy,
demons and the heavens.

The neoplatonist system therefore allowed Ronsard a choice
of images all of which claimed for such human activities as
music, poetry and study a status they had not necessarily hither-
to enjoyed. The elevated source from which these activities
derived, and from which they were 'inspired', had the great
advantage of being clearly mythological in character, and
therefore not impinging on a rigidly orthodox and serious
theology. In Ronsard's serious poetry, as in Apollinaire's, God
becomes an image, as for Ronsard do the nymphs and Muses.

In the end Ronsard naturalizes the preternatural sources of
human emotions and activity by relating them to identifiable
human emotional states, at the same time retaining for those
states the overtones associated with their preternatural derivation. An early tendency towards allegory yields to a more
consistent use of metaphor as Ronsard, always writing about
his own experience in the physical world, strives to link its
terrestrial dimensions to a transcendental significance expressed
in mythological imagery. Of the two sorts of available system,
theological and mythological, Ronsard clearly preferred to

The role of neoplatonism

explore the enhanced status of poetic activity in mythological terms (see below, chapter 4, pp. 187 ff. Of the mythologies available and widely understood, the neoplatonist system as developed by Ficino offered him the most fruitful images for exploring what he wished to explore. The *Symposium* commentary of Ficino is itself a poetic rather than a philosophical work, and Ronsard exploited the legacy of Ficino primarily as a myth rather than a truth.

Ronsard had always attached much aesthetic importance to the musical settings of his verse (see below, chapter 5, *passim*, on Ronsard's attitude to music and his use of musical imagery). This fact explains the emphasis placed by Ronsard and Du Bellay on metre and rhyme schemes, and Ronsard no doubt felt simply that poetry set to music produced an emotional reaction that was surer, swifter and more appropriate than the reaction produced by a printed page or a spoken voice could ever have been. However, the neoplatonist tradition offered several readily available explanations of why the effects of poetry were necessarily enhanced by a musical setting. There was a well-known series of biblical and classical stories in which music had achieved extraordinary effects. Amphion had moved with his music the rocks to build the walls of Thebes, Orpheus had moved to moral perfection those whom he soothed with his music, and David had achieved the spiritual perfection of his audience with the Psalms.[1] Theoretically, the importance of setting verse to music came to centre on the idea that musical harmonies, like the structure of the cosmos itself, were founded on numerical proportions. This was a rationalization, or an image, to explain how receptivity to music

[1] On the Renaissance catalogue of music's preternatural effects, see Frances Yates, *The French Academies of the Sixteenth Century* (London, The Warburg Institute, 1947), especially pp. 36 ff., and D. P. Walker, 'Orpheus the theologian and Renaissance platonists' in *The Journal of the Warburg and Courtauld Institutes*, 16 (1933), pp. 100–20. Ronsard could also elaborate the 'fureur double' of painting and poetry. See the eleventh ode of the fifth book (*L* III, 178; *Pl* I, 617–18) where a eulogy of painting is added to those of poetry and music. In the *Préface* to the 1560 *Livre de meslanges,* Ronsard assimilates music to poetry and painting.

necessarily re-established the harmony of the human soul with the cosmos and its creator, thereby conducing to the soul's moral perfection, since the numerical proportions underlying the laws of the cosmos and the laws of music derived alike from the mind of the world's creator, and the composer, performer and hearer of music necessarily aligned themselves with the laws impressed by the creator on the universe.

The importance which Ronsard attached to musical settings is partly attested by the frequency of his references to the lyre and the lute in his verse. But he also affirms in a preface to a book of *chansons* the association of a taste for music with 'la philosophie', virtue, 'le maniement des affaires politiques' and 'le travail des guerres'. Ronsard recites the list of magical effects achieved by music, 'petite partie de celle qui si armonieusement (comme dit Platon) agitte tout ce grand univers' and commits himself, perhaps a little hurriedly, to the mythology of the divine frenzies which he is careful not to equate with grace, 'Aussi les divines fureurs de Musique, de Poësie, et de Paincture ne viennent pas par degrés en perfection comme les autres sciences, mais par boutées et comme esclairs de feu' (*L* XVIII, 486; *Pl* II, 980). Ronsard is maintaining that the significance of the creative act is extraordinary by mythologizing its psychology in neoplatonist terms. The 1565 *Abbregé de l'art poëtique françois* repeats the need to join music to poetry, 'car la Poësie sans les instruments ... n'est nullement aggreable, non plus que les instrumens sans estre animez de la melodie d'une plaisante voix' (*L* XIV, 9; *Pl* II, 997). It is Ronsard's conviction of the importance of adding music to poetry which explains the frequency of his allusions to Orpheus. To express his view that poetry should be set to music in order to achieve its full effect, he naturally drew on neoplatonist theory.

The early *Ode à Michel de l'Hospital* (1552) identifies the Muses with 'musiciennes' and describes the three sorts of music they sang.[1] Ronsard is inspired by Hesiod when Calliope, who according to Pontus de Tyard represents the 'entiere sym-

[1] *L* III, 128–37; *Pl* I, 386–406. See also Pontus de Tyard, *Solitaire premier,* ed. Baridon (Geneva, Droz, 1950).

The role of neoplatonism

phonie' of eight spheres over each of which one of her sister Muses presides, prays in the ode to her father on behalf of her sisters:

> Fay nous Princesses des Montaignes,
> Des Antres, des Eaux et des Bois. . . .
> Donne nous encor davantage,
> La tourbe des Chantres divins,
> Les Poëtes, et les Devins
> Et les Prophetes en partage.
>
> (*L* III, 138–9; *Pl* I, 394 ff.)

Calliope goes on to ask for the power

> D'arracher les ames dehors
> Le salle bourbier de leurs corps.

Jupiter consents, giving the Muses the power to 'ravir' the 'poëtes saincts' who, in their turn, will 'ravir' 'la tourbe estonnée', and he goes on to specify the four neoplatonist 'fureurs' ('Prophétie', 'Poesies', 'Mysteres', 'Amours'). To receive these 'fureurs', the human heart must be

> Pure de vice, et reparé
> De la vertu precieuse.

The poets are to be the 'Interpretes des Dieux', although the people will regard them as 'sotz, et furieux'. All these elements are selected from Ficinian neoplatonism and subsequently developed in such a way as to make the 'fureurs' images of properly divine inspiration, and hence powerfully to upgrade the activities which require moral purity and which, in the poem, the Muses are seen to preside over. Ronsard is presumably talking in images, just as he will do much later when he claims to have been washed nine times by Euterpe and to have had his hair standing on end in the early part of the *Hymne de l'automne*. The number nine had, of course, a special mystical significance in neoplatonist mythology. In the *Ode à Michel de l'Hospital* Ronsard himself prays

Ronsard the poet

que tousjours j'espie
D'œil veillant les secretz des cieulx.

His references to the poetic frenzy in this ode clearly draw on some parts of Ficino's theory. The exact channels of transmission are not so important as Ronsard's own selectivity in exploiting the neoplatonist tradition and the level of commitment to Ficinian theory observable. Ronsard later associates poetic activity with prophecy, supernatural knowledge, fasting, penance, virtue and a knowledge of the divine mysteries in the first section of the *Hymne de l'autonne* (*L* XII, 46 ff.; *Pl* II, 239 ff.). Richard Le Blanc's preface to the *Io* translation of 1546 had already identified poetic inspiration, even in pagans, with divine grace. But how are we to understand Ronsard? Is this a credal affirmation or merely a string of images to probe the difficulty, delicacy and importance of the poet's task? Why did Ronsard exploit the Ficinian doctrine of the frenzies in everything but his love poetry, where his view was far too earthy to permit him to enhance the status of his experience by discussing it in neoplatonist terms?

Ronsard, building on the views of Thomas Sebillet and others, is careful to associate poetic activity with prophecy, ascetic practice and moral virtue. But he avoids the directly theological statements of Richard Le Blanc's preface to the *Io* translation and of Sebillet's *Art poétique* of 1548. He is merely appealing to an obviously mythological framework, developed at this point from Ficino by such near-contemporaries of Ronsard's as Pontus de Tyard, in order to enhance the status of poetic activity. He will later make it clear that poetic inspiration by the neoplatonist *fureur* results in, and is perhaps to be identified with, the psychological experience of being moved emotionally and being able to communicate emotion. Du Bellay had made emotional power the chief criterion of the true poet in the *Deffense* after a period in which court poetry had largely been reduced to verbal acrostics, when the communication of emotion in poetry was still comparatively new. Poetry was still commonly considered to be a form of rhetoric, often merely decorative, and not exclusively concerned with stirring the emotions.[1]

As Ronsard's career developed, his enthusiasm for exploiting the neoplatonist mythologies of music and poetic inspiration waned as, after the first books of *Hymnes*, his confidence started to diminish. He could still use substantially as wide a mythological spectrum, but the tone changes as the range of emotion narrows and a hint of disillusion creeps in.

Some of the early poems exploit neoplatonist themes for merely decorative purposes. The *Hymne triumphal* on the death of Marguerite de Navarre draws on the terms of her own *Discord par la contrariété de l'esprit et de la chair*, opposing spirit to *volupté* in a facile compliment to Marguerite's own early views. Later in the *Tombeau de Marguerite de Valois* of 1551, in spite of his earlier praise of the 'chanson Chrestienne', Ronsard reverts to a mythological view of heaven, contrasted not with hell but with Hades (*L* III, 45, 85; *Pl* I, 590, 607). Even in the context of the neoplatonist psychology of the *Hymne de la mort*, Ronsard is careful to use a mythological rather than a theological concept of heaven.[2]

The 1552 *Ode à Michel de l'Hospital* does, however, exploit a neoplatonist theme which was frequently to recur in Ronsard's verse. Ronsard in this poem follows Hesiod in celebrating memory as the mother of the nine Muses, as he did in the 1555 *Hymne de la mort*, although Pontus de Tyard's *Solitaire premier* records in 1552 that memory was considered first one of three and then one of seven Muses. Ronsard's view of the functions of memory and, in particular, the relationship he, with so many

---

[1] The final criterion for the poet is enunciated by Du Bellay in the *Deffense* of 1549, after Cicero, as follows: 'Celuy sera veritablement le poëte que je cherche en nostre Langue, qui me fera indigner, apayser, enjouyr, douloir, aymer, hayr, admirer, etonner, bref, qui tiendra la bride de mes affections, me tournant ça et la à son plaisir. Voyla la vraye pierre de touche, ou il fault que tu epreuves tous poëmes, et en toutes Langues' (ed. H. Chamard, Paris, Marcel Didier, 1961, part 2, chapter 2, pp. 179–80).
[2] *L* VIII, 164; *Pl* II, 282, and see also *L* VIII, 233–4 (suppressed in 1584); *L* XVII, 122; *Pl* I, 183, for clearly mythological images of the afterlife.

others, envisages between memory and the Muses, is a pillar of the conceptual universe on which he drew to communicate his poetic vision of the world, but he exploited different and incompatible philosophical doctrines involving memory. Like Héroët, he occasionally used the neoplatonist doctrine of the soul's reminiscence of prenatal heavenly knowledge, particularly to explain the sharp, sudden impression made on him by female beauty in the 1552 *Amours*.[1] But, as if to confirm that he was merely using an established poetic convention, current in the Renaissance from Petrarch to Desportes, Ronsard alludes both to the platonist doctrine of reminiscence and to a psychology incompatible with it in the first madrigal of the *Sonets et madrigals pour Astrée* (L XVII, 181–2; *Pl* I, 206).

For the scholastics, the memory had been closely associated with the imagination. Both were related to the *sensus communis* but, while the memory merely stored and reproduced what was recorded, the imagination drew on the store to produce new combinations of the data which had originally derived from sense impressions. Ficino had given much greater importance to the imagination than to the memory in the thirteenth book of the *Theologia Platonica*, and in Ronsard's day the scholastic distinction was on the point of breaking down.[2] Since Ronsard so frequently used the interrelated concepts of *invention*, *fantaisie*, *fureur*, *frénésie* and *imaginer,* it is important to be clear about the underlying psychology, which also related the memory to the imaginative power. In its grand lines, Ronsard's psychology of the memory derives from Jacques Peletier Du Mans, whose views on the importance of developing the vernacular we know to have been incorporated into Ronsard's poetic programme.

In Peletier the memory escapes from its confusion with the

[1] See for instance L IV, 126–7; *Pl* I, 71. See also L VIII, 141; *Pl* II, 190; and the reference in 1560 to those who 'ne se souvenant de la celeste armonie du ciel' are 'engourdiz, paresseux, et abastardiz en ce corps mortel' (L XVIII, 481; *Pl* II, 978). Cf. Merrill and Clements, *Platonism in French Renaissance Poetry* (New York University Press, 1957), p. 57.
[2] See the *Theologia Platonica*, ed. R. Marcel, volume II (Paris, Les Belles Lettres, 1964), pp. 196 ff. and 227–8.

imagination and is the faculty by which the poet, innately endowed with the numerical proportions which underlie the cosmos, can reconstitute within his own mind the external world. The poet rediscovers within himself what is true in the external world and reconstructs from what he finds within himself the metaphysical essence of the cosmos, so penetrating its secret forces and properties, which Dorat was to teach Ronsard to communicate in fables and myths. The psychology is neoplatonist, and it explains why Ronsard so often has recourse to neoplatonist theory to expound the poet's function and status. The psychology enables Ronsard to assume that poetic inspiration must necessarily enjoy prophetic status, because poetic invention is a rediscovery of universal cosmic and divine laws.[1]

For Peletier, as for Ramus, invention was the discovery of appropriate material in the memory. Ronsard regards invention as deriving from the imagination, the source both of poetry and of error induced by the senses and the emotions. In the *Abbregé de l'art pöetique* he therefore distinguishes between the 'imagination concernant les Idées et formes de toutes choses qui se peuvent imaginer tant celestes que terrestres' and the 'inventions fantasticques et melencoliques, qui ne se rapportent non plus l'une à l'autre que les songes entrecoupez d'un frenetique, ou de quelque patient extremement tourmenté de la fievre'.[2] The necessity for Ronsard to distinguish between two different sorts of imagination, the sources respectively of poetic invention and of raving frenzy, suggests an inadequate set of

[1] On Peletier, see especially Hans Staub, *Le Curieux Désir* (Geneva, Droz, 1967), pp. 16–21. Peletier is supported not only by Pontus de Tyard, his close friend, but also by Thomas Sebillet, who justifies the sanctity and even the divinity of poets by reference to 'quelque don divin, et céleste prérogative, laquéle est clérement montrée par lés nombres dont les Poétes mesurent leurs carmes, la perfection et divinité desquelz soutient et entretient l'admirable machine de cest univers', *Art poétique françoys*, ed. Gaiffe (Paris, Droz, 1932), p. 10.
[2] *L* XIV, 12–13; *Pl* II, 999. On the contrast between Peletier and Ronsard, see also Grahame Castor, *Pléiade Poetics* (Cambridge University Press, 1964), pp. 172–3.

Ronsard the poet

psychological categories, confirmed by the Spanish doctor Huarte, whose *Examen de Ingenios* (1575), as translated by Chappuys in 1580 under the title *Anacrise*, has to attribute to the specifically 'bonne imagination', 'la Poesie, l'Eloquence, la Musique et sçavoir prescher'. The function of the imagination had become ambiguous since it was capable of producing morally elevating poetry and morally degrading frenzy.

In the *Ode à Michel de l'Hospital* Ronsard repeatedly alludes to the inspired poetic *fureur* with the gifts of knowledge and virtue it brings and which contrast with the *art*, *sueur* and *peine* of the mere versifiers. In the ode's potted history of poetry we are told that the 'saincte ardeur antique' is attenuated in the later poets whom the Muses' grace 'plus lentement agitoit' and who therefore struggled less efficaciously with ignorance.[1] Ronsard's vocabulary here includes words like *fureur*, *ravir* and *agiter* to convey, inside his mythological framework, divine inspiration and moral elevation. They were later to lose some of their savour. Already in 1553 the *Elegie à M. A. de Muret* used the terms *fureur* and *rage* in a playfully pejorative sense (*L* V, 228 and 230; *Pl* I, 101-2). Even in the early verse the *Fureurs* can stand for the vengeful Erinyes of Greek mythology, and *fureur* can be equated simply with sin.[2] But at this date Ronsard, especially in the *Hymnes*, is still confident that poetic inspiration, *fureur*, can mediate virtue, knowledge and religious fulfilment. The *daimons*, mythological intermediaries between the human and the divine, act on the fantasy in the 1555 *Les Daimons*. In 1556 the *Epistre* to the Cardinal de Lorraine claims that the poet's love of the Muses

> Tout furieux d'esprit me ravist nuict et jour,
> Découvrant leurs secretz aux nations Françoises.

[1] *L* III, 143 ff.; *Pl* I, 396-7. The *Solitaire premier* of Pontus de Tyard also contains a history, or mythology, of the diminishing inspiration of successive generations of poets.
[2] See the *Hymne de la philosophie* and the *Hymne du ciel* both of 1555 (*L* VIII, 92 and 147; *Pl* II, 203 and 192 where the reference to sin was removed in 1584).

The role of neoplatonism

In the 1556 *Elegie* to Chretophle de Choiseul, Ronsard maintains that poetry is 'un don venant de Dieu . . . qui ne tombe en toute fantaisie' and in the 1559 *Hymne* for the Cardinal de Lorraine, the poet's praise of his subject is 'Des fureurs d'Apollon sainement offencée' (*L* VIII, 122–3, 349, 353–4 and IX, 30; *Pl* II, 169, 862, 430, 175 variant).

With the onset of the wars of religion, there is a loss of confidence in the poetic mission. In the second book of *Meslanges* (1559) Ronsard is as optimistic as ever, confidently expressing his function in terms of the neoplatonist mythology:

> Ainsi nostre ame sort quand nostre corps repose,
> Comme d'une prison où elle estoit enclose,
> Et en se promenant et joüant par les Cieux,
> Son païs naturel, devise avec les Dieux. . . .
> Si tost qu'elle est rentrée, elle luy communique
> Ce qu'elle apprend de Dieu, luy monstre la pratique
> Du mouvement du Ciel, luymerque les grandeurs
> Des astres etherez, leur force, et leurs splendeurs.
>
> (*L* X, 103; *Pl* II, 467)

But by 1560 Ronsard is regretting that the poetic *fureur* is given only in youth (*L* X, 293; *Pl* I, 885) in an elegy dedicated originally to L'Huillier but later changed when L'Huillier became a Huguenot. The poetic pride is presented in a markedly lower register in the *Elegie* for Pierre L'Escot (1560), and the elegiac mood continues through the *Elegie* for Cardinal de Chastillon with its reference to the 'folastre mestier de nostre poesie' (*L* X, 335; *Pl* II, 466) until, in the *Elegie* for Guillaume Des Autels of the same date, *fureur* is what Ronsard ascribes to the Lutherans he opposes and 'fantastique' becomes a quality of the 'esprit sombre et melancolique' (*L* X, 355 and 358; *Pl* II, 567–8).

After the political and satirical verse of 1562–3 the ambiguity in Ronsard's use of 'fureur' and its associated terms becomes if anything even more pronounced. In the 1563 *Epistre* prefacing the *Recueil des nouvelles poësies* Ronsard refers to the 'fantaisies de mes calomniateurs' (*L* XII, 5; *Pl* II, 984), although in the *Hymne de l'autonne* of the same year Ronsard claims that the 'Daimon qui preside aux Muses . . . me . . . haussa la fantaisie' (*L* XII, 46; *Pl* II, 239). *Fureur, fantaisie* and *frénésie* are all associated with love in the 1563–4 collection, often light-heartedly, but the 'furieuse ardeur' of the poet still makes an appearance which is intended to be understood in the full seriousness of its setting in neoplatonist mythology (*L* XII, 176; *Pl* I, 867), although the same poem can go on to bewail the lack of support received by the poet, whose poetry is said by the 'devin' to be 'un mal de cerveau qu'on nomme frenaisie' (*L* XII, 185; *Pl* I, 871).

Later on the neoplatonist mythology is used less confidently in Ronsard's attempts to elevate the poet's status. In the 1561 *Elegie à Jacques Grevin*, Ronsard can still confidently contrast the 'inventeurs de vers' with

> ceux qui ont la fantasie
> Esprise ardentement du feu de Poësie
> Qui n'abusent du nom, mais à la verité
> Sont remplis de frayeur et de divinité.[1]

But by 1569, even when Ronsard refers in his 'poëme' *La Lyre* for Belot to the four *fureurs,* he goes on to complain of his dependence on erratic inspiration (*L* XV, 18–19; *Pl* II, 322) (see also below, chapter 4, pp. 192, 197–8) and the references to inspiration become playful in the 1569 *La Salade* for Jamyn, the *Discours d'un amoureux desesperé* and the *Cartels* of the same year. By 1575 Ronsard, mourning the death of his patron and friend Charles IX in 1574 in an *Elegie* the following year to Henri III, announces his intention of giving up the 'mestier Heroïque, Lyrique, Elegiaq' for the 'Satyrique'. 'Furieux' becomes a synonym for 'fiévreux' (*L* XVII, 90–1; *Pl* I, 803). Thereafter Ronsard's rare appeals to the poetic *fureur* become despondent

---

[1] Ronsard broke with Grevin in 1563, and his *Elegie* appears only at the front of Grevin's *Théâtre*. See *L* XIV, 193–9; *Pl* II, 920–4.

The role of neoplatonism

attempts to fight a losing battle for patronage and esteem, as in some of the new pieces for the 1584 *Œuvres*.

The way in which Ronsard's exploitation of the neoplatonist mythology of inspiration changes its register, reflecting a lack of confidence as his career proceeds, shows something of how Ronsard could and did exploit myths of all sorts in different ways, at different times and for different purposes. But whether early or late, whether dashing off a frivolity or composing the richest and densest of the *Hymnes*, and whatever his mood, the use of myth shows the stylized nature of the poetry. Ronsard is acting out a formal role – at some times more clearly than at others – however exciting the resulting poetry. What changes is not so much the views expressed in his philosophical poetry as Ronsard's changing relationship to his own poetic *je*, as he now playfully, now seriously and now despondently draws on his broad mythological spectrum for different purposes and with different degrees of conceptual commitment.

*

*   *

*

What can be seen from Ronsard's treatment of the poetic *fureur* is confirmed by an examination of his use of all the other strands of neoplatonist theory and mythology which appear in his poems. The poems afford very little evidence about Ronsard's philosophical, as distinct from his religious, beliefs. He uses neoplatonism, and other systems incompatible with it rather less often, as a mythology on which he draws for the articulated structure of his imaginative universe in order to communicate his own poetic vision of the world and his experience.

In particular he frequently exploits the superhuman beings with whom, with some neoplatonist encouragement, he populated the spiritual realm between man and God. As the neoplatonist *fureurs* allowed Ronsard to elevate the poet's status without necessarily suggesting that he was inspired by grace, so the mythological inhabitants of this intermediary spiritual realm

Ronsard the poet

can elevate the importance of certain human states, emotions and activities while neatly sidestepping any formally theological framework. The reformers had taken exception to Ronsard's polemical verse at the outbreak of the wars of religion, but the scholastics were not interested in where the fairies lived, or in any but formally theological attempts to revise their views about the relative merits of the different emotional states and activities of which men were capable. Ronsard and his companions were reproached for using a 'pagan' frame of reference, but quite unjustly. They might have claimed credit for examining established values and attitudes in mythological terms, so taking the discussion well away from the hazardous seas of theological controversy.

Ronsard naturalizes the inhabitants of his middle realm between heaven and earth by giving a psychological correlative to the effects its inhabitants accomplish. When in the 1555 *Hymne de la justice* Themis begs God to inspire his sybils and prophets to attack injustice on earth, Ronsard is doing no more than project his passion for justice poetically, by indicating that it is a virtue of superhuman provenance. Quasi-supernatural characters such as Themis and Clemence intercede with God on man's behalf. The framework is mythological, but the poetic point is clear.

When the mediators are not clearly preternatural creatures, like angels and demons, they are invariably lifted above the ordinary human estate by their sacred characters and the specially numinous gifts which isolate them among men. In order to portray their mediation as efficacious, they are often also linked to recognizably human feelings, virtues, needs and even geographical settings.[1]

[1] T. C. Cave in 'The triumph of Bacchus', *Humanism in France,* ed. A. H. T. Levi (Manchester University Press, 1970), p. 260, points out how careful Ronsard is to situate the divine fury on a recognizably human basis, even to siting Bacchus' camp in the Loir valley. This could be interpreted as an elaborate compliment by Ronsard to himself, his friends and his patrons. It nevertheless betrays a typical concern to show how, where and in what circumstances the spiritual realm mediates between God and man, linking the intermediaries to identifiable psychological states.

The role of neoplatonism

It is in the 1555–6 *Hymnes* that Ronsard most deliberately exploits the intermediate spiritual realm of neoplatonist cosmology in order to point to the divine origins of the earthly qualities, emotions and virtues whose importance he wishes to emphasize. The *Hymne de la justice* almost indiscriminately mixes the term 'Dieu', safe enough in this context, with 'Jupiter' until, in line 473, Ronsard hastily covers his imaginative inconsistencies:

> Car Jupiter, Pallas, Apollon, sont les noms
> Que le seul DIEU reçoit en meintes nations.
>
> (*L* VIII, 69; *Pl* II, 165)

When there is no danger of theological heterodoxy, Ronsard would as soon escape the charge of paganism. But his lines are not cogent. Whatever might be thought in his 'meintes nations', the French Renaissance knew perfectly well how to distinguish between God and Jupiter. In this hymn it is Jupiter who acts out the role ascribed to God in Genesis, and it is by the population of the intermediary realm 'par songes, par Daimons, par cometes sanglantes' that Clemence urges God to warn humanity so that justice might be restored and the 'siècle d'or' might return. The 'confusion' between God and Jupiter is quite deliberate and poetically effective, suggesting a Christian frame of reference while safeguarding all the advantages of a mythological one.

It is the function of philosophy in the *Hymne de la philosophie* to lead the imprisoned soul to the astral realm so that, contemplating the 'merveilles des Cieux' the soul should not only comprehend the nature of the universe but also should aspire to know the nature of God. Scientific knowledge is a prize wrested from God, and only the virtuous may pretend to have access to it. In *Les Daimons* Ronsard draws on the Ficino translation of Psellos for his cosmology. As the fish fill the seas and men the land, so the *daimons* fill the air and the angels the heavens. The angels are totally spiritual, free of passion, omniscient, immortal, while the *daimons* have a 'corps leger':

Ronsard the poet

Ilz sont participants de Dieu, et des humains.[1]

The *daimons*, who can take any form they wish, therefore act as intermediaries. Without any particular cosmological consistency, Ronsard goes on to say so:

> Des hommes et Dieu, les Daimons aërins
> Sont communs en nature . . .
> Et sont bons ou mauvais tout ainsi qu'ilz s'affectent.
>
> (*L* VIII, 125; *Pl* II, 170)

Demons, angels, philosophy, stars and heavens occupy no consistent position in Ronsard's different neoplatonist cosmologies, but they all inhabit the intermediate realm between the purely spiritual and the material worlds. They signify the possibility of God's communication with men and of man's spiritual fulfilment in self-transcendence, and they poetically probe its modalities. The *daimons* end up, however, by explaining a purely natural experience in preternatural terms by providing a numinous cause for the vagaries of 'nostre fantasie'. The neoplatonist mythological apparatus is used in 1555–6 to draw attention to some forms of human experience whose importance Ronsard projects poetically in terms of the mediation of divine favour. Discussion is removed from theology into the realms of poetry, even when Ronsard talks about God. The aim, like the poetic register, is clear. Poetry, justice and music are invested with a numinous significance by poetic reference to a preternatural source, but they do not compromise the poet's theological orthodoxy or cosmological beliefs.

The occult powers can wreak evil as well as good. The formal prayer commencing 'O Seigneur' at the end of *Les Daimons* asks that the *daimons* should be dismissed from Christendom, so preserving orthodoxy while providing a rhetorically satisfactory conclusion which does not detract from the poetic content of the hymn. The *Hymne du ciel* goes further than most of the

[1] *L* VIII, 123; *Pl* II, 169. Ronsard is here following Plato's *Symposium* quite closely.

hymns in using the incarnation as an image of man's potential perfectibility by divine grace (*L* VIII, 146; *Pl* II, 191–2). The world is in the perfect form of the sphere. Its bodies demonstrate the

discordans accordz de leurs diversitez,

thereby creating harmony out of the sounds generated by independent movement. The harmony of the spheres and the roundness of the earth are images by which Ronsard projects an optimism about man's experience on earth, at least potentially and under propitious circumstances, rather than affirmations of cosmological theory. Later in the poem he attacks the Averroist contention of a world existing eternally by affirming a creation *ex nihilo,* and vehemently denies the possibility of other worlds in order to make the poetic point that experience in this world is unique and providentially controlled, again without wishing to commit himself to scientific hypotheses about the origin of matter. He merely uses a convenient cosmological system, which he regards as at least semi-mythical, to probe into the meaning of human experience in the world.

Each of the remaining hymns of 1555–6 really requires individual analysis. In the present context however it need only be mentioned that the stars in the *Hymne des astres* become the gates to heaven. Like the demons, the stars give access to heaven, while their influence on men is reduced to effects on the body which leave the soul untouched. This optimistic view about the human power of self-determination, expressed with the help of a neoplatonist theory, was to be called into question in the *Elegie* incipit 'Si le ciel' of the 1564 *Nouvelles Poësies* and admitted again, on a much less committed note, in the 1575 *Estoilles à M. de Pibrac* (on this poem, see also below, chapter 7, pp. 295–300). If the *Hymne des astres* stresses the influence of the stars on the bodily humours, it rejects alchemy, which would detract from the idea of divine providence which floods the poem and, since the immortal stars convey divine messages, they are exempted from suffering terrestrial influence, which would have compromised the poetic function with which Ronsard endows them.

It is perhaps the *Hymne de la mort* which makes most clear the way in which Ronsard uses philosophical systems as poetic vehicles, as the poem is clearly a mock encomium, as ironic as Panurge's praise of debt or Erasmus's *Praise of Folly*. But the praise of death raises at another level fundamental questions about values which give the poem a deeper significance than its somewhat perfunctory philosophical reflections might at first seem to suggest. Ronsard's attitude to death is well illustrated by the fact that the *Hymne de l'or*, of the same date as the *Hymne de la mort*, makes death the feared companion of Peste and Famine. The *Hymne de la mort* does however inevitably lead Ronsard to move from pagan to Christian imagery, so that the ironic mask drops, as it does when, in Erasmus's *Praise of Folly*, Erasmus praises the Christian folly of the Cross after the light-hearted banter of the earlier sections of his satire, so transforming a mock encomium into a real one. With Ronsard, as with Erasmus, we have to be sensitive to poetic registers. As Ronsard moves to Christian imagery, the poem's statements become more simple, and the degree of commitment, reflected in the adoption of a more serious tone, becomes unmistakably deeper. Death, whose panegyric starts out as a technical challenge, becomes, as the poem proceeds, the necessary path to human fulfilment.

The *Hymne de l'or* is a similarly serious *tour d'esprit*. It is dedicated to Dorat, the latinized form of whose name suggested the title. Ronsard makes much of his own poverty, and even goes so far as to connect riches with virtue. But once again we have a stylized poem, with Ronsard playing a role, never totally committed to what he says, just as in the *Hercule chrestien* he adopts the well-used convention of depicting Christ as Hercules in order to make of him a semi-mythological mediator between God and men without trespassing into the non-poetic realm of conceptual theology. In deference, however, to the use of Christ as an intermediary figure, and perhaps partly to counter the accusations of purely pagan imagery,

The role of neoplatonism

Ronsard's imaginative register is graver, and his intellectual commitment more serious.

The exploitation of the intermediary realm between man and God which remains mythological is perhaps the central characteristic of the hymns. The register is more lighthearted again in the *Epistre à Charles de Pisseleu*, but more serious in the *Hymne de l'eternité*, where the neoplatonist tradition, including that of Nicholas of Cusa, contributes more to the structure of Ronsard's imaginative universe. The *Hymne de Calaïs et de Zetes* makes the poetic function of the intermediary realm clear. By means of what is almost an allegory of sin, forgiveness and divine clemency, it links men, with their need to achieve self-transcendence, to God, who can fulfil their deepest aspirations, but it does so in poetic and mythological terms, so that Ronsard can project what is in fact an essentially Christian view of human experience poetically, tentatively assaying what the theologians asserted and constructed a conceptual calculus to support. Phinée, deprived of sight 'pour trop profetizer', has learned his lesson. The will of the gods cannot be pre-assured. The gods veil their oracles 'de je ne sçay quels obstacles' to assure that 'les humains/Dressent toujours au Ciel et le cœur et les mains' (*L* VIII, 285; *Pl* II, 139). The correlative of clemency from on high is aspiration from below.

The *Epistre* to the Cardinal de Lorraine from the second book of hymns in 1556 had contained a long complaint at the lack of royal support for the *Franciade*, with more than a touch of world-weariness. In 1557 Ronsard retired from court, and took to extolling the pleasures of country life. He published nothing new for two years until in 1558 he was awarded a royal pension and began to publish more court verse. The references to the poetic *fureur*, to nymphs, fauns, Muses and dryads are again lighthearted. Love, once again, becomes the *vinculum mundi*, as it had been in the *Hymne de l'eternité*.

The 1559 *Elegie*, written as a preface for a translation of Livy, once again affirms the importance of intellectual and artistic achievements including Livy's gift for writing history, by claiming for them in terms of a clearly recognizable neoplatonist psychology a divine origin. But Henri II died in 1559. In the 1560 collected *Œuvres*, the Muses do not feed their favourites, and the tone of the new pieces, like the *Elegies* for L'Huillier and L'Escot, is pessimistic. References in these poems to neoplatonist mythology, a creation of optimism about the world, become more rare and occasionally ironic:

> Les mondains amoureux vivent en indigence
> Desirant la beauté.

(L X, 345; Pl I, 907)

The perfect lover in *La Vertu amoureuse* (1560) is indistinguishable from the stoic sage, and the *Elegie* for Guillaume Des Autels attacks ecclesiastical corruption and looks forward already to the wars of religion. Ronsard's personal fortunes were at this date improving, but the new poetry announces a wave of disillusion which was to cut deeper with the polemical verse in the *Discours* of the following years.

Charles IX came to the throne in 1560. The first of the religious wars was over in 1563 with the peace of Amboise. Ronsard had received orders from the court to cease attacking the Huguenots. The *Nouvelles Poësies* of 1563–4 were probably written earlier, although not before 1560, and their tone could not contrast more vividly with the *Discours*. Between 1560 and 1563 Ronsard was writing bitterly disillusioned poetry at the same time as he was writing his most elaborate hymns, those to the seasons, as if to remind us that the *je* of an accomplished poet inevitably represented a variety of moods, and authentic feelings, rather than a settled intellectual commitment. In the *Epistre* prefacing the 1563 *Recueil* Ronsard refers to his 'soudaine mutation d'escriture'.[1] But even the hymns to the seasons, with all the panoply of neoplatonist mythology to emphasize the poet's status, are defensive in tone. The mythology is now supported by the additional element of neoplatonist number mysticism, but Ronsard emphasizes the obloquy which poets

---

[1] *L* XII, 3 ff.; *Pl* 984 ff. Ronsard is defending himself primarily against Florent Chrestien, and dropped the *Epistre* in 1578 in deference to their reconciliation.

and prophets have to expect in the richly elaborate *Hymne de l'autonne*:

> Mais courage, Ronsard, les plus doctes poëtes,
> Les Sybilles, Devins, Augures et Prophetes,
> Huiez, siflez, moquez des peuples ont esté:
> Et toutefois, Ronsard, ils disoient verité.
>
> (*L* XII, 49; *Pl* II, 241)

It is at this point that Ronsard goes on to remember how Dorat taught him the use of mythology in poetry, the need to

> feindre et cacher les fables proprement,
> Et à bien deguiser la verité des choses
> D'un fabuleux manteau dont elles sont encloses.

We could scarcely wish for a clearer statement of his poetic technique in so far as it is relevant to Ronsard's need to probe and communicate his understanding of the world in poetic and mythological terms that avoided the theological arguments and difficulties.

The myth of autumn's marriage to Bacchus is magnificently elaborated, although the *Hymne de l'hyver*, in which Ronsard distinguishes between heavenly and terrestrial philosophy, limited to a knowledge no longer of the heavens but of the virtue 'des herbes et des plantes', shares the new defensive note. The truths of even this terrestrial philosophy need to be covered with 'un voile bien subtil' (*L* XII, 70–1; *Pl* II, 251–2).

The register of the *Hymne de l'autonne* is mythopœic. The wedding of Bacchus and autumn is a splendidly rich conception in which the wedding becomes the celebration of an intoxicating fertility which is portrayed as morally uplifting and life-enhancing. In his elaborately neoplatonist proem Ronsard is merely announcing that his poemium should be understood as myth, and that its affirmations should be understood as bearing that relationship to truth which was expected of myth and is now, in Ronsard's verse, to be expected of poetry. Ronsard, in other words, states poetically that he expects to be understood as saying that, as a poet creating myths, there is something underneath the magnificent ornamentation which he wishes seriously to suggest. It is only by communicating through his often neoplatonist mythology that Ronsard can successfully elude the rigid orthodoxy of established systems of thought and imaginatively enlarge them. If he uses myth, it is

> A fin que le vulgaire ait desir de chercher
> La couverte beauté dont il n'ose approcher.
>
> *(L* XII, 72; *Pl* II, 252)

The problem is one of poetic register. Ronsard, like Montaigne, can depict death poetically as a release or as an enemy. Today we are still capable of regarding it as both. His attitude to gold is poetic and ambivalent. His nymphs can be the merest poetic backdrop or they can signify the supernatural import of what occurs in their company, or in those who have access to them. After the death of Charles IX in 1574 the defensive stoicism and the tone of disillusion become more pronounced, but there are new elements of neoplatonism even in the 1584 *Œuvres.* In that collection the *Discours* for Cheverny from *Le Bocage royal* reiterates the need to wrap truth prudently in fable. Although Ronsard does not say so, it was the only way to enlarge our understanding of truth. Only the imagination could satisfactorily probe the meaning of a changing world and changing experience at a time when 'truth' was thought to be rigidly encapsulated in an intellectual orthodoxy. It was in the end by recourse to neoplatonist tradition that Ronsard was able to vindicate the necessity of poetry as well as to practise it.

Ronsard's mythological universe

TERENCE CAVE

To examine Ronsard's use of mythological imagery is to gain
an insight into his poetic universe as a whole. It represents in
quintessential form his humanist practice of 'imitation', of
adapting themes, images and styles from the poets of classical
antiquity; it reflects traditions and fashions in the visual arts as
well as in literature; it raises questions germane to the history of
Renaissance thought and the changing sensibility of the sixteenth century; it mirrors the world of the court, the world of
scholarship, and the contemplative life of the poet in solitude.
Above all, the storehouse of classical mythology provided
Ronsard with a medium through which he could explore – and
interconnect – many different areas of experience. His endorse-
ment of its value as an instrument of the imagination cannot be
doubted, since it constitutes his prime mode of figurative
expression. Yet the status of myth was in his day far from
secure. It was interpreted in some quarters as a symbolic
language in which the profoundest truths had once been – and
could still be – expressed; for others, it was a lie, at best
frivolous, at worst evil and corrupting. Its sensuous qualities
were widely appreciated, but they were also distrusted and
despised. Since Ronsard set out to write poetry of enduring
value, comparable with the literary achievements of Greece
and Rome, it was virtually inevitable that he should have been
led to explore the relationship between myth and truth. Terms

Ronsard the poet

which polarize the antithesis too sharply are unhelpful: it is
nearly always an oversimplification to ask whether Ronsard
'really believed in' Apollo, the Muses, Bacchus, Venus and the
rest. What we are dealing with is a shifting territory situated at
the point where reality and illusion, truth and fiction, life and
art converge. It is indeed the realm within which all literature
can be said to operate; but it is also one of Ronsard's principal
claims to greatness that his poetic experiments delineate the
contours of this terrain. In consequence, the two sections of
this chapter – which correspond to the categories established
by Ronsard in a famous passage of the *Hymne de l'autonne*
(*L* XII, 50, lines 77–82; *Pl* II, 241) – should not be seen as
distinct and contrasted entities: starting from different points
on the line drawn between 'mythical surface' and 'hidden
truth', they work towards one another and, in the end, towards
the definition of a single creative centre.

THE FABULOUS MANTLE

In *Le Ravissement de Cephale*, one of Ronsard's earliest poems,
Neptune puts on a richly woven cloak to attend the marriage
of his daughter Thetis to Peleus (*L* II, 134–6; *Pl* I, 546–8). The
cloak is blue, woven in silk and gold thread by a group of
nereids, and it is decorated with an appropriate series of motifs:
a storm at sea, a shipwreck, and Neptune himself ('brodé d'or')
intervening to save the sailors. Ronsard was to use this device
again: in the *Hymne de Calaïs et de Zetes*, Castor and Pollux wear
a purple robe woven by their mother Leda, again from silk and
gold thread, and bearing a group of scenes connected with their
supernatural birth and subsequent career (*L* VIII, 263–4; *Pl* II,
128–9); while in the first book of the *Franciade* Ronsard depicts
Andromache presenting to her son Francus a 'riche habit',
once the possession of Hector, which is made of the same
material and embroidered with images of Troy, Mount Ida,
and the abduction of Ganymede (*L* XVI, 80–1; *Pl* I, 670).
Each of these cloaks is, quite literally, a 'fabuleux manteau';
each incorporates a mythological landscape into a rich surface

[160]

texture, lending an ostentatious elegance to the wearer. Moreover, such decorated surfaces abound in the work of Ronsard: the mythological paintings on his own 'guiterre', described in another early ode (*L* I, 230–1; *Pl* II, 700), include a Ganymede scene phrased much as in the passage from the *Franciade*; Leda's basket in *La Defloration de Lede* (*L* II, 71–4; *Pl* I, 517–18) and a basket belonging to one of the pastoral figures in a *Chant pastoral* of 1559 (*L* IX, 86–7; *Pl* I, 960) are decorated with mythological scenes, as are the elaborately worked goblets described in two other pastoral poems (*L* XII, 148–9, XIII, 85–7; *Pl* I, 982–3, 922–3), while a lyre supposedly given to Ronsard by his friend and patron Belot represents a *tour de force* of decorative ingenuity in that it is covered on both sides with a series of scenes from the myths of Apollo and Bacchus (*L* XV, 29–37; *Pl* II, 328–31).

Classical models can be adduced for all of these passages: the description of a decorated cloak is a device which Ronsard borrowed from Apollonius of Rhodes or one of his Latin imitators; carved and painted objects are described by Theocritus and Moschus and by Sannazaro, their Italian successor in the pastoral genre. Overshadowing them all – though never directly imitated by Ronsard – is the famous description of the shield of Achilles in the *Iliad*. This particular configuration of models is important in that it suggests an affiliation between Ronsard's taste and that of the so-called Alexandrian poets: that is to say, the Greek and Latin poets who cultivated an ornate and stylized manner of writing by contrast with the relatively sober classicism of the Attic and Roman tradition. Although Ronsard is too rich and varied a poet to be forced into a single category, and although Alexandrianism is not a very precise label, the mode of writing illustrated by the examples given so far provides one of the essential co-ordinates for a definition of the role of myth in Ronsard's poetry. For it represents a 'mythological style' which appears to be wholly ornamental, sensuous or picturesque: even gratuitous, perhaps.

To understand it more fully, however, one must first consider it in relation to some of the factors which determined the

Ronsard the poet

taste, both literary and artistic, of Ronsard and his contemporaries. As a court poet Ronsard was familiar with the world of plastic decoration within which the French court moved, and which was constantly being extended and elaborated throughout his career. The walls of Fontainebleau, of Anet and of many other châteaux, like the façade of the Louvre, were covered in a rich mantle of scenes and motifs, predominantly mythological; the king possessed objects like the famous salt-cellar of Benvenuto Cellini, encrusted with mythological decoration; and the public fêtes and the court entertainments which became increasingly frequent and elaborate under the direction of Catherine de Médicis combined the love of decorated surfaces (triumphal arches and the like) with a dramatized presentation of similar mythological tableaux. The aesthetic principle which is most apparent throughout is one of multiplicity and abundance: each surface is profusely covered, not with a single scene or motif but with a series of interrelated decorations, often executed in different media. Moreover, although each group of images is fundamentally unified (visually by a central panel or motif, intellectually by an underlying symbolic pattern), the spectator's attention is constantly fragmented by the diversity of details and techniques, while the series of 'image clusters' is often extended in a constantly evolving progression in which it is difficult to find a point of repose. The patrons who commissioned these elaborate projects and the artists who designed and executed them were no doubt in some sense involved in a propaganda exercise, since their constant theme is the glorification of France and its rulers: the monarchy needed to present to its European rivals, as well as to the nation itself, an image of inexhaustible wealth and power, manifested through its cultural resources. Yet the love of parade and ostentation goes deeper than this: whereas a single painting or sculpture exists in a self-contained realm of art, surrounded by a reality which it may comment on but never wholly transform, the decoration of Fontainebleau and the fêtes seems designed, by its very profusion and multiplicity, to cover the real world and thereby transform it. Thus a desire

Ronsard's mythological universe

to create an ideal 'supernatural' milieu, which had in earlier centuries been limited principally to sacred art and architecture, now invades the secular world: monarchs and courtiers move though a décor which mirrors them, not as they are, but as they might be; and in the festivals, they themselves play the role of gods and goddesses.[1]

Ronsard's role as witness, and indeed designer, of this kind of artistic activity is by now relatively well documented.[2] We shall see later how much of his poetry is explicitly or implicitly designed to transpose living people and events into a transcendent world and hence to confer upon them an immortal

[1] On these aspects of the visual arts, see John Shearman, *Mannerism* (Harmondsworth, Penguin Books, 1956); *Les Fêtes de la Renaissance,* ed. J. Jacquot, 2 volumes (Paris, Centre National de la Recherche Scientifique, 1956 and 1960); E. Panofsky, 'The iconography of the Galerie François Ier', *Gazette des beaux-arts,* 52 (September 1958), pp. 113–77. A superb collection of contemporary engravings based on the work of the school of Fontainebleau is provided by H. Zerner, *École de Fontainebleau: gravures* (n.p., Arts et Métiers Graphiques, 1969). Analogies between mannerist art and French poetry in this period are analysed by Marcel Raymond, 'La Pléiade et le maniérisme' in *Lumières de la Pléiade* (Paris, Vrin, 1966), pp. 391–423, and more recently in the introduction to his anthology *La Poésie française et le maniérisme,* prepared in collaboration with A. J. Steele (Geneva, Droz; Paris, Minard, 1971); the first section of the present chapter owes a great deal to Raymond's insights. A specific connection between a mannerist painting and a poem by Ronsard is discussed by R. A. Sayce, 'Ronsard and mannerism: the *Elegie à Janet*', *L'Esprit créateur,* 6 (1966), 234–47. F. Joukovsky-Micha, *La Gloire dans la poésie française et néolatine du* xvie *siècle des rhétoriqueurs à Agrippa d'Aubigné* (Geneva, Droz, 1969), is illuminating on the nature and function of 'triumphal' poetry; the mingling of court reality with mythical fantasy is analysed by F. Bardon, *Diane de Poitiers et le mythe de Diane* (Paris, Presses Universitaires de France, 1963); and some helpful remarks are made by M. M. McGowan, 'The French court and its poetry', in *French Literature and its Background,* ed. J. Cruickshank, volume I: *The Sixteenth Century* (Oxford University Press, 1968), pp. 63–78.

[2] See the articles by Frances Yates and V-L. Saulnier in *Les Fêtes de la Renaissance* (mentioned above, note 1); also W. M. Johnson, and V. E. Graham, 'Ronsard et la *Renommée* du Louvre', *Bibliothèque d'humanisme et Renaissance,* 30 (1968), pp. 7–17. An example can be found in *L* XV, pp. 389 ff., *Bref et sommaire recueil . . .* (not reproduced in *Pl*).

Ronsard the poet

destiny; meanwhile, even at the level of 'mythological style', there are striking resemblances between the Fontainebleau manner and the way in which Ronsard incorporates his decorated surfaces into a complex scheme of description and narration. This may be rapidly demonstrated by a consideration of a group of odes from the 1550 collection. The ode entitled *Des peintures contenues dedans un tableau* (L I, 259–64; *Pl* II, 704–7) purports to be a description of a real painting: to this extent, it operates on a somewhat different level from the decorated objects derived from a purely literary tradition, but in practice the analogies between the two kinds of presentation are strong. Characteristically, the *tableau* is a composite one, containing several more or less independent *peintures*: purely mythological scenes (the forge of the Cyclops, the seduction of Jupiter by Juno) are juxtaposed with historical ones (the Emperor Charles V sailing towards Tunis, the entry of Henri II into Paris), and no unifying thematic schema is at any point made explicit. Furthermore, it is virtually impossible to integrate the episodes described in the last two stanzas into the *tableau* proper, since they take place on land, whereas Ronsard had earlier referred to the ocean as delimiting the *tableau* (although the reading is uncertain here). One could perhaps take the phrase 'Tout au bas' which introduces these two stanzas as indicating, not a further element in the same composition, but rather a separate pair of *cartouches* at the bottom of the *tableau*, much as one finds in the frescoes of the Galerie François Ier. The decorative impact of the ode thus arises from the rapid succession of contrasted, discontinuous motifs, each of which is treated in some visual detail. Similarly, of the three mythological scenes which decorate the guitar in *A sa guiterre*, those depicting Apollo and Orpheus are clearly related to the musical theme, while the Ganymede episode – which is treated at greater length than the others – seems divergent. In *La Defloration de Lede*, most of the second section or 'pose' is given over to the description of the scenes painted on Leda's basket: two mythological motifs and two pastoral motifs are represented, none of which is overtly related to the others or to the story of Leda, while their arrangement on the surface of the basket is only sketchily indicated. *Le Ravissement de Cephale* is divided into three 'poses': the first describes Neptune's cloak, the second and longest narrates the story of Aurora's love for Cephalus, and the third contains Themis' prophecy of the future greatness of Achilles, who will be born to Peleus and Thetis; the poem thus forms a triptych of disparate episodes, the title referring to the central 'panel' only.

Such poems give an impression of decorative richness and abundance; they suggest a love of surface ornament, of changing patterns and textures. Their structure is largely determined by this multiplicity: the different levels of narrative and description are simply juxtaposed. In most cases it would no doubt be possible to demonstrate some unifying principle: encomiastic allegory in *Des peintures*,[1] sensuous and psychological tonality in *La Defloration*; but the immanence of any such unity in no way cancels out the immediate aesthetic impact.

At this point the analogy between Ronsard's structures and aspects of the contemporary visual arts must be complemented and corrected by a further consideration of the literary context within which Ronsard was working, and of his own assumptions as a writer. In the first place, the fact that these poems are odes is intrinsically important: one of the principal characteristics of the Pindaric – and to a lesser extent of the Horatian –

[1] Charles V's Tunis expedition marked one of the peaks of the emperor's career: he had persuaded an impressive number of European powers to accompany him on this 'crusade' against the Turks. In *Des peintures,* the representation of this episode is juxtaposed with the humiliation of the emperor at the hands of the new French monarch: 'Tout au bas, d'une couleur palle/Est repaint l'Empereur Romain', fearful of Henri II, whose 'lance/Ja ja captif le traine dans la France' (a piece of wishful thinking). This deflation, together with the description of the entry of Henri into Paris, celebrates the glory of the French king as the supreme monarch of Europe. The preceding mythological motifs allegorize the transition from belligerence (i.e. the wars with the empire and England) to love and peace; the presence of the myth of Juno disguising herself as Venus in order to regain her husband's attentions may be a discreet reference to the rivalry between Catherine de Médicis and Henri's mistress Diane de Poitiers.

[165]

ode is the discontinuity of its structure and the multiplicity of its themes and imagery. These are precisely the qualities which Ronsard singles out in a famous passage of the 1550 preface to the *Odes* as both typical of the genre and liable to disconcert the reader:

> Je ne fai point de doute que ma Poësie tant varie ne semble facheuse aus oreilles de nos rimeurs, et principalement des courtizans, qui n'admirent qu'un petit sonnet petrarquizé, ou quelque mignardise d'amour qui continue tousjours en son propos: pour le moins, je m'assure qu'ils ne me sçauroient accuser, sans condamner premierement Pindare auteur de telle copieuse diversité, et oultre que c'est la sauce, à laquelle on doit gouster l'Ode. Je suis de cette opinion que nulle Poësie se doit louer pour acomplie, si elle ne ressemble la nature, laquelle ne fut estimée belle des anciens, que pour estre inconstante, et variable en ses perfections.
>
> (*L* I, 47; *Pl* II, 973)

Likewise, the sense of a richly worked fabric woven of many strands is evoked by the first stanza of the *Ode à Michel de l'Hospital* (*L* III, 118–19; *Pl* I, 386).

This principle of 'copieuse diversité' was to form the basis for a great deal of Ronsard's work throughout his career, spreading out from the odes to embrace a wide range of other forms and genres. Thus many of his later mythological poems are analogous in structure to those we have already considered. In the second book of *Hymnes*, the two poems describing the exploits of fabulous twins (Calaïs and Zetes, Castor and Pollux) can be seen as two panels in a mythological or legendary diptych, especially as both are derived from the story of the Argonauts; moreover, the *Hymne de Pollux et de Castor* is further divided into two, each half recounting the exploit of one of the twins. Similarly, the visit of Orpheus to the cave of the centaur Chiron in *L'Orphée* (*L* XII, 126–42; *Pl* II, 64–72) (a further episode from the voyage of the Argonauts) introduces two separate mythological narratives. Or again, the narration of Hylas's drowning in the poem *Hylas* (*L* XV, 234–53; *Pl* II,

381–91) (yet another Argonaut motif) is preceded by an extended (and apparently gratuitous) description of Hercules pulling a full-grown pine out of the ground: there is a sharp contrast here between the violence and brute strength of Hercules and the decorative, 'feminine' mood which pervades the story of his young cupbearer.

All these poems are constructed on a larger scale than the early odes: they are in fact epic fragments rather than mythological miniatures or vignettes, and their style is based on an expansive cumulation of couplets (predominantly alexandrine) rather than the self-contained stanzaic units of the ode. This is admittedly only a broad distinction: the movement of the ode often flows over the borderlines created by the metric division. It seems, however, that in his 'middle period' (roughly, from the *Hymnes* to the *Franciade*), Ronsard developed a sinuous, constantly expanding rhythm which could knit together a wide range of thematic material and imagery into a single ornate texture.[1] Yet the underlying aesthetic preoccupation remains constant: the theory of the epic as outlined by Ronsard indicates his continuing preference for variety, abundance and rich texture:

> ils [les vers Alexandrins] ont trop de caquet, s'ils ne sont bastis de la main d'un bon artisan, qui les face autant qu'il luy sera possible hausser, comme les peintures relevees, et quasi separer du langage commun, les ornant et enrichissant de Figures, Schemes, Tropes, Metaphores, Phrases et periphrases eslongnees presque du tout, ou pour le moins separees, de la prose triviale et vulgaire (car le style prosaïque est ennemy capital de l'eloquence poëtique) et les illustrant de comparaisons bien adaptees de descriptions florides, c'est à dire enrichies de passements, broderies, tapisseries et entrelacements de fleurs poëtiques, tant pour representer la chose, que pour l'ornement et splendeur des vers . . .
>
> (*L* XVI, 331–2; *Pl* II, 1018–19)[2]

[1] See Marcel Raymond, 'La Pléiade et le maniérisme', pp. 416 ff.
[2] See also *L* XVI, 336 and 340 (*Pl* II, 1021–2 and 1024–5), an extract from which is quoted below, p. 178. In the passage quoted here, Ronsard

Ronsard the poet

Indeed, one may perhaps attribute his failure to complete his projected epic in part to his tendency to focus on richly worked episodes rather than on narrative design on a grand scale: his taste for the Alexandrian Apollonius of Rhodes in itself indicates a liking for the wayward and fragmented narrative.

To these theoretical testimonies from the beginning and end of Ronsard's career one may add the following passage which occurs in the *Abbregé de l'art poëtique* of 1565:

> tu te doibs travailler d'estre copieux en vocables, et trier les plus nobles et signifians pour servir de ners et de force à tes carmes, qui reluyront d'autant plus que les mots seront significatifs, propres et choisis. Tu n'oubliras les comparaisons, les descriptions des lieux, fleuves, forests, montaignes, de la nuict, du lever du Soleil, du Midy, des Vents, de la Mer, des Dieux et Déesses, avecques leurs propres metiers, habits, chars, et chevaux: te façonnant en cecy à l'imitation d'Homere, que tu observeras comme un divin exemple, sur lequel tu tireras au vif les plus parfaictz lineamens de ton tableau.

(L XIV, 15; Pl II, 1002)

This statement once again stresses the need for 'copiousness' of vocabulary and image (including mythological reference). The word 'copieux' here and in the phrase 'copieuse diversité' from the 1550 preface is not used at random. The notion of *copia* in style, originating with the Latin rhetoricians, was developed into a specific technique by Erasmus, whose *De Copia Rerum et Verborum* became one of the most successful humanist handbooks of the sixteenth century.[1] According to Erasmus,

---

is ostensibly defending his preference for the decasyllabic line over the alexandrine as an epic metre; but the advice he gives for the avoidance of slack prolixity ('caquet') is equally applicable to his notion of epic style *per se*.

[1] The importance of this treatise, and its possible influence on Rabelais and others, is briefly indicated by R. R. Bolgar, *The Classical Heritage and its Beneficiaries* (Cambridge University Press, 1954; New York, Harper Torchbooks, 1964), pp. 272–5, 297–8, 320 ff. P. Laumonier, in his

Ronsard's mythological universe

stylistic *copia* should be acquired by the systematic exploitation of both the material and the vocabulary of classical writers: the student should work his way through the whole range of classical literature, compiling a notebook both of 'things' (*exempla, sententiae,* images and stock themes) and of words, and should then use his storehouse of materials to enrich his own style. This technique, which is a specific interpretation of the humanist notion of imitation, was bound to result in a stylistic texture totally opposed to the purist 'Ciceronian' aesthetic: at the level both of the individual sentence and of the overall structure of a work, the emphasis would be on proliferation and variety (as in Erasmus's *Praise of Folly* or his *Adages*). Whether or not through the direct influence of Erasmus, the principle of *copia* is fundamental to the aesthetic of the leading vernacular writers of the French Renaissance, to Rabelais, to Montaigne, and not least to Ronsard himself, who appears to be referring to *copia* of words and images in the passage from the *Abbregé* quoted above. Ronsard's humanist studies, directed from the outset by Dorat, consisted primarily in the exhaustive reading of classical literature: each successive phase of his poetic creation bears the mark of some newly discovered vein of source-material. Moreover, his use of sources seldom takes the form of line-by-line imitation, even in his earliest works: several parallel passages from different poets will be exploited to produce a new synthesis. Indeed, it looks very much as if he must have compiled his own notebooks in the *copia* manner, since the virtuosity with which the technique is commonly carried out scarcely suggests the random operation of memory: simply by sampling the footnotes of Laumonier's edition one can rapidly acquire an impression of the extraordinary variety of Ronsard's materials. It seems likely, also, that Ronsard used contemporary compilations as a source of mythological and other classical material – Robert Estienne's *Dictionarium Nominum Propriorum*, for example, or the mythographical manuals of Italian humanists such as

Ronsard, poète lyrique (Paris, Hachette, 1909), pp. 379 ff., refers to what is in effect the *copia* technique as taught by Dorat and practised by Ronsard.

Ronsard the poet

Comes[1] – and in this way supplemented his own collection of 'things' and words.

Two further quasi-theoretical passages from different phases of Ronsard's career throw light on his method. The first, from the *Ode de la paix* of 1550, follows a longish excursion into myth and legend, which explains the tone of 'self-correction' (borrowed from Pindar):

> Tousjours un propos deplaist
> Aus oreilles attendantes,
> Si plein outre reigle il est
> De parolles abondantes.
> Celui qui en peu de vers
> Etraint un sujet divers,
> Se mét au chef la couronne:
> De cette fleur que voici,
> Et de celle, et celle aussi,
> La mouche son miel façonne
>
> Diversement . . .
>
> (*L* III, 23; *Pl* I, 362–3: see Laumonier's
> note on the punctuation)

The tension between expansion and compression which is apparent here is characteristic of Ronsard: his prose theory contains similar recommendations to check unwarranted extravagance. Yet the phrase 'un sujet divers', followed immediately by the celebrated 'bee' image (a commonplace of Renaissance imitation theory, derived originally from Pindar) and by the heavily stressed 'Diversement', shows that abundance, or multiplicity of subject, is not in question. In fact, as we have seen, Ronsard's use of *copia* tends to be highly concentrated: his eclecticism produces a closely woven texture, a

---

[1] See J. Seznec, *The Survival of the Pagan Gods* (New York, Pantheon, 1953; Harper Torchbooks, 1961), pp. 307–9, with references to Laumonier and de Nolhac.

kind of stylistic *discordia concors*.[1] Some twenty years later, Ronsard was to use the bee image again:

> Mon Passerat, je resemble à l'Abeille. . . .
> Ainsy courant et fueilletant mes livres,
> J'amasse, trie et choisis le plus beau,
> Qu'en cent couleurs je peints en un tableau,
> Tantost en l'autre: et maistre en ma peinture,
> Sans me forcer j'imite la Nature . . .
>
> (*L* XV, 252; *Pl* II, 390–1)

Once again, the notion of colourful diversity is strongly emphasized, mirroring the technique used in *Hylas*, from which the passage is drawn, and indeed in the majority of Ronsard's mythological poems. The secondary reference in this instance to 'peinture' also deserves comment, since, as we saw earlier, Ronsard's poetic manner runs parallel to the current vogue for elaboration and diversification in the plastic arts. It is true that the analogy between poetry and painting, derived from Horace's dictum 'ut pictura poesis', is again a commonplace in this period, and that it is only applied in a loose, metaphorical sense, even where the poem is explicitly 'imitating' the visual arts (as in *Des peintures*). Yet its repeated appearance in Ronsard's work gives it a special weight, particularly where it is associated with *copia* references.[2] It seems, indeed, that the orientation of the *copia* method towards a decorative multiplicity – as distinct from the philosophical or burlesque multiplicity of Erasmus and Rabelais – finds its theoretical expression precisely in this analogy.

At the level of both style and structure, therefore, the *copia* technique of imitation helps to explain the closely woven fabric and the discontinuous form of many of Ronsard's

[1] Cf. below, p. 194. This analogy deserves further discussion, since it represents one of those key areas in which Ronsard's stylistic preferences coincide with an aspect of his world-view (cf. also below, p. 191, and the first section of chapter 7).

[2] Cf. the quotations from the *Abbregé* and the *Franciade* preface, above, pp. 167–8; also *L* I, 117 (*Pl* I, 410); *L* III, 177 ff. (*Au Conte d'Alsinois*, *Pl* I, 617 ff.), and many other examples.

mythological poems. It also has a bearing on his use of mythological allusion and periphrasis. The complex play of erudite allusion for which Ronsard used to be ridiculed may in part be ascribed to a wilful exclusiveness, but it is also the result of an encyclopedic technique which places at the poet's disposal a range of nuances hardly accessible to the ordinary reader, whether of his day or ours (hence the commentaries which contemporary humanists such as Muret supplied for his works). 'Obscurities' of this sort characteristically take the form of periphrasis, which is in effect itself a *copia* device when used liberally, since it draws on material not directly provoked by the context and thus opens a window, however briefly, on a new perspective; indeed, it represents in its most extreme form the 'compressed' *copia* referred to above. An example which Laumonier quotes – with some disapproval – in his *Ronsard, poète lyrique* occurs in *La Defloration de Lede*, immediately after the description of the basket:

> L'une [des nymphes] arrache d'un doi blanc
> Du beau Narcisse les larmes,
> Et la lettre teinte au sang
> Du Grec marri pour les armes:
> De crainte l'œillet vermeil
> Pallit entre ces piglardes,
> Et la fleur que toi soleil
> Des cieus encor tu regardes . . .

(L II, 74; Pl I, 518)

The convoluted texture of these lines is simply an extension of the introspective movement of the poem as a whole into a self-contained world of myth; furthermore the metamorphoses they allude to awaken echoes of love and suffering which add a further dimension to the poem's psychological import. Once again, one may take the decorated cloaks – in particular those of Castor and Francus – as the epitome of Ronsard's method: for they are in effect a form of visual periphrasis, clothing the hero in an emblematic complex of allusions and thus transporting him beyond the narrative moment into the realm of his destiny.

Ronsard's mythological universe

It is true that periphrasis and other forms of allusion create tensions, interrupting the flow of the poetic argument; but Ronsard's aesthetic flourishes on such tensions, and any criterion which rejects them cannot do justice to his work.[1]

The aesthetic disposition which on the theoretical level is represented by *copia*, or by the bee image as Ronsard uses it, is of course not simply a question of technique. It will be recalled that, in the 1550 preface, Ronsard attributes the need for 'copieuse diversité' in poetry to nature itself, which is 'inconstante, et variable en ses perfections'; and the conclusion of the passage from *Hylas* has a similar implication. The cornucopian abundance of the natural world recurs as a central theme throughout Ronsard's poetry, whether it is applied to the realm of cosmology, pastoral landscape or national wealth;[2] and it will be apparent at once that such references to the 'imitation of nature' are as much a metaphor as the analogy with painting discussed earlier. For their sense is determined, not by some verifiable 'real world' outside the poem, which imposes its colours, shapes and textures on the poet's style, but rather by a nature imaginatively transformed and already integrated into a poetic universe, whether by Homer (see the passage from the *Abbregé* quoted above, p. 168) or by Ronsard himself.

[1] This analysis, emphasizing the density and convolution characteristic of Ronsard's manner at certain points, should not be taken to indicate that his mythological style is predominantly static. On the contrary, it is a sense of dynamism which prevails; the passages in which the texture is densely allusive, when incorporated into this movement, tend only to create moments of turbulence. Ronsard's 'dithyrambic' style, epitomized in the *Dithyrambes* of 1553 and the *Hinne de Bacus* of 1554, provides the most striking examples of such effects; cf. M. Morrison, 'Ronsard and Catullus: the influence of the teaching of Marc-Antoine de Muret', *Bibliothèque d'humanisme et Renaissance,* 18 (1956), pp. 240–74. The 'dynamism' of Ronsard's world-view and of his style is discussed in detail in chapters 1 and 7 of the present volume, pp. 26–34, 288–302.

[2] See, for example, L I, 26 ff. (*Pl* II, 686 ff.) on the natural riches of France; L VIII, 148 (*Pl* II, 192) on cosmic fertility; L IX, 80 ff. (*Pl* I, 956 ff.) for imagery of abundance connected with poetry and eloquence in a pastoral setting; and the first three seasonal hymns, *passim*. Cf. also chapter 2 of the present volume, pp. 86–7, 92, 95.

Ronsard the poet

When Ronsard describes an object painted or engraved with mythological scenes, he often indicates the 'lifelike' quality of the representation, implying that the visual arts reach perfection when the scene 'comes alive' for the spectator. Whatever else 'imitation of nature' may mean for the poet,[1] this animation of a scene in all its detail is certainly one of the functions of poetry as sixteenth-century theorists saw it, and it is in this sense precisely that the analogy between poetry and painting is most often stressed. What Peletier Du Mans has to say on the rhetorical procedure of hypotyposis is relevant here;[2] within the work of Ronsard, the most explicit exposition of the theory is to be found, once again, in the posthumous preface to the *Franciade*. Yet this preface is equally concerned with the 'ornamentation' of poetry, with devices like periphrasis which seem to remove it from direct contact with a living scene. This duality is already apparent in the passage quoted earlier where the 'flowers of rhetoric' which Ronsard recommends the poet to use in such profusion have a double purpose: 'tant pour representer la chose, que pour l'ornement et splendeur des vers'. If one recalls further that Ronsard, drawing an analogy with 'les peintures *relevees*', has just insisted on the need for the poet to separate his work as far as possible from the 'langage commun', it becomes clear that the word 'representer' has a special meaning for him. The representation of reality in poetry takes place within the framework of a language designed specifically to eliminate the common, the ordinary and the trivial; thus the objects and scenes which are to be represented 'au vif' must be both pre-selected for their rarity or special interest and endowed by poetic language with a prestige which fits them for the higher world of art.

This interpretation of Ronsard's theory throws light on many of the mythological subjects portrayed in his poetry. The

---

[1] Cf. Grahame Castor, *Pléiade Poetics* (Cambridge University Press, 1964), chapter 5.

[2] Jacques Peletier Du Mans, *Art poëtique,* ed. A. Boulenger (Paris, Les Belles Lettres, 1930), pp. 133–5; cf. also p. 130, on the function of comparison.

cloaks, goblets, baskets, musical instruments and paintings he describes are themselves luxury objects, indeed works of art, and his depiction of the scenes that decorate them is at several removes from reality. Not only are the scenes rendered in a poetic language heightened by the technique of *copia*; they are also imagined as painted, woven or engraved (that is to say, they have been shaped by a second aesthetic medium), and they are predominantly drawn from a mythological universe which is by definition 'non-real'. The description of objects and the animation of scenes thus becomes an elaborate game, purporting to reflect reality but in fact taking the reader deeper and deeper into the world of the imagination.[1] Nowhere is this more apparent than in the pastoral poems where, as in his classical and Italian models, Ronsard's shepherds wager prized objects (such as the engraved goblets) in a gratuitous rivalry of poetic skills. The whole scenario has the character of a game played with poetry: the poet, imagining a contest of eloquence between shepherd-poets, gives his own virtuosity free rein both in the contest itself and in the depiction of the 'stakes'; and it is in this setting that the jewel-like mythological miniatures seem, deceptively and even ironically, to 'come alive'.

'Mimesis', defined thus, has an importance beyond the confines of detailed description and virtuosity of technique. Since it tends to make the borderline between the everyday world and the imagined world fluid, both by presenting fantasy scenes in sharp focus and by endowing physical objects with the prestige of art, it cannot fail to give a special colouring to another category of 'reality', namely historical personages, events and circumstances. If the world of Fontainebleau and the fêtes is an attempt to disguise everyday court life in the mantle of fable, to transpose it into an ideal realm in which tensions are resolved and destinies consecrated, then much of Ronsard's poetry can be said to fulfil an analogous function. The transition from myth to history in *Des peintures* is no longer

[1] For an illuminating analysis of this process in the work of a contemporary of Ronsard, see M. Jeanneret, 'Les œuvres d'art dans *La Bergerie* de Belleau', *Revue d'histoire littéraire de la France,* 70 (1970), pp. 1–13.

abrupt if it is presumed that there is a continuity between the
two levels: the categories 'myth' and 'history' themselves
become blurred, so that human events are seen as reflecting a
supernatural order. Elsewhere the movement into – or out of –
the mythological landscape may be signalled by a 'threshold'
device which participates in both worlds. The 'grotte de
Meudon' at the château of the Cardinal de Lorraine fulfils this
function in the epithalamium *Chant pastoral* of 1559. The landscape of the poem and the protagonists are throughout idealized according to the pastoral convention; the *grotte* itself, as a
real building, reaches back into the historical world of Ronsard
and his patrons, but at the same time it is the entrance, within
the pastoral, to a yet higher realm of experience:

> Apres qu'ilz [the 'shepherds' Du Bellay and Ronsard]
>   eurent fait aux deux coings de la porte
> Le devoir à Pallas qui la Gorgonne porte,
> Et à Baccus aussi, qui dans ses doigs marbrins
> Laisse pendre un rameau tout chargé de raisins:
> Ilz se lavent trois fois de l'eau de la fonteine,
> Se serrent par trois fois de trois plis de vervene,
> Trois fois entournent l'Antre, et d'une basse voix
> Appellent de Meudon les Nymphes par trois fois,
> Les Faunes, les Sylvains, et tous les Dieux sauvages
> Des prochaines forests, des mons, et des bocages,
> Puis prenant hardiesse, ilz entrerent dedans
> Le sainct horreur de l'Antre, et comme tous ardans
> De trop de Deité, sentirent leur pensée
> De nouvelle fureur saintement insensée.
>   Ilz furent esbahis de voir le partiment,
> En un lieu si desert, d'un si beau bastiment:
> Le plan, le frontispice, et les pilliers rustiques,
> Qui effacent l'honneur des colonnes antiques,
> De voir que la nature avoit portrait les murs
> De crotesque si belle en des rochers si durs,
> De voir les cabinets, les chambres, et les salles,
> Les terrasses, festons, guillochis et ovales,

Ronsard's mythological universe

Et l'esmail bigarré, qui resemble aux couleurs
Des préz, quand la saison les diapre de fleurs,
Ou comme l'arc-en-ciel qui peint à sa venue
De cent mille couleurs le dessus de la nue.

(*L* IX, 77–8; *Pl* I, 955–6)

The juxtaposition in this passage of the stylized classical rituals performed by the poets with the architectural description of the *grotte* provides a key to Ronsard's superimposition of imagination on reality, in this poem and many others. The elaborate ceremony, derived from a foreign world and a foreign religion, reflects notions commonly associated by the Pléiade with poetic inspiration (moral purification, the animation of nature and insight into its mysteries),[1] and prepares the poets for the supernatural *fureur* which descends on them in the *grotte* itself. By contrast, the description of the building, with its proliferation of architectural detail, transfers one's attention to the visual world and thus to something much nearer to tangible reality. Yet, although the details are precise, and thus in a sense 'concrete', the overall impression is diffuse: the imagination recreates a bewildering variety of spaces, shapes and decorations rather than a solid building. Indeed, the description finally moves into the realm of fantasy as the columns and masonry of the *grotte* give way to an enamelled surface which is itself dispersed amid the flowery abundance of spring and the shimmering colours of the rainbow.

In terms of aesthetic imagination this rendering is in sympathy, once again, with contemporary manifestations of the plastic arts; it is also curiously similar in tone, and in some details, to a passage in the posthumous preface to the *Franciade* where Ronsard describes the workings of the poetic imagination by means of a visual analogy:

[1] A central example of these themes is provided by the request of the Muses and the reply of Jupiter in the *Ode à Michel de l'Hospital*; they are expounded at greater length in the *Solitaire premier* of Pontus de Tyard (1552). Cf. F. Joukovsky-Micha, *Poésie et mythologie au* xvie *siècle. Quelques mythes de l'inspiration chez les poètes de la Renaissance* (Paris, Nizet, 1969); and see below, pp. 187–8, 193–5.

Ronsard the poet

C'est le faict d'un Historiographe d'esplucher toutes ces considerations, et non aux Poëtes, qui ne cherchent que le possible: puis d'une petite scintille font naistre un grand brazier, et d'une petite cassine font un magnifique Palais, qu'ils enrichissent, dorent et embellissent par le dehors de marbre, Jaspe et Porphire, de guillochis, ovalles, frontispices et piedsdestals, frises et chapiteaux, et par dedans de Tableaux, tapisseries eslevees et bossees d'or et d'argent, et le dedans des tableaux cizelez et burinez, raboteux et difficile à tenir és mains, à cause de la rude engraveure des personnages qui semblent vivre dedans. Apres ils adjoustent vergers et jardins, compartimens et larges allees . . .

(*L* XVI, 340; *Pl* II, 1024)

If one bears in mind both this passage and the earlier one from the same preface (above, p. 167), one may more easily grasp the internal relationship between the two apparently discontinuous parts of the 'grotte de Meudon' quotation. In the first place a link is provided by an interpretation of the poetic *fureur* in psychological terms: the sense of awe which overtakes the poets as they enter the *grotte* is at first attributed to a supernatural inspiration, but it is then manifested in the purely human astonishment provoked by the architectural marvels of the building. In the second place, the decorative abundance of the description itself, prolonged into the realm of simile, illustrates and even, in a sense, represents that expansion of the poetic fantasy which inspiration releases. Furthermore, the invocatory language of the opening raises all that follows above the level of common experience so that the descriptive arabesque, introduced 'tant pour representer la chose, que pour l'ornement et splendeur des vers', can dissolve the tangible stonework and frescoes of the real *grotte* (an artificial structure 'imitating' nature) into the more fluid medium of poetry.[1]

---

[1] In certain important respects, the function of the decorated lyre in *La Lyre*, consecrated in a 'temple' which may be identifiable with Saint-Cosme, is analogous to that of the *grotte* in this poem; see below, pp. 190–2; and chapter 5 (pp. 218–25) on instrumental metaphor.

Ronsard's mythological universe

In this instance the mythological and inspirational themes are introduced first, colouring one's reading of the 'mimetic' passage. Elsewhere, by contrast, the narration of a purportedly real situation may gradually acquire the prestige of fable. This occurs in the later part of the *Voyage de Tours* of 1560, where the poet, watching his mistress leave the celebrations with her mother and take the river ferry, embroiders the scene with aquatic myths and then indulges in fantasies of metamorphosis:

> j'avisé sa mere en haste gagner l'eau,
> Et sa fille emmener avecq elle au bateau. . . .
> En guise d'un estang, sans vagues paresseus
> Aille le cours de Loyre, et son limon crasseus
> Pour ce jourd'huy se change en gravelle menue,
> Pleine de meint rubi et meinte perle esleue.
>
> Que les bords soient semez de mille belles fleurs
> Representant sur l'eau mille belles couleurs,
> Et le tropeau gaillard des gentiles Nayades
> Alentour du vaisseau face mille gambades,
> Les unes balloyant des paumes de leurs mains
> Les flots devant la barque, et les autres leurs seins
> Descouvrant à fleur d'eau, et d'une main ouvriere
> Conduisant le bateau du long de la riviere. . . .
> Que ne puis-je muer ma resamblance humaine
> En la forme de l'eau qui cette barque emmeine!
> J'irois en murmurant sous le fond du vaisseau,
> J'irois tout alentour, et mon amoureuse eau
> Bais'roit ore sa main, ore sa bouche franche,
> La suivant jusqu'au port de la Chapelle blanche:
> Puis, forçant mon canal pour ensuivre mon vueil,
> Par le trac de ses pas j'yrois jusqu'à Bourgueil,
> Et là, dessous un pin, sous la belle verdure,
> Je voudrois retenir ma premiere figure.
>
> N'y a-t-il point quelque herbe en ce rivage icy
> Qui ait le gous si fort qu'elle me puisse ainsi
> Muer comme fit Glauque en aquatique monstre,
> Qui, homme ny poisson, homme et poisson se montre?
>
> > (*L* X, 222–5; *Pl* I, 144–6)

Ronsard the poet

Once again, as in the epithalamium, the landscape of the poem as a whole is idealized by pastoral convention; throughout, real places, people and events are woven into a decorative style which heightens the colours of reality and confers an aura of *mignardise* on the poet's amorous adventures. The passage quoted illustrates the process of transition; at the same time, it moves beyond even the pastoral fantasy into the realm of myth itself as the mud of the Loire is transformed into rubies and pearls, the river nymphs appear and the poet dreams of escaping from human contingency (see above, chapter 1, pp. 42–3, and chapter 2, pp. 90–6). At this point, the would-be metamorphoses of the lover mirror the function of the poem itself, which is to compensate for the intractability of reality by transforming it into fable. Ronsard himself recognizes the illusory quality of the fantasy and deflates it: 'Or cela ne peult estre . . .' (line 253); but later, after a bout of copious drinking (lines 267–74), his imagination conjures up new dreams of pastoral bliss in which – like the poet-god Apollo in love with Admetus – he will abandon his poetic pretensions and become a shepherd in Anjou.

It is by the creation of such complex and fluctuating relationships between different levels of experience that Ronsard surpasses his models. The fabulous mantle is never *merely* decorative, since even where its ornamentation is most gratuitous, it already embodies a significant exploration of the shifting pattern of relationships between art and ordinary reality. Ronsard moves beyond the crude categories of myth and reality (or history), image and meaning, surface and content: what is important is not the distinctions between them, but rather their reciprocal action. Hence his 'mythological style' is a means of mediation, gathering into itself both the real world and the world of fantasy. Yet the meanings which it can thus independently convey cannot, in the end, be dissociated from that further area of significance represented by the notion of an 'enclosed truth'; nor can its mediating function be properly understood without an analysis of the criteria by which the value of the mythological universe as a whole may be measured. Is it the world of poetic insight which is 'true', or the ordinary world in which Ronsard, as a historical personage, lived his life? Is inspiration really a divine gift, providing supernatural intelligence, or is it simply a delusion, a product of uncontrolled imagination? And these questions provoke others: how far can an idealized view of the history and destiny of a nation give direction to the political realities of a particular point in time? Can transient experience be immortalized? Can the pleasures of love and conviviality be reconciled with the pursuit of a higher truth? In other words, what is at stake here is the status and function of poetry itself, as represented by a mythological imagination. It is to these problems that we must now turn our attention, beginning with a brief outline of the forms of mythography which offered to a sixteenth-century poet both theory and material for the exploitation of myth within a safe conceptual framework.

THE ENCLOSED TRUTH

Ronsard and his contemporaries inherited a long and still flourishing tradition of mythological exegesis which can broadly be termed 'allegorical'.[1] Within this tradition, classical myths were interpreted not in terms of archaeology, anthropology or the history of religions, but rather as an imaginative masking of truth. At one end of the scale a myth might be rationalized in historical or 'scientific' terms, so that the gods become simply princes or heroes deified by tradition, or allegories of the seasons, the elements, or the heavenly bodies; alternatively, it might be given a moralizing interpretation, the judgement of Paris representing for example the triumph of lust over wisdom and civic virtue; while in some works –

[1] For an overall view of the history and character of mythological allegory in the Middle Ages and the Renaissance, Seznec's *The Survival of the Pagan Gods* is indispensable. G. Gadoffre, *Ronsard par lui-même* (Paris, Éditions du Seuil, 1960), pp. 103–17, gives a succinct and intelligent account of Ronsard's position in this context. G. Demerson, *La Mythologie classique dans l'œuvre lyrique de la 'Pléiade'* (Geneva, Droz, 1972), appeared as this volume was about to go to press; unfortunately, no account could therefore be taken of it in the composition of the present chapter.

[181]

Ronsard the poet

notably the various versions of the *Ovide moralisé*, still popular in the sixteenth century – it might acquire a biblical or theological sense (Hercules defeating the hydra prefigures Christ's victory over Satan; Bacchus embodies the action of divine grace). The mythographers of this tradition commonly summarize the stories and attributes connected with each figure, and then provide allegorical interpretations at two or more levels. The result is a catalogue of unrelated attributes and allegorizations such as one finds in Boccaccio's *De Genealogia*; furthermore, the procedure of translating mythological material into a series of explicit conceptual equivalents immobilizes its meaning and deprives it of the ambiguities, tensions and imponderables which are essential to most forms of poetic discourse.

While remaining remarkably persistent in its older forms, this tradition of mythography also evolved in various ways during the Renaissance: the classical sources quoted for each myth become far more wide-ranging, so that mythographies begin to play the role of *copia* handbooks, while the allegorical apparatus, still present, tends to become less extensive and elaborate.[1] The most important reorientation of the tradition was, however, brought about by the Florentine neoplatonists. Ficino and his colleagues, following the method of early Christian neoplatonists like Plotinus, constructed a unifying theory of classical myth which restored both its religious and its poetic content. In their view, the earliest Greek poets were in contact with the fundamental mysteries of religion, consecrated later by the Christian revelation; these poets devised the language of myth as a means of making ineffable truths manifest, and at the same time of preventing the uninitiated from gaining too intimate a familiarity with them. Myth was thus originally a form of poetic theology, although later it was debased by writers who had lost contact with the fount of truth: the pagan gods represent the powers of the true God as

[1] A good example of both developments is provided by the *Mythologiae* of Natale Conti (Comes), first published in 1551 (see references in Seznec, op. cit.).

they are manifested in the universe and in man; they are the divine unity bodied forth in the whole range of physical and psychological processes which keep the created world in motion. Hence the schematic, didactic form of allegorization is dropped in favour of a more flexible approach which allows metaphysical, psychological, moral and physical insights to interpenetrate as part of a pattern which represents the single universal truth. Each myth is 'dynamic' in that it embodies the force which animates the world; and since it is never wholly comprehensible, its content is never exhaustively defined. Finally, its aesthetic integrity is guaranteed by the platonist identification of the good and the beautiful, and by an elevated hedonism which celebrates the joy of the soul in its pursuit of truth.[1]

Ronsard's affiliation to the neoplatonist view of myth is evident in the statements which occur in the opening pages of the *Abbregé de l'art poëtique*:

Sur toutes choses tu auras les Muses en reverence . . . comme les filles de Jupiter, c'est à dire de Dieu, qui de sa saincte grace a premierement par elles faict cognoistre aux peuples ignorans les excellences de sa majesté. Car la Poësie n'estoit au premier age qu'une Theologie allegoricque, pour faire entrer au cerveau des hommes grossiers par fables plaisantes et colorées les secrets qu'ilz ne pouvoyent comprendre, quand trop ouvertement on leur descouvroit la verité . . . Car les Muses, Apollon, Mercure, Pallas et autres telles

[1] Neoplatonist allegory was a source of inspiration for much of the finest art of the Italian Renaissance; see in particular E. Wind, *Pagan Mysteries in the Renaissance,* new and enlarged edition (Harmondsworth, Penguin Books, 1967; London, Faber and Faber, 1968). The marriage of aesthetic beauty with 'philosophical' meaning is apparent too in the work of the school of Fontainebleau, although here neoplatonism plays a less central role (see the article by Panofsky cited on p. 163, note 1, in this chapter). The second section of chapter 3 of the present volume ('Ronsard's other poetry') discusses in detail, in a somewhat different perspective, the relation between myth and neoplatonism in Ronsard's poetry: the two accounts should be considered as complementary.

Ronsard the poet

deitez ne nous representent autre chose que les puissances de
Dieu, auquel les premiers hommes avoyent donné plusieurs
noms pour les divers effectz de son incomprehensible
majesté.

(L XIV, 4, 6; Pl II, 997–8)

Most of his other references to allegory reflect the same
notions, or are at least compatible with them.[1] It seems likely
that he had read the preface of Richard Le Blanc's translation
of the *Io* (1546), in which the poetic fury is equated with
Christian grace:[2] he himself refers in the *Abbregé* to the
'saincte grace' of God which is projected through the Muses.
In addition, the *Solitaire premier* of Pontus de Tyard, published
in 1552, made available to him a development of precisely the
same form of allegory, derived this time principally from
Ficino's commentary on the *Symposium*.[3]

This evidence, supported by what we know of Dorat's
allegorical teaching and its influence on Ronsard,[4] might lead
us to expect a consistently allegorical intention in his mythological poetry. Yet it is precisely this consistency of approach
which is lacking, so much so that critics like Pierre de Nolhac
and Henri Weber have asserted categorically that his treatment
of myth is in the main free from the 'contamination' of allegorical method. It is true that he commonly identifies his
patrons with mythological and legendary figures; that certain
of the hymns portray in terms of myth the workings of the

[1] See *L* VIII, 68–9 (*Pl* II, 165); *L* XII, 50 and 70–2 (*Pl* II, 241 and 251–2);
L XVIII, 96–8 (Pl I, 909–10).
[2] This preface is reproduced in A. Lefranc, *Grands Écrivains français de la
Renaissance* (Paris, Champion, 1914), pp. 125–6.
[3] Cf. also L. Le Caron, *Les Dialogues* (Paris, Sertenas, 1556), dialogue 4:
Ronsard. Ou, de la poësie (fs. 127 r°–149 v°). Although Ronsard's presence
as interlocutor in this dialogue is fictitious, as Le Caron himself indicates,
it gives a useful account of contemporary arguments for and against the
use of 'fable', the status of inspiration, and other aspects of poetic theory.
[4] See P. de Nolhac, *Ronsard et l'humanisme* (Paris, Champion, 1921), pp.
69–73; Nolhac quotes a Latin poem by Dorat on the allegorization of
Homer in connection with Ronsard's acknowledgement of his debt to
Dorat in this respect.

Ronsard's mythological universe

universe; that some of his mythological narratives – *L'Hymne de Calaïs et de Zetes, L'Adonis, Le Satyre, Le Pin* – are concluded with a brief moralization, or with a sketchy indication of the myth's allegorical sense; and that the *Hercule chrestien* systematically allegorizes the labours of Hercules in terms of the life of Christ. But amid the extraordinary range and variety of poems based on mythological themes, it is hard to detect any unifying intention, any systematic exploration of universal truth through the medium of myth. The fragmentary, episodic nature of many of the mythological narratives operates against such a conception: mythological figures are evoked, acquire their own momentum within a carefully delineated landscape and then disappear, leaving one in most cases with the sense rather of an intuitive insight than of an underlying conceptual framework. Where a specific allegorization appears, it is frequently secondary to the structure of the poem as a whole, forming part of a wider complex of meaning.[1] Ronsard's allegorical intention as expressed in his theory thus remains unresolved, in the sense that the meanings he incorporates into his mythological poems cannot easily be reduced to a single interpretative schema. His practice in this respect reflects the love of oblique allusions and juxtapositions that one finds throughout his work, particularly in the earlier years. It can also no doubt be attributed in part to his instinctive tendency to retain the aesthetic integrity of the image, to develop the imaginative energies it contains, rather than to make it conform to a pre-established pattern of ideas.[2]

In a sense Ronsard's theory allows for such ambiguities and expansions in that the *fureur* of poetic inspiration frees the poet from rational constraints and allows him to explore universal experience intuitively. The poet's intellectual or contemplative

---

[1] A good example is provided by *La Lyre* (L XV, 22; *Pl* II, 324) where Ronsard gives an explicit interpretation of the birth of Pallas Athene.

[2] On this ambivalence, see Joukovsky-Micha, *Poésie et mythologie*, especially p. 183: 'Dans ses plus belles réussites, elle [la Pléiade] semble avoir respecté la nature du mythe, intermédiaire entre l'explication systématique et l'ignorance totale. Le rôle du mythe dans l'œuvre de la Pléiade est souvent d'exprimer les efforts de l'homme pour plonger dans le mystère, non pas de donner des solutions.'

[185]

Ronsard the poet

disposition is thus displayed not so much through a conscious structure of ideas for which myth provides a convenient illustration as through the intrinsic meaning which each myth acquires in the inspired use of poetic language. In this way the poet may hope to renew the experience of the earliest Greek theologian-poets and hence to put into practice the true 'theologie allegoricque', assuming always that divine grace, in the form of inspiration, guarantees the 'truth' of what the mythical cloak conceals. Yet in practice the guarantee is virtually impossible to demonstrate once schematic allegorization has been abandoned: the allegories of the *Hercule chrestien* are too 'safe' to admit of inspiration, while the Bacchic *fureur* of the *Hinne de Bacus* is simply self-assertive, renouncing rational verification.

One consequence of this situation is the need to adopt a flexible approach to the exegesis of Ronsard's mythological poems. Sometimes a 'key' may be found which reveals one or more hidden levels of meaning within a poem: this is true of *Des peintures*, the *Ode à Michel de l'Hospital*, the seasonal hymns, and many others; the allegorical method and its commonplace notations undoubtedly form a living part of Ronsard's poetic imagination. 'Allegory-hunting' on this level must however be undertaken with caution, since it may lead one to distort the character of the poem in order to make it fit into a convenient schema. Even where a poem's extrinsic relationship with a given historical circumstance or set of ideas can be established, it is always its intrinsic range of significance, the specific structure which the use of myth creates from experience, which must be the principal object of analysis.

At the same time, Ronsard's stance in respect of allegory provides a paradigm for the 'criterion' problem outlined at the end of the first section of this chapter. Ronsard proclaimed and endorsed a system which seemed to provide 'certainty', a secure external correlative for the proliferation of his poetic imagery; yet the poems themselves fragment and obscure the certainty. The remainder of this chapter will attempt to show how the problem manifests itself, in terms of myth, in some of

Ronsard's mythological universe

the central areas of Ronsard's poetic creation. We shall examine first the ideal of a fulfilled poetic destiny towards which he appears to be working, and then point to the flaws in the structure, the ways in which the ideal proved unrealizable.

*

*   *

*

Two of Ronsard's major poems, the *Ode à Michel de l'Hospital* and *La Lyre*, develop in mythological imagery the theme of the poet's function, drawing into their orbit at the same time a wide range of related preoccupations. Although they are separated in time by nearly twenty years (the *Ode* was published in 1552 and may have been sketched out earlier, while *La Lyre* appeared in 1569), they both analyse the nature of poetic inspiration in a manner analogous with the *Abbregé*. The central episode of the *Ode* – the request of the Muses and the response of Jupiter – provides in mythical terms an explanation of how divine power is transmitted through the medium of poetry to men. The principle of diversification outlined by Jupiter in strophe 13 (*L* III, 142; *Pl* I, 396) is in this instance derived directly from Plato's *Io*, while it clearly anticipates the *Abbregé* theory also. Its function here is to provide a structure which clarifies the preceding request of the Muses (ibid., 138–40; 394–5): the animation of nature, the healing powers, the cosmic insight, the spiritual and moral elevation, the civilizing culture which they ask to be allowed to bestow – all these powers, comprehensible at the level of human experience, are invested in poetry by a single supernatural principle.

The stanzas which set out in schematic form this platonizing theory must however not be isolated from the fabric of the poem as a whole. For Ronsard is preoccupied, from the very beginning, with the making of poetry, with its colours, its abundance, and its complex structure (see above, p. 166); while a sense of creative energy is apparent throughout, whether in the richly textured description of the Muses' journey, in the exuberance of their song, which develops into a self-contained

G   [187]

epic fragment, or in the passages depicting the creation of
Michel de l'Hospital himself: the image of the Parcae weaving
his life-thread is reminiscent of the poem's 'woven' structure,
referred to in the first and last stanzas of the poem. The creative
momentum which sustains the poem through its many themes
and episodes is presumably for Ronsard a manifestation of that
force of inspiration which the theoretical passages analyse.
Yet it seems to be epitomized also in the description of the
underwater palace in which the Muses meet Jupiter at a feast
given by the Ocean (ibid., 125–6; 389–90): Jupiter is here
associated with another source of power, 'des vives fontaines /
Le vif Sourgeon parannel'. One might be tempted to recall in
this context the Muses' own Pierian spring, the most celebrated
image of inspiration, were it not for the absence of any reference to this image elsewhere in the poem (except for line 460,
where the water is associated rather with purification). However, in strophe 5, Ronsard alludes specifically to the generative
force of the ocean:

> Là, sont divinement encloses
> Au fond de cent mille Vaisseaux,
> Les semences de toutes choses,
> Eternelles filles des eaux.

The ocean is the fount of life, reflecting at the level of physical
matter Jupiter's own function as the originator of spiritual
energy.[1] Thus the generation of poetry, embodied in the Muses
themselves, arises from a conjunction of the two extremes of
the creative spectrum, just as the *Ode* is compounded of a
theoretical schema and a rich use of poetic language and structure.

If this poem is primarily about the nature of poetic creation,
there is nevertheless a second outgrowth of meaning connected

---

[1] There are important parallels for this motif of physical generation in
Ronsard's 'seasonal' hymns; one finds in the same context instances of
the motif of children visiting their father, which could be seen as an
image of the exploration of the supernatural meanings inherent in human
experience.

with the cultural situation at the French court. The song of the Muses opens with an allusion to the myth of Minerva and Neptune disputing the sovereignty of Athens, Neptune here representing war and Minerva peace (ibid., 128–9; 390). It then moves rapidly through a mythical representation of the extent of the cosmos to an account of the battle between Jupiter and the Giants. The theme of war is further evoked later, first when Mars is sent to sleep by the song itself (antistrophe 10; compare Jupiter's slighting reference to Mars in strophe-antistrophe 12), and then in connection with the armies of Ignorance which drive the Muses from the earth, only to be themselves overcome by Michel de l'Hospital. These disparate references are united by two themes: the defeat of the forces of darkness, and the subsequent triumph of peace. To understand them fully, one must recall that the *Ode* was written in the early years of the reign of Henri II, when Ronsard's poetry was repeatedly heralding a new era of peace and cultural progress; this was to be marked both by the long-desired triumph of France in its struggles with the Empire and England, and by the liquidation of all opposition to the innovations of Ronsard and his colleagues. Hence the triumph of peace over war, of Jupiter over the Giants, of l'Hospital over Ignorance operates both on a political and a cultural level, particularly if one identifies the Jupiter of the Gigantomachy with Henri II himself.[1] In this context, the reference in the theoretical section of the poem to the benefits bestowed by the Muses on monarchs who honour

---

[1] The identification of Jupiter with Henri II is frequent in Ronsard's poetry and contemporary iconography; see in particular the *Hymne de Henri II*. Cf. D. and E. Panofsky, *Pandora's Box: the changing aspects of a mythical symbol,* 2nd ed. (New York, Harper Torchbooks, 1965), on Ignorance, the motif *ex utroque Caesar,* and other topics; M-R. Jung, *Hercule dans la littérature française du* xvie *siècle. De l'Hercule courtois à l'Hercule baroque* (Geneva, Droz, 1966), on similar politico-cultural themes in the context of the myth of Hercules; I. Silver, 'Ronsard, the theological reaction, and the creation of a national poetic language', *L'Esprit créateur,* 10 (1970), pp. 95–103; and F. Joukovsky-Micha, 'La guerre des dieux et des géants chez les poètes francais du xvie siècle (1500–1585)', *Bibliothèque d'humanisme et Renaissance,* 29 (1967), pp. 55–92.

them takes on its full force: if poetry must draw its creative power from a supernatural principle, it can only flourish at a particular moment in history when the nation flourishes and when it is protected by enlightened patrons. One might add that these themes are further linked, within the structure of the poem, by the quasi-historical schema of the 'descent of poetry' which reduplicates the metaphysical schema (ibid., 148–52; 399–401).

La Lyre, unlike the *Ode*, consists almost entirely of an analysis of the nature and functions of poetry. Once again, a patron forms a 'figurehead' for the poem, providing an excuse for a comprehensive summary of Ronsard's attitude to poetic creation and of his career as a poet: for now the first-person references, which were only marginal in the *Ode*, dominate the poem. At the same time the imagery is highly mythological, not only in the concluding section, which describes the scenes on the lyre itself, but also in the opening analysis of the waxing and waning of Ronsard's inspiration. Bacchus plays a central role in both sections, while Apollo, to whom the lyre is dedic-ated, has pride of place in its decorations. More precisely, it is dedicated to 'le Gaulois Apollon' (*L* XV, 28–9; *Pl* II, 327), by which Ronsard seems to designate either French poetry (or the Pléiade) in general, or himself in particular. Laumonier inclines to the second interpretation, principally on the grounds that the 'temple' where the instrument will be hung can be identified in some sense with the priory of Saint-Cosme. If so, this is a characteristic example of Ronsard's manner of moving from the real to the mythological world; and it presupposes also that the Apollo of the decorations represents, in transposed form, aspects of Ronsard's own experience. This seems indeed to be the case: for certain of the scenes are analogous to out-standing phases of Ronsard's career. In the first scene, for example, Apollo appears at the feast of the gods, harmonizing with his music 'cette vieille discorde' between Pallas and Neptune: this expansion of the first song of the Muses in the *Ode* reflects the role of poetry (or of Ronsard himself as poet) in absorbing political tensions and in resolving them, ideally, in terms of a superior culture. Similarly, the sequence of scenes closes with a reference to Apollo singing of the defeat of the Giants, explicitly interpreted this time as an allegory of the fortunes of the Huguenots: this final episode could well refer to Ronsard's recent activities in the field of polemical poetry. Overall, what is important here is the synthesis of different aspects of poetic activity. Apollo represents the poet in his public role at court or as defender of the establishment; but he is also a god turned shepherd for the love of Admetus, and is depicted next to the dance of Venus, Love and the Graces: in this capacity he recalls the amorous and pastoral modes cultivated by Ronsard, and, in more general terms, the pursuit of beauty and pleasure through the medium of poetry. The autumnal scene of Bacchus pouring forth from his cornucopia a rich profusion of fruits follows appropriately upon the scene of Love throwing golden apples at the Graces. Within the context of a decorative fresco so closely linked with the nature of poetry, Bacchus inevitably evokes the creative abundance which is a major aspect of the *Ode* and which is apparent in this poem also, particularly in the elaborate description of the lyre: the cornucopian motif at the level of theme and image is reflected in the *copia* of the style. This interpretation of Bacchus as a god of poetic abundance is endorsed by the Bacchic passage earlier in the poem, where Ronsard depicts himself cultivating the vine and being rewarded with the gift of Bacchic *fureur*.[1] Finally, like Apollo, Bacchus holds the balance between war and peace, reconciling military vigour with the pleasures of the dance.

The lyre, then, draws together and 'harmonizes' various areas – sometimes conflicting ones – within which the poet operates. Furthermore, since the passages on inspiration at the beginning of the poem refer to the four platonic furies as aspects of a single transcendental force, the unification of experience in the crucible of poetry is made possible by the

[1] L XV, 17–18; *Pl* II, 322. Cf. also the image of the river in flood (19–20; 323). For another cornucopian representation of Bacchus, see the *Hymne de l'autonne*; in this instance, however, no explicit connection is made between Bacchus and poetic inspiration.

Ronsard the poet

divine gift of inspiration, the source of all creation and harmony. Apollo and Bacchus thus give the poet access to a world of permanent values and endless creativity, represented by myth itself; through the scenes depicted on it, the votive lyre consecrates synchronously his whole range of activities. The transformation is all the more potent because the beginning of the poem stresses the *discontinuity* of inspiration, and the sense of sterility which arises when it is absent. The writing of the poem itself, according to Ronsard, followed upon just such a sterile period:

> J'avois l'Esprit qui le labeur desdaigne,
> Depuis un peu tout en friche et brehaigne,
> Sterile et vain, ou soit qu'il fust lassé
> De trop d'enfans conceuz au temps passé,
> Soit qu'il cherchast le repos solitaire:
> Il m'assuroit de jamais plus ne faire
> Rime ny vers ny prose ny escrit,
> Voulant sans soing vivre come un Esprit . . .
>
> (*L* XV, 22–3; *Pl* II, 324)

One might say, then, that *La Lyre* attempts to counteract the periodicity of inspiration by synthesizing a myth of permanent creativity.

Hence the Muses, Apollo and Bacchus are central to Ronsard's poetry in that they embody a range of significance which includes the theory of inspiration but goes far beyond it. Bacchus is himself particularly relevant to the problem that mythological poetry poses on the level of moral values: how can the overtly sensuous and morally suspect character of many classical myths be reconciled with a poetic which stresses the dignity and quasi-religious nature of poetry? It is known that this question and others like it were raised by his opponents, particularly in the Calvinist camp;[1] it could not be answered by reference to an allegorical system which extracts an arbitrary

---

[1] See in particular the *Elegie à Loïs des Masures* (1560) (*L* X, 362–70; *Pl* II, 570–3); Ronsard's defence of the 'pompe du bouc' in the *Responce . . . aux injures* (*L* XI, 141 ff.; *Pl* II, 605–6); and below, chapter 6, pp. 258 ff.

meaning and discards the 'surface' of the myth. For Ronsard retains the sensuous presence of his deities, elaborating it indulgently, and yet offers them as the product – even the symbol – of an inspiration analogous to the grace of God. In the *Hinne de Bacus* of 1554 this problem appears in a particularly clear form since Ronsard explicitly defends Bacchus against charges of effeminacy and moral turpitude, then depicts him as the leader of a frenetic and disorderly company of devotees, only to associate him later with moral purification and divine insight. What seems to be implied here is that Bacchus affirms a continuity between human and transcendental experience; he represents the recognizably earthly joys of drinking and conviviality, yet at the same time directs the momentum of these energies towards a higher end. The poet is specially equipped to understand this connection, since the Bacchic dynamism is another form of inspiration, one of the 'puissances de Dieu' operating through man.[1]

The moral purification which contemporary theory sees as an essential prerequisite for true inspiration and which is often associated with the Muses does not therefore prescribe to the poet an overtly moralizing approach, or the avoidance of morally ambiguous material, since inspiration itself directs the use of the material and is supposed to guarantee its ultimate propriety. The ritual washing in the fountain of the Muses is perhaps primarily a metaphor for the poet's need to set himself apart from material preoccupations and to give his whole attention to the act of poetic creation as an end in itself. Hence this theme is often allied with the notion that the poet works best in solitude, avoiding social pressures and drawing closer to the forces immanent in the natural world with which the Muses themselves are intimately linked.

[1] For a more detailed analysis of this poem, see my article 'The triumph of Bacchus and its interpretation in the French Renaissance: Ronsard's *Hinne de Bacus*', in *Humanism in France at the end of the Middle Ages and in the early Renaissance,* ed. A. H. T. Levi (Manchester University Press, 1970), pp. 249–70. The aesthetic character of the poem is finely analysed by Marcel Raymond, *Baroque et Renaissance poétique* (Paris, Corti, 1955), pp. 97–100.

Ronsard the poet

In the famous introductory section of the *Hymne de l'autonne* all these themes are present, while the myths recounted in the four seasonal hymns imply an ethic based on exuberant creativity, which is shown to transcend ordinary moral categories.[1] Although the mythical narratives themselves contain no explicit references to poetic creation, they show in a particularly vigorous way how the 'abundance' principle so often asserted by Ronsard in other realms is manifest in cosmic process. Given this analogy and the overtly theoretical introductions of the third and fourth hymns, it only requires a slight shift of register to understand the seasonal cycle in terms of the poet's own activity.[2] Hence the divine furies as embodied in Bacchus and the Muses provide a structure within which the poet's use of hedonistic themes and imagery is morally consecrated, and which allows him to place poetic creation at the centre of the spectrum of human experience.

The analogy between the cosmic and the poetic domains is further encouraged by the belief that inspired poetry is in effect a privileged form of philosophy, giving access to the secrets of the universe. Like Cybele in *Le Pin*, and like Philosophy herself in the *Hymne de la philosophie,* the Muses, Bacchus and Apollo all have this function; once again, they mediate between heaven and earth, this time in the realm of knowledge. What they reveal is expressed in greater detail in the cosmic and seasonal hymns: that the universe is based on a *discordia concors* which reconciles unity with multiplicity; that all the hierarchies of beings, things and processes in the universe are linked by the 'chain of Jupiter' which assures a dynamic continuity between the principle of creation and all its manifestations; that the structure of the cosmos reflects divine per-

[1] See in particular the *Hymne de l'esté* (L XII, 35–45; *Pl* II, 234–9), and the interpretation of the seasonal hymns by D. Stone, *Ronsard's Sonnet Cycles: a study in tone and vision* (New Haven and London, Yale University Press, 1966), pp. 107 ff.

[2] For more detailed evidence, see my article, 'Ronsard's Bacchic poetry: from the *Bacchanales* to the *Hymne de l'autonne*', *L'Esprit créateur,* 10 (1970), pp. 104–16.

fection; and that man, subjected by original sin to time and mortality, cannot through his own powers perceive the full eternal sequence of cause and effect which makes 'history' part of a transcendental pattern.[1] Poetry in its philosophical capacity provides its own physics and metaphysics.

One would have expected mythology to play a major part in the concrete representation of this synthesis. Curiously enough, however, its role is purely ancillary in the principal cosmic hymns (*de la philosophie, des astres, du ciel, de l'eternité*), where it provides notations for features of the cosmos or decorative expansions, but is seldom used at length to embody its essential workings. Ronsard seems to prefer a more explicit language in this context, or at most a use of personification which may occasionally be itself quasi-mythological, as in the *Hymne de l'eternité*; unlike his models Callimachus and Marullus, he seldom addresses his hymns to a prominent deity (the only major exceptions being the early *Hinne de Bacus* and the late *Hynne de Mercure*). Mythology comes into its own rather at the lower end of the spectrum, explaining the natural processes of generation and change in terms of a supernatural principle: this is the function, for example, of Venus in the *Hymne de la mort* and the *Hymne de l'eternité*; elsewhere, as we have seen, it symbolizes the forms of psychological experience which provide access to higher insights.

Thus one could say that Ronsard's mythological universe is centred at the threshold of supernatural experience, or conversely at the limits of purely human experience: it expresses a heightened sense of 'reality', reflecting the world of men yet releasing it from contingency. In this respect his mythological figures are often analogous with the *daimons* which he describes at length in the well-known hymn from the 1555 collection. For the *daimon* is both subject to passions, like mankind, and

[1] See *L* VIII, 143, line 40 (*Pl* II, 191, modified); ibid., 89–90, 148 (202–3, 192); ibid., 142 (191); ibid., 253–4 (124–5). Cf. also *Le Chat* (*L* XV, 39–47; *Pl* II, 331–6), and the late ode *Les Estoilles* (analysed in detail below, chapter 7, pp. 295–300).

immortal; he lives in the sublunar world, the world of change and imperfection, but inhabits the air, while man is bound to the earth (*L* VIII, 123, 125; *Pl* II, 169–70). Indeed, Ronsard interprets certain lesser deities – nymphs, satyrs and the like – as *daimons* (ibid., 129–30, 133; 171–2, 173). Furthermore one may recall that the speech of Jupiter in the *Ode à Michel de l'Hospital* refers to the *daimon* who will be assigned to each poet to guide his creative activity (*L* III, 146; *Pl* I, 398: cf. ibid., 150; 400), while Ronsard speaks of his own guiding *daimon* at the opening of the *Hymne de l'autonne*. This latter case is particularly interesting in that Ronsard calls him 'le Daimon qui preside/Aux Muses', and in a later edition makes the reference wholly explicit by substituting 'Apollon' for 'le Daimon' (*L* XII, 46; *Pl* II, 239). Similarly in the *Dithyrambes* of 1553 Bacchus is referred to as a *daimon* (*L* V, 74; *Pl* II, 772). At this point mythological figures are something more than metaphors or allegories: for if Ronsard indeed believed in the real existence of *daimons*, then Apollo, Bacchus, the nymphs of Gastine and the Loir, perhaps the Muses also, may take on an analogous mode of existence, dropping the cloak of fiction to become participants in an actual hierarchy of beings.

Thus far, then, we have considered primarily the functions of myth in Ronsard's poetry in pointing towards a total interpretation of man and the universe, viewed within the perspective of poetic creation. This synthesis, in so far as it is realized by Ronsard, would involve the proper ordering of the state, both politically and culturally, and an understanding of contemporary events in terms of the nation's history and destiny; it would present an interpretation of man's moral experience in terms of a metaphysical frame of reference; it would represent the processes of the physical world as an integral part of a supernatural cosmic system; and it would show how, through poetry, man can gain insight into all the realms of truth. Yet any reader of Ronsard will perceive at once that no such universal synthesis is achieved in his poetry, that in nearly every case the utopian ambition is hedged in with doubts and problems;

Ronsard's mythological universe

we must now, therefore, look at the reverse of the coin.

we must now, therefore, look at the reverse of the coin.

*

*   *

*

The first problem arises in the context of inspiration itself. The sustained belief in the insights mediated by Apollo, Bacchus or the Muses as 'powers of God' depends on the extent to which such powers manifest themselves within the human experience of writing a poem: at times of creative energy Ronsard was doubtless able to believe that he was in reality possessed by a supernatural force. Yet such moments tend to be shortlived: as we have seen, he is often preoccupied with the periodic nature of his inspiration. This in itself produces a discontinuity in the poet's perception of the 'other world', a discontinuity stressed particularly in the middle years of Ronsard's career (roughly, the 1560s): the wholly personal sense of sterility which pervades the opening of *La Lyre* has no parallel in the youthful *Ode à Michel de l'Hospital*. At about the same time, moreover, it seems that Ronsard came to question the inherent validity even of the 'creative' periods themselves. He had always been fascinated by the products of the uncontrolled fantasy: from the eighth *folastrie* (*Le Nuage, ou l'ivrogne*) to the *Nues ou nouvelles* of 1565, and thence to the posthumous preface of the *Franciade,* he evoked the limitless nebulous forms that the imagination can produce when not governed by reason.[1] Sometimes he condemns them, either directly, as in the *Franciade* preface (*L* XVI, 334; *Pl* II, 1020), or by using a burlesque tone (as in *Le Nuage*). In these instances, reason is apparently the criterion by which 'truth' is determined. Yet the divine furies assert the superiority of irrational insights; indeed, Ronsard frequently specifies the fantasy as the faculty through which inspiration itself operates, raising it

[1] See above, chapter 1, pp. 43–9; and chapters 3 and 6, pp. 147–9 and 255 ff. on the whole question of Ronsard's 'crisis of confidence' in the 1560s.

Ronsard the poet

from the realm of fiction to the perception of truth.[1] Hence there is a dualism here which already implies an uneasiness about the status of inspiration. It can be detected also in a passage of the *Responce aux injures* (*L* XI, 159–63; *Pl* II, 613–15), where he speaks of the uncontrolled, will-o'-the-wisp character of his inspiration, and defends it as having a divine origin; but then he totally discounts the truth of his poetry, using his favourite image of fantasy shapes seen in the clouds:

> Tu sembles aux enfans qui contemplent es nues
> Des rochers, des Geans, des Chimeres cornues,
> Et ont de tel object le cerveau tant esmeu,
> Qu'ils pensent estre vray l'ondoyant qu'ils ont veu,
> Ainsi tu penses vrais les vers dont je me joüe,
> Qui te font enrager, et je les en avoüe.
>
> (ibid., 163; 615)

Two years previously Ronsard had expressed the same ambivalence towards inspiration in the *Elegie à Jacques Grevin*. His view here is that man is too imperfect to gain full access to divine perception (*L* XIV, 193; *Pl* II, 920); he himself, moreover, has exhausted himself in the attempt to write, and his poetic creativity fails to compensate adequately for the erosion of his vitality (ibid., 195; 922). True inspiration, and with it the 'theological' significance of fable, is relegated to the realm of early Greek poetry, to a long-distant past (ibid., 196–7; 922–3); in this instance, no Michel de l'Hospital seems to be at hand to lead the Muses triumphantly back to earth. Although there are certainly affirmations of inspiration in Ronsard's later work,[2] he never fully recovered his confidence in its authenticity and fruitfulness. At the end of his career he wrote a bitter and ironic epilogue to the story. In the *Discours ou*

---

[1] See *L* I, 145 (*Pl* I, 420); VI, 190 (II, 281); XII, 46 (II, 239); XIV, 196 (II, 922). Ronsard's interest in *daimons* belongs very much to this area of his poetic experience. Cf. Grahame Castor, *Pléiade Poetics,* chapters 13–15, on the imagination.

[2] See, for example, the *Panegyrique de la Renommée*, discussed below, chapter 5, pp. 220–1, and chapter 7, pp. 311–12.

Ronsard's mythological universe

dialogue entre les Muses deslogées, et Ronsard, the poet meets the
Muses, who have been exiled from Greece by the Turkish
invasion; they are dishevelled and poorly dressed, and Ronsard
sees in them the deflated image of his inspiration:

> Je pensois qu'Amalthée eust mis entre vos mains
> L'abondance et le bien, l'autre ame des humains :
> Maintenant je cognois, vous voyant affamées,
> Qu'en esprit vous paissez seulement de fumées,
> Et d'un titre venteux, antiquaire et moysi,
> Que pour un bien solide en vain avez choisi. . . .
> Que vous sert Jupiter dont vous estes les filles ?
> Que servent vos chansons, vos Temples et vos villes ?
> Ce n'est qu'une parade, un honneur contrefaict,
> Riche de fantaisie, et non pas en effect.
>
> (*L* XVIII, 92–3; *Pl* I, 819)

It is true that the Muses reply, taxing him with ingratitude for
the gifts and glory they have bestowed on him; but Ronsard
holds them at arm's length, and the poem ends ambig-
uously.

Ronsard's difficulties in obtaining patronage and full recognition of his poetic stature seem to have played a major role in
this crisis of confidence. Of equal importance is his claim, in
the Grevin elegy and elsewhere, to be endowed with a melancholic temperament. For melancholy in Ronsard's day – or
more specifically since the rehabilitation of the temperament by
the Florentine neoplatonists – was seen as having a dual mode
of operation. On the one hand it could produce fever and
delusions, resulting from an inflamed fantasy; on the other,
it might take the form of a contemplative disposition, open
to the insights conferred by true inspiration: Socrates, for
example, was held to have been a Saturnian. By associating
himself with this temperament, Ronsard was in a sense assuming the Ficinian persona of the artist, which had become commonplace; but it seems that the ambiguity of melancholy also
provided a framework within which he could clarify his own

profound uncertainty about the nature of his poetic activity.[1]

A particularly interesting variant of the ambivalence inherent in the poet's role as 'philosopher' is provided by *Le Pin*, another poem from the 'middle period'. The myth of Atys is interpreted as an allegory of the philosopher's withdrawal from society, his search for solitude and moral purity; thus far, it is wholly compatible with the motifs of purging and pastoral solitude often associated with the Muses. Yet there is a tension between the serenity of the austere philosopher and the anguish of Atys, separated from society by an action which goes against both reason and the natural forces which replenish the universe (compare *L* XV, 180–2; *Pl* II, 368–9 with ibid., 184; 370: there is a clear discrepancy between the mythological narrative and its interpretation). The poem thus expresses in a most cogent form the situation of a poet whose creativity is purely mental: Ronsard's defective health, and perhaps also his celibacy and isolation, create an anguish which poetry can

---

[1] On this question, see D. Wilson, *Ronsard, Poet of Nature* (Manchester University Press, 1961), chapter 4; my article 'Ronsard's Bacchic poetry'; and, on the history of the melancholic temperament, R. Klibansky, E. Panofsky and F. Saxl, *Saturn and Melancholy: studies in the history of natural philosophy, religion, and art* (London, Nelson, 1964). The question is made more complex by Ronsard's recurrent image of himself as a 'poëte gaillard', a phrase which suggests both mental and physical vigour; there is an unresolved tension between such indications of optimism and exuberance on the one hand, and the darker energies of the melancholic temperament on the other. One is once more reminded of the periodicity of Ronsard's inspiration as he himself saw it, and a corresponding oscillation between a sense of physical wellbeing and the awareness of decay. For an overall view of Ronsard's 'self-portraiture', see the following: *L* X, 293 ff. (*Pl* I, 885–6, shortened); ibid., 300–5 (II, 422–4); ibid., 334–5 (II, 465–6); XI, 116–76 (II, 595–621), *passim*, especially 159–62 (613–14); XII, 46–50 (II, 239–41: 'gaillard' in line 3 replaced by 'subtil'); XIV, 142–5 (I, 824–6); ibid., 194–5 (II, 921–2); XV, 15–21 (II, 321–4). Note that all these passages occur in poems published between 1560 and 1569; they could easily be supplemented by reference to poems written both before and after, but they nevertheless represent a particularly intensive period of self-awareness.

only spasmodically transcend;[1] the doubts about inspiration are aggravated by a discrepancy between spiritual energies and the contingencies of physical existence.

Hence the divine fury is in the last analysis unable to provide continuity of insight, a reliable criterion for judging the truth of what poetry reveals, or a means of redeeming the poet's subjection to time and circumstance. It remains the embodiment of his desire to probe the limits of human experience, but even at this level it reflects his fluctuating commitment to his art, the characteristic cycle of elation and despondency. The platonizing structure outlined in the *Ode à Michel de l'Hospital* thus remains an ideal, a conception of 'pure poetry' far removed from the fragmented explorations which the poems themselves realize. Likewise, the myths – Apollo, Bacchus, the Muses – even as images of divine power or as *daimons*, can at most point to a wished-for transcendence.

Indeed in many of Ronsard's mythological poems the movement towards the supernatural seems to be reversed. The gods lose their aura of divinity and submit, in part at least, to human limitations; or they become simply entertaining 'fictions'. An early example is provided by the *Defloration de Lede*, where Jupiter's metamorphosis into a swan has no metaphysical implications: it embodies rather the qualities of subtle sensousness and persuasion with which Ronsard, as lover, wishes to approach Cassandre. Likewise, in the burlesque *A son lict* (*L* I, 257–9; *Pl* II, 704), Mars and Venus appear as the erotic epitome of the poet's own lovemaking; while the overall tone of the poem is determined by the first and last stanzas which elevate the bed itself to a dignity of cosmic proportions. This burlesque mood recurs throughout Ronsard's work: it appears,

[1] According to Ronsard's secretary Amadis Jamyn, the poetry written at Saint-Cosme in the late 1560s and published in 1569 was provoked by a 'fiebvre quarte' which Ronsard suffered for some eighteen months; see *L* XV, 14 (liminary sonnet by Jamyn, not reproduced in *Pl*); ibid., 59–60, 177, 185 (*Pl* II, 342, shortened; 366–7, with a significant variant of line 90; 371). In the love poems of 1569, the theme of fever recurs, often connected with fantasy, distortion of vision, and solitude. On the Cybele–Atys myth in *Le Pin*, see also above, chapter 1, p. 56.

for example, in a sonnet of the *Continuation des amours*, where
Jupiter's furious celestial activities are deflated by a humorous
conceit:

> Tu as beau, Jupiter, l'air de flammes dissouldre,
> Et faire galloper tes haux-tonnans chevaus,
> Ronflans deçà delà dans le creux des nuaus,
> Et en cent mille esclats tout d'un coup les descoudre,
>   Ce n'est pas moi qui crains tes esclairs, ni ta foudre
> Comme les cœurs poureus des autres animaus:
> Il y a trop lon tems que les foudres jumeaus
> Des yeus de ma maitresse ont mis le mien en poudre.
>   (*L* VII, 164–5; *Pl* I, 155. Cf. *L* XV, 199–200; *Pl* I, 42)

This lighthearted attitude towards myth may be determined,
particularly in the mid-1550s, by the exploitation of Latin
elegiac poets and the pseudo-Anacreon; hence it cannot be
taken to signify any profound disillusionment with the inherent
value of mythological imagery. Yet when, in a similar vein,
Ronsard depicts a gay and slightly frivolous Venus who uses
rose water as a cosmetic (*L* VII, 184; *Pl* I, 119), the door is
opened to an equivalence between the human and the mythical
worlds which cannot but affect the status of myth. In a sense,
the 'Argonaut' fragments from the second book of hymns
(1556) point in the same direction. If they are allegorical, the
frame of reference is historical rather than transcendental;
moreover the mythical aspects of the protagonists and their
exploits are treated pragmatically: the winged twins have the
same difficulty in taking to flight as large birds (*L* VIII, 275;
Pl II, 134), while Amycus is depicted as a crude bully rather
than as a fabulous monster (still less as an allegory of wrath or
pride) (ibid., 304–7; 218–20). Parallels may be found in *Hylas*,
but it is perhaps the *Adonis* of 1563 which carries the 'human-
ization' process furthest. Venus – like Apollo in the Admetus
fable – abandons her divinity in order to share the pastoral
way of life of Adonis; her passion, her lamentations, her
ultimate inconstancy operate wholly on a mortal level, while

Ronsard's mythological universe

the jealousy of Mars is identifiable with the psychological reflexes of any cheated lover.[1]

In these instances, instead of using myth as a means of exploring the supernatural world, Ronsard transposes 'downwards': the myth moves so far into the realm of familiar human experience that its function as a symbol of further realities disappears. This does not, of course, mean that it becomes poetically ineffective. On the contrary, poems such as the *Adonis*, precisely by renouncing any claim to represent a 'theologie allegoricque', take on a purely psychological and picturesque interest which will endear them – rather than the more ambitious experiments in 'inspired' mythology – to later generations of readers.

It is, however, in the extensive domain of court poetry that the problem of the status of myth is posed in its most acute form, for the mythification of experience here comes into conflict with the intractable realities of personalities, politics and historical circumstance. Reduced to its most trivial level, this is apparent in the sometimes extravagant mythological hyperboles which Ronsard uses to eulogize his patrons; he himself hints at this in an early ode:

> La fable elabourée
> Decrite heureusement
> Par la plume dorée
> Nous trompe doucement:
> A l'un donnant la gloire
> Qu'il n'a pas merité,

[1] See J. C. Lapp, 'Ronsard and La Fontaine: two versions of *Adonis*', *L'Esprit créateur*, 10 (1970), pp. 125–44, to which I owe my comments on this poem, and 'The potter and his clay: mythological imagery in Ronsard', *Yale French Studies*, 38 (1967), pp. 89–108. Cf. Marcel Raymond, 'La Pléiade et le maniérisme', pp. 410–11. Specifically 'human' details of characterization, gesture and situation are often present in the mythological scenarios of the seasonal hymns. Cf. also below, chapter 7, pp. 308–9, on the distancing of mythological figures; and above, chapter 2, pp. 106–7, for an example of ironic deflation in connection with Hélène.

Ronsard the poet

Faisant par le faus croire
Qu'on voit la verité.

(L I, 131–2; Pl I, 415)

Yet there is no doubt that in assembling a system of Olympic notations for court personages – illustrated in its most comprehensive form by the *Hymne de Henri II*[1] – he was not simply indulging in flattery for the sake of material reward. Such transpositions reflect a desire to realize a dream of national and cultural greatness, of a new golden age, which his poetry would triumphantly celebrate. Hence his vision of Henri II, and later Charles IX, at the head of a new empire, fulfilling the royal motto 'donec totum impleat orbem';[2] hence also his recurrent invocation of peace as the source of all joy and abundance, his hope that Mars might finally be banished and the languishing Muses revived. This vision is already fully developed in the copious *Ode de la paix* of 1550 (L III, 3–35; Pl I, 358–67), which, by means of a complex structure, integrates it into both a historical and a cosmic schema; and in spite of the political setbacks of the 1550s it is renewed in 1559 when the treaty of Cateau–Cambrésis is being negotiated and celebrated.[3] The irony and the pathos of the situation is in retrospect self-evident: when France is on the point of losing two monarchs in as many years and of being plunged into thirty years of civil

[1] A close parallel for this particular Olympus is provided by the celebrated fresco at Tanlay (reproduced in Gadoffre, op. cit., pp. 110–11). E. Bourciez, *Les Mœurs polies et la littérature de cour sous Henri II* (Paris, Hachette, 1886; Geneva, Slatkine, 1967), is still useful on questions of this kind. Ronsard continued to update his mythological identifications, and to add new ones, throughout his career (see, for example, L IX, 193 ff.; Pl II, 869 ff.: the context here is that of a court entertainment in which monarchs and courtiers play the role of gods). See also below, chapter 6, pp. 243–5.

[2] See, for example, L I, 17–23 (Pl II, 682–5); IX, 194 (II, 869); XV, 395–6 (not in Pl). Cf. F. Bardon, *Diane de Poitiers et le mythe de Diane*, pp. 42 ff.; E. Armstrong, *Ronsard and the Age of Gold*, pp. 7–9, etc.; and the articles by Saulnier and Yates in *Les Fêtes de la Renaissance*, volume I, pp. 31–58, 61–82.

[3] See L IX, 15–26, 103–16, 131–41 (Pl II, 436–41, 441–6, 862–6).

wars, Ronsard celebrates the new era of joy and glory which is now finally to be established. Yet in spite of the series of disasters which immediately followed the *opuscules* of 1558–9, Ronsard regained some of his confidence during the reign of Charles IX. A series of poems written in close conjunction with the court festivals of this period reflect the conciliatory policies which Catherine de Médicis built into the festivals themselves: the use of pastoral setting, of mythological and legendary motifs, transports the tensions of the present into an ideal landscape where they may be harmlessly worked out, while the imperial dream is resurrected for the marriage of Charles with Elizabeth of Austria.[1] Yet again the flimsy fabric of Ronsard's mythification dissolves, together with the fêtes themselves, in the face of harsher realities: the wars are incessantly renewed, and the celebrations of 1571 and 1572 are followed not by the harmonies of a golden age but by massacre. The posthumous *Caprice* reveals the extent of Ronsard's ultimate disillusionment, of his disgust with the decadence of Henri III's reign; even here, however, he looks beyond his own lifetime to the reign of Henri IV, which will bring peace, abundance and the Muses back to France (*L* XVIII, 322–4; *Pl* II, 678–9) . . .

If one assumes an equivalence between myth and legend in the sense that both transpose human experience into a universal realm ('synchronic' in myth, 'diachronic' in legend), it is legitimate to consider the *Franciade* project as the supreme example of Ronsard's ambition – and his failure – to achieve such a transposition.[2] The subject matter is already outlined in the 1550 *Ode de la paix*; while at two key points in the *Ode à Michel de l'Hospital* Ronsard refers to his embryonic epic in terms which suggest that it will surpass the *Ode* itself and finally realize the theories contained therein (*L* III, 148, 163; *Pl* I,

---

[1] See below, chapter 6, pp. 275–85. Insight into many aspects of these court festivals and the intentions underlying them is given by Frances Yates, *The Valois Tapestries* (London, Warburg Institute, 1959), an iconographical essay of unsurpassed brilliance.

[2] The introduction to *L* XVI provides a useful summary of how the project developed.

[205]

399, 405). This dream of a definitive *œuvre* runs like a leitmotive through his poetry; indeed it becomes at times a criterion in the light of which all his other poetic experiments appear as fragments, as temporary substitutes for the real thing.[1] It seems likely, given this evidence, that what he envisaged was not simply a legendary history of the origins of France but rather a universal poem, analogous to the Homeric epics as Dorat interpreted them (see above, p. 184, note 4). If this is so, then his failure to complete the *Franciade* is a failure not only of the epic ambition but also of the allegorical ambition. The periodicity of his inspiration, the resulting fragmentation of his poetic insights, the intrusion of adverse historical circumstance (in this instance, the death of Charles IX) – all these factors contributed to the deflation of his ideal; while the same creative problem is manifest at the aesthetic level in the Alexandrian discontinuities discussed in the first section of this chapter.[2]

The verse preface which introduces the book of *Poëmes* for the first time in the 1587 edition distinguishes between 'poësie', a unified collection of different 'arguments' like the epic of Homer, and the 'poëme', which is a fragment taken from the same structure (*L* XVIII, 283–4; *Pl* II, 662–3). Ronsard's defence of the 'poëme' in this short piece seems to point beyond the book of *Poëmes* itself to an awareness, at the end of his life, of the tendency towards fragmentary and discontinuous structures which is central to his poetry in the domains of both aesthetic creativity and signification. His poetry, like nature as he had defined it in the 1550 preface, is 'inconstante, et variable en ses perfections': it reaches its

[1] This mood is already present in the 1550 ode *A sa lire,* where Ronsard speaks of lyric poetry (symbolized by the lyre itself) as a genre which he has discarded in favour of 'un euvre plus divin' (*L* I, 164; these lines were suppressed in 1584).

[2] The *Sonets pour Helene* provide an ironic epilogue to the *Franciade* fiasco: for, having chosen the name of the Trojan princess as that of his final inamorata, he uses the epic motif to refer—often in a burlesque tone not far from bitterness—to his own advancing age and exhaustion (see above, chapter 2, pp. 108–9).

highest point of achievement in the suggestive yet elusive patterns created by a rich variety of surfaces and textures, rather than in a monolithic world-view. Whatever reasons one assigns to the failure of the *Franciade* project, it mirrors his inability to construct through myth a systematic image of the world and of man's place in it. He is too conscious of the presence of immediate reality and its limitations, too uncertain – ironically, one might think – of the origin and meaning of his own poetic vocation, to arrive at the comprehensive synthesis achieved by a Homer, a Dante or a Milton.

*
*   *
*

In the last analysis, then, the conception of poetry as a 'theologie allegoricque' proves impossible to realize, although there is little doubt that it acted as a catalyst for his poetic imagination, and that without it his work would have been much less rich in significance. Once the supernatural framework begins to fall away, poetry is left with no guarantee other than its own intrinsic power to create, to maintain the dialogue between reality and the imagination, and thus to compensate in some measure for the deficiencies and intractabilities of ordinary experience. In this sense, the role of myth is the role of poetry itself: it evokes a magical world which is unreal and which nevertheless seems to comprehend truths fundamental to reality.

In *La Promesse*, a poem full of doubts and ambiguities arising from Ronsard's dependence on patrons, the personification Promesse herself is made to say: 'La parolle, RONSARD, est la seule magie . . .' (*L* XIII, 10; *Pl* II, 100). In its context, this statement is not part of a conscious theory of the status of poetry, or of language, particularly as the personification does not necessarily speak with the voice of Ronsard himself. Yet, as the antithesis of the 'theological' view of poetry, it represents the ultimate position which any poet who questions the supernatural guarantee must adopt, and thus crystallizes a cardinal aspect of Ronsard's image of himself as poet. Nostalgic for a total world-view in which myth might consecrate and redeem history, and in which the poet would consequently be the mediator of a transcendent reality, Ronsard was at the same time susceptible to the erosion of time as demonstrated by the *faits divers* of history and biography. But the very tensions inherent in this divided sensibility helped him to develop and explore the mythological imagination as a medium partaking of both natural and supernatural experience, yet in the end independent of both. Precisely because he conceived of myth neither as wholly religious nor as wholly fictitious, he was able to multiply inexhaustibly the meanings inherent in the autonomous domain of aesthetic creation. The mythological cloak does not simply disguise, decorate or make manifest elements of some external conceptual system: it is itself a microcosm, with its own copious beauties and its own elusive modes of significance.

The idea of music in Ronsard's poetry

BRIAN JEFFERY

RONSARD'S attitude to music is essentially and poetically ambivalent. On the one hand in his poetry we find a certain awareness of music as contemporary sound, as an actual activity, connected with the rich musical life of France in the sixteenth century. Demonstrable on many levels, this awareness is evident on the simplest level in his quite frequent references to performers, composers, pieces and especially instruments of his day, and is developed on occasion by special imagery and by the special purposes of individual poems, as we shall see. But in addition, and more frequently and importantly, we find a more metaphorical attitude towards music, seen above all in his formulations of the classical musical myths of Apollo, Orpheus, Chiron and so on, and continually directed towards the idea of *music as a metaphor for writing poetry*. The two attitudes are never clearly defined separately, nor can they or should they be so defined: it is precisely as a fusion of the two that Ronsard uses the theme of music and that it becomes central to his poetic sensibility and to his idea of the nature of poetic composition.

A merely philosophical approach to the question, then, is insufficient, for Ronsard did take notice of the musical practice of his day. But a merely practical approach is even less sufficient, given the importance of musical myths and imagery in his poetic creation. In this chapter, I shall try to take the

Ronsard the poet

widest view possible, and by examining both the practical details and the broader ideas, shall inquire into the ways in which he has used the theme of music to enrich his poetry, and also relate him to the musical civilization of his day.

*

*　　*

*

Let us be quite clear about one thing: Ronsard was far *less* involved with the actual music-making of his time and *less* knowledgeable about its professional realities than were many of his predecessors. Clément Marot not only worked closely (it would appear) with the composer Claudin de Sermisy, but even edited his own chansons specially for publication in a large collection of chanson verse entitled *Les Chansons nouvellement assemblées*. Ronsard's rival Saint-Gelais owed part of his reputation to singing to the lute. Marguerite de Navarre wrote *contrafacta* (new poems to old tunes); while even that delightfully bad poet Eustorg de Beaulieu composed musical settings of his own verse, some of which still survive.[1] Ronsard did none of these things as far as we know. Statements that he was a practising musician, or even a skilled lutenist, can certainly not be disproved but have no basis in historical evidence.[2] His poems were indeed set to music by many musicians; yet, enormously important though this is in the history of sixteenth-century taste, the fact has little significance for the poetry of Ronsard himself. His references to musical practice show no special skill, no awareness of the special demands of the art; they are no more than the sympathetic

[1] On Beaulieu, see Nanie Bridgman, 'Eustorg de Beaulieu, musician', *Musical Quarterly*, 37 (1951), pp. 61–70.

[2] Apart from references in his poetry which, as we shall see, are largely metaphorical, the only authority is his biographer Binet, who wrote that he 'aimoit à chanter et à ouyr chanter ses vers'; but quite apart from the vagueness of these words, Binet's unreliability in such matters is well known. Nevertheless modern writers still sometimes make this assertion, for example: 'il continuera . . . de jouer de la guitare' (R. Lebègue), or 'a skilled lutenist' (N. C. Carpenter).

The idea of music in Ronsard's poetry

and intelligent comments of a courtier and poet. No shame to Ronsard, for his achievement lies elsewhere; but the fact must be made clear at the outset. We shall examine later his close involvement with certain court festivities in which music played an important part – an involvement in which he figured strictly as a poet, with no personal or professional musical function – and his specific mentions of music-making, above all in the courtly context.

The closest Ronsard ever came to a professional association with music was perhaps very early in his career, with the publication of the musical supplement to his *Amours* of 1552. In this volume after the text of the poems there follows a section of printed music, being musical settings of nine poems by Ronsard, all of them by his contemporaries and all of them for four voices.[1] The settings are the following:

J'espere et crains [sonnet]	P. Certon
Bien qu'à grand tort [sonnet]	P. Certon
Errant par les champs de la grace [*Ode à Michel de l'Hospital*]	C. Goudimel
Quand j'aperçoy [sonnet]	C. Goudimel
Qui renforcera ma voix [*Hymne triumphal*]	C. Goudimel
Las, je me plains [sonnet]	M. A. Muret
Qui vouldra voir [sonnet]	C. Janequin
Nature ornant la dame [sonnet]	C. Janequin
Petite Nymphe folastre [*Amourette*]	C. Janequin

Before, during and after the music, there appear certain comments and instructions for performance, because of which this musical supplement appears to the unwary to take on a certain

[1] The bibliographical data may be found in *L* IV, introduction and 187–250, where parts of the separate printings of the supplement are also reproduced in facsimile. The nine settings were well transcribed by J. Tiersot in his *Ronsard et la musique de son temps* (Leipzig, Breitkopf & Härtel; Paris, Fischbacher [1903]; itself now a rare book); and H. Expert also transcribed seven of them, less well than Tiersot, in his *La Fleur des musiciens de P. de Ronsard* (Paris, Cité des Livres, 1923; New York, Broude Brothers, 1965).

Ronsard the poet

specific importance for Ronsard. Briefly, the *Advertissement* at the beginning, signed by A.D.L.P. (Ambroise de la Porte, the printer's son), states that our poet 'a daigné prendre la peine de les [the poems] mesurer sur la lyre' and that the reader can if he wishes use the music to sing 'une bonne partie du contenu' of the book. And the instructions list fourteen other sonnets in the *Amours* which may be sung to the music of 'J'espere et crains', three to 'Quand j'aperçoy', ninety-two to 'Qui vouldra voir', and sixty to 'Nature ornant la dame'.[1] In other words, the settings of these four sonnets are being used as *timbres* (the technical term for old tunes or settings employed for the musical performance of new words – as, in England, the many new poems 'To the tune of Greensleeves'). And when we analyse the lists of sonnets to be sung to each setting, we find that the sonnets in each list share the same rhyme scheme and alternation of masculine and feminine endings in the successive lines. So it really could seem that here is a serious humanist endeavour to recreate the classical Greek and Roman performance of lyric poetry with music, with Ronsard taking care to regularize his verse to make it suitable for the purpose, and collaborating with the musicians of his day to make this possible.

Not a bit of it. Perhaps Ronsard tried. But a close examination of the supplement reveals that while we have here nine interesting settings of nine good poems – certainly a worthwhile thing in itself – the idea of a serious humanist endeavour does not hold water. It is suspicious, for example, that the *Advertissement* is signed by the printer and not by Ronsard. Then the alternation of masculine and feminine endings on which the whole grouping of sonnets depends, however significant it may be for the poetry, is quite simply not important when it comes to musical settings.[2] And most importantly the

[1] Slight variations in these figures, sometimes quoted, are due to certain errors in the original lists printed in 1552 and 1553.
[2] The doubtful reader should simply compare the cadences in 'Nature ornant la dame' with those in 'Qui vouldra voir', whose line endings are different, and he will find that there are no essential differences.

The idea of music in Ronsard's poetry

four sonnet settings mentioned above are not neutral enough to be *timbres*: they are quite obviously settings of *single* poems of Ronsard and nothing more. Attempts to sing the other poems listed to this same music sometimes lead to ludicrous results. For example, 'Ces flotz jumeaulx' (sonnet CLX), a poem in praise of Cassandre's breasts, is one of the poems listed to be sung to the music of 'Nature ornant la dame'. What happens if we attempt this? We find that at line 9 of 'Nature ornant la dame', Janequin has set the words 'Du ciel à peine elle estoit descendue' perfectly aptly to a descending phrase of music; but at line 9 of 'Ces flotz jumeaulx' we should find ourselves singing to this same descending phrase of music the words 'Là deux rubiz hault eslevez rougissent' – a rather contradictory procedure! As Tiersot wrote as long ago as 1903, 'Son projet de faire chanter soixante sonnets—que dis-je? quatre-vingt-treize! – sur la même musique savante rentrait en effet dans le domaine des chimères.' (*Ronsard et la musique de son temps,* p. 26.) Tiersot's remark is perhaps extreme, for as Gilbert Gadoffre has pointed out in this connection, the same melody has been known to serve widely disparate texts, notably in the works of J. S. Bach,[1] but at least it seems to me to be proved that whatever Ronsard or his printer may have intended, his *musicians* merely set *single* poems to music.

It may well be that this endeavour induced Ronsard to discipline his sonnets so that the cycle included no more than four different rhyme schemes (as opposed, say, to the sixty-one used by Du Bellay), and if so then music has indirectly exercised a very important effect on Ronsard's poetry and indeed on all subsequent French poetry. But it would be a paradoxical effect, for music does *not* necessarily require the versification of a poem to be more strict, as a glance at the chanson verse of the earlier century will show.

In the case of the two ode settings the humanist intention is evident, for the two poems set are ones which stress the divinity, the Apollonian frenzy, of the lyric poet's activity, to

---

[1] *Ronsard par lui-même* (Paris, Éditions du Seuil, 1960), p. 91.

which music is by theoretical definition an essential accompaniment. Both the poems are long and ambitious. For the *Ode à Michel de l'Hospital,* it would be necessary to sing some of Goudimel's music forty-eight times, and some of it twenty-four times, an almost unimaginable thing to do, no matter how much allowance we may make for differences of taste, or for variety in such things as instrumentation or ornamentation. As D. P. Walker has said, Ronsard's intention is obvious, but in attempting to make actual sixteenth-century music conform to his theoretical ideas about the role of that art, he made a disastrous mistake.[1]

In the musical supplement of 1552, then, perhaps there was some kind of humanist endeavour, maybe not directly by Ronsard himself but probably with his approval since he allowed the supplement to be published in the same volume with his poems; but if so, it was not a well-informed endeavour. Rather than a significant neoclassical achievement, this musical supplement is more modestly a collection of nine good settings of nine poems by Ronsard.

Such settings appeared in floods later in the century. The earliest known musical setting of a Ronsard poem is that by his friend M. A. Muret, the humanist, of 'Ma petite colombelle'; the 1552 supplement comes next; and then there follow so many others that our poet becomes probably the most frequently set of all French poets of the later sixteenth century.[2] After 1552 these settings always appeared in separate music books, frankly addressed to musicians. The most famous settings today are perhaps those by Antoine de Bertrand of poems from the *Amours,* some of which have been recorded;

[1] 'Le chant orphique de Marsile Ficin', in *Musique et poésie au XVIe siècle,* ed. J. Jacquot (Paris, Centre National de la Recherche Scientifique, 1954), p. 27. In the same volume, p. 88, Geneviève Thibault made a similar point.

[2] These settings have been listed in the fine work by G. Thibault and L. Perceau, *Bibliographie des poésies de P. de Ronsard mises en musique au XVIe siècle* (Paris, Droz, 1941). The setting by Muret mentioned below is printed as an appendix in that work; the original poem may be found at L I, 246–8; *Pl* I, 453–4.

and by Lassus and others. As I have said above, such settings are important in the history of music and of sixteenth-century taste, and their quality is sometimes high; but their significance for Ronsard's poetic creation remains low.

*

    *   *

*

Having cleared the ground to this extent, let us turn to see what Ronsard himself has to say about music in his theoretical writings. At the very outset of his career, in 1550, he mentions it in the preface to his *Odes,* saying that he has previously written odes but that (speaking of one of them) such an ode was 'imparfaite, pour n'estre mesurée, ne propre à la lire'. His odes now, he says, are regular, so that they can be set to music. This appears to be the same chimerical idea of regularity which he or his printer tried to put into practice two years later in the musical supplement. He mentions the mythical origins of the lyre, and the position and importance of lyric poets, and he writes, '[je] ferai encores revenir (si je puis) l'usage de la lire aujourdui resuscitée en Italie laquelle lire seule doit et peut animer les vers, et leur donner le juste poix [i.e., *poids*] de leur gravité.' (*L* I, 48; *Pl* II, 974.)

These same ideas about the desirability of musical performance of poetry, about the metrical regularity which he claims is necessary, and about the union of music and poetry in classical antiquity, recur throughout his work. In the *Abbregé de l'art poëtique françois* of 1565, he writes:

> tu feras tes vers masculins et fœminins tant qu'il te sera possible, pour estre plus propres à la Musique et accord des instrumens, en faveur desquelz il semble que la Poësie soit née: car la Poësie sans les instrumens, ou sans la grace d'une seule ou plusieurs voix, n'est nullement aggreable, non plus que les instrumens sans estre animez de la melodie d'une plaisante voix. Si de fortune tu as composé les deux premiers

vers masculins, tu feras les deux autres fœminins, et para-
cheveras de mesme mesure le reste de ton Elegie ou chanson,
afin que les Musiciens les puissent plus facilement accorder.

(*L* XIV, 9; *Pl* II, 999.)

Later in the same treatise, he adds that short lines are more
suitable for music than long ones; and that is all there is about
music in the treatise.

Longer is a preface which he wrote to a collection of musical
settings of poems (only five of them, incidentally, being his
own): the *Livre de meslanges, contenant six vingtz chansons* . . .
(Paris, Le Roy and Ballard, 1560). This preface's classical
sources are amply commented on in Laumonier's edition and
in an article by N. C. Carpenter.[1] It begins with generalities
about music derived from Plato, Boethius and other classical
authors (the harmony of the spheres, the influence of music
over the passions, and so on). It continues with a strange
passage attempting to justify the age of the chansons in the
collection (some of them were over fifty years old) as being
nearer to the age of gold than present-day chansons – a doubtless
circumstantial passage, considering how firmly Ronsard in
fact rejected the art of his predecessors. Then, finally and surprisingly, Ronsard gives a precise and accurate list of the finest
and most famous composers from Josquin des Prez (died
c. 1521) to the present day. About the relationship between
music and poetry in Ronsard's day: nothing. The whole
passage is theoretical. Now in Ronsard's day it was conventional in a prose discourse to use classical ideas rather than
modern ones, to build your treatise upon citations. Any
reader of the early Montaigne knows that. Ronsard obeys the
demands of the form, just as he did in the three *discours* printed
immediately before this preface in Laumonier's edition, *Des
vertus intellectuelles et morales, De l'envie,* and *De la joie et de la*

---

[1] The only known copy was inaccessible to Laumonier during the First
World War, and was apparently destroyed during the Second. See *L*
XVIII, 480 ff. (*Pl* II, 979 ff.), where the preface is printed from a later
edition (1572) of the same work. Carpenter's article is 'Ronsard's *Préface
sur la musique*', *Modern Language Notes,* 75 (1960), pp. 131 ff.

The idea of music in Ronsard's poetry

tristesse. So it is no wonder that we find no practical or modern ideas here, only derivative ones: undoubtedly, for Ronsard the medium of the prose *discours* was the message.

Ronsard's enthusiasm for uniting music and poetry, then, is certain. For someone closely associated with the foundation of the Académie de Poésie et de Musique, this is not surprising. But this often quoted enthusiasm is purely theoretical. He himself played a decisive part in finalizing the professional separation of the two arts: a fruitful separation perhaps, leading to some fine musical settings of his verse, but still a separation. As a definition of Ronsard's attitude and position in time, I cannot do better than quote the words of Jean Chantavoine, written in 1924 but despite all recent research still as perceptive and true as they were then:

> Ronsard vient au lendemain du jour où la poésie et la musique en France, intimement unies chez les troubadours, se sont émancipées pour de bon l'une de l'autre. A l'instant de ce congé réciproque et chacune croyant n'aller que vers l'avenir, c'est le passé qui les ramène un moment l'une à l'autre. Passé moins lointain, moins mort que ne le dit Ronsard, quand il se prétend disciple et rénovateur de Pindare, il n'est que le petit-fils et l'héritier d'Adam de La Hale ou de Guillaume de Machault sans être comme eux musicien autant que poète. Son appel à la musique est, au fond, un adieu.[1]

It may be taken as established, then, that Ronsard (unlike many of his predecessors) had little or no professional dealing with music, and that his theoretical writing about the subject is impractical indeed. Lyric poetry and music in theory remained closely linked, yet in practice became more and more the separate provinces of increasingly specialized professionals.

[1] *Revue musicale* (1 May 1924), p. 85.

Ronsard the poet

Ironically, a flourishing union had existed not long before in the French chanson of the fifteenth and early sixteenth centuries, a genre in which poetry and music were inextricably linked, yet which Ronsard rejected as part of the 'vulgaire poesie' which in the preface to the *Odes* of 1550 he was so eager to leave behind him.

Wherein, then, lies the importance of music in Ronsard? Above all: in his continual use of musical ideas, more than any other kind of idea, to construct a highly extended *metaphor for the writing of poetry*. This metaphor runs centrally through his work, from his earliest beginnings to the end of his life. It is expressed in certain direct and recurring ways, and once Ronsard has established these ways he embroiders on them and elaborates them more and more as the years go by. The procedure is essentially a technique of variation like that which I described in my study of French Renaissance comedy.[1]

One of the simplest ways in which Ronsard expresses this metaphor, and by far the most frequent, is by the image of musical instruments. Now this metaphorical use of instruments is not a self-evident procedure. Other poets might talk about poetry as simply poetry – whether spoken, written, read, or published. To speak of one's lute, or one's trumpet, or one's flageolet, as different aspects of one's muse, is perfectly understandable and a most fruitful poetic idea, but it is not self-evident. It is not, of course, original, for Ronsard took it from classical sources and his contemporaries such as La Péruse and Belleau shared it; but it is true to say that he seems to have preferred and developed it. He makes no direct references to *singing* his own poetry, for instance (the famous reference to his 'mauvaise voix' is in an ecclesiastical context);[2] none to *speaking* it; only some few to *writing* it with a pen; but an almost infinite number to *playing* his poetry on an instrument.

Nor are instruments the obvious aspect of music for him to choose. He could have stressed sacred or secular composi-

[1] See the third part of my *French Renaissance Comedy* (London, Clarendon Press, 1969).
[2] *Responce . . . aux Injures*, lines 589–90 (*L* XI, 147; *Pl* II, 608).

The idea of music in Ronsard's poetry

tions or techniques of composition of all sorts, music's use in ceremonies or pageants, its supposed power over the passions, classical musical myths – yet though he does mention all of these things, instruments take pride of place for him. They represent in some way the life of his own poetry, and lead readily into and across the ambiguous borderland between the real and the metaphorical.

Certain writers insist on taking the image literally and even warn against interpreting it in a figurative way, for example D. B. Wyndham Lewis in his *Ronsard* (London, Sheed and Ward, 1944), p. 6: 'When, like Horace, Ronsard addresses his lute, he means no metaphor but the actual stringed instrument which stood at every elbow.' But, as I have said, the musical metaphor in Ronsard is ambivalent and fruitful, meaning at once its *signifiant* and its *signifié*; an exclusively literal interpretation is simply not possible.

Three instruments or families of instruments appear throughout Ronsard's works, from the beginning to the end. The merest mention of any of them implies and describes a certain kind of poetry. The lute, or lyre, or sometimes the guitar, stand for lyric poetry in general, but especially for poetry on a medium or small scale and for love poetry. Here is the beginning of the *Hymne de France* (1549):

> Sus, luc doré, des Muses le partaige,
> Et d'Apollon le commun heritaige,
> De qui la voix, d'accord melodieux,
> Chante le loz des hommes et des dieux.
>
> (*L* I, 24; *Pl* II, 685)

The *luc* (or *luth*, or *lut*) translates here the Greek and Latin λύρα, lira, κἴθάρα, cithara. Whether or not in Pindar or in Horace an actual instrument was involved need not detain us here; certainly it would be naïve to think that Ronsard literally and imperatively meant that a lute should accompany his poem, any more than Wyatt did when he wrote 'My lute, awake!' It is true that the lute was the accompanying instrument *par excellence* in Ronsard's day; and this is the reason

why he chose the term to translate Pindar or Horace, not a
reason to take the image exclusively literally.

In these same four lines of the *Hymne de France* appear other
ideas which will be developed in later years: thus, the lyre's
invention by Mercury and its adoption by the Muses are described in his *Ode à Michel de l'Hospital* a year or two later. The
final line above, 'Chante le loz des hommes et des dieux',
describes the poet's function as a bestower of immortality. Let
us trace some developments of such ideas about lyric poetry,
expressed in terms of this musical instrument. Here is the final
epode of the *Ode au seigneur de Carnavalet* of 1550:

> Mais la mienne [*ma lirique*, see below] emmiellée
> Qui sçait les lois de mon doi,
> Aveq' les flutes meslée
> Chassera l'oubli de toi.
> Les neuf divines Pucelles
> Gardent la gloire chez elles,
> Et mon luc qu'els ont fait estre
> De leurs secrés le grand prestre,
> Bruiant un chant solennel,
> Epandra de sus ta face
> Le dous sucre de sa grace,
> Dont le gout semble eternel.
>
> (*L* I, 98; *Pl* I, 382)

In this passage, his 'lirique' is already ambivalently his *lyre* or
his *lyric poetry*; he speaks of it as an *instrument*, while at the same
time promising immortality to his patron through *verse*.
Ronsard calls his lute the divine gift of the nine Muses, the
same idea as in the *Ode à Michel de l'Hospital*. The gift defines
the poet's function as a bestower of immortality. The instrument of Apollo, indeed, is the central element in many of
Ronsard's descriptions of poetry. There is a fine late formula-
tion of the poetic frenzy in the *Panegyrique de la Renommée* of
1579, in which Ronsard says, 'J'entens dessus Parnasse
Apollon qui m'appelle,/J'oy sa lyre et son arc sonner à son

The idea of music in Ronsard's poetry

costé . . .' (*L* XVIII, 1; *Pl* I, 787) (see below, chapter 7, pp. 311–12).

Ronsard sometimes develops the metaphor further by citing apparently technical details of instrumental musicmaking which all refer to various aspects of writing poetry. In the passage from the *Ode au seigneur de Carnavalet* just cited (line 2), Ronsard speaks, technically correctly, of using his 'doi' (his finger) to play the instrument. In the ninth line he speaks of the lute's 'chant', its voice; instead of being supposedly simply an accompaniment, the lute now stands for, in a certain sense *is*, Ronsard's poetry. In Ronsard there is no clear distinction between performing a poem *on an instrument* and performing it *with instrumental accompaniment,* because neither idea is literal. Both are images about the composition of poetry.

Opposed to the lute very frequently in Ronsard, but not developed metaphorically to the same extent, is the trumpet. This instrument signifies war poetry, the lute signifying either poetry in general or specifically love poetry. Here is a typical opposition; Ronsard, in the *Elegie à Chretophle de Choiseul* of 1556, is recalling his younger days:

> Du regne de HENRY, cinq ou six seulement
> Vindrent, qui d'un acord moderé doucement,
> Et d'un pouce atrempé firent doctement bruire
> Maintenant la guitterre, et maintenant la lyre,
> Et maintenant le luc, et oserent tenter
> Quelque peu la trompette affin de haut chanter.
>
> (*L* VIII, 352; *Pl* II, 430, modified)

The third family of instruments are specifically pastoral ones. The mere writing of an eclogue or of any bucolic poem means, for Ronsard, bringing in the *chalumeau* or *chalemie* (a kind of flute), the *musette* or *cornemuse* (bagpipes), or the *flageol* (another kind of flute), as well as nymphs and satyrs and dryads dancing by moonlight, trees, fields and streams, the shepherds' flocks, and the whole pastoral arsenal. In these poems, to play any one of the above instruments (or one or two others) is to write pastoral poetry, just as to play the lute is (as we saw) to write lyric poetry. Take the *Eclogue Du Thier* of 1559, in which Ronsard, Du Bellay and Belleau appear, thinly disguised as Perrot (for Pierre), Bellot and Bellin. At the very beginning, Perrot and Bellot are called players of 'chalumeaux' (flutes); then we hear of Perrot's 'musette' and 'flageol', and then of Bellin's 'musette'. Here is the beginning:

Les pasteurs. Bellot, Perrot, Bellin

De fortune Bellot et Perrot, desous l'ombre
D'un vieil chesne touffu, avoient serré par nombre
L'un à part ses brebis, et l'autre ses chevreaux,
Et tous deux sur la levre avoient leurs chalumeaux.
L'un et l'autre tenoit son échine appuyée
Sur l'escorce d'un chesne, et la jambe plyée
En croix sur la houlette, et leur mastin estoit
Couché pres de leurs pieds, qui les loups aguettoit:
Ce pendant que Bellot chantoit sa DIANETTE,
Et que Perrot faisoit aprendre à sa musette
Le sainct nom de CHARLOT, et d'ANNOT, que les bois
Les fleuves et les monts ont ouy tant de fois
Redire à son flageol, que mieux ils le cognoissent,
Que ne font les troupeaux le thin, dont ils se paissent:
Voicy venir Bellin, lequel avoit erré
Tout un jour à chercher son bellier adiré,
Qu'à peine il remenoit, ayant lié sa corne
A un lasset coullant d'un tortis de viorne.
　　Or ce Bellin estoit de chanter bon ouvrier,
D'habits et de façons il sembloit un chevriet:
Il avoit en la main une houlette dure,
Sa musette pendoit du long de sa ceinture . . .

　　　　　　　　　　(*L* X, 50–1; *Pl* I, 973–4)

Now Bellin has lost his voice, and the 'anche' of his 'bourdon' (a part of his bagpipe) has been stolen; Bellot yesterday had his 'chalemye' and his 'pipeau d'aveyne' stolen; and as for Perrot, he has lost his 'loure' (again a kind of bagpipe); and all of this is a metaphor for the theft of their poetic ideas by

[222]

The idea of music in Ronsard's poetry

other poets. These examples are only a few among very many metaphorical uses of musical instruments in this poem – and, of course, among very many other pastoral 'props' which Ronsard brings in. One may say that the musical 'props' are particularly important because they stand for poetic composition, that central idea for Ronsard. Later in his career he makes exquisite use of them as part of the whole pastoral backdrop:

> Pasteur, qui conduiras en ce lieu ton troupeau,
> Flageolant une Eclogue en ton tuyau d'aveine,
> Attache tous les ans à cest arbre un Tableau,
>   Qui tesmoigne aux passans mes amours et ma peine:
> Puis l'arrosant de laict et du sang d'un agneau,
> Dy, Ce Pin est sacré, c'est la plante d'Heleine.
>
> (*L* XVII, 253; *Pl* I, 246)

Ronsard's poetic achievement, though, is far too rich for the metaphor of instruments, or for any such metaphor, to be merely automatic. Certainly, the essential procedure is that of variations upon a norm, but Ronsard goes beyond this. His father, represented as denigrating Homer's achievement, speaks scornfully of his 'Troyenne viëlle' – the 'viëlle' in the mid-sixteenth century being an outdated medieval instrument (*Elegie à Pierre L'Escot,* 1560, line 41: *L* X, 302; *Pl* II, 423). Or take the development of the pastoral idea for comic purposes in the description of Polyphemus in *Le Cyclope amoureux* of 1560 (a poem borrowed from Ovid, true, but still individual). Since Polyphemus is a shepherd, naturally he must have shepherd's musical instruments; and so he has, but their size is far from normal:

> Il tenoit en son poing, au lieu d'une houlette,
> Un sapin tout entier, il avoit sa musette
> Bruyante à cent tuyaulx, et du hault du collet
> Jusqu'au bas des genoulx pendoit son flageollet,
> Comme un baston de buis, duquel il menoit paistre
> Sur le bord de la Mer son gras troupeau champestre.
>
> (*L* X, 279; *Pl* I, 991)

Ronsard the poet

It must be said that Ronsard's development of this metaphor of musical instruments for the writing of poetry, when taken too literally, does lead to some curious and sometimes perhaps unintentionally comic results. Here, for example, is a shepherd singing to his own bagpipe accompaniment, a musical solecism unwarranted even by the deliberately grotesque tone:[1]

> A cent couleurs il tire une musette,
> La met en bouche, et les levres enfla,
> Puis coup sur coup en haletant soufla
> Et resoufla d'une forte halenée
> Par les poulmons reprise et redonnée,
> Ouvrant les yeux et dressant le sourci:
> Mais quand par tout le ventre fut grossi
> De la chevrete, et qu'elle fut esgalle
> A la rondeur d'une moyenne balle,
> A coups de coude il en chassa la voix,
> Puis çà puis là faisant saillir ses dois
> Sur les pertuis de la musette pleine,
> Comme s'il fust en angoisseuse peine,
> Piteusement avec le triste son
> De sa musette, il dict telle chanson . . .
>
> *(Chant pastoral à madame Marguerite*, 1559:
> L IX, 176–7; *Pl* I, 967, modified)

Sometimes Ronsard carelessly talks of playing the lute with a bow.[2] And later in his career, the metaphor is so established for him that he can describe himself as 'singing' with his 'pen' (L XVII, 203; *Pl* I, 219). Or he can substitute *guiterre* for *luth* or for *lire,* for merely metrical reasons, even when ostensibly addressing the god (Mercury) who in legend invented the lyre (L II, 80–2; *Pl* II, 717–18). Nor is even the music/poetry metaphor totally consistent, for in 1569 he opposed one to the other: 'Mais ne pouvant chanter,/D'escrire en vers il me

[1] For further comments on the bagpipe (and the lyre) in Ronsard's poetry, see above, chapter 1, p. 55.
[2] L VI, 134; *Pl* I, 558. Cf. L VI, 130 (from a poem by Olivier de Magny).

The idea of music in Ronsard's poetry

faut contenter' (*Le Soucy du jardin*, lines 93–4: *L* XV, 177; *Pl* II, 367).

But such petty details are unimportant. The metaphor is a serious one, and must be accepted as valid. Take these fine closing lines of the four books of *Odes* of 1550, wherein Ronsard acknowledges his fruitful imitation of Pindar and Horace while yet remaining French, combining the rich fertility image with the living sound of instruments:

> Je volerai tout vif par l'univers,
> Eternizant les champs où je demeure
> De mon renom engressés et couvers:
> Pour avoir joint les deus harpeurs divers
> Au dous babil de ma lire d'ivoire,
> Se connoissans Vandomois par mes vers . . .
>
> (*L* II, 152–3; *Pl* I, 650, modified)

*
*   *
*

Musical instruments, then, are the most frequent and most obvious aspect of music in Ronsard's poetry. We shall return briefly to them when discussing our poet's role in court entertainments. But also of great significance in his poetic achievement is his treatment of various classical myths about music.

Very simply and very importantly, if Ronsard is considering music as poetry, or poetry as music, then immediately the whole range of classical mythology dealing with music becomes available to him to apply to poetry and to his own endeavours. His store of imagery immediately becomes richer. He can take over to poetry the legends about Orpheus moving trees and plants, about the power of music over the passions, and so on. Ronsard is not slow to follow the example of his classical predecessors in doing just this. And his treatment of these musical myths, by their relevance to poetic creation, is central to the whole important function of mythology in his

[225]

poetry (see also above, chapter 3, pp. 139–41, on music and myths of music in the context of neoplatonism).

I have mentioned the invention of the lyre (or lute). In the *Ode à Michel de l'Hospital* (1552) Jupiter speaks to his daughters, the nine Muses, about poetry and its sacred mission; and his final act before sending them off on this mission to earth is to give them 'Le Luth qu'avoit façonné/L'ailé Courier Atlantide' (lines 506–7: *L* III, 117; *Pl* I, 398), that is, the instrument invented by Mercury. When they sing with an instrument (sometimes called a lute, sometimes a lyre and sometimes a harp), they sing about lighter subjects on the 'chanterelle' (the highest and thinnest string), and about graver subjects such as the Gigantomachia 'sus la plus grosse corde' (the deepest and thickest string) – metaphors respectively for the subjects and for the tone of their poetry.

Perhaps the best-known classical myth about music is that of Orpheus. In Ronsard it appears quite often, sometimes with some unusual features, but only once in a fullscale treatment of the myth.[1] Frequently Ronsard associates Orpheus with the Argonauts' expedition, an association derived from Apollonius of Rhodes. It comes, for example, in the *Hymne de Calaïs et de Zetes* of 1556, in which in a most beautiful passage Orpheus encourages the rowers with his music, and even the timbers of the ship *Argo* listen to him as did the living trees, according to legend:

> Là, descendit apres le chevelu Orphée,
> Qui tenoit dans ses mains une harpe estophée
> De deux coudes d'ivoire, où par rang se tenoient
> Des cordes, qui d'en haut inegalles venoyent
> A bas l'une apres l'autre, en biaiz chevillées:
> Ne plus ne moins qu'on voit les ailes esbranlées
> Des faulcons en volant, qui despuis les cerceaux
> En se suivant depres vont à rangs inegaux.

[1] A penetrating study of Ronsard's use of the Orpheus legend and of the related ideas of poetic composition may be found in Eva Kushner's 'Le personnage d'Orphée chez Ronsard', *Lumières de la Pléiade* (Paris, Vrin, 1966), pp. 271–302.

The idea of music in Ronsard's poetry

Ce noble Chantre avoit par sur touts privileges
Ne tirer l'aviron. Seulement de son siege
Tout au haut de la proue avecque ses chansons
Donnoit courage aux Preux, les nommant par leurs noms,
Maintenant de ses vers rappellant en memoire
De leurs nobles ayeus les gestes et la gloire,
Maintenant se tournant vers Argon la hastoit
D'un chant persuasif que le boys escoutoit.

(*L* VIII, 258–9; *Pl* II, 126–7)

Orpheus again travels with the Argonauts in the long poem
L'Orphée of 1563 (*L* XII, 126–42; *Pl* II, 64–72). Only the
loosest overall structure fashions this poem, in which the
Argonauts' adventure forms the framework for two stories
sung respectively by Chiron (Achilles' centaur tutor and himself a musician) and by Orpheus. Orpheus' story is his own
well-known adventure of his descent into the Underworld to
free Eurydice, and her disappearance when he inadvertently
turns to look at her. Ronsard follows closely his classical
sources, and gives no special or original metaphorical significance to Orpheus' looking back; but in the closing lines
spoken by Orpheus one may see, I think, Ronsard's own
attitude to poetry:

De jour en jour suyvant s'amenuisoit ma vie,
Je n'avois de Bacus ny de Ceres envie,
Couché plat sur la roche, et de moy ne restoit
Qu'une voix qui ma femme en mourant regretoit,
Quand, oyant d'Helicon ma pleinte si amere,
Aveques ses huit sœurs, voicy venir ma mere,
Qui me leva de terre et repoussa la mort,
Qui desja de mon cœur avoit gaigné le fort.
    Mon fils, ce me disoit, l'amour qui est entrée
Dans ton cœur s'en fuyra en changeant de contrée:
En traversant la terre, et en passant la mer,
Tu perdras le soucy qui vient de trop aymer.

[227]

Ronsard the poet

Pour ce, si le desir de loüenge t'anime,
Reveille la vertu de ton cœur magnanime,
Et suy les nobles Preux, qui loing de leur maison
S'en vont de sur la mer compagnons de Jason.
    Ainsi pour me garir me disoit Calliope,
Ainsi, fuyant amour, je vins en cette trope,
Non tant pour voir la mer, ses vens et ses poissons,
Que pour te voir, Chiron, et oyr tes chansons.
    A tant se teut Orphée, et les bestes sauvages
Erroient devant la porte: oyseaux de tous plumages
Volletoient de sur luy, et les pins, qui baissoient
Les testes pour l'oyr, devant l'Antre dansoient,
Tant leur plaisoit le son d'une si douce Lyre,
Que depuis dans le Ciel les Dieux ont fait reluire.

Orpheus, the most famous of mythological musicians, has lost
his love Eurydice; yet he still sings, serves the Muses, travels,
aims at fame, is the companion of the great, listens to other
musicians (poets), makes nature listen to him—and eventually
will gain divine immortality. Poetry (or music) in this poem
has a number of functions: it is a purpose, a pleasure to the
listener, an encouragement to valiant enterprises, a comfort to
the singer himself (lines 221-2, 'Sans cesse je pleurois, soula-
geant sur ma Lyre,/Bien que ce fust en vain, mon amoureux
martyre'). Ronsard, who compared himself to Orpheus on
more than one occasion, in recreating this classical myth in
French, is using it for his own ideas of what poetry is, or should
be: ideas which he developed all his life.

Ronsard's treatment of the Orpheus myth, then, is significant
and expressive in its details. Other musical myths recur in his
poetry, the harmony of the spheres for example: addressing
'Le Ciel' as it guides the heavenly bodies, he writes:

Ainsi guidant premier si grande compagnie
Tu fais une si douce et plaisante harmonie,
Que noz lucz ne sont rien aux prix des moindres sons
Qui resonnent là haut de diverses façons . . .

(L VIII, 143–4; Pl II, 191)

The idea of music in Ronsard's poetry

Sometimes the movement of the universe is described as a great *bal*, an idea used most beautifully in the poem *La Charite,* as we shall see below. The dance of wood nymphs and dryads, too, recurs many times, as in the *Ode à la fonteine Bélerie* (1553):

> Toujours les belles Naiades
> Oreades, et Dryades
> S'entreserrant par les mains,
> Jointes avec les Sylvains
> Puissent rouër leurs caroles
> Autour de tes rives moles:
> Pan retrepignant menu
> De son argot mi-cornu,
> Guidant le premier la dance,
> Au dous son de la cadance.
>
> (*L* V, 240; *Pl* I, 624)

Such references are frequent and significant, but Ronsard devotes no major poem to any one of them. Sometimes he produces some unusual variations on the myths, as when he has the *Muses* (instead of the evils of the world) escaping from Pandora's box. Sometimes he will use a classical idea on music to develop some special theme: thus, when it suits his purpose to develop a stern morality in the *Discours à maistre Julien Chauveau,* he uses these ideas from Plato:

> Contemple moy de ton temps les Musiques:
> Quand elles sont et fortes et rustiques,
> D'un masle son, croy que telle Cité
> Doit longtemps vivre en sa felicité:
> Et la Cité sera bientost ruinée
> Où la Musique est toute effœminée:
> "Toujours la voix ensuit les passions,
> Les passions font les mutations."
>
> (*L* XV, 159; *Pl* II, 378–9)

(Music here, incidentally, far from influencing the passions, a classical idea more common in Ronsard, is seen as a symptom of them.)

Ronsard the poet

But of all the poems about music or even mentioning music in Ronsard's works, one of the finest—need we be surprised? – is devoted to a musical instrument, *La Lyre* of 1569. This long poem or *Elegie* has been analysed in chapter 4, pp. 190–2, so I shall not repeat the analysis. Suffice it to say that in this description of a finely carved instrument, Ronsard is describing many aspects of French poetry and particularly his own. At the beginning of his career he had written the odes *A son luc* (L II, 155–62; *Pl* II, 725–8) and *A sa lire* (L I, 162–6; *Pl* I, 427–9), using the comparatively simple technique of an instrument standing for his poetry, while in the ode *A sa guiterre* (L I, 229–34; *Pl* II, 699–701) he described a painted instrument, the paintings on it representing apparently random mythological scenes (see chapter 4, pp. 161, 164). In *La Lyre,* twenty years later, the carved images themselves represent aspects of literary creation: images within images, poetry within poetry within poetry.

*
*   *
*

As is well known, much of Ronsard's poetry is occasional verse, created as a direct result of his employment as a court poet. Some of this occasional verse has musical connections of one sort or another. Such are, for example, certain poems which actually were sung at certain court functions. In 1569 Ronsard wrote a *Chant triomphal pour jouer sur la lyre* celebrating the victory over the Hugenots at Jarnac. It was set to music by Nicolas de la Grotte (and the fact that de la Grotte's setting is for four voices, in apparent contradiction of the poem's title, supports my contention that 'jouer sur la lyre' has nothing necessarily to do with real instruments).[1] Another such poem

---

[1] The poem is printed in *L* XV, 61 ff. (*Pl* II, 193 ff.), with notes explaining the subsequent adaptation to cover the battle of Moncontour. De la Grotte's setting has been published by H. Expert in his *La fleur . . .*, pp. 56–7. Performance with instruments is of course possible, but that is the musicians' decision and has nothing to do with Ronsard.

The idea of music in Ronsard's poetry

is called *Stances prontement faites pour jouer sur la lyre, un joueur repondant à l'autre*, written for a baptism and again set to music by Nicolas de la Grotte.[1]

Such poems take their place along with other occasional verse by Ronsard, such as *mascarade* poetry, *cartels* (stylized 'defiance' verse for use at tournaments) and so on. Thus in 1567 he wrote one of the pieces of verse which were performed at court between the acts of Baïf's comedy *Le Brave* (exactly how these verses were performed, or *recitez*, is not known).[2] Earlier, he had been employed in the festivities at Fontaine-bleau in 1564, in which some of the poetry was certainly sung. Much work remains to be done on French Renaissance poetry of this kind before a proper evaluation of the roles of poetry and music can be made; but it is certain that in writing such verse Ronsard was playing an important part in a new and rich fusion of the arts which was to lead from the medieval and Renaissance entry, through court ballets and masques, to the development of opera in the seventeenth century.[3]

Sometimes Ronsard wrote about specific musicians and compositions. In the *Amours de Cassandre* (1552) there is a very unusual and delightful sonnet in which he creates a medieval atmosphere by using medieval terms of music and dancing, and he even refers to the old chanson 'Allegez moy madame' still popular at that time but going back at least fifty years to a setting by Josquin des Prez:

[1] L XV, 136 ff. (*Pl* II, 903 ff.); for the setting, see Thibault and Perceau, *Bibliographie* . . . For other such poems, see L XIII, 222 ff. (*Pl* I, 1005 ff.) and XV, 346 ff. (I, 1014 ff.).

[2] L XIV, 201–2 (*Pl* II, 931); and see my *French Renaissance Comedy*, pp. 18–19.

[3] Much remains to be done on court festivities at this time. But see H. Prunières, 'Ronsard et les fêtes de cour', *Revue musicale*, 1924, pp. 27–44; the introduction and notes to L XIII; Frances Yates, *The French Academies of the Sixteenth Century* (London, Warburg Institute, 1947); *Les Fêtes de la Renaissance,* ed. J. Jacquot (Paris, Centre National de la Recherche Scientifique, 1956); and Margaret McGowan, *L'Art du ballet de cour en France (1581–1643)* (Paris, Centre National de la Recherche Scientifique, 1963).

Ronsard the poet

Hà, Belacueil, que ta doulce parolle
    Vint traistrement ma jeunesse offenser
    Quand au premier tu l'amenas dancer,
    Dans le verger, l'amoureuse carolle.
Amour adonq me mit à son escolle.
    Ayant pour maistre un peu sage penser,
    Qui des le jour me mena commencer
    Le chapelet de la danse plus folle.
Depuis cinq ans dedans ce beau verger,
    Je voys balant avecque faulx danger,
    Soubz la chanson d'Allegez moy Madame:
Le tabourin se nommoit fol plaisir,
    La fluste erreur, le rebec vain desir,
    Et les cinq pas la perte de mon ame.
(L IV, 132; Pl I, 73–4, tercets substantially rewritten)[1]

He establishes the medieval atmosphere at the beginning of the
sonnet with the allegorical figure Belacueil from the *Roman
de la rose* and with the old word 'carolle' for 'dance'. The instruments, too, are medieval: flute and drum (that is to say, pipe
and tabor) and the old-fashioned rebec. The 'cinq pas' are not
only dance steps, but the medieval five points of love. That the
young Ronsard, while rejecting his predecessors, could still
have written this deliberately old-fashioned poem, in which old
musical terms are used so precisely and significantly, can only
be seen as a deliberately virtuoso achievement. He has transformed the old elements through his poetic imagination.[2]

In 1554 he published an epitaph for the royal lutenist Albert
de Rippe, but this is a poor poem, overfull of the classical
musical clichés. Better than this is a charming description of

---

[1] On Josquin's setting, see my article, 'The literary texts of Josquin's
chansons', *Proceedings of the International Josquin Festival-Conference* (to be
published by Oxford University Press).
[2] It is true that he does on two occasions actually use the old technique
of *timbres*, but I have been unable to trace either of the tunes concerned.
They are 'Saint-Augustin' (L X, 116 ff.; Pl I, 166 ff.) and 'Te rogamus
audi nos' (L XVIII, 275 ff.; Pl II, 658 ff.).

The idea of music in Ronsard's poetry

the musician Alfonso Ferrabosco and his two brothers, singing to their lutes:

> Mon Dieu que de douceur, que d'aise et de plaisir
> L'âme reçoit alors qu'elle se sent saisir
> Et du geste, et du son, et de la voix ensemble
> Que ton Ferabosco sur trois lyres assemble,
> Quand les trois Apollons chantant divinement,
> Et mariant la lyre à la voix doucement,
> Tout d'un coup de la voix et de la main agille
> Refont mourir Didon par les vers de Vergille,
> Mourant presques eusmesme, ou de fredons plus haux
> De Guines et Calais retonnent les assaux,
> Victoires de ton frere: adonques il n'est ame
> Qui ne laisse le corps, et toute ne se pasme
> De leur douce chanson, comme là haut aux cieux
> Soubs le chant d'Apollon se pasment tous les Dieux,
> Quand il touche la lyre, et chante le Trofée
> Qu'eleva Jupiter des armes de Typhée.
>
> (L IX, 53–4; Pl II, 184)

They are singing of the death of Dido (perhaps the text 'Dulces exuviae' from the *Aeneid*, book IV, which was indeed often set to music at this time) and of more recent political events. Classical elements come yet again in a sonnet addressed to the royal lutenist Vaumeny, and in a number of other such occasional poems.

More interesting than these last are others in which Ronsard assimilates more closely into his verse the very extensive music-making at the court and in the French society of his day. When he writes of his first sight of Cassandre Salviati at Blois in 1545—she a young and aristocratic lady, he an aspiring poet, the two of them in a traditional and essentially social relationship to each other—he shows her engaging in a social pastime: she is playing on a lute (or speaking, or singing; Ronsard, perhaps not surprisingly, is ambiguous on this point) a *branle de Bourgogne*.

[233]

Ronsard the poet

Ne plus, ne moins, que Juppiter est aise,
   Quand de son luth quelque Muse l'apaise,
   Ainsi je suis de ses chansons épris,
Lors qu'à son luth ses doits elle embesongne,
   Et qu'elle dit le branle de Bourgongne,
   Qu'elle disoit, le jour que je fus pris.

                     (*L* V, 138–9; *Pl* I, 49)

The *branle de Bourgogne* was a courtly formation dance. Here is what Thoinot Arbeau, our principal source, has to say about it:

> Les joueurs d'instruments sont tous accoustumez à commencer les dances en un festin par un branle double, qu'ils appelent le branle commun, et en aprez donnent le branle simple, puis aprez le branle gay, et à la fin les branles qu'il appellent branles de Bourgoigne, lesquels aucuns appellent branles de Champaigne. La suyte de ces quatre sortes de branles est appropriée aux trois differences de personnes qui entrent en une dance. Les anciens dancent gravement les branles doubles et simples. Les jeusnes mariez dancent les branles gayz. Et les plus jeusnes comme vous dancent legierement les branles de Bourgoigne.[1]

He also gives instructions on how to dance it, and these instructions may be found in the English translation of his book, *Orchesography*, translated by C. W. Beaumont (London, 1925; reprinted, Dover Books, 1968), pp. 117–18. Examples of the *branle* are known from earlier in the century, but the earliest *branles* that are specifically *de Bourgogne* are very close in time to this poem by Ronsard. Here is a 1551 setting for lute solo of

---

[1] *Orchésographie* (Langres, 1589), f. 69; quoted from Daniel Heartz, *Preludes, Chansons and Dances for Lute* (Paris, Société de Musique d'Autrefois, 1964), p. xli, q.v. for more information on the *branle*. See also Mabel Dolmetsch, *Dances of England and France, 1450–1600* (London, Routledge and Kegan Paul, 1949), chapter 4.

The idea of music in Ronsard's poetry

the dance which Ronsard wants us to think of Cassandre Salviati playing when he first set eyes on her:[1]

BRANLE DE BOURGOGNE

In the long poem *La Charite* of 1572 (L XVII, 166–73; *Pl* I, 346–54), Ronsard expresses most exquisitely the parallel between a court dance and the divine ballet of the spheres. In this poem, while Marguerite de Valois, queen of Navarre, dances a 'volte Provençalle', one of the Graces descends from

[1] From A. le Roy's *Premier Livre de tabulature de luth* (1551); taken by kind permission from the modern edition by A. Souris *et al*. (Paris, Centre

Ronsard the poet

heaven and enters into her. So close is the parallel between a mythological and a courtly figure that Ronsard describes the two becoming one during the courtly/divine dance. The luxurious beauty of this scene, in which the older Ronsard uses his mature technique to apply his rich mythological ideas to a courtly festivity, seems to me one of the poet's greatest achievements. Nowhere does he apply more richly his fruitful and ambiguous combinations of illusion and reality, of the classical past and the present, of fantasy and current politics.

The 'volte Provençalle' in that poem was in 1572 a thoroughly modern dance, and the musicians are playing violins, at that time thoroughly modern instruments. At some time in the mid-century the *volta,* originally from Provence, was adopted by the French court. Ronsard accurately describes its distinguishing feature: throwing the lady up in the air. He uses it again in another divine parallel in *Les Amours d'Euryme-don et de Callirée*: 'Tous deux dansans la Volte, ainsi que les Jumeaux [the constellation Gemini],/Prendrions place au sejour des Astres les plus beaux' (*L* XVII, 147; *Pl* I, 194).

Dances of various kinds in fact appear quite often in Ronsard's verse. In the *Sonets pour Helene,* II, sonnet XXX (quoted in full above, chapter 2, p. 114; see also below, chapter 7, p. 293), we find a whole court ballet used for yet another application of the courtly/divine parallel. And 'branles nouveaux' appear in his description of a would-be golden age in a late preface to his *Hymnes* (*L* XVIII, 263–4; *Pl* II, 652). In an *Elegie* to Robert Dudley, Earl of Leicester,

---

National de la Recherche Scientifique, 1960), p. 66. I have changed the barring slightly in accordance with my own interpretation. This may actually be the earliest known *branle de Bourgogne*; see the introduction to the 1960 edition, pp. xvii–xxi and xxiv–xxvii. It is certainly remarkably close in time to Ronsard's poem and to his first meeting with Cassandre; it comes from the very first publication of the house of Le Roy and Ballard, the publishers who were to dominate French music-printing for two hundred years; and this particular one is the first dance of a suite of nine lively and contrasting *branles de Bourgogne* in the book. It is not too hard to play, nor would it have been even for the 14-year-old Cassandre Salviati.

The idea of music in Ronsard's poetry

Ronsard praises his skill in the dance, but without being very precise as to the kind of dance ('branles' is a general term, and neither kind of galliard mentioned is very specific):

> Nul mieux que toy ne tombe à la cadance,
> Quand main à main tu guides une dance,
> Soit decoupant ou les branles Anglois,
> Ou les Flamans, ou les nostres François,
> Ou soit balant d'une jambe soudaine
> Une gaillarde Espagnole ou Romaine,
> Montrant la greve et le corps bien adroit
> Que pour espoux une Nymphe voudroit.
>
> (*L* XIII, 71; deleted in 1584)

Like these specific dances, certain instruments continually reappear, not only in the metaphorical ways already discussed, but also in connection with certain courtly and social functions. Thus, we find fifes, drums and oboes at a public rejoicing; fifes, cornets and oboes at a wedding; fifes, drums and trumpets signifying war; brass instruments for a tournament; and lutes and cornets in a religious procession.[1] A whole rich orchestra of instruments appears in a poem connected with the 1564 Fontainebleau celebrations:

> Quand oyrons nous au matin les aubades
> De divers lutz mariés à la voix,
> Et les cornets, les fifres, les hauts boys,
> Les tabourins, les fluttes, espinettes
> Sonner ensemble avecques les trompettes?
>
> (*L* XIII, 147; *Pl* I, 875)

In Castiglione's *Courtier,* music was one of the social accomplishments demanded of a gentleman. So it is in Ronsard, as well as a leisure activity, a *délassement,* for the great. These ideas were almost obligatory in the Renaissance social and courtly context. He mentions music on occasion as an accomplishment like another, like for example tennis playing or a

[1] Respectively *L* IX, 131 (*Pl* II, 862–3); XIV, 170 (I, 898) and XVIII, 120 (II, 9); X, 82 (I, 307); XVII, 74 (II, 486); and XVIII, 280 (II, 661).

[237]

knowledge of botany; and he shows us Mary Queen of Scots playing the lute as relaxation after affairs of state, just as he shows us Charles IX using literature for the same purpose. But such references are rare indeed compared to his far more frequent concern with music as a metaphor for the high purpose of poetry.

*

* *

*

It remains to ask: to what extent did Ronsard's attitude to music change during his life? I have already mentioned one or two ways in which it appears to do so.

The theoretical idea that poetry should be sung remains constant, though it comes to be expressed less and less often. In the early and middle years, as we saw, it was common. At the very end of his life, we still find the following statement (printed in the posthumous 1587 edition):

> Les vers Sapphiques ne sont, ny ne furent, ny ne seront jamais agreables, s'ils ne sont chantez de voix vive, ou pour le moins accordez aux instruments, qui sont la vie et l'ame de la Poësie. Car Sapphon chantant ses vers ou accommodez à son Cystre, ou à quelque Rebec, estant toute rabuffée, à cheveux mal-agencez et negligez, avec un contour d'yeux languissants et putaciers, leur donnoit plus de grace, que toutes les trompettes, fifres et tabourins n'en donnoient aux vers masles et hardis d'Alcée, son citoyen, et contemporain, faisant la guerre aux Tyrans.
>
> (L XVIII, 227–8; Pl II, 1018)

The essential and central idea of music as a metaphor for poetry also never disappears. But it is strongest at the beginning, then fades away, and then fluctuates in the middle and later periods. The *Odes* (if one may say so) harp on it; the *Amours* of 1552–3 have it quite a lot; the *Continuation des amours* of 1555 and the *Nouvelle Continuation des amours* of 1556 contain hardly a single reference to music of any kind; the varied

The idea of music in Ronsard's poetry

poetry of the 1560s uses the idea a good deal; the *Franciade* makes only some formal gestures towards music; while the late poems, as one would expect, use the idea in a mature fashion.

Conversely, in the middle and later periods the metaphorical idea gives way somewhat to a more mature recognition of music as a reality, and especially as a part of the civilization of the court at which Ronsard was employed. References to music in processions, *mascarades* and other social functions are more common. Music is cited as a pastime, a *divertissement,* a social accomplishment—things which the earnest young Ronsard seldom mentioned. Also, it seems to me that by the 1560s Ronsard has accepted the professional dichotomy between poets and musicians, and so while remaining professionally aloof from music, still sees it as a reality, essentially a courtly reality, perhaps somewhat removed from the ideal of his youth.

In the late period, there are no new musical ideas: only an increasingly superb technique, more apparent relaxation, occasional subtle and beautiful developments. This is true, of course, not only of music but of all aspects of Ronsard's art. The idea of earthly music and dancing as a parallel to celestial harmony and movement is a commonplace with him; yet how superb an expression of it is *La Charite* (1572), compared with poems of twenty years earlier.

*

*   *

*

The theme of music, then, is one which may be traced all through Ronsard's work. Music, especially the instruments of music, seems to have aided him in his creation of an individual and profound fusion of the real and the supernatural, the real and the metaphorical. It functions both as an essential neo-classical metaphor and as an aspect of sixteenth-century courtly civilization. The business of music itself he left to other professionals; but the idea of it was one of the most fertile elements in his own poetic achievement.

[239]

6

Ronsard's political and polemical poetry

FRANCIS M. HIGMAN

FROM the very beginning of Ronsard's poetic career (*Avant-entree du Roi treschrestien à Paris,* 1549) to the end (*Caprice: au seigneur Simon Nicolas,* 1584, published 1609), Ronsard wrote poetry directly connected with the political events and movements of his time. It has become fashionable to stress that Ronsard, as well as being a love poet and a poet-philosopher, was also a courtier actively involved in the political wranglings, power struggles – even the physical battles – of the particularly violent period in which he lived. But discussion of the *nature* of the poetry which Ronsard created in response to the evolving historical situation is less common, though more important, than a mere catalogue of his political poetry.[1] The aim in this chapter is to situate Ronsard, as a person, in the social and political life of his time, and to see how the political tensions to which he was subjected conditioned the nature of his poetry, and his view of poetry. There is a constant tension between, on the one hand, ideals of poetry (whether as a quest for beauty, or as allegorical theology) and the persona of the poet which such ideals imply, and, on the other hand, the political realities of the period and the demands those realities

[1] The one outstanding study of this transformation of historical reality into poetic form is Henri Weber's penetrating analysis of the *Discours des miseres de ce temps,* in *La Création poétique au seizième siècle en France* (Paris, Nizet, 1955), pp. 559–600.

[241]

Ronsard the poet

impose on the practising poet. This tension underlies Ronsard's thought about his art, and expresses itself in the qualities of much of his poetry.

We shall explore the historical situation of Ronsard at a number of particularly significant points in his career, and juxtapose the historical exposition with an analysis of the poetry composed in that situation. Thus the plan of this chapter is chronological, since we are dealing with a historically evolving situation. We shall concentrate on the decade from 1555 to 1565, which represents both the period of most dramatic evolution in French politics during Ronsard's life, and the period of his deepest involvement in the political scene.

THE MUSE AND THE NATION

Our starting point is that landmark in Ronsard's career, the *Hymnes* of 1555, about which a number of points may be made to extend the fuller treatment given to these poems elsewhere in the present volume (chapter 3, pp. 150–5).

The collection consists of fifteen long poems on serious subjects – the *Hymne de Henri II*, the *Hymne de la justice*, the *Hymne de la philosophie*, the *Hercule chrestien* among others. Two things go hand in hand in this volume, and both are fundamental to the poetic aspirations of the disciples of Dorat: the creation of philosophical, intellectual poetry, and the glorification of the French nation. On the one hand, poetry here rises above decorative court entertainment, above elegant *badinage* to amuse the ladies: it is the work of the scholar, the thinker, the visionary. It expresses the profundities of human and divine truth—not, it should be stressed, by the rationalities of argument (since the human mind cannot directly grasp the nature of the divine), but veiled by image, picture, fable. The poet is thus a sort of painter: not only in his verbal creation of illustrations, but in the very nature of his symbolic representation. The *Hercule chrestien,* which so offended the Calvinists by its confusion (in their eyes) of pagan fable and Christian truth, is to Ronsard a 'pictorial' representation of values: the truth of Christ

Ronsard's political and polemical poetry

is properly expressed in the symbol of the mythological hero.

On the other hand, the creation of such a poetry is a contribution to a patriotic end: for to create great poetry is to add to the cultural heritage of the nation. Moreover, without the poet to record and interpret the greatness of the French nation, the country is doomed to oblivion.[1] Just as Homer 'created' the Greece we know, and Virgil 'created' Augustan Rome, so also Ronsard is conscious of creating the France of the Valois. Thus the *Hymnes* as a whole are a patriotic action on Ronsard's part.

In particular, of course, this is true of the *Hymne du treschrestien Roy de France Henry II. de ce nom* (*L* VIII, 5 ff.; *Pl* II, 142 ff.). Here we have a systematic assimilation of Henri II and his court to the deities of Mount Olympus, and the heroes of Homeric epic: Henri is a greater warrior than Achilles, combines the respective skills in horsemanship and fencing of Castor and Pollux, and so on. The court of Henri II is superior to that of Jupiter in that, while Jupiter has but one Mars, one Mercury, one Apollo, Henri II has in his service not only a Mercury as eloquent (Charles de Lorraine), but also a hundred warriors, a thousand Apollos. This mythological material is interwoven with descriptions of the French provinces, their variety and riches, and a history of Henri's military triumphs, in particular at Boulogne and Metz.

What are we to make of this lavish paean, which seems so sycophantic to the modern reader? Firstly, it belongs to a genre, the encomium or composition in praise of an individual, the ordering and techniques of which were set out in the manuals of classical rhetoric.[2] More importantly, the particular form of the encomium here, the mythological assimilation, is a working out, in terms of the nation, of the system of values and significances discussed above, which was already a commonplace

[1] Cf. the theme of Du Bellay's *Deffense et illustration*; and see the *Hymne de Henri II*, lines 731–6 (*L* VIII, 44; *Pl* II, 153–4).
[2] See for example the *Rhetorica ad Herennium,* III, vi. 10–viii. 15, where all the topics which appear in panegyrics are categorized; and cf. the equally misunderstood encomium by Eudemon in *Gargantua,* chapter 15.

Ronsard the poet

of patriotic language before Henri II came to power.[1] To express it most strongly, one could say that in fact the poet, by the assimilation of the court of Henri II to a mythological universe, is *investing* the facts of history with significance through his poetry. The court, in itself, is merely a collection of individual human beings; a war, in itself, is merely a large-scale brawl. It is the poet who elevates events and people to their true significance by stressing the congruence of the individual event or person with the archetypal model in mythology or Homeric epic. Poetry, therefore, is an activity of the utmost seriousness and importance, for it is poetry which validates actions and personalities.

The status of the poet in this process is of course paramount. He is the painter of the fresco, the creator of the fabulous mantle, the inspired formulator of truth. The poet-*vates* has it in his power to bestow significance on mere reality; it is also given to him to bestow immortality through his verse. Which leads us to another essential element in Ronsard's poetry in the *Hymnes*: the need for patronage. For all his familiarity with the Muses, he did not live on Mount Parnassus; and although he constantly proclaims the proud independence of the true poet he has somehow to obtain his bread and butter.[2] Two of Ronsard's most important patrons are prominent in the *Hymnes*: Charles, Cardinal de Lorraine, and Odet de Coligny, Cardinal de Chastillon.

[1] See as an extreme example the mythological portrait of François I by Niccolò da Modena in the Bibliothèque Nationale, Paris, with its inscription: 'Francoys en guerre est un Mars furieux / En paix Minerve et diane a la chasse . . .' Cf. also the Olympic frescoes at Tanlay.

[2] The first major inflation of modern times, gradual in the first half of the century, accelerated rapidly after 1550, and even more in the period 1560–70. See the *Response de Jean Bodin à M. de Malestroit* (1568), ed. Henri Hauser (Paris, Colin, 1932), pp. xix–xxiv. The figures quoted by Hauser could be reduced roughly to the following scale : a cost-of-living index of 100 in 1520 would have become 110 by 1550; 120 by 1560; 180 by 1570 (a 60 per cent rise in 10 years); 230 by 1580. The income Ronsard received from his benefices of Challes and Evaillé was in the 1550s rapidly becoming inadequate, especially for someone hoping to cut some sort of figure at court.

Ronsard's political and polemical poetry

To Charles, Cardinal de Lorraine, brother of François, Duc de Guise, and fellow student with Ronsard at the Collège de Navarre, Ronsard dedicates the *Hymne de la justice*, which is at the same time an encomium of the cardinal and a glorification of the virtue of justice (which, Ronsard says, Charles has eloquently and successfully advocated to Henri II). What is important is that Charles de Lorraine has been *incorporated* into Ronsard's mythological universe of values: Justice (rather like the Muses in the *Ode à Michel de l'Hospital*), having been driven from the face of the earth after the golden age, is finally sent back by Jupiter himself, after an Olympic debate, to occupy the person of the cardinal.

In the same way Odet de Coligny, the nephew of the Connétable Anne de Montmorency and brother of Gaspard de Coligny, is incorporated, with his family: one may note the significant title of the fourth poem of the volume, *Le Temple de messeigneurs le Connestable, et des Chastillons*. Indeed Odet de Coligny occupies a unique place in the *Hymnes*: of the fifteen poems, no less than six are dedicated to the Montmorency/Chastillon family, four of them being to Odet himself (including the *Hymne de la philosophie*, and the *Hercule chrestien*); in addition, the volume as a whole is dedicated to him.

The *Hymnes*, therefore, represent a network of relationships and concepts: the poet-*vates*, creator of significance, contributes to the glory of the nation both directly, by the praise of France and the king, and indirectly, by extending the intellectual and cultural achievements of the French nation; as part of this work, he incorporates into his cultural fresco his patrons, thus bestowing immortality on them, in exchange for the favours he has received (or hopes to receive) from them.[1]

THE VOICE OF THE NATION

There is no doubt that, with the publication of the *Hymnes*, Ronsard consolidated his position as *the* poet of France (further assured after the death of Mellin de Saint-Gelais in 1558). However, success exacts a price; and the second stage of our

[1] Cf. *Priere à la fortune*, lines 29–38 (*L* VIII, 104; *Pl* II, 840).

analysis leads us to the deeper involvement of Ronsard in the political affairs of France which results from his undisputed pre-eminence among French poets.

For nearly two years after the publication of the *Deuxième Livre des hymnes* and the *Nouvelle Continuation des amours* in 1556 Ronsard seems to have rested on his laurels, at least as far as actual publication is concerned. His next published poems exemplify clearly one of the new challenges that went with the status Ronsard had acquired. From August 1558 to April or May 1559 he composed and published a series of pamphlets or *plaquettes,* closely connected to the political developments of the period: *Exhortation au camp du Roy pour bien combattre le jour de la bataille* (late August 1558); *Exhortation pour la paix* (late September or early October 1558); *Chant de liesse au Roy*; *La Paix, au Roy* (first third of 1559). Other *plaquettes* published in the same period include the *Hymne de tresillustre prince Charles, Cardinal de Lorraine* and its *Suyte,* and a *Discours à Mgr le duc de Savoie.*

The political background of these poems first needs to be explored, as they illustrate vividly the drama and tension of Ronsard's position in this period.

The *plaquettes* are related to the final, disastrous stage of the Spanish war, and the treaty of Cateau-Cambrésis (April 1559) which ended the war. In 1557 the French had been shocked by the defeat inflicted by the Duc de Savoie at Saint-Quentin, during the siege of which the Connétable Anne de Montmorency and Gaspard de Coligny had been captured. In early 1558 François de Guise had somewhat restored French fortunes by the capture of Calais from the English, and in June had taken the supposedly impregnable town of Thionville; on the other hand, the Maréchal de Termes had suffered a bloody defeat at Gravelines. In late August Henri II and Philippe II of Spain joined their respective armies on the river Authie, and all seemed set for a full-scale battle. It is in this situation that Ronsard composed the *Exhortation au camp.*

However, the battle did not take place. Both Henri II and Philippe II were desperately short of money with which to continue the war. Moreover Henri had particular reasons for desiring an end to hostilities. In the power vacuum left by the absence of his favourite minister Montmorency, the successes of François de Guise, a national hero after Calais and Thionville, were a threat to the king's authority. While he could not admit the latter reason publicly, the king was wanting peace, at more or less any price, from the end of August 1558 on. Montmorency, from his prison, was in fact negotiating with the Spanish; and he was now encouraged secretly by Henri, who urgently needed the return of Montmorency to counter the Guise influence. Henri wrote to Montmorency as follows:

> Mon ami . . . je vous assure que M. de Guyse ne desire la pays, me remonstrant que j'e plus de moyens de faire la guerre que je n'us james et que je n'an saroys tant perdre, faisant la guerre, que j'en rans, sy vous venés d'accort. . . . Faytes ce que vous pourés afin que nous ayons la pays; et ne monterés séte lestre qu'au Maréchal Saynt André et la brulés apres. Ledit personnage [Guise] que je vous nomme dans ma lectre a dyst icy à quelquun que, tant que la guerre durera, pas ung de vous ne sortirés jamès de prison et, pour ce, pansési, comme chose qui vous touche.
>
> (Lavisse, *Histoire de France,* V, 2, 176)

So the initial negotiations were undertaken by Montmorency, secretly encouraged by the king, and against the will of François de Guise (seconded by his brother Charles de Lorraine). It was only in mid-October that official plenipotentiary negotiators were appointed; on the French side these were Montmorency, Saint-André and – appearing for the first time – the Cardinal de Lorraine.

Now, Ronsard's *Exhortation pour la paix* is dated by Laumonier to September or early October 1558, and thus before the 'peace policy' had become public. While it could be seen to come from circles connected with the king,[1] there is no

[1] Already in the *Exhortation au camp* Ronsard had affirmed that he had been appointed official chronicler of the battle by the king.

Ronsard the poet

mention in the poem of its political source – indeed, there is a prayer in it to 'rompre l'ire des Rois', as if Henri needed persuading. The *Exhortation pour la paix* appears to be a *ballon d'essai*, preparing the nation in advance for the abrupt change of official policy in mid-October. This would explain the obvious change of heart on Ronsard's part, following the *Exhortation au camp* by a directly contrary poem only one month later. It thus emerges that Ronsard was very closely associated with the propagation of royal policies at this period. In the jargon of the modern political commentator we might speak of an 'informed source'.

The peace negotiations, officially opened in October, went on throughout the winter of 1558–9. In January Montmorency was released on payment of a huge ransom which scandalized many Frenchmen. In April the treaty of Cateau-Cambrésis was signed. When its terms were known there was an outburst of anger at what was clearly a highly disadvantageous settlement for France. Once again we find Ronsard in a public-relations role: in the period immediately preceding, or coinciding with, the signing of the treaty he published the *Chant de liesse,* rejoicing at the prospect of peace, and *La Paix, au Roy*, with the same message (and also hailing the release of Montmorency as a triumph). As part of the peace settlement Philibert, Duc de Savoie, the man who defeated the French at Saint-Quentin, and thus far from a favourite with the French, married the sister of the French king – another unpopular provision. So, to mark the occasion, Ronsard published one of his most skilful exercises in diplomacy, the *Discours à Mgr le duc de Savoie*. Thus, throughout this period Ronsard is seen as a spokesman conveying in persuasive tones an unpalatable royal policy. It is no coincidence that we find, in the *privilège* of the *Discours au duc de Savoie* (dated 23 February 1559, new style), the first description of Ronsard as 'Conseiller et aumonier ordinaire du Roy et de Madame de Savoye'. Ronsard has become the voice of the nation, the propagandist of the government.

This new status has considerable implications for Ronsard's poetry. What is to become of the poet-*vates*, servant of none

Ronsard's political and polemical poetry

but the Muses, when he is called on to serve the government, and to transmit a message formulated by others? How is Ronsard, the poet who constantly professes to despise the *vulgaire,* to address the army as a whole, or the nation at large?

The *Exhortation au camp . . . pour bien combattre le jour de la bataille* treads the familiar path of martial poetry: bloodthirsty encouragements to trample on mounds of dead enemies, imaginative evocation of a battle scene, glorification of courage and condemnation of cowardice – the themes are commonplaces of war poetry from Homer on. Yet there is a difference. In accordance with the precept of epic poetry which he defines in the 1587 preface to the *Franciade* (L XVI, 344; *Pl* II, 1024) he describes the battle which is to come:

> Je voy desja, ce semble, en ordre nos gendarmes,
> J'oy le bruit des chevaux, j'oy le choquer des armes,
> Je voy de toutes pars le fer etinceller
> Et jusques dans le ciel la poudre se mesler,
> Je voy comme foretz se herisser les piques,
> J'oy l'effroy des cannons, œuvres diaboliques,
> J'oy faucer les harnoys, enfonser les escus,
> J'oy le bruit des vainqueurs, j'oy le cry des vaincus,
> J'oy comme lon se tue, et comme l'on s'enferre,
> Et dessous les chevaux les Chevaliers par terre,
> Je voy dans un monceau les foibles et les fortz
> Pesle-mesle assemblez, et les vifs et les morts.
>
> (*L* IX, 7–8; *Pl* II, 434)

If we compare this battle scene with the heroic narrative of the *Ode à Michel de l'Hospital,* antistrophe 7–epode 9 (L III, 131–6; *Pl* I, 391–3), the simplicity of syntax, the directness of vocabulary, the absence of comparisons are immediately striking. The poetic diction is far less magnificent; the effect is derived from the panting, repetitive syntax, and the use of sound – much of the description is of sound rather than of sight, and it is heightened by the unharmonious consonants ('choquer', 'etinceller', 'piques') and the aspirated *h* ('se herisser', 'les harnoys').

[249]

Ronsard the poet

Another point of comparison for this poem is the *Harangue que fit monseigneur le duc de Guise aus soudards de Mez*, of 1553 (*L* V, 203 ff.; *Pl* II, 304 ff.), a poem composed with a purpose identical to that of the *Exhortation*. But the *Harangue* is worlds apart poetically. It begins with a magnificent description of the duke's armour, piece by spectacular piece.[1] This purely descriptive grandeur has no counterpart in the *Exhortation*. The speech itself in the *Harangue* (an avowed imitation of Tyrtaeus) relies heavily on mythological allusions which place the soldiers in a relationship to Ronsard's cosmic vision (they are the descendants of Hercules and Francus), and it assumes an understanding of references to the Cyclops, Midas, Mars, Mercury . . . The sentiments expressed in the two poems are very similar; but in 1558 there is not a single mythological allusion, reference to destiny, or elaborated image.[2] They are replaced by references to past victories of the French, by simplicity of syntax and vocabulary – in fact by a form of poetry with closer affinities to the speech or declamation, less properly poetic (in Ronsard's terms) than the 1553 poem was. The poet-painter is being replaced by the poet-orator.

The epic comparison is of course not entirely banished from these patriotic poems. In the *Discours au duc de Savoie*, for example, Philibert's attack on the French at Saint-Quentin is described in these terms:

> Aussi soudain qu'un torrent des montagnes
> A gros boüillons tombe sur les campagnes,
> Perdant l'espoir du povre laboureur:
> Aussi soudain tout rempli de fureur,

---

[1] Another constituent element of the epic model, cf. again the *Franciade* preface; see above, chapter 4, pp. 160–1, for further examples of richly decorated garments and objects.

[2] Marcel Raymond, *L'Influence de Ronsard sur la poésie française (1550–1585)* (Paris, Champion, 1927), volume I, p. 381, suggests that Greek mythology was misplaced in patriotic poetry; the *Exhortation au camp* illustrates Ronsard's attempt to forge a new, indigenous model for patriotic appeals.

Ronsard's political and polemical poetry

> D'ire, d'ardeur, de cueur et de proüesse,
> Tu renversas la Francoise jeunesse
> La lance au poing, et pavas tous les champs
> De mors occis sous tes glaives tranchans.
>
> (*L* IX, 165–6; *Pl* I, 847)

The image is sufficiently developed to suggest the impetuosity of Philibert's attack, but does not extend to an elaboration for its own sake. We may contrast this passage from the *Hymne de Charles de Lorraine,* also of 1559, in which a quite incidental reference to the Alps invites Ronsard to six lines of amplification:

> Comme luy [Ulysse], ny le froid des grandz Alpes cornues,
> Qui soustiennent le ciel de leurs croupes chenues,
> Nourices de meint fleuve, à qui les grans torrens
> Du menton tout glacé jusque aus piedz vont courans,
> Qui portent en tout temps sur leurs doz soliteres,
> Les neges, les frimas, les vens herediteres,
> Ny les dangers marins, ne t'ont point engardé
> Qu'à Romme tu ne sois à la fin abordé
> Mercure des François, de faconde si rare,
> Pour faire entendre au Pape, à Venise, à Ferrare,
> Le tort qu'on fait au Roy, et pour les animer,
> En gardant son party, de justement s'armer.
>
> (*L* IX, 43; *Pl* II, 179–80)

An element of the poet's quasi-priestly function which survives in some of these politically instigated poems is Ronsard's assumption of the role of moral adviser.[1] In *La Paix*, for instance (evidently aware that the king wants peace anyway), Ronsard reproaches Henri with his warlike ambitions, extols peaceful activities such as building the Louvre, reading and hunting, and ends with an apostrophe:

---

[1] As R. Lebègue says ('Ronsard poète officiel', in *Studi in onore di V. Lugli et D. Valeri* (Venice, Neri Pozza, 1961), volume II, p. 582): 'Ronsard ne cherche pas seulement dans le thème imposé l'occasion d'écrire de beaux vers, mais aussi de donner une haute leçon morale et politique.'

Ronsard the poet

Il suffist, il suffist, il est temps desormais
Fouller la guerre aux pieds, et n'en parler jamais.
Pensez vous estre Dieu, l'honneur du monde passe,
Il faut un jour mourir quelque chose qu'on face,
Et apres vostre mort, fussiez vous Empereur,
Vous ne serez non plus qu'un simple laboureur.

(*L* IX, 114–15; *Pl* II, 445)

Ronsard was not to know that his words would become reality within three months.

But here, as elsewhere in this series of pamphlets, much has changed in the texture of Ronsard's poetry. Gone are the *copia* of poetic effects (the literary allusions, the richness of image or of vocabulary) discussed in chapter 4 above, and which are so much in evidence in the *Hymnes*. Instead, we find a richness of *invention* in the rhetorical sense, the amassing of a series of arguments in favour of a policy or attitude. The clearest example here is the *Exhortation pour la paix,* based on an appeal to the Christian faith common to both sides in the war; war is decried as being fit only for tyrants, lions and wolves; strife is incited by 'la meschante Discorde' to lighten the burden of humans weighing on the earth; war is unnatural to mankind since, unlike lions and tigers, men are not created with natural armaments and defences; the invention of iron, fire and gold are cursed, the age of Saturn nostalgically evoked. But these are only references, not pictures. Only once, at the end of the poem, does he revert even briefly to a picture, in describing the joys of peace:

Bien vivre en vos maisons sans armes, et avoir
Femme tresbelle et chaste entre vos bras, et voir
Vos enfans se joüer au tour de la tetine,
Vous pendiller au col d'une main infantine,
Vous frisoter la barbe, ou tordre les cheveux,
Vous appeller papa, vous faire mille jeux . . .

(*L* IX, 24; *Pl* II, 440)

No more than a sketch, this short glimpse seeks the unpretentious simplicity of the family scene, enhanced by the domesticity of the language (*pendiller, frisoter, papa*); yet in it Ronsard speaks to the imagination of the reader in a way he does not elsewhere in the *Exhortation*.

In the new persona of the poet which emerges from these poems all is not, however, loss by comparison with his earlier poetry. There are positive qualities. There is, for example, the remarkable skill with which Ronsard assembles his arguments. How for instance is he, in a poem for a French public, to sing the praises of Philibert de Savoie, when all Philibert's greatness was won in battle at the expense of the French?

Ronsard incorporates the whole progress of the duke, from his impoverished beginnings to his triumphant alliance with France and restoration of his lands, into a plan of divine providence. He opens the *Discours au duc de Savoie*:

> Vous Empereurs, vous Princes, et vous Roys,
> Vous qui tenez le peuple sous vos lois,
> Oyez icy de quelle providence
> Dieu regit tout par sa haulte prudence . . .
>
> (*L* IX, 157; *Pl* I, 843)

The tone is biblical.[1] Ronsard is not merely describing a political settlement: he leads us into a new form of cosmic power structure. Philibert did not defeat the French at Saint-Quentin by superior tactics: Fortune had taken pity on him, and sent her minions Le Bonheur and La Victoire to lead him (and Ronsard makes it quite clear that he might not have won without their aid). The peace settlement was not the action of an impoverished monarch acting through imprisoned negotiators: Divine Peace herself, in obedience to God, intervened to inflame the hearts of Lorraine and Montmorency. Such an interpretation, stressing the dependence of man on celestial forces for all the actions of life, provides a very diplomatic version of the situation, acceptable to both sides (although the interplay of the distinctly ambiguous minions of Fortune, helping Philibert, and the Peace of the Christian God, working

[1] Cf. Ps. ii. 10: 'Be wise now therefore, O ye kings; be instructed, ye judges of the earth.'

[253]

through the French, is interesting); it also exemplifies a new type of value system in Ronsard's poetry, derivative, but different, from the mythological system of the *Hymnes*.

Derivative, in that the poet's task remains the interpretation of visible events in terms of superior values. Different, firstly in that the whole tone of this poem, and of the others in the series of *plaquettes,* is argumentative far more than visionary. Ronsard is aware that he is presenting a case, not creating an image. Different also in the nature of the values to which he appeals. The *Discours au duc de Savoie* maintains the biblical tone with which it opened. The providence of God makes shepherds into kings (David), and kings into beasts of the field (Nebuchadnezzar); God is the Great Potter, moulding as He wills His passive clay (Jeremiah xviii).

In addition to these allusions to biblical values, the 'characters' in the divine drama Ronsard creates are personified,[1] in just the way that virtues and qualities were personified in a medieval morality play; La Fortune, Le Bonheur, La Paix all speak, and La Victoire is also given physical existence:

> Victoire avoit de grans aelles dorées,
> Bien peu s'en fault des Princes adorées:
> Son œil estoit douteux et mal certain,
> Son front sans poil, inconstante sa main.
>
> (*L* IX, 165; *Pl* I, 847)

The world forces we move among in these poems are much more familiar within the French tradition (and thus much more accessible to the wider audience Ronsard must have had in mind); they belong to genres quite different from the forces which march through the *Hymnes*. They are also much less ambitious than the splendid fresco-like visions of the *Hymnes*. The poet-orator, charged with the transmission of a message, must keep his poetic universe in a secondary place, subordinated to the argument which he is propounding.

---

[1] For an analysis, in a different perspective, of Ronsard's handling of such personifications, see above, chapter 1, pp. 51–4, 67–8.

Ronsard's political and polemical poetry

If we have spent a seemingly excessive time on these apparently unimportant pamphlets, it is because they form a crucial stage in the development of Ronsard's public poetry. They all relate to a brief period of his life; but this period prepared all the problems and tensions which beset Ronsard for many years beyond.

The brevity of the period is firstly due to the death, in June 1559, of Henri II. Ronsard had scarcely received his new title of *conseiller et aumonier ordinaire du Roy* than the king was killed in a tournament; with a sickly child (François II) on the throne, France inevitably fell a prey to the competing ambitions of the great feudal families. Ronsard had not had time to consolidate his position (and his income) before the opportunity was lost.

Second, and even more gravely, the families of Ronsard's two most important patrons – Odet de Coligny and Charles de Lorraine – were more and more in opposition to each other, in the 'feudalization' of French politics after 1559. Already in the negotiations preceding the 1559 treaty we saw Montmorency (Odet's uncle) and the Guises in conflict with each other. The tensions this produced in Ronsard's loyalties are perceptible in the pamphlets he composed in 1559. The pamphlet *La Paix* contained three poems: one to Henri II, one celebrating the return of Montmorency, and the third written for a tournament organized by François de Guise. The favours are carefully balanced. In *La Bienvenue de monseigneur le Connestable* (L IX, 117 ff.; *Pl* II, 447 ff.) Ronsard gives all the credit for the peace to the Connétable; but a few months later, in the *Suyte de l'hymne de . . . Charles Cardinal de Lorraine* (L IX, 145 ff.; *Pl* II, 873 ff.), it is to the cardinal, he says, that the praise is due. During the course of this year in which, at royal behest, he was extolling a policy opposed to that of the Guise family, he was hard at work producing a *Chant pastoral sur les nopces de Mgr Charles duc de Lorraine et madame Claude*; *XXIIII inscriptions en faveur de quelques grands seigneurs lesquelles devoyent servir en la comedie qu'on esperoit representer en la maison de Guise, par le commandement de Mgr le Cardinal de Lorraine*; and, most important, the *Hymne de tres illustre prince Charles, Cardinal de Lorraine* (the only *Hymne* Ronsard composed in honour of a living individual apart from Henri II). Comment has already been made on the style of this poem (p. 251 above), which marks a fleeting return to the high poetry of the 1555 *Hymnes*. The parallelism of diction and thought between the *Hymne de Charles de Lorraine* and the poems to Odet de Coligny in the 1555 collection[1] speaks volumes about Ronsard's efforts to keep a balance between his patrons.

His efforts were wasted. The Cardinal de Lorraine failed to provide the material rewards Ronsard had hoped for (see *Le Procés . . .* , 1562, published 1565: *L* XIII, 17 ff.; *Pl* I, 851 ff.); and in 1560, Odet de Coligny became a declared Calvinist, with the result that Ronsard could no longer dedicate any poems to him and retain a place at court. His hopes had come to naught, his ambition was thwarted, his position as national poet jeopardized. True, his place as *aumonier ordinaire* assured him of a modest income; but his aim was higher. In terms of his poetry also, he had forsaken the freedom with which, as an independent follower of Apollo, he drew from his inspiration an imaginary world of poetic truth, and had instead given his pen in the service of the state, to argue a policy and persuade a nation. As a result, inspiration has left him; he is no more than a 'demy-poëte'.

Such is the burden of a number of poems written in this period. In the celebrated *Complainte contre fortune* in the 1559 *Second Livre des meslanges* (*L* X, 16 ff.; *Pl* II, 399 ff.), one of the last poems he dedicated to Odet de Coligny, Ronsard associates his obsessive attachment to the false values of the court (ambition, riches, intrigue) with the loss of his poetic ability, since he has renounced his singlehearted devotion to the

---

[1] Cf. *Hymne de Charles*, line 9 (*L* IX, 29; *Pl* II, 174) and *Vers heroiques* (1555), line 1 (*L* VIII, 3; *Pl* II, 832); *Hymne de Charles*, lines 81–2 (*L* IX, 33; *Pl* II, 176), and *Prière à la fortune* (1555), lines 1–5 (*L* VIII, 103; *Pl* II, 839).

Ronsard's political and polemical poetry

Muses. In the *Elegie à Loïs des Masures*, with which volume III of the 1560 *Œuvres* closes, the ghost of Du Bellay advises Ronsard to withdraw to his house and avoid the seductions of the court. In the poem to L'Huillier in the same collection (*L* X, 292 ff.; *Pl* I, 885 ff.) he laments the loss of his youthful inspiration; and in the *Elegie* with which he prefaced Jacques Grevin's *Théâtre* in 1561, he longs for 'un mestier moins divin que le mien'.

Thus Ronsard's poetic disillusionment goes hand in hand with the ominous turn in the political scene, which had direct implications for his personal position.

One final point in this summary of the political developments of these years is characterized by the fact that not only Odet de Coligny, but also many others of Ronsard's friends were being converted at this period to Calvinism: of those just mentioned, Jacques Grevin almost before the 1561 *elegie* was composed, Loïs Des Masures some time earlier. How many more would desert the faith of their fathers? Moreover, the spread of reformed doctrines, at its most rapid just in this period, was presenting a new and threatening aspect: the religious movement was taking on political overtones (the Amboise conspiracy, an attempt by the 'heretics' to kidnap the king, in March 1560, was the first clear manifestation of the new turn of events). The threat of civil war was obvious.

The Calvinist movement also had literary implications which involved Ronsard directly, indeed personally. Memorialists of the period, for example Florimond de Raemond, and also the Cardinal Du Perron in his funeral oration for Ronsard,[1] stress the contribution of books to the growth of Calvinism in France. Translations of the Bible, theological treatises, devotional works, satirical pamphlets, polemical poems pouring off the presses of Geneva were among the most effective means of spreading the new doctrines. In the face of this tidal wave, the response of writers in defence of the traditional church was, before 1560, pitifully inadequate. In the *Elegie à Guillaume des Autelz* (from the 1560 *Œuvres*: *L* X, 348 ff.; *Pl* II, 564 ff.)

[1] See P. Perdrizet, *Ronsard et la réforme* (Paris, Fischbacher, 1902), pp. 5 ff.

[257]

Ronsard the poet

Ronsard expresses the need to reply in books to the subversive books of the opposition. In this Calvinist challenge a demand is once again being made on Ronsard to subordinate literature to an end other than autonomous poetic creation; for just as Ronsard had been called on in 1558–9 to transmit a message handed down from a political source, so the Calvinists asserted that literature was the handmaid of theology, and that the poet's function was to transmit a message given to him from above.

The aesthetic principles implied in the Calvinist view of literature have been well studied by Marcel Raymond[1] and Mario Richter.[2] We find, of course, a preoccupation with simplicity, in view of the propaganda purpose of Calvinist literature; the constant emphasis by Calvin and Bèze on a style 'point eslongné du language commun' (Calvin), which will not 'espoventer les simples gens' (Bèze) is in direct contrast to the élitist preoccupations of the early Pléiade, seeking to cultivate a poetic language 'du tout eslongné du vulgaire' (Ronsard). But this simplicity goes beyond the mere desire to be understood. To Calvin and his followers, the message which they are expressing has its own beauty and power (Calvin contrasts the forcefulness of the Gospels, unadorned by any literary pretensions, with the artificiality of effect-seeking human rhetoric);[3] the function of the poet is to transmit that message and its beauty with the utmost transparency. Human style, in fact, is counterproductive in divine subjects.

Contrast this view of literature as the undistorted transmission of an intrinsically beautiful message with all that has been said above about poetry as investing mere reality with significance. Or take the following remark from Ronsard's *Abbregé* of 1565:

[1] *L'Influence de Ronsard,* volume I, pp. 342 ff.
[2] 'La poetica di Theodore de Bèze e le *Chrestiennes Meditations*', *Aevum,* 38 (1964), pp. 479–525.
[3] See L. Wencelius, *L'Esthétique de Calvin* (Paris, Les Belles Lettres, 1937); and F. M. Higman, *The Style of John Calvin in his French Polemical Treatises* (Oxford University Press, 1967).

Ronsard's political and polemical poetry

Elocution n'est autre chose qu'une propriété et splendeur de
paroles bien choisies et ornées de graves et courtes sentences,
qui font reluyre les vers comme les pierres precieuses bien
enchassées les doigts de quelque grand Seigneur.

(*L* XIV, 15; *Pl* II, 1000)

As the choice of words is to the power of the verse, so the
verse itself is to the reality it evokes: the fingers are not
particularly beautiful in themselves; it is the rings of poetry
that create the beauty.

The particular question of the use of mythology is the
clearest example of this aesthetic collision. Ronsard, as we
have seen, sees mythology as a system of symbolized values
which can express pictorially the significance to be attached
to the individual person or event inserted into that system:
the fabulous mantle for the expression of the concealed truth.
To the Calvinists, the relation of 'pagan fable' and 'divine
truth' is quite different; the Synod of Sainte-Foy in 1578 put it
thus:

> Ceux qui mettent la main à la plume pour traiter en poésie
> l'histoire de l'Ecriture sainte sont avertis de n'y mesler les
> fables poetiques et de n'attribuer à Dieu le nom des faux
> dieus et de n'ajouter ou diminuer à l'Ecriture sainte, mais
> de se tenir à peu pres à ses termes.[1]

The opposition is complete between Ronsard and the
Calvinists.

Perhaps the most influential work yet produced by the
Calvinists was the Marot/Bèze *Pseaumes de David mis en rime
françoise*.[2] Their popularity was enormous; for a generation
and more, the Psalms of Marot and Bèze were the hallmark of
Protestant worship, and the marching song of Huguenot
soldiers going into battle. One of the signs taken as indicative
of the atmosphere of tolerance fostered by Catherine de

[1] Quoted by Perdrizet, op. cit., pp. 61-2.
[2] See M. Jeanneret, *Poésie et tradition biblique au* XVIe *siècle* (Paris, Corti,
1969), for an excellent analysis of the poetic qualities of the *Pseaumes*.

Ronsard the poet

Médicis in 1561, the period of the Colloque de Poissy, was that the singing of the Psalms was fashionable at court.

Early editions of the psalter, from the partial edition of 1553 until the 1560s or 1570s, contained a liminary poem by Bèze which is worth quoting at some length. It sums up the challenge of the Calvinist aesthetic; and it is couched in terms particularly directed at Ronsard himself:

> Sus donc, esprits de celeste origine,
> Monstrez ici votre fureur divine,
> Et ceste grace autant peu imitable
> Au peuple bas, qu'aux plus grands admirable.
> Soyent desormais vos plumes adonnées
> A louer Dieu, qui vous les a données.
> C'est trop servi à ses affections,
> C'est trop suivi folles inventions.
> On a beau faire et complaintes et cris,
> Dames mourront, et vous, et vos escrits!
> Flattez, mentez, faites du Diable un Ange:[1]
> Vos dieux mourront, vous et vostre louange.
> Resveillez vous, amis, de vostre songe,
> Et m'embrassez verité pour mensonge.
> Ne permettez, gentilles creatures,
> Vos beaux esprits croupir en ces ordures,
> Chercher vous faut ailleurs qu'en ce bas monde
> Dignes sujets de vostre grand'faconde.
> Mais pour ce faire, il faut premierement
> Que reformiez vos cœurs entierement.
> Vos plumes lors, d'un bon esprit poussées,

[1] Ronsard took the remark personally. In the *Remonstrance au peuple de France* he replied:
> Mais je suys plain d'ennuy et de dueil quand je voy
> Un homme bien gaillard abandonner sa foy,
> Quand un gentil esprit pipé huguenotise,
> Et quand jusque à la mort ce venin le maistrise.
> Voyant cette escriture ils diront en courroux,
> Et quoy, ce gentil sot escrit doncq' contre nous!
> Il flatte les Seigneurs, il fait d'un diable un ange...
>
> (L XI, 94; Pl II, 586)

Decouvriront vos divines pensées.
Lors vous serez poëtes veritables,
Prisés des bons, aux meschants redoutables.
Sinon, chantez vos feintes poësies,
Dames, amours, complaintes, jalousies,
Quant est de moy, tout petit que je suis,
Je veux louer mon Dieu comme je puis.

The complexity of Ronsard's position in the face of the Calvinist challenge comes from the fact that that challenge imposed itself irresistibly on him at just the period when he was already in doubt about his own position as a poet. The Ronsard that Bèze is attacking is the Ronsard of the *Odes*, the *Amours* and, in anticipation, the *Hymnes* (though this last collection was published two years after Bèze's poem). The 'demy-poëte' of 1561 believes he has already lost his *fureur divine* – not by praising false gods, as Bèze would have it, but by subordinating his poetic talent to an external authority. The Calvinists would have him go further along the same, unpoetic path. Must the poet-*vates*, now a mere poet-orator, go on to become a poet-preacher?

PATRIOTISM AND POETRY

During the first war of religion (1562–3), Ronsard composed a further series of *plaquettes,* later assembled under the collective title *Discours des miseres de ce temps.*[1] It is in this series that Ronsard finds his answers to the multiple problems, personal, political and poetic, that faced him in 1560. Two consecutive answers emerge, in fact; in the *Discours,* the *Continuation du discours* and the *Remonstrance au peuple de France,* all composed during the period of armed conflict, he develops further the tendencies of the 1558–9 pamphlets, in the line of national, oratorical poetry. Then immediately after the peace of Amboise (March 1563) he changes his theme and, in the *Responce aux injures,* looks for an answer to the poetic problems with which he was faced.

[1] See *L* XI; *Pl* II, 544 ff. for the individual titles of the series.

Ronsard the poet

In one sense, Ronsard provides no answer at all to the Calvinist challenge. Quite simply, he does not provide a poetry of theology or devotion; he does not 'chanter de Jesus-Christ'. Not because he neither knew nor cared about religious questions, as some have asserted; but because he took the perfectly orthodox view that such questions are properly discussed by fully trained specialists only, involving as they do mysteries beyond human comprehension. One of his major complaints against the Huguenots, echoing many similar sentiments in the period, is that all and sundry, women and children, presume to speak of theology (see *Remonstrance*, lines 567–72: L XI, 93; *Pl* II, 586). To engage in theological discussion would be to accept the Huguenot principle.

It is true that at least once in these poems (*Remonstrance*, lines 109–42: L XI, 68; *Pl* II, 576) he touches on a properly theological point; but, after summarizing the arguments of the Cardinal de Lorraine at the Colloque de Poissy, he rapidly moves on to insist on the mystery of these insoluble questions, and to attack the pride of the Huguenot doctors in claiming to have all the answers.

The place of strictly religious matters in these poems is small indeed. Of far greater importance is the place of political argument. As in the pamphlets of 1558–9, Ronsard is giving expression to a political viewpoint in these poems. The *privilège* which appears with each of the *plaquettes,* granted by François II in 1560, continues to describe Ronsard as the king's 'feal Conseiller et Aulmosnier ordinaire'. Much of the argument of the poems is an appeal to patriotic sentiment – a lamentation on the devastation of France, the tragedy of civil war, the unpatriotic recourse by the Huguenots to foreign troops, and the hope and faith that Catherine and Charles IX will be able to restore order. The voice of the government spokesman, one might say, evoking in the people the sense of national unity.

But this is not all; for simple appeals to patriotism offer little in the way of positive action. Once again, in 1562 as in 1558, we find Ronsard advocating a royal policy – now that of the queen mother, to whom Ronsard addresses the *Discours* and the

Ronsard's political and polemical poetry

Continuation. But the policy was by now much more complex since, instead of the two poles of peace or war in 1558–9, there was now a welter of policies, and the allegiances of the great of the land varied from one month to the next. M. Lange has shown[1] the similarity of ideas and expression between many passages of the *Discours* cycle and the policies advocated, in the assemblies of Fontainebleau and Orleans in 1560, by Michel de l'Hospital, newly appointed *chancelier,* and Jean de Montluc, bishop of Valence (and brother of the memorialist). These men were the leaders of the 'Gallican' party at court, which also included, in 1560–2, Charles de Lorraine and Marguerite de France. They represented a middle way between persecution of heretics on the one hand, and recognition and acceptance of the Calvinists on the other.

To the modern mind, accustomed to a radical division between Catholic and Protestant, the attitude of the Gallican *réformistes* is difficult to grasp.[2] Thanks to Calvin's *Excuse aux Nicodemites,* we have been led to believe that all reformist sentiments in this period must be equated with secret Protestantism, the 'Nicodémisme' of Calvin's terminology. We expect Catholicism to be equated with support of the papacy, with rigidity of doctrine and of church practice. Such a view makes the position of a man like Montluc incomprehensible; for he is as outspoken in his attacks on ecclesiastical abuses as the most convinced Calvinist, he defends the singing of the Psalms in the vernacular, he admires the courage and learning of Calvinist ministers, he rejects the policy of persecution – partly because the heretics are too numerous (he assesses their numbers at 400,000 at least), partly because it is counterproductive, since the Huguenot martyrs die so well. And yet there is no trace in his mind of an acceptance of Calvinist

[1] 'Quelques sources probables des *Discours* de Ronsard', *Revue de l'histoire littéraire de la France,* 20 (1913), pp. 789–816.
[2] The following comments owe much to discussion with Professor G. Gadoffre, who is making an important study of French Gallican policies in connection with a future publication on Du Bellay. See also Frances Yates, *The French Academies of the Sixteenth Century* (London, Warburg Institute, 1947), pp. 199 ff.

teachings; he affirms the continuity of faith of the true church, from which the *novateurs* have separated themselves; he proposes that the pastors should be interrogated on their faith 'afin d'essaier s'il y avoit order de les ramener ou reduire, ou pour le moins de les convaincre . . .'; he demands the convening of a general council or, failing that, a national council; and defines the purpose of the Colloque de Poissy as either to bring the lost sheep back to the fold, or if not, to remove the complaint that they had never had a hearing.[1]

A Gallican policy, such as is expressed with particular clarity in Montluc's arguments, was favoured by Catherine de Médicis throughout this period, an attitude which was only weakened during the actual hostilities of the first war. This is the background against which to assess the repeated attacks by Ronsard on ecclesiastical abuses – in the *Elegie à Guillaume des Autelz*, the *Remonstrance* and the *Responce*. Where, to the modern mind, Ronsard seems to be weakening his own case against the Huguenots by interspersing his diatribe against them with an echo of some of their own complaints, he is in fact being consistent with the religious policy of the Gallican party. Although in 1562 his view of the Huguenots and their ministers is nowhere near as sympathetic as Montluc's was in 1560, he is free in his criticism of the papacy (*Remonstrance*, lines 277 ff.) and the prelates of the Council of Trent (*Remonstrance*, lines 421 ff.), the awarding of offices to children and courtiers (*Elegie*, lines 79 ff.), the greed and avarice of the clergy (*Responce*, lines 441 ff.). But, as he goes on to assert in this last passage, his abhorrence of abuses in the church does not lead him to schism, but to a desire to reform the church. In all this, Ronsard is promoting a royal policy just as he was in the pamphlets of 1558–9.

However, there is a profound difference. In 1558 the persona

[1] These points are made in Montluc's speech at the Fontainebleau assembly, summarized at length by Pierre de la Place, *Commentaires de l'estat de la religion, et republique soubs les Roys Henry et François seconds, et Charles neufieme.* [Paris], 1565, and in the *Apologie contre certaines calomnies mises sus à la desfaveur et desavantage de l'estat des affaires de ce roiaume*, 1562, ascribed to Montluc.

Ronsard's political and polemical poetry

adopted by Ronsard was that of official spokesman, exposing arguments which do not affect him personally and immediately. In the *Discours* cycle, on the contrary, the exposition of government attitudes is absorbed into a much more personal expression of feeling. Appeals to national unity, exposition of Gallican policy, support for the queen mother, are channelled into the poet's irrepressible urge to express his own fervent emotions – grief, anger, hope, despair. The persona of the poet in these compositions is that of Pierre de Ronsard, ordinary Frenchman and patriot, not the poet claiming divine inspiration, nor the spokesman granted an official status.

The result is a poetry which, while originating in the genre of the earlier official poetry, has a quite different character.[1] In the *Discours* cycle the first person singular is omnipresent. The phrasing of the opening lines of the *Continuation* ('Madame, je serois ou du plomb ou du bois,/ Si moy, que la nature a fait naistre François . . .'), the constant expression of personal dislike of Huguenot ideas ('Je suis plain de despit quand . . .', 'Je meurs quand les enfans . . .', 'Je suis remply d'ennuy . . .', 'J'ay pitié quand je voy . . .'; see *Remonstrance,* lines 545–87), the place given to Ronsard's experience of a Huguenot meeting (*Continuation,* lines 144 ff.) – examples of the new tone in these poems could be multiplied indefinitely.

This irruption of the individual and his emotions into the public poem results in a number of new characteristics by comparison with earlier public poetry. Ronsard is much freer in his invention: whereas, in the *Discours au duc de Savoie,* he had created a rather intellectualized series of celestial beings, here he displays a whole gamut of imaginative personifications – 'le monstre Opinion', born of Jupiter and Dame Presomption, who perverts the minds of theologians and spreads discord in France (*Discours*) and who, inflaming the mind of Luther, poisons his heart with a venomous serpent (*Remonstrance*); the pitiable state of France, torn by civil strife, becomes a vision of 'l'idole de la France' – 'Son poil estoit

[1] For a much more extensive study of the qualities of the *Discours* than is possible here, see Weber, *La Création poétique,* pp. 559–600.

hydeux, son œil have, et profond,/Et nulle magesté ne lui hausoit le front' (*Continuation*, lines 329–30) – just as, in the *Elegie à Loïs des Masures,* the ghost of Du Bellay had appeared to him to give supernatural advice. Indeed the plethora of visions evoked by Ronsard to formulate in imaginative pictures the abstractions of idea and sentiment produced the jibe from his Calvinist opponents: 'On diroit proprement, depuis que tu es Prestre,/ Qu'un million d'esprits te viennent apparoistre.'[1]

Most of all, the persona of the poet as an individual results in the remarkable variety of tone in these poems. Examples here must be selective. In the first *Discours* Ronsard embroiders in a tone of lament on the ship of state image:

> Las! Madame, en ce temps que le cruel orage
> Menace les François d'un si piteux naufrage,
> Que la gresle et la pluye, et la fureur des cieux
> Ont irrité la mer de vens seditieux,
> Et que l'astre jumeau ne daigne plus reluyre,
> Prenez le gouvernail de ce pauvre navire,
> Et maugré la tempeste, et le cruel efort
> De la mer, et des vens, conduisez-le à bon port.
>
> (*L* XI, 21; *Pl* XI, 545)[2]

But later the tone is frequently more violent:

> Et quoy! bruler maisons, piller et brigander,
> Tuer, assassiner, par force commander,
> N'obeir plus aux Roys, amasser des armées,
> Appellez vous cela Eglises reformées?
>
> (*Continuation:* ibid., 37; 551)

The brutality of the language, the antithesis of the final 'reformées', the rhetorical questions, forcefully convey the indignation and disbelief of the poet.

---

[1] *Response aux calomnies contenues au Discours . . . ,* 1563, f. g. 3v.
[2] See Yates, *French Academies,* p. 247, note 3, on the use of this image of the ship guarded by Castor and Pollux to represent France, in previous poems by Ronsard and others.

Ronsard's political and polemical poetry

Elsewhere violence of language, without the irony of the question form, makes the anger even stronger:

> Ils n'ont pas seulement, sacrileges nouveaux,
> Fait de mes temples saincts, estables à chevaux,
> Mais comme tormentés des Fureurs Stygialles,
> Ont violé l'honneur des ombres sepulchrales,
> A fin que par tel acte inique et malheureux
> Les vivans et les morts conspirassent contre eux.
>
> (ibid., 57; 558)

Or a thunderous invocation to the Almighty, shocking by its apparent questioning of the wisdom of God, creates a sense of the cataclysmic scale of the crisis both by its allusion to the ends of the earth, and by the breadth of the rhetorical periods:

> O Ciel, ô Mer, ô Terre, ô Dieu pere commun
> Des Chrestiens, et des Juifs, des Turc, set d'un chacun:
> Qui nourris aussi bien par ta bonté publicque
> Ceux du Pole Antarticq', que ceux du Pole Artique:
> Qui donnes et raison, et vie, et mouvement,
> Sans respect de personne, à tous egallement,
> Et fais du ciel là haut sur les testes humaines
> Tomber, comme il te plaist, et les biens, et les peines.
>   O Seigneur tout puissant, qui as tousjours esté
> Vers toutes nations plain de toute bonté,
> Dequoy te sert là haut la foudre et le tonnerre,
> Si d'un esclat de feu tu n'en brusles la terre?
>   Es tu dedans un trosne assis sans faire rien?
> Il ne faut point douter que tu ne saches bien
> Cela que contre toy brassent tes creatures,
> Et toutesfois, Seigneur, tu le vois et l'endures!
>
> (*Remonstrance*: ibid., 63; 573)

A quite different tone is that of satire. Ronsard's portrait of the model Huguenot, like the satirical portraits of Du Bellay's *Regrets,* is a caricature created by the enumeration of well-chosen, typifying details:

Ronsard the poet

Il faut tant seulement avecques hardiesse
Detester le Papat, parler contre la messe,
Estre sobre en propos, barbe longue, et le front
De rides labouré, l'œil farouche et profond,
Les cheveux mal peignez, un soucy qui s'avalle,
Le maintien renfrongné, le visage tout palle,
Se monstrer rarement, composer maint escrit,
Parler de l'Eternel, du Seigneur, et de Christ,
Avoir d'un reistre long les espaules couvertes,
Bref estre bon brigand et ne jurer que certes.

(ibid., 73; 578)

The use of direct speech, in particular in the *Continuation*, gives Ronsard the framework within which to create verse of unequalled fluidity and almost conversational ease, in which rhetorical questions, frequent enjambments and popular imagery combine to provide an unbroken, flowing continuity of movement:

Adonq je respondi: apellés vous Athée
La personne qui point n'a de son cœur ostée
La foy de ses ayeux? qui ne trouble les loix
De son pays natal, les peuples ny les Roys? . . . .
Apellés vous Athée un homme qui deteste
Et vous et vos erreurs comme infernalle peste?
Et vos beaux Predicans, qui fins et cauteleux
Vont abusant le peuple, ainsi que basteleurs,
Lesquels enfarinés au mi-lieu d'une place
Vont jouant finement leurs tours de passe passe?

(*Continuation:* ibid., 45; 553)

The liveliness of tone, the ease of reading, the flow of the verse in these poems, represent for Ronsard at the same time an outstanding achievement and a danger. The achievement lies in the mastery he shows of a popular, accessible verse form. The *Discours* cycle is by far the most successful group of public poems composed by Ronsard. The fact that Cardinal Du Perron, in his funeral oration for Ronsard, gave particular

Ronsard's political and polemical poetry

prominence to the *Discours* poems is indicative at least in part of the esteem in which they were held at the time (as are also the numerous ripostes these poems evoked from the Huguenots). And certainly today, their verve, resonance and variety make them some of Ronsard's most readable poems.

Yet, for Ronsard, they were also a danger; for they represent a move still further away from his original ambitions. Where, now, is the poet-*vates*? Where now is inspiration? Where the concept of poetry as veiled theology? Where the aspiration towards an ideal form? Instead of these fundamental elements of the Ronsardian poetic, we have the poet in the persona of a patriotic individual, not as any sort of mediator of truth or even of policy; poetry in these poems is closely allied to rhetoric, and has lost the visionary elements by which the Pléiade had hoped to differentiate poetry fundamentally from rhetoric; and the basic structure of the discourse, determined by the need to present an argument and state a case, militates against the fashioning of a poetic form determined by aesthetic considerations only. The features which make the *Discours* cycle so easily accessible and acceptable to the modern reader are those least in keeping with Ronsard's own poetic pre-occupations.[1]

The *Responce de Pierre de Ronsard aux injures et calomnies de je ne sçay quels predicans et ministres de Geneve sur son Discours et Continuation des miseres de ce temps* is a crucial poem in Ronsard's poetic evolution. The peace of Amboise, signed in March 1563, ended the armed conflict, and relieved pressure on Ronsard to concern himself so singlemindedly with the political situation. On the other hand, the earlier poems of the *Discours* series had provoked a number of replies from the

---

[1] In the *Abbregé* of 1565 (L XIV, 25; *Pl* II, 1004), the 1572 *Advertissement de la Franciade* (L XVI, 9; *Pl* II, 1011), and the posthumous preface to the *Franciade* (L XVI, 331–2; *Pl* II, 1015), Ronsard makes the same comment with slight variations: that alexandrines, unless they are filled with rich and dignified vocabulary, 'sentent trop leur prose'. The *Discours* poems, uniformly in alexandrines, and avoiding richness of vocabulary, are prime examples of this danger.

Ronsard the poet

Calvinists,[1] in particular the *Response aux calomnies contenues au Discours et Suyte du discours sur les miseres de ce temps, faits par messire Pierre Ronsard, jadis poëte et maintenant prebstre*, by 'A. Zamariel' and 'B. de Mont-Dieu' (believed to be Antoine la Roche-Chandieu and Bernard de Montméja). This pamphlet was in the tone of personal vituperation common to sixteenth-century polemics; the authors accused Ronsard of atheism, and of being a priest (two heinous crimes compounded); as was inevitable in the period, he is said to be suffering from syphilis; and his poetic abilities are questioned. Taking their cue from Ronsard's own remarks two years earlier, they claim he has lost his poetic gift, and they add that he uses overblown language, lacks order in his thought, and has failed to acknow-ledge huge poetic debts to the Greeks, to Dorat, to Du Bellay . . . In short, a poetic has-been who vastly overrates himself.

The effect on Ronsard is dramatic. In his *Responce,* while continuing the argument about the religious crisis, Ronsard resolves to refute the criticisms of his poetic powers by giving a demonstration of those powers. He is deliberately showing off.

The result is a poetic *tour de force.* While replying point by point (and, it must be said, with a certain lack of order) to the accusations of his detractors, Ronsard ranges, perhaps more widely than in any other poem, over a vast variety of tones and styles. Each Huguenot jibe is refuted in a style of its own. To the accusation that he is a priest, he answers jokingly that he wishes he was, with a large ecclesiastical income (*L* XI, 120–2; *Pl* II, 596–7); one of his first tasks as a priest, indeed, would be to exorcize the devils which have invaded his detractors (ibid. 124–8; 598–600). His answer to the accusation of atheism breaks from the knockabout comedy tone to provide a magnificent, solemn amplification of the Creed (ibid., 135–8; 603–5). The grandeur of the Ronsardian periods in this section (some sentences run to fourteen lines) maintains

[1] See F. Charbonnier, *Pamphlets protestants contre Ronsard, 1560–77* (Paris, Champion, 1923).

the seriousness of tone for almost 100 lines before it is suc-
ceeded by a new outburst of polemical vigour. The Huguenots
accuse him of leading a depraved life. He replies with a
beautifully naïve timetable of his day, in simple, unadorned
language (ibid., 144–8; 606–8).

So, for over 1,000 lines of verse, he continues this sparkling
reply. But since, in this wide range of tones, Ronsard is inten-
tionally giving a poetic display, it is perhaps justifiable to
regard the passages where Ronsard answers the criticisms of
his poetry as being the most significant of all. Two rather
different attitudes emerge. On the one hand, Ronsard's desire
to disengage himself from the overserious involvement of
poetry in the religious quarrel leads him to propose an unusually lighthearted view of poetry:

> Ny tes vers ny les miens oracles ne sont pas,
> Je prends tanseulement les Muses pour ébas,
> En riant je compose, en riant je veux lire,
> Et voyla tout le fruit que je recoy d'escrire,
> Ceux qui font autrement, ils ne sçavent choisir
> Les vers qui ne sont nés sinon pour le plaisir.
> Et pour ce les grands Roys joignent à la Musique,
> (Non au Conseil privé) le bel art Poëtique.
>
> (ibid., 163; 615)

But, on the other hand, this is not to say that there is no
qualitative difference between Ronsard and his opponents;
in answer to the accusation that his poetry lacks order, he
reasserts the autonomy of poetic inspiration; true poetry
wanders at will, unrestrained by the petty arts of preachers and
rhymers:

> En l'art de Poësie, un art il ne faut pas
> Tel qu'ont les Predicans, qui suivent pas à pas
> Leur sermon sceu par cueur, ou tel qu'il faut en prose,
> Où toujours l'Orateur suit le fil d'une chose.

[271]

Ronsard the poet

Les Poëtes gaillards ont artifice à part,
Ils ont un art caché qui ne semble pas art
Aux versificateurs, d'autant qu'il se promeine
D'une libre contrainte, où la Muse le meine.

(ibid., 160; 614)

He concludes with a contrast between mere *versificateurs* 'Qui ne sont seulement que de mots inventeurs,/Froids, grossiers, et lourdaux, comme n'ayant saisie/L'ame d'une gentille et docte frenaisie', and the true, wellborn poet, favoured by the heavens.

Here, then, despite the disclaimer of oracular status for poetry, we find some familiar concepts being reasserted for the first time for some years: the Muses, poetic *fureur,* the divine source of inspiration; strictly poetic criteria of form, differentiated from the rules of rhetoric. As in the *Elegie à Jacques Grevin,* the true poet is opposed to mere versifiers; but now Ronsard reasserts his claim to belong to the former category. He rehearses his poetic achievements in raising the status of French poetry to equality with that of Greece and Rome (ibid., 167; 617); that he is indeed the prince of poets is demonstrated, he says, by the fact that his opponents themselves are plagiarists of his work. The Ronsard who, in 1561, was saying that he is a mere 'demy-poëte', now has this to say:

De ma plenitude
Vous estes tous remplis: je suis seul vostre estude,
Vous estes tous yssus de la grandeur de moy,
Vous estes mes sujets, et je suis vostre loy.
Vous estes mes ruisseaux, je suis vostre fonteine,
Et plus vous m'espuisés, plus ma fertile veine
Repoussant le sablon, jette une source d'eaux
D'un surjon eternel pour vous autres ruisseaux.

(ibid., 168; 617–8)

In the face of criticism, Ronsard finds new resources of self-confidence; when others, writing in the same form of argumentative poetry as he had used in the *Discours* series, have the temerity to doubt his poetic gifts, Ronsard reasserts his power – and, having done so, breaks abruptly from the type of poetry exemplified in the *Discours*.

For the *Responce* is the last poem that Ronsard wrote on the religious troubles (later additions to the series were entirely about military events, not religious and social issues). It is also the last of this series of 'popular' poems addressed to the nation at large. Ronsard's rediscovery of himself as a poet involves a casting off of the personae of government spokesman or patriotic individual.

In part, of course, non-literary developments contributed to the new orientation. The peace of Amboise seemed to promise a durable settlement; the need for the *Discours* type of poetry faded. Moreover, an edict of September 1563 forbade the publication of inflammatory literature. Ronsard used this as an excuse for withdrawing from the polemical exchange, in the prose *Epistre au lecteur, par laquelle succinctement l'autheur respond à ses calomniateurs,* which he wrote in October 1563 for the *Trois Livres du recueil des nouvelles poësies* (1563–4). The burden of this preface, as Marcel Raymond has pointed out,[1] is an assertion of the poet's liberty – liberty to choose whatever subject he wishes, to write, free of the political pressures which would make demands on his thought and dictate his subject matter.

He was, moreover, at this period becoming freer than ever before of his financial worries, and the consequent dependence on patronage. His position of *aumonier ordinaire du Roy* assured him of a regular income; and in 1564 he was to receive the more substantial reward of the abbey of Bellozane, exchanged in 1565 for the priory of Saint-Cosme, and followed the next year by that of Croixval as well. Consequently he was able, when the Cardinal de Lorraine lost his influence at court, to bid him farewell without much regret.[2]

One of his last begging letters expressing his need for financial support is the *Compleinte* he addressed to Catherine (*L* XII,

---

[1] *L'Influence de Ronsard,* volume I, p. 371.
[2] See the *Procés* (*L* XIII, 17 ff.; *Pl* I, 851 ff.).

172 ff.; *Pl* I, 865 ff.) in the same *Recueil*, which provides a further illustration of the new confidence Ronsard feels in the status of the poet. The *Compleinte* juxtaposes two themes which are familiar in Ronsard's poetry, but which at first sight accord ill with each other. On the one hand he repeats his attack on ecclesiastical abuses as in the *Discours*, in particular the giving of high offices in the church to unworthy people; on the other hand, he laments the lack of reward, in the form of ecclesiastical preferment, for himself and his fellow poets. It may seem ironical that Ronsard's financial hopes so constantly depended on the continuation of precisely the sort of abuse he criticized. But the irony is only apparent. It is clear from this poem that he genuinely believes that poets should rightly be called to church office. The words he uses are these:

> Et nous, sacré tropeau des Muses, qui ne sommes
> Usuriers, ny trompeurs, ny assassineurs d'hommes,
> Qui portons Jesuchrist dans le cueur aresté . . .

> (ibid., 181; 869)

The inspiration of the Muses is the same thing as the inspiration of God: the demand for ecclesiastical preferment is thus justified by the status of the poet as inspired priest. Thus one of the last requests he had to write to the queen, granted at last in 1564, bears witness to the fact that Ronsard, after his interlude as poet-orator, is once again asserting the role of the poet-*vates* in terms reminiscent of those of the early 1550s. The only difference is that he is now more careful to make explicit the religious significance, in Christian terminology, of the mythological concepts he uses.

The *Hymne de l'automne* (L XII, 46 ff.; *Pl* II, 239 ff.), also from the same *Recueil*, provides one of Ronsard's most emphatic assertions ever of the doctrine of poetic *fureur*, of the nature of poetry as truth veiled in a fabulous mantle – and of Ronsard's own inspiration, which he claims to have received 'le jour que je fu né' (line 1); there is no hint here that he had at any time doubted his powers, or that only two years previously he had been lamenting his degradation to the status of 'demy-poëte'.

[274]

Ronsard's political and polemical poetry

Likewise, the *Abbregé de l'art poëtique françois,* published in 1565, marks a full return to the exalted view of poetry expressed in the *Ode à Michel de l'Hospital,* again with the rider that the mythological world of the poet is simply one way of expressing religious truth: 'Car les Muses, Apollon, Mercure, Pallas et autres telles deitez ne nous representent autre chose que les puissances de Dieu, auquel les premiers hommes avoyent donné plusieurs noms pour les divers effectz de son incomprehensible majesté' (*L* XIV, 6; *Pl* II, 996). Poetry is in origin an allegorical theology clothed in 'fables plaisantes et colorées'; the poet must reverence the Muses and not involve them 'à choses deshonnestes, à risées, ny à libelles injurieux' (no more *Responces*); the poet has a moral responsibility, and must therefore be of an unimpeachable life, intellectually, morally and socially.

THE POET AND THE COURT

In the years following the first war, then, Ronsard turned from the line of development he had followed during the previous five years, and returned with all the more conviction to his original view of the status of poetry and of the poet. How does this renewed faith affect his further production of politically involved poetry?

In 1565 Catherine was assiduously cultivating relations with England. The English who, in 1562, had signed the treaty of Hampton Court with the Huguenot rebels, and who had been driven out of Le Havre in 1563, were now so much friends and allies that a marriage between Elizabeth and Charles IX was being mooted. As Ronsard had written to justify the alliance with the recent enemy Philibert de Savoie in 1559, so again he is called on to aid the diplomatic effort now: in the preface to his *Elegies, mascarades et bergerie,* dedicated 'à la majesté de la Royne d'Angleterre' in 1565, he says that he is publishing the volume at royal command, to bear witness to the 'amitié et fidelité tresassurée' of the two queens.[1]

[1] For a detailed study of this collection, see M. C. Smith, 'Ronsard and Queen Elizabeth I', *Bibliothèque d'humanisme et Renaissance,* 29 (1967), pp. 93–119.

Ronsard the poet

But one would look in vain in this volume for the type of argumentative, rhetorical discourse found in 1559. The destination of this collection is different: these are court poems, intended not primarily for the nation at large but for the élite reader. The poet makes no attempt, as in the *Exhortation pour la paix,* to argue a case for the new alliance; instead, Ronsard creates a mythological framework which provides a strictly imaginative (not to say imaginary!) interpretation of the relationship between England and France. And thirdly, only a few of the poems are directly composed for the immediate purpose of dedication to the English court; a greater proportion were composed for other occasions, in particular for festivities and events of the French court. The contribution of the poet to political events is here becoming, not a direct intervention as if he were an orator, but the indirect transformation of real life into a poetic, visionary world in which conflicts can be faced and resolved without the dire consequences of physical action.

To develop these three points further: unlike the public poetry of the period 1558–63, the poems composed for Queen Elizabeth, Dudley and, in particular, Cecil clearly show that Ronsard is writing, as he considers poetry should be written, not for the *vulgaire* but for the initiated who are able to understand the sign language of poetic fable. The opening lines of his poem *Au seigneur Cecille, secretaire de la Royne d'Angleterre* fully illustrate the sphere in which this poetry moves:

> Docte Cecille, à qui la Pieride
> A fait gouter de l'onde Aganippide,
> A descouvert les Antres Cirrheans,
> A fait danser sur les bords Pimpleans,
> A mené voir baigner en la fonteine
> Sur Helicon cette belle neufvaine
> Que Juppiter en Memoire conceut,
> Et pour sa race en pompe la receut.
> Je te confesse heureux en mille sortes,
> Non pour le nom si fameux que tu portes . . .

Ronsard's political and polemical poetry

[I omit eighteen lines of mythological allusions]

> Non pour autant que la Muse latine,
> Angloise, et Grecque a mis en ta poitrine
> Je ne sçay quoy de grand et de parfait,
> Qui passe en France, et reverer te fait
> De ces espritz à qui rien ne peut plaire
> S'il n'est du tout eslongné du vulgaire . . .
>
> (*L* XIII, 159–61; *Pl* I, 880–1)

The example is an extreme one; but it shows well the new tone that Ronsard is adopting in these poems. The poet is not aiming to sway the hearts and minds of the populace, but to write as one learned man to another, thus building the concept of alliance on the fact of a culture common to the élite on both sides of the Channel.

Poetry, then, is a form of communication between superior souls. And the superiority of the poet manifests itself—as it did in the *Hymnes,* and earlier – in his role of mythmaker: his handling of the materials from the mythological storehouse provides a visionary expression of profoundly 'true' relationships. The first poem in the *Elegies, mascarades et bergerie,* a eulogy of England addressed to Elizabeth, illustrates this reversion to the mythological vision. England, says Ronsard, was originally a floating island; Neptune, at the request of his son Proteus, attached it to a section of France, which he carved out to form an anchor. Proteus then prophesies the characteristic qualities of the land (including an amusing, but unconvincing, panegyric of English ale) and the achievements of the English nation and, finally, gives a warning against discord with France over the 'anchor'. Thus—as in the *Discours au duc de Savoie* – the material facts, such as the problem of Calais, the anchor, are incorporated into a supernatural plan; but, unlike the earlier poem, there is here no overdirect allegorization of historical events. It is a timeless image, a statement of how things are, not a narrative of how the events developed. The poet creates a picture, the contemplation of which is intended to inspire a proper attitude of 'amitié et fidelité' in the royal reader.

Ronsard, in these poems, is withdrawing from the too immediate involvement with political events which had led him to the rhetorical, argumentative poems of the preceding period. The poet is not an orator, but a painter; his task is not the direct comment on the events of the day, but the inspired, visionary assertion of underlying forces and truths. He must step back from the actual historical moment, the brutal reality of which too easily swamps the poetic vision (as in the *Discours*); instead, the vision must be a transformation of that reality, must dominate it in order to act beneficially upon it.

So it is that the *Elegies, mascarades et bergerie* do not appear in large part to be directly connected with politics at all. As Ronsard says in his preface, they contain 'les Joustes, Tournoys, Combatz, Cartelz, et Masquarades, representées en divers lieux par le commandement de sa Majesté, pour joindre et unir davantage, par tel artifice de plaisir, noz Princes de France qui estoient aucunement en discord' (*L* XIII, 36; *Pl* II, 995).

Catherine's hope of reuniting the warring families of the kingdom by bringing them together in court festivities, jousts, carnivals, ballets and the like is well known; and it easily looks like an aristocratic version of 'bread and circuses', an attempt to distract attention from the real problems of the country. In fact the policy was more seriously conceived than may appear, and was based on an application to politics of the belief in the moral and intellectual effects of culture – poetry, music, the plastic arts – propounded by the poets of the Pléiade, and lucidly analysed by Frances Yates in *The French Academies of the Sixteenth Century* (see above, chapters 3 and 4, pp. 139–40, 205), The trappings of jousts, *ballets de cour* and so on may appear trivial and childish to us; but in the period one can understand why Ronsard, precisely because he believed in the lofty status of the poet, and in the fundamental importance of poetry, should lend his pen to the composition of *cartels* (stylized challenges to joust), verses for the king in fancy-dress costume, and so on. It is all part of a serious contribution to the peace and unity of the kingdom, overcoming the violence and hatred of the preceding years in a feast of uplifting poetry and music.

In chapter 11 of her book ('The academies and court entertainments'), Dr Yates studies the particular application of academic theories to the court entertainments of the period. Her study, moving from the theory to the practical result, is based primarily on the fullest exploitation of the theory, the *Ballet comique de la Reine* of 1581. She then traces elements of this form of entertainment in earlier court festivities – the earliest being the fêtes at Fontainebleau in 1564.

From a rather different perspective, our interest here is to see how the form of the 1564 festivities arises out of the political situation of the moment, and how, in that situation, Ronsard sets about the transformation of reality in terms of his poetic theory.[1] There are several different guises for this transformation; but they all involve some form of acting out or dramatization of events, removing them from the plane of direct expression. In the context of an imaginary world, the forces, attitudes and emotions of reality can be handled safely.

The most fruitful type of transformation among these court poems is in fact only a partial transformation. It is the *Bergerie*, composed at Fontainebleau in the spring of 1564. Only one year after the cessation of hostilities which had led to so much hatred, bloodshed and devastation, to the death of Antoine de Bourbon and the assassination of François de Guise, this poem raises all the issues about which the war had been fought, in the presence of the surviving protagonists. Considerable delicacy was obviously called for.

The transformation of reality which Ronsard lights on is in the setting. He has recourse to the now familiar genre of the

[1] On the political use of the *ballet de cour* in general, see Margaret M. McGowan, *L'Art du ballet de cour en France (1581–1643)* (Paris, Centre National de la Recherche Scientifique, 1963).

eclogue;[1] this is a pastoral idyll, the participants are 'sauvages pasteurs' and, just as the beauty of nature surpasses the efforts of human artifice, he says the simple song of his shepherds will be more pleasing

> Qu'une plus curieuse et superbe chanson
> De ces maistres enflez d'une Muse hardie,
> Qui font trembler le Ciel sous une tragedie
> Où d'un vers enaigri d'une colere voix
> Jappent apres l'honneur des peuples et des Roys.

(L XIII, 77; Pl I, 918)

I have not been able to identify any specific dramatic production to which this might refer; perhaps rather, Ronsard is alluding to the bitter polemics which resulted from the *Discours* series, and stressing the new departure represented by this treatment of contemporary themes.

So we are to be treated to a rustic concert – indeed, a song contest; for each of the participants offers a rustic prize for the best song.

Another element in the setting is the choice of the 'shepherds' and 'shepherdess': Orleantin (the future Henri III, aged twelve); Angelot (François d'Anjou, aged nine); Navarrin (Henri de Navarre, later Henri IV, aged ten); Guisin (Henri de Guise, aged thirteen); and Margot (Marguerite de Valois, future wife of Henri de Navarre, aged eleven). What could be better calculated to touch the hearts of the court than the sight of the royal children playing their innocent games?[2]

Ronsard's transformation of reality in fact comes more or less to an end with this pastoral setting; for the songs of the five performers, the core of the *Bergerie,* are surprisingly direct in their treatment of the recent past. However, he now avoids

---

[1] On the genre as a whole, see A. Hulubei, *L'Églogue en France au* XVIe *siècle* (Geneva, Droz, 1938). As Ronsard remarks at the end of the *Bergerie,* he is conscious of the innovation he is introducing by using a pastoral poem for such immediately political ends.

[2] It is generally agreed that the *Bergerie* was not actually performed; but it was clearly composed with a performance in view. See *L* XIII, xv–xvii.

Ronsard's political and polemical poetry

the argument and the narrative which had formed a large part
of earlier political poems; he relies here on description and a
pathetic appeal. He creates a series of word-pictures – the
desolation of France, the greatness of Henri II, the lost age of
gold, the dawning golden age under Charles, the splendour of
France. Each of these themes allows Ronsard scope for
imaginative amplification, for rich vocabulary, for the weaving
of images, periphrases, mythology, into a texture of harmonious sound. Part of Ronsard's description of the future
golden age exemplifies this poetry well, and shows the marked
contrast with the 'prosaic' verse of the *Discours*:

> Les pins, vieux compagnons des plus hautes montagnes,
> En navires creusez ne voirront les campagnes
> De Neptune venteux, car sans voguer si loing
> La terre produira toute chose sans soing,
> Laquelle ne sera comme devant ferüe
> De rateaux bien dentez, ny de soc de charüe:
> Car les champs de leur gré, sans toreaux mugissans
> Souz le joug, se voirront de froment jaunissans.
> Les vignes n'auront peur de sentir les faucilles,
> De leur gré les sommetz des arbres bien fertilles
> Noirciront de raisins, et le clair ruisselet
> Ondoira par les fleurs et de vin et de laict.
>
> (L XIII, 109; Pl I, 934)

The historical events are thus transformed and elevated into
the higher sphere of poetic vision, here in the frame of the
golden age theme so commonly met in Ronsard's work.[1]

This poem, one of the finest written by Ronsard for political
purposes, shows one way in which he transposes the political
situation from a direct handling to an indirect approach. The
too sensitive issues are removed to an imaginary world in
which they can be safely handled, and in which the beauty of
the poetry and music (in addition to the speeches quoted, there
are stanzas for part-singing in the composition) can incline

[1] See E. Armstrong, *Ronsard and the Age of Gold* (Cambridge University
Press, 1968).

the hearers towards peace and friendship. In fact not only is this poem remarkable in itself, but it is of great historical interest; for, as has been suggested by H. Prunières,[1] the hybrid genre of music and poetry Ronsard here created is perhaps the first prefiguration of the English masque, and even has links with the growth of opera.

The *Bergerie* is the poem from this series of courtly compositions which has best stood the test of time. Apart from the intrinsic beauty of the verse, this is also due to the fact that, while the *Bergerie* is a complete performance in itself, the other court poems of the collection are contributions by Ronsard to larger productions, and do not make full sense out of context; moreover, they are productions which rely as much on music and on spectacle as they do on poetry, and it is difficult to judge the full effect when we only have a printed text before us. It is thus easy to dismiss the *cartels,* as G. Cohen does, with the remark: 'On pourra s'étonner ou s'indigner que la Cour ait employé à cela un si grand poète' (*Pl* I, 1126). But it is worth looking further at these productions, to see other elements in Ronsard's transformation of political reality into his poetic world.

Les Sereines, représentées au canal . . . de Fontainebleau (L XIII, 231 ff.; *Pl* I, 1010 ff.) is Ronsard's contribution to a larger work which also included an appearance by Neptune in a car drawn by four seahorses, and an artificial rock which opened to reveal a nymph, all with songs and instrumental music. The theme of the whole, as it is of Ronsard's two poems, is that the gods and spirits of nature had been driven into hiding in caves, rocks and underwater by the civil war; in the new era of peace being ushered in by Charles IX and his mother, they are now returning to the face of the earth. Here, then, the transformation of reality, more extensive than in the *Bergerie,* makes appeal (visual as well as verbal) to the familiar treasury of classical mythology. The political fact of peace is shown to signify at a deeper level the harmony, in time of peace, between man and natural and supernatural forces.

[1] 'Ronsard et les fêtes de cour', *Revue musicale* (May 1924), p. 35.

Ronsard's political and polemical poetry

Most curious of all, especially from the pen of so convinced a classicist as Ronsard, is the medieval tradition which is pressed into the service of the state. Perhaps we can still bear with Ronsard when he writes a *cartel* ('Apres avoir pour l'Amour combatu': *L* XIII, 197 ff.; *Pl* I, 997 ff.) for a knight prepared to give battle for his perfect love – for the neo-platonists give ample justification for seeing deep significance in that theme. But what are we to make of Ronsard composing a poem for a dramatization of episodes from that ever-popular novel despised by all good humanists, *Amadis de Gaule*? For the *cartel* 'Demeure, Chevalier, et en la mesme place' was written for an entertainment in which an enchanted castle guarded by six knights was attacked by six other knights; the message of Ronsard's poem is that the enchantment makes the castle impregnable to all except those who have remained perfectly loyal to their lady.[1] How are the mighty fallen . . .! The key lies in the *dramatis personae* of the performance itself: the six knights guarding the castle were the Prince de Condé, leader of the Huguenots, and his friends; the victorious attackers were Charles IX and his companions. In the fantasy world of medieval chivalry, the battles of yesteryear are defused by being transformed into sport.[2]

It is in this vein of the full transformation of political reality into medieval or classical pageant or entertainment that much of Ronsard's later political poetry was written. He composed *cartels* for a tournament at Bar-le-Duc, poems for the Bayonne interview of 1565, songs for Cupid and Mercury at the wedding of Henri de Navarre and Marguerite de Valois in 1572, and contributed to the celebrations at the wedding of the Duc de Joyeuse in 1581. In the form in which they survive, divorced from the musical and visual context for which they were designed, these poems form an unimpressive conclusion indeed to the career of the poet of the *Discours* and the *Bergerie*. By

[1] See Laumonier's notes for the sources in *Amadis* of this encounter.
[2] Childish it may seem, but we might compare it with the philosophy behind the modern Olympic Games, and the place of table-tennis in Chinese diplomacy in 1971.

Ronsard the poet

their nature they are necessarily short, piecemeal contributions to a larger whole. Moreover, despite the grandeur of the theory that cultural activities could make a positive contribution to the state of the nation, there was the obvious tendency for the pageantry and display to become an end in itself, losing the symbolism which first inspired it, degenerating into mere entertainment; as Francis Bacon later wrote of the English masque, 'These Things are but Toyes.'

Finally, the aspiration to peace through poetry was bitterly refuted by events. The marriage of Henri de Navarre and Marguerite de Valois was the occasion for a whole month of entertainments of the sort we have been examining; at the end of the month the costumes were cast off, and the fairytale makebelieve turned into the real-life massacre of St Bartholomew. One has only to look at the fates in the 1580s of 'Orleantin', 'Guisin', and 'Navarrin' from the *Bergerie* to see writ large the failure of Catherine's policy of peace through court entertainments, and the failure of the Pléiade and the Academy actually to achieve any moral effects through music and poetry.

Ronsard himself seems to have been conscious of the inadequacy of this resolution of his problem of the poet and the state. We learn from the *Estreines au Roy Henry III* (L XVII, 85 ff.; *Pl* I, 800 ff.), presented to the king in December 1574, that he had offered to write satirical poetry for Charles IX, but that Charles's death had put an end to the project. Had Ronsard been intending a return to the genre of the *Discours*? At least it would have given more scope than court ballet did to the poet's persona of moral mentor to the great. He renewed the offer to Henri III, in his *Estreines*, but Henri did not take it up. Indeed, the moral and political advice Ronsard gave Henri in his *Discours au Roy* (1575), reminiscent of the *Institution du Roy Charles IX*, appears to have displeased the royal ear. Lebègue suggests this as the reason why 'soixante-sept vers d'objurgations' (lines 183–249; L XVII, 28–30) were excised from the second edition.[1] Instead, Ronsard, like Baïf, Pontus

[1] 'Ronsard poète officiel', p. 585.

de Tyard and Desportes, was called on to give discourses – in prose – on the intellectual and moral virtues to the Palace Academy, in a context so totally divorced from current realities that criticism of these debates was widespread.[1]

In the final years of his life the most significant political poems Ronsard wrote were the ones he did not publish: a poem to Moreau, 'trésorier de l'Espargne' (*L* XVIII, 299 ff.; *Pl* II, 667 ff.), the verses *Au Roy Charles IX* (*L* XVIII, 403 ff.; *Pl* II, 964 ff.) and the *Caprice: au seigneur Simon Nicolas* (*L* XVIII, 315 ff.; *Pl* II, 674 ff.), all of them published after his death. As poetry they are unimpressive enough to have made some editors doubt their authenticity; but it is interesting to see that Ronsard's disillusion with political affairs leads him to turn his satire against the royal house he had so faithfully served.

Ronsard's exploration and experimentation in the field of political poetry is a story which ends in a sort of defeat. The final resolution of the conflict between poetic ideal and political requirement is singularly unsatisfying, and runs out in the sands of courtly makebelieve. Yet in the course of the story, Ronsard achieved some of his most original creations. From the tensions which surrounded him, from the irreconcilable exigencies of political intrigue, religious belief, poetic convictions, personal finance and social status, Ronsard was led to formulate a range of remarkable poems – the *Discours,* the *Remonstrance,* the *Responce,* the *Bergerie* – which were central to his reputation in his own age, and which still represent high points in the vast corpus of his works. As is so often the case, the most outstanding work is the product of unresolved tensions, not the product of problems solved.

[1] See Yates, *French Academies,* pp. 32–4.

Ronsard's later poetry

ODETTE DE MOURGUES

The first ten years in Ronsard's poetic production are so rich and so varied that they seem both to contain and to herald all the rest of his work – with perhaps the exception of his political poems and of the *Franciade*. Even more than being a triumphal arch opening up the succession of poetic achievements, they reveal the perspective of the long colonnade and determine its main structural features, down to the very end of the vista. I am here concerned with the western arch, the last ten years in the poet's life – that is roughly with his works published or written between 1574 and 1584 – and am constantly tempted to look back to earlier poems.

Some of the later masterpieces possess the same degree of typically Ronsardian perfection as did the best among the more youthful poems. The same qualities of poise, restraint and delicate stylization are equally present in the famous sonnet 'Comme on voit sur la branche' (1578) and in the no less famous ode to Cassandre, 'Mignonne, allon voir . . .' (1553). Such basic qualities undoubtedly need further examination. But the more closely we look at the texts, the more we notice to what a surprising extent Ronsard has been faithful not only to certain themes but also to certain techniques, to certain stylistic preferences. This does not mean that the vein of inspiration is exhausted. There are subtle changes and we all know that Ronsard constantly corrected and modified his works. Moreover, and this is perhaps the most interesting point, this

terminal arch, so harmoniously integrated in the whole architectural complex, bathes in a different light – the poet is only
too conscious that it faces the setting sun.

It is this double aspect of Ronsard's later poetry – permanence and alteration – which I propose to consider. Not
that I can do so in an exhaustive manner. I shall only examine
a few aspects of the poet's art which are particularly significant.

MOVEMENT AND SOLIDITY

Movement seems one of the most important elements in
Ronsard's poetry, and by that I mean at the same time his
preference for a world picture in motion and his recurrent
choice of a dynamic structure for a line or a poem (see also
above, chapter 1, pp. 26–34).

From the very beginning of his career the beauty and sensuous appeal of a woman's hair is given through the suggestion
of moving water and of a capricious dance of curls:

> Soit que son or se crespe lentement
> Ou soit qu'il vague en deux glissantes ondes,
> Qui ça qui là par le sein vagabondes,
> Et sur le col, nagent follastrement . . .
>
> (*L* IV, 77; *Pl* I, 40)

We note also in those early love sonnets the vigour in the
rendering of movements, either downwards:

> Quand le Soleil à chef renversé plonge
> Son char doré dans le sein du viellard
>
> (ibid., 51; 26)

(the boldness of the semi-personification of the ocean being
intensified by the giddy violence of the charioteer who drives
into it) or upwards:

> Nét, libre, et nud, je vole d'un plein sault,
> Oultre le ciel, pour adorer là hault
> L'aultre beaulté dont la tienne est venue.
>
> (ibid., 135; 75)

Ronsard's later poetry

Would another poet have translated so paradoxically the craving of the soul for a platonic heaven in terms of the muscular vertical movement of a young athlete's body leaping beyond the stars to land among the gods?

Throughout the years the Ronsardian landscape remains characterized by the flight of birds, by flowing rivers and swaying boughs. This concern for the fascinating mobility of the natural world leads to the adoption of some devices well-suited to express the harmony of recurrent movements. I shall look more closely at one, among many others, of his favourite devices. It is particularly successful in the following lines, taken from *L'Hylas,* published in 1569, in which Ronsard describes the teasing game of the wind playing with the shadows of trees over the surface of a pool:

> Un ombre lent par petite secousse,
> Erroit dessus, ainsy que le vent *pousse,*
> *Pousse* et *repousse* et *pousse* sur les eaux
> L'entrelassure ombreuse des rameaux . . .
>> (*L* XV, 244; *Pl* II, 386:
> the italics are mine in this and the following examples)

This technique of repetition, plus variations, keeps reappearing in the later poems. It may again be connected with water:

> J'aimois le cours suivy d'une longue rivière,
> Et voir *onde sur onde* allonger sa carrière,
> Et *flot à l'autre flot* en roulant s'attacher,
>> (*L* XVIII, 34; *Pl* I, 276)

or it may render the swift purposeful flutter of the bees:

> gentilles avettes,
> Lesquelles en volant de *sillons en sillons,*
> De *jardins en jardins* . . .
>> (*L* XVII, 381; *Pl* II, 50–1)

or on the contrary the slow, insidious and powerful twining of ivy round a tree, with its sensual suggestion of the tightening pressure of a close embrace:

Ronsard the poet

Vous triomphez de moy, et pource je vous donne
Ce lhierre, qui coule et se glisse à l'entour
Des arbres et des murs, lesquels *tour dessus tour,*
Plis dessus plis il serre, embrasse et environne.

(L XVII, 327; Pl I, 254)

It may even be found in connection with abstract material, for instance the progressive accumulation of misfortunes in the royal family:

Des deux freres à peine estoit clos le tombeau,
Que voicy *dueil sur dueil, pleur dessus pleur* nouveau,
Trespas dessus trespas, misere sur misere.

(L XVII, 71; Pl II, 484)

One might be tempted to think of the pattern as being by this time a mannerism of Ronsard, a convenient device, too convenient in fact not to be suspected of facility. This is only partly true. The recurrence of this rhetorical pattern has a deeper significance: like a minor echo of the music of the spheres, it seems to have been for Ronsard a way to catch and stylize the delicate beat in the pulse of nature, so that it becomes for him, consciously or unconsciously, the familiar rhythm of what in the world flows, flies, runs, creeps, throbs, increases or decreases.

The device is never used crudely. It is sometimes no more than one of several elements destined to express a movement; thus it combines with sound effects and pauses in the line to conjure up the death of the rose:

Languissante elle meurt *fueille à fueille* déclose . . .

(L XVII, 125; Pl I, 184)

Also Ronsard's technique to suggest movement is not restricted to a few devices. Undoubtedly his inventiveness in matters of rhythm or vocabulary and his skill in the placing of a word or the use of a run-on line give him immense resources. At the beginning of the sonnet from which the last quotation is taken – 'Comme on voit sur la branche au mois de May la rose' – the art with which the poet delays the mention of the rose until the very end of the line not only sets the flower in evidence but

Ronsard's later poetry

also, coming after the lilt of a ternary rhythm, the rose seems to sway gently at the extremity of a flexible stem, as the word does at the end of the line.[1] We are bound also to remember the well-known passage in the elegy *Contre les bucherons de la forest de Gastine* where Ronsard uses imitative music (among other elements) to illustrate the gentle yet powerful undulation produced by an invisible zephyr over a large mass of trees:

> et en lieu de tes bois,
> Dont l'ombrage incertain lentement se remue . . .
> > (*L* XVIII, 145; *Pl* II, 117)

Nature is not prone to erratic steps or unpredictable jerks, and she rarely stumbles. What appeals to Ronsard both as an artist and as a Renaissance thinker is her harmonious regularity, the seemingly effortless perfection of her dynamism. It is not surprising therefore that the dance motif should attract Ronsard as a pattern and even as a theme in itself. In fact this was partly implied in the device of repetition which I have mentioned. This theme of dancing is very much in evidence in the later works. It was certainly present in the early poems but the passing reference to 'le bal de tant d'astres divers' in one of the sonnets to Cassandre (*L* IV, 29; *Pl* I, 13) was only the germ of what becomes an elaborate cosmic ballet, the 'danse éthérée' of the stars in the ode *Les Estoilles* published in 1575 (*L* XVII, 37–44; *Pl* II, 196–200).

The dance of the heavenly bodies is impressively majestic. More humble citizens in the natural world can also dance and Ronsard does not overlook the graceful rhythmical flitting of the will-o'-the-wisp:

> Un prompt Ardent sur les eaux esclairant,
> Tantost deça, tantost delà courant
> De place en place, et repos ne se donne . . .
> > (*La Charite*: *L* XVII, 172; *Pl* I, 350, somewhat modified)

[1] Cf. the analysis of this sonnet by Marcel Raymond, *Baroque et Renaissance poétique* (Paris, Corti, 1955), pp. 111–15. The whole chapter devoted to Ronsard should be read; the present study owes much to Marcel Raymond's views on the problems of structure in Ronsard's poetry.

Ronsard the poet

The lightness of the dance of the will-o'-the-wisp is mentioned in the poem as a comparison, to illustrate the 'bonds légers' of Queen Marguerite dancing 'la volte Provençalle' with her brother, the king (see above, chapter 5, pp. 235–6).

Dancing was obviously a favourite pastime at the court and it is very understandable that Ronsard as a court poet should celebrate such an event as a ball like any other pageant, and he did so in several poems. It would be wrong, I think, to dismiss this aspect of his later poetry as being no more than pandering to the frivolous tastes of royal patrons. The theme proves singularly rich in suggestions attractive to the poet.

Perhaps for human beings dancing is a way of escaping the clumsy heaviness of their ordinary pace, a chance to come halfway between their earthly condition and that of the gods who can fly and whose steps are miraculously attuned to a harmonious cadenza:

> Comme une femme elle ne marchoit pas,
> Mais en roulant divinement le pas,
> D'un pied glissant couloit à la cadance.
>   L'homme pesant marche dessus la place,
> Mais un Dieu vole, et ne sçauroit aller:
> Aux Dieux legers appartient le voler,
> Comme engendrez d'une eternelle race.

(ibid.)

Man can, however, invent most intricate ballets with complicated evolutions and a kaleidoscopic succession of figures. Such is the fascination for the eye and for the mind of a mock-tournament patterned as a ballet, in which the movements of horses and riders, both co-ordinated and unpredictable, dazzle the spectator by their endless variations:

> Tantost vous les voirrez à courbettes danser,
> Tantost se reculer, s'approcher, s'avancer,
> S'escarter, s'esloigner, se serrer, se rejoindre
> D'une pointe allongée, et tantost d'une moindre,
> Contrefaisant la guerre au semblant d'une paix,
> Croizez, entrelassez de droit et de biais,

Ronsard's later poetry

Tantost en forme ronde, et tantost en carrée,
Ainsi qu'un Labyrinth, dont la trace esgarée
Nous abuse les pas en ses divers chemins.
   Ainsi qu'on voit danser en la mer les Dauphins,
Ainsi qu'on voit voler par le travers des nuës
En diverses façons une troupe de Grues.

(L XVIII, 111; Pl I, 1034)

Note the final comparisons with dolphins and cranes. Just as dancing mirrors in a fragile but precious way the harmonious movements of deities, this essentially artificial creation reproduces, unconsciously, the most beautiful moving patterns in nature.

In one of the sonnets to Hélène (L XVII, 270–1; Pl I, 262; see also above, chapter 2, pp. 114–15) we find, in a superbly condensed form, all those elements which make dancing a *moment privilégié* among the various activities of man: the loveliness of the ever-changing pattern, the imitation of nature – be it the winding meanders of a river or the flight of birds – and the divine spark which magically transfigures the dancer:

Le soir qu'Amour vous fist en la salle descendre
Pour danser d'artifice un beau ballet d'Amour,
Voz yeux, bien qu'il fust nuict, ramenerent le jour,
Tant ils sceurent d'esclairs par la place respandre.
   Le ballet fut divin, qui se souloit reprendre,
Se rompre, se refaire, et tour dessus retour
Se mesler, s'escarter, se tourner à l'entour,
Contre-imitant le cours du fleuve de Meandre.
   Ores il estoit rond, ores long, or' estroit,
Or' en poincte, en triangle, en la façon qu'on voit
L'escadron de la Gruë evitant la froidure.
   Je faux, tu ne dansois, mais ton pied voletoit
Sur le haut de la terre: aussi ton corps s'estoit
Transformé pour ce soir en divine nature.

The dance motif implies tight control over movements,

Ronsard the poet

balance in the laying-out of poetic material, and as such connects the element of fluidity in Ronsard with another important feature of his art: the extreme care for solidity in the structure of a poem. This was also apparent in his first poetic productions. The building up of the Pindaric odes, heaping Pelion upon Ossa, as a lofty pedestal for the Muses, required, given the massive quality of the substance chosen, an exact calculation of the weight each stanza should carry and an impeccable sense of proportion – despite the poetic fallacy of inspired frenzy.

Concern for solid structures can be seen throughout the poet's career, even in the poems where the lightness of rhythm and the near-absence of rhetoric give to the resilient framework a kind of transparency. This basic order and stability enable Ronsard to experiment boldly with dynamic patterns, the boldest experiment being perhaps a mid-career masterpiece, the first fifty-two lines of the *Elegie à Marie Stuart* (*L* XIV, 152–4; *Pl* II, 293–5). These lines, published in 1567, which have been admirably analysed by Marcel Raymond (*Baroque et Renaissance poétique*, pp. 140–4), offer an extreme complexity of structure as they deal simultaneously with three different planes: the portrait of Marie Stuart, the memory of Marie Stuart walking in the park of Fontainebleau, and the vision of the galleon sailing on the waves to take the queen away from France. The constant shifting of elements in this three-dimensional picture is organized, through rhythmical devices and apposite imagery, into a spiral movement which might suggest a restless succession of metamorphoses if it were not that the equilibrium of the poem is strongly secured by the tightness of crossreferences and the unity of colour; a 'rapsodie en blanc mineur', to use Marcel Raymond's words.

The later works also offer some remarkable illustrations of the search for unified structures: the plan of the elegy *Contre les bucherons de la forest de Gastine* may well have been, as Professor McFarlane has shown,[1] partly dictated by a risky mosaic

[1] I. D. McFarlane, 'Neo-Latin verse: some new discoveries', *Modern Language Review*, 54 (1959), pp. 24–8.

of elements borrowed from different sources. The result, however, achieves unity and progression.

But the most interesting poems are those in which dynamism and stability appear as two complementary elements. My first illustration is the ode, *Les Estoilles*, which I have briefly mentioned already. It is a long poem and, in quoting it, I shall leave out a few stanzas but will supply the missing links.

Les Estoilles envoyées à Monsieur de Pibrac
en Polonne

Ode

O, des Muses la plus faconde
Ma Calliope conte moy
L'influs des Astres, et pourquoy
Tant de fortunes sont au monde.
    Discourant mille fois
    Ensemble par les bois,
    Emerveillés nous sommes
    Des flambeaux de la nuict,
    Et du change qui suit
    La nature des hommes.

Chante moy du ciel la puissance,
Et des Estoilles la valeur,
D'où le bon-heur et le mal-heur
Vient aux mortelz dés la naissance.
    Soit qu'il faille deslors
    Regarder que noz corps
    Des mottes animees,
    Et des arbres crevés,
    Nasquirent eslevés,
    Comme plantes semees:

Soit qu'on regarde au long espace
De tant de siecles empanés,
Qui legers de pieds retournés
Se suyvent d'une mesme trace

[295]

Ronsard the poet

On cognoistra que tout
Prend son estre et son bout
Des celestes chandelles,
Que le Soleil ne void
Rien ça bas qui ne soit
En servage sous elles.

De là, les semences des fleuves
Sortent et rentrent dans la mer:
De là, les terres font germer
Tous les ans tant de moissons neuves:
 De là, naissent les fleurs
 Les glaces, les chaleurs,
 Les pluyes printanieres:
 De là, faut que chacun
 Souffre l'arrest commun
 Des Parques filandieres.

En vain l'homme de sa priere
Vous tourmente soir et matin
Il est trainé par son destin,
Comme est un flot de sa riviere,
 Ou comme est le tronçon
 D'un arraché glaçon,
 Qui roule à la traverse,
 Ou comme un tronc froissé
 Que le vent courroucé
 Culbute à la renverse.

Bref les humaines creatures
Sont de Fortune le jouët:
De sus le rond de son rouët
Elle tourne noz avantures.
 Le sage seulement
 Aura commandement
 Sur vostre espaisse bande,
 Et sur vous aura lieu
 L'homme sainct qui craint Dieu,
 Car Dieu seul vous commande.

Ronsard's later poetry

Nostre esprit, une flame agile
Qui vient de Dieu, depend de soy,
Au corps vous donnez vostre loy,
Comme un potier à son argile.
    Du corps le jour dernier
    Ne differe au premier
    C'est une chaisne estrainte:
    Ce qui m'est ordonné
    Au poinct que je fu né
    Je le suy par contrainte.

. . . .

L'un de la mer court les orages
Enfermant sa vie en du bois,
L'autre, pressant le Cerf d'abbois
Devient Satyre des bocages.
    L'un sans peur de meschef
    Bat d'un superbe chef
    Le cercle de la Lune,
    Qui tombe outrecuidé
    Pour n'avoir bien guidé
    Les brides de Fortune.

L'un valet de sa panse pleine,
Pourceau d'Epicure otieux,
Mange en un jour de ses Ayeux
Les biens acquis à grande peine.
    Ce guerrier qui tantost
    Terre et mer d'un grand Ost
    Couvroit de tant de voiles,
    Court de teste et de nom
    Pendille à Mont-faucon:
    Ainsi vous plaist, Estoilles.

Et toutesfois loing des miseres
Qu'aux mortels vous versez icy,
Vous mocquez de nostre soucy
Tournant voz courses ordinaires,

Ronsard the poet

Et n'avez peur de rien
Tant que le fort lien
De la saincte Nature
Tient ce monde arresté,
Et que la magesté
Du grand Juppiter dure.

Du Ciel les ministres vous estes
Et agreable n'avez pas
Qu'un autre face rien ça bas
Ny là haut, si vous ne le faictes.
Astres qui tout voyez,
Ou soit que vous soyez
Des bosses allumees,
Ou des testes de cloux
Ardantes de feu roux
Dans le Ciel enfermees:

Je vous salue, heureuses flammes,
Estoilles filles de la Nuict,
Et ce Destin qui nous conduit,
Que vous pendistes à nos trames.
Tandis que tous les jours
Vous devidez voz cours
D'une dance aetheree:
Endurant je vivray,
Et la chance suyvray
Que vous m'avez livree.

(*L* XVII, 37–44; *Pl* II, 196–200)

The first stanza gives the double theme of the poem: belief in astrology and admiration for the beauty of the stars. Stanzas 2, 3 and 4 deal with the power of the stars over nature. Stanzas 5, 6 and 7 are devoted to their influence on man in general, and stanzas 8, 9 (these two being omitted), 10 and 11 their influence on some particular individuals. The next three stanzas praise the serene indifference, the supreme power and glory of the stars. I have left out the last two stanzas in which the poet asks those arbiters of fate, despite their implacable aloofness, to protect France and his friend Pibrac.

What is immediately striking in this ode is the range of material Ronsard includes and more especially the great difference in size between the various objects he mentions. Some are impressively large: the sun, the moon, the sea, time measured by centuries, whereas others are comparatively – or even by any standard – very much smaller: clods of earth, flowers, an icicle, a tree trunk. As a rule the result of placing in a poem, side by side, large and small things is to reduce automatically the larger items to the size of the smaller. (It may be a deliberate technique on the part of the poet or an unconscious distortion in his poetic vision.)[1]

Here we find nothing of the sort. The proportions of the world have not altered. We are not faced with a diminutive universe, but with a vast picture in which the space taken by each item seems exactly right according to our normal scale. This successful effect is achieved first by the constant movement which links each thing mentioned with the next. Objects are not juxtaposed, but born out of each other and they change according to the will of stars. Our bodies have their germs in lumps of earth and dead trees, water originates from the sea, falls as rain, gathers into rivers and goes back to the sea. Centuries follow each other in endless succession; so do the seasons, cold, wet and warm in turn, and every year the earth yields its bounty of flowers and corn. And man's fate follows the same ineluctable course. There is no break in the sequence of events, no pause.

Verbs and images stress the element of movement. The 'Parques filandieres', the 'rouët' of Fortune, the words 'trame' and 'devidez' bring three times into the poem the suggestion of the unwinding of a thread. Man is like a plaything dragged by the strong current of a river and the pressure of the wind. The rhythm helps to produce the impression of unbroken movement. This is particularly marked in the fifth stanza

[1] Some examples of this can be found in the landscape painting of the Libertin poets and in Théophile Gautier's *Émaux et camées*.

where a long sentence, made up of a succession of subordinate clauses with strongly articulated and repeated conjunctions, suggests a rolling motion which could go on for ever. Order rules this unceasing movement. Its harmonious nature is underlined by the pattern of a dance, by the stress on regular recurrence and by the general impression of a closed circuit. The winged feet of centuries 'se suyvent d'une mesme trace'. Water comes from the sea and goes back there. Several images conjure up the idea of the circle: 'le rouët' of fortune, 'le cercle de la lune'; and the circle is the symbol of perfect unity.

The unity and solidity of the universe are also preserved by the rhythmical structure of the poem, through the pattern of the stanzas. Although each stanza seems to follow the preceding one without interruption, as if gently sliding forward, the recurrent octosyllabic lines secure the wholeness of the basic unit. The impeccable balance between dynamism and solidity does not detract from the feeling of wonder at the mysterious beauty of the stars. Their light illuminates the poem. And here again we find movement and stability: light appears either as the lively nimbleness of a flame or as blazing bosses solidly affixed to the sky.

My second illustration is a much shorter poem, taken from the *Sonets pour Helene*:

Afin qu'à tout jamais de siecle en siecle vive
La parfaite amitié que Ronsard vous portoit,
Comme vostre beauté la raison luy ostoit,
Comme vous enlassez sa liberté captive:
Afin que d'âge en âge à noz neveux arrive,
Que toute dans mon sang vostre figure estoit,
Et que rien sinon vous mon cœur ne souhaitoit,
Je vous fais un present de ceste Sempervive.
Elle vit longuement en sa jeune verdeur.
Long temps apres la mort je vous feray revivre,
Tant peut le docte soin d'un gentil serviteur,

Ronsard's later poetry

Qui veut, en vous servant, toutes vertus ensuivre.
Vous vivrez (croyez moy) comme Laure en grandeur,
Au moins tant que vivront les plumes et le livre.

(L XVII, 248; Pl I, 243)

The general meaning of the sonnet is fairly straightforward
and the theme is a familiar one: the poet's verse will give
immortality to the lady. But the structure of the poem reveals
an interesting complexity.

The first seven lines are marked by a continuous ascending
movement, with just a breathing space at the end of the first
quatrain. The rhetorical devices – repetition of the 'Afin que',
the dignified lilt of the echoing 'siecle en siecle', 'âge en âge'
emphasize the lofty and triumphant assurance of this motion
upwards. In spite of the element of repetition, the symmetry
between the first and second quatrain is only partial symmetry:
the gentle if insistent movement of the third and fourth lines
('Comme vostre beauté . . . Comme vous enlassez . . .') is
replaced by the more vigorous effect of the conjunctions 'Que
toute . . . Et que . . .' This affects the quality of the progression
and adds a note of urgency, the more so as the stress falls on
words as abrupt in sound and absolute in meaning as 'toute'
and 'rien'.

The movement stops at the eighth line, as if on the flat top
of that kind of step pyramid which has been built up from the
beginning of the poem, and there the poet lays his offering of
the symbolical plant, the 'Sempervive'. Then movement starts
again but becomes linear: the next four lines focusing on an
indeterminate stretch of time, a long, long time going beyond
death, made to appear even longer because the sentence of the
first tercet goes on into the second. The final line closes the
vista of endless time by setting a limit to survival and, so to
speak, freezes the whole movement towards immortality,
leaving us with the solid and only evidence of the poet's victory
over time, 'le livre'.

The variations in movement, the pause at the centre of the
sonnet to set off the apparent simplicity of a deceptively simple

offering, the balance between harmonious movement and self-assured stability are very much connected with Ronsard's particular attitude to the theme. Pride is inherent in the subject. Hélène's immortality, although linked with some personal qualities (her beauty), is essentially dependent on the will and fame of Ronsard; the mention of the poet himself in the second line, of 'mon sang', 'mon cœur' and even more the assertion of a gratuitous gift 'je vous ferai revivre' leave no doubt of it. But the vicarious life promised to Hélène is not as secure as it might seem. In spite of the reassurance given by the repeated use of the verb 'vivre' (in key positions in the general structure of the poem), survival becomes a matter for speculation, and at best for wishful thinking. The magnificent hyperbolical opening of the sonnet, the uncompromising assertions, the absolute tenor of words such as 'à tout jamais', 'parfaite', 'toute', 'rien' give place to more relative affirmations. The plant which, in essence, is everlasting, 'Sempervive', is then viewed in terms of protracted youth, the 'à tout jamais' becomes 'Long temps apres la mort'. The last line of the poem, both triumphant and subdued, suggests an ambiguous victory, a curtailed immortality. Books may not live for ever and yet they are the only answer to the threat of oblivion.

This sonnet, in a different way from *Les Estoilles,* shows Ronsard's complete mastery over the complex structure of a poem, and the perfect balance he can achieve between movement and solidity, whether he deals with a large cosmic picture or with a short meditation on *gloire*.

NEARNESS AND DISTANCE

However near to reality a poem happens to be there is always, of necessity, a gap between the subject matter chosen by the writer – be it a landscape, a feeling or a commonplace – and its poetic treatment. I am not concerned here, at least not directly, with the question of deciding to what extent Ronsard was abiding by the Renaissance theories on close imitation of nature and the criterion of truth,[1] but rather with a more general problem of perspective which affects the poetry of any period and is specially interesting in the case of Ronsard. For it seems that the impression of rich variety given by his works depends much less on the variety of subjects than on the variety of treatment and more particularly the different degrees of closeness or distance, which introduce considerable modifications inside an already familiar poetic world. The same theme may be endowed with such a lifelike quality as to bring it within reach of tangible experience, may even suggest a very personal concern on the part of the writer, or it may assume a quality of extreme remoteness or else be poised halfway between convention and reality, keeping us wondering about the amount of seriousness the poet intended to convey. The distance which separates a subject from its aesthetic expression is of course carefully measured and reveals, in its variations, not only the flexibility of Ronsard's technique, but also certain shifts of emphasis in the way he looks at the world and at himself.

Perspective changes with age. The last period of his life brings oscillations and readjustments in the distancing and focusing of his poetic vision, as all the themes he has so often sung – nature, mythology, the court, love and death – either recede into a fictional background or, on the contrary, come to the foreground.

The concrete world – colours, forms, textures, scents and sounds – has constantly been present in the poetry of Ronsard and it is when he deals with material objects, natural or man-made, that we might expect the closest approach, the strongest impression of immediate experience. But it is not always so. In fact what we find is a skilful 'dosage' of the concrete element so that it should fit exactly into the overall composition of a given poem. Stylization may transfer the rose into a beautiful symbol and retain of its appearance only either the colour, a regal crimson ('Mignonne, allon voir si la rose . . .'), or its

---

[1] For a *mise au point* of this question I refer the reader to Grahame Castor's *Pléiade Poetics* (Cambridge University Press, 1964), and more particularly to chapter 5, 'Imitation of nature'.

pervading scent ('Comme on voit sur la branche . . .'); and link for ever 'la vigne' and 'l'ormeau' to sensual love in nature or in man.

At other times, on the contrary, an appearance of realism implies a direct approach to flowers and plants. In the poem *La Salade,* published in 1569, Ronsard invites his secretary, Jamyn, and the reader to go into a country kitchen garden, and to follow him closely:

> Lave ta main blanche, gaillarde et nette,
> Suy mes talons, aporte une serviette,
> Allon cueillir la salade. . . .
>
>   Tu t'en iras, Jamyn, d'une autre part
> Chercher songneux, la boursette toffuë;
> La pasquerette à la fueille menuë,
> La pimprenelle heureuse pour le sang,
> Et pour la ratte et pour le mal de flanc,
> Et je cueill'ray, compagne de la mousse,
> La responsette à la racine douce,
> Et le bouton de nouveaux groiseliers
> Qui le Printemps annoncent les premiers.
>
> (*L* XV, 76, 77; *Pl* II, 347)

The brisk opening of the poem, the individualization of each plant through its name, its distinctive features and its medicinal properties (rather than its beauty) compel us to bend down and look for the burnet, the daisy or the lamb's lettuce. The homeliness of the atmosphere (underlined by the suggestion of old wives' remedies), the tone of unsophisticated alacrity add to the impression of a familiar everyday reality.

I have used the term 'realism' – probably rashly, as it is so anachronistic; but the precision of botanical terms reminds us that the use of technical vocabulary may be one way of achieving a faithful and objective picture of a thing and a means of bringing it nearer to the reader.[1] It is certainly the case here.

[1] Du Bellay in his *Deffense et illustration* had advocated the use of proper words borrowed from the specialized terminology of arts and crafts. Ronsard also, judging from his *Art poëtique* and the preface to *La Franciade,* insisted on this form of realistic accuracy, particularly in the epic.

Ronsard's later poetry

However, the result may be quite different. Ronsard's later poetry contains some interesting examples of the curious effect an extreme technicality in the choice of words can produce:

> C'estoit un Meleagre au mestier de chasser:
> Il sçavoit par-sur tous laisser *courre* et *lancer,*
> Bien *demesler* d'un Cerf les ruses et la *feinte,*
> *Le bon temps, le vieil temps, l'essuy, le rembuscher,*
> *Les gangnages, la nuict, le lict* et *le coucher,*
> Et bien prendre *le droict,* et bien *faire l'enceinte.*
> Et comme s'il fust nay d'une Nymphe des bois,
> Il jugeoit un vieil Cerf à la *perche,* aux *espois,*
> A la *meule, andouillers* et à *l'embrunisseure* . . .
> *(Amours d'Eurymedon et de Calliree;* L XVII, 150–1;
> *Pl* I, 196) (italics are mine)

I shall not quote any further and refer the reader to the footnotes of the Laumonier edition for the elucidation of the italicized words. Whatever the quibbles of the experts as to whether Ronsard was strictly accurate or slightly fanciful in his selection of technical terms, there is no doubt that the intention here is to provide his mythical hero with a solid and forceful sixteenth-century background, based on the contemporary sport. This form of realism can only appeal to the initiated and this one would presume the court circle to be. But even those conversant with this highly specialized vocabulary would not have the illusion of being present at the kill; the concrete reality of the huntsman and of the stag is pushed back, out of sight, behind the closely knit screen of technicalities, which becomes an end in itself and is no more than an abstract tribute to the noble art of hunting.

Yet, as a rule, during the last period of Ronsard's life his evocation of the natural world – animals, plants or trees – is very much in keeping with the subtle handling of concrete elements which characterizes all his work. Whatever the distance stylization and ornamentation can create between

[305]

nature and its poetic rendering, a slight but skilful touch will preserve some precious quality of the real world:

> Ne vois-tu d'autre part les Nymphes dans ces prez
> Esmaillez, peinturez, verdurez, diaprez,
> D'un poulce delicat moissonner les fleurettes . . .
>
> (*L* XVII, 381; *Pl* II, 50)

The precise, careful gesture of the nymph breaks the glittering solidity of the overdecorated meadows and gives back to the flowers their lifelike fragility without detracting from the stylized loveliness of springtime.

It is clear when we come to some of the last masterpieces that the Ronsardian landscape has in the course of the years developed features of its own, that it is regulated by an inescapable symbolism coloured by reminiscences not only of classical poets but also of Ronsard's own works. More skill is needed to balance the various elements and to calculate the ideal distance between reality and imagination.

A poem like the *Stances de la fontaine d'Helene* shows admirably the composite nature of such a landscape. The poem is in principle a love poem and the fountain is used not only to glorify Hélène but also as a convenient prop for petrarchan antitheses:

> Tantost ceste fontaine est froide comme glace,
> Et tantost elle jette une ardente liqueur.
> Deux contraires effects je sens, quand elle passe,
> Froide dedans la bouche, et chaude dans mon cœur.
>
> (*L* XVII, 287; *Pl* I, 272)

The sufferings of the lover are not overstressed, however, and our attention is directed towards the various creatures, real or imaginary, which inhabit the stream and the waterside. Literary reminiscences are present in every stanza (Theocritus, Virgil, Horace, Ariosto and many others) and classical mythology very much in evidence: nymphs, dryads and hamadryads, Echo and inevitably Narcissus. But the lightness with which the convention of the unhappy lover is blended with classical allusions prevents either artificial element from weighing too heavily over the clear fountain:

> Vous qui refraischissez ces belles fleurs vermeilles,
> Petits freres ailez, Favones et Zephirs,
> Portez de ma Maistresse aux ingrates oreilles,
> En volant parmy l'air, quelcun de mes souspirs.
>
> (ibid.)

The latinism 'Favones' (the west wind), probably straight from Lucretius or Catullus, is partly neutralized by the proximity of the familiar and tender 'Petits freres ailez'. Even more significant is to find in the same stanza (lines 29–32) a bird belonging to a noble classical tradition, Philomèle, the nightingale, together with the 'Gadille' (a term which in the dialect of Anjou is used for a redbreast).

In order to retain some concrete details of an actual landscape Ronsard does not hesitate to use a negative process:

> Grenouilles qui jasez quand l'an se renouvelle . . .
> Ce lieu sacré vous soit à jamais interdit.
>
> (ibid., 288; 273)

> Ny Cannes ny Roseaux ne bordent ton rivage
>
> (ibid., 289; 273)

as well as the positive mention of one of his favourite plants 'le gai poliot' (the pennyroyal), an aromatic plant with golden flowers.

But the general effect of delicate balance is mostly produced by the lightness of the rhythm and the recurrent reference to movement; it is certainly the flowing stream which in this essentially artificial landscape miraculously brings the strongest suggestion, and the beauty, of stylized concreteness:

> Ainsi que ceste eau coule et s'enfuyt parmy l'herbe,
>
> (ibid., 286; 272)

> Ains comme un beau Crystal, tousjours tranquille et nette,
> Puisses tu par les fleurs eternelle couler.
>
> (ibid., 290; 274)

Ronsard the poet

This is a very typical Ronsardian landscape but here already, as we can perceive, the transparency of the landscape tends to become more marked. The concrete world becomes an elusive presence and the triumph of such transparency, of this unassessable poetic distance, is the famous elegy *Contre les bucherons de la forest de Gastine* (L XVIII, 143–7; *Pl* II, 116–18) in which the quintessence of what the theme of the forest meant to Ronsard[1] is given perfect expression. As for the art with which Ronsard manages to give the concrete feel of the forest (greenness, coolness, swaying of the foliage) without mentioning any detail, I can only refer the reader to D. B. Wilson's analysis.[2] One may also wonder whether the mythological universe has not partly lost the quality of a living and immediate presence, whether it is not viewed from a certain distance, taken for granted perhaps, and treated with a certain amount of irony.

The personification of spring in the *Elegie du printemps* of 1578 is a very pale image of what the mythical god was in the *Hymne du printemps* of 1563. He was then the vigorous and powerful hero of a beautiful myth in a world constantly transformed and made alive by the multiple activities of other gods or demi-gods. In the *Elegie* Spring is used to pay a hyperbolical compliment to Astrée whose beauty provokes a violent resentment in the god's heart. In this new light the poetic value of the personification has altered but is no less successful:

> Et quoy, disoit ce Dieu, de honte furieux,
> Ayant la honte au front, et les larmes aux yeux,
> Je ne sers plus de rien, et ma beauté premiere
> D'autre beauté veincue a perdu sa lumière:
> Une autre tient ma place, et ses yeux en tout temps
> Font aux hommes sans moy tous les jours un Printemps:
> Et mesme le Soleil plus longuement retarde
> Ses chevaux sur la terre, afin qu'il la regarde:

[1] For the importance of the theme of the forest in Ronsard's poetry consult E. Armstrong's *The Age of Gold* (Cambridge University Press, 1968), pp. 183–94.

[2] *Ronsard, Poet of Nature* (Manchester University Press, 1961), pp. 57–8.

Ronsard's later poetry

Il ne veut qu'à grand peine entrer dedans la mer,
Et se faisant plus beau, fait semblant de l'aimer.

(*L* XVII, 192; *Pl* I, 213–14)

The selfpitying lamentations of Spring, the pathetic fallacy involving the sun are treated with a mixture of irony and sympathy. The diction verges on the abstract and the melodious elegance of the alexandrines gives an impression of sophisticated naturalness. The gods seem to have moved already to the place assigned to them later by the classicists and the lines I have just quoted may well bring to mind the exquisite limpidity of La Fontaine's verse in *Adonis*.

In the *Sonets pour Helene* we can also perceive an ironical detachment from classical myths. This is hardly surprising as irony is important in that sequence of sonnets and its use raises many questions. Is love too receding at a distance, shelved in the world of petrarchan conventions? Irony is a powerful tool to explore critically the attitudes of the lover and of the lady. But the test may result in bringing the problems of love nearer to reality and nearer to the poet himself, or, on the contrary, in rejecting them into a world of makebelieve. The question deserves a thorough investigation for which there is no room in this chapter. Regretfully I leave it to the reader to choose among the different assessments the *ronsardisants* have made of the *Sonets pour Helene* and refer him more particularly to the critics who have shown a keen interest in the value of irony: to Donald Stone in his book *Ronsard's Sonnet Cycles,*[1] and chapter 2 of the present volume.

What emerges however among the complexity of attitudes to be found in the work is Ronsard's pride and his concern for the durable value of poetry. This was clearly perceptible in the sonnet 'Afin qu'à tout jamais . . .' which I analysed from the point of view of its structure. It is not a new preoccupation for Ronsard. The idea that the poet has the power to confer immortality on his friends, his mistress and himself is basic to his conception of poetry.

[1] *Ronsard's Sonnet Cycles: a study in tone and vision* (New Haven and London, Yale University Press, 1966).

Ronsard the poet

Immortalizing Hélène may be immortalizing a fiction. However, the process of idealization will operate as well on real human beings such as the royal family of the Valois and perhaps the poet himself.

A great deal of the poetry published during the last period of Ronsard's life is destined to build and decorate a pantheon of illustrious personages. It is his privilege, and his official task, to hand over to posterity an impressive image of those kings and queens who were or still are his patrons. Already in 1560 in the *Elegie au seigneur L'Huillier* he had stressed how important to him was this aspect of his poetic works:

> Et la Muse jamais en un cœur ne se prit
> Si ardant que le mien, pour celebrer les gestes
> De noz rois, que j'ay mis au nombre des Celestes.
>
> (*L* X, 295–6; *Pl* I, 886)

Such deification implies the art of distancing. The poetic representation of Charles IX, Henri III and the two queens Marguerite requires a transmutation of their real selves into nobler beings, larger than life, with something like the seal of eternity affixed on the portrait.

The more straightforward technique is to embody in them, through hyperbolic praise, the quintessence of kingly virtues and achievements. But although Ronsard does not neglect such an obvious approach he seems determined to lavish on his creation of semi-gods the riches of his poetic storehouse and thus to introduce complexity and variety into what might have been a rather crude process.

Some of his devices to place his poem, from the start, far above the atmosphere of the everyday world may not appear very successful. In the first lines of *Le Tombeau de Marguerite de France, duchesse de Savoye*:

> Ah! que je suis marry que la Muse Françoise
> Ne peult dire ces mots comme faict la Gregeoise,
> Ocymore, dyspotme, oligochronien:
>
> (*L* XVII, 65; *Pl* II, 480)

the use of the three Greek adjectives to translate the sad fate
of the Valois family, who seem doomed to sudden death, misfortunes and too short a life, provides an element of strangeness
without really lifting the tone to the heights of an acknowledged hellenic tradition.

One may equally think that the fiction of poetic frenzy is
overdone at the beginning of the *Panegyrique de la Renommée*, a
poem destined to glorify Henri III:

> Tout le cœur me debat d'une frayeur nouvelle:
> J'entens dessus Parnasse Apollon qui m'appelle,
> J'oy sa lyre et son arc sonner à son costé.
> Quelque part que mon pied vagabond soit porté
> Ses Lauriers me font place, et sens ma fantasie
> Errante entre les Dieux se souler d'Ambrosie. . . .
>
>   J'ay les yeulx esblouyz, tout le cerveau me tremble,
> J'ay l'estomac panthois . . .
>
>   (*L* XVIII, 1–2; *Pl* I, 787)

Yet the lines expressing the wandering flight of the poet's
imagination (4–6) are very beautiful and exaggeration is after
all a requisite of this type of poetry.

More interesting perhaps is the fact that, in the same poem,
the impressive beginning is only the first stage in the distancing
of the subject. The inspired poet is not going to describe
straightaway the achievements of the king. The allegory which
gives its name to the poem is introduced: the all-knowing
Fame, with her hundred eyes and hundred mouths, a redoubtable
and austere judge of rulers. Then comes the third stage when
we are taken even further from reality; for when Ronsard at last
mentions Henri III we witness a stupendous enlargement of
the canvas. The poet, praising the king's intellectual qualities,
conjures up the loftiest aspects of scientific knowledge[1] and
gives Henri a background of cosmic proportions which
includes the earth, the sea and the heavens:

---

[1] Ronsard's interest in the sublime and mysterious beauty of the cosmos
appears early in his works and we are here very much reminded of his
Hymne de la philosophie, published in 1555.

Ronsard the poet

Il a voulu sçavoir de ce peult la Nature,
Et de quel pas marchoit la premiere closture
Du Ciel, qui tournoyant se ressuit en son cours,
Et du Soleil qui faict le sien tant au rebours.
  Il a voulu sçavoir des Planettes les danses,
Tours, aspects, et vertus, demeures, et distance . . .
Il a cogneu du Feu la nature volage,
Il a pratiqué l'Air combien il est subtil . . .

(*L* XVIII, 10–11; *Pl* I, 792)

Here – and also in the *Tombeau de Charles IX*, when the king becomes, like Pollux, a star in the sky (*L* XVII, 10, lines 165–71; *Pl* II, 478) – the distance between the real man and the poem is almost to be measured in light years. We lose all sense of perspective. Instead of the hero of the apotheosis standing out in sharp relief, the idealized personality becomes blurred as if flattened against the grandiose but remote horizon.

It is only when the princely figure is a woman that Ronsard finds the perfect distance which combines idealization and the illusion of presence, because he can give to the idealized personage the precise outlines of physical beauty. In *La Charite* (the Grace), written in praise of Marguerite de Valois, queen of Navarre, the central part of the poem is devoted to a detailed description of a lovely body. In the *Elegie à Janet peintre du Roy*, written in 1555, Ronsard had already given a very similar picture of a type of feminine beauty which R. A. Sayce has shown to have 'close affinities' with the painting of the time.[1] There is in this picture an obvious distancing from reality both in the stylization of certain features in keeping with a contemporary ideal (elongation of arms, legs and hands,

---

[1] 'The *Elegie à Janet* shows close affinities with one mannerist picture' ('Ronsard and mannerism: the *Elegie à Janet*', *L'Esprit créateur*, 6 (1966), p. 247). I do not propose to go into the question of mannerism in Ronsard. Dr Sayce in this most interesting article is very careful in weighing the evidence. Marcel Raymond, however, would not hesitate to consider *La Charite* as a typical mannerist poem (cf. his article 'Aux frontières du maniérisme et du baroque' in the *Cahiers du Centre International de Synthèse du Baroque*, No. 3 (Montauban, 1969), p. 80).

sophisticated arrangement of hair in curls and ringlets) and in the constant use of decorative metaphors (flowers and precious stones) yet nevertheless a touch of sensuality suggests the warm softness of real flesh:

> Ses mains estoient blanches, longues, *douillettes,*
> Qui tressailloient en veines et rameaux,
> Puis se fendoient en cinq freres jumeaux
> Environnez de cinq bords de perlettes.
> (*L* XVII, 170; *Pl* I, 348: the italics are mine)

Artificialization of the human body remains the dominant impression, and this graceful artificiality is still further enhanced by the fairytale characteristic of the rest of the poem, by the narrative which starts with Venus sending one of the three Graces, Pasithee, to a ball at the French court. The description I have commented upon is that of Pasithee, but as soon as the Grace reaches the ballroom, she becomes, by a mysterious process, identified with Marguerite. The room is filled with delicious and exotic perfumes and, while the queen-goddess dances, her ambiguous identity becomes more and more evanescent through 'cent metamorphoses'.

It is certainly in this poem that Ronsard's technique of changing one of his royal patrons into something 'rich and strange' is most elaborate and, I think, poetically most successful. Elsewhere we may see the danger of the fanciful decorative element leading to too much prettifying. This is so in the following lines taken from the *Tombeau de Marguerite de France* where pathetic fallacy assumes too sugary a flavour:

> Pour marquer sa grandeur puissent à l'advenir
> Les rochers de Savoye en succre devenir,
> En canelle les bois, les torrens en rosée . . .
> (*L* XVII, 83; *Pl* II, 490)

As we linger in the ornate and magnificent pantheon we notice at last the presence of the poet himself 'tel qu'en lui-même enfin l'éternité le change':

Ronsard the poet

Je veux, pour n'estre ingrat, à sa feste ordonnée . . .
Comme un antique Orphée en long surpelis blanc,
Retroussé d'une boucle et d'un nœud sur le flanc,
Chanter à haulte voix d'une bouche immortelle . . .

(ibid.)

More than once Ronsard looks at himself at a distance measured
by pride and intimations of future glory. There may be a shade
of irony when he says to Hélène:

Je seray ton Orphee, et toy mon Eurydice

(*L* XVII, 264; *Pl* I, 259)

but the irony is probably directed at Hélène and there is a
quiet assurance in:

Par les ombres Myrtheux je prendray mon repos.

(ibid., 266; 260)

Yet the distance between Ronsard and the poetic image of
himself is not always an idealization, in place and time, which
transcends the biographical reality. Old age may lend itself to
some ennobling process; but it may also be translated as a
close and bitter experience and nowhere perhaps more forcefully than in the last lines of the *Discours au Roy* when the poet
expresses what retirement from active life could be for him:

Il fera comme fait un cassé mortepaye,
Qui confinant ses jours dans quelque vieux chasteau
Apres avoir pendu ses armes au rateau,
Inutile à soymesme enrouille de paresse
Avecques son harnois les ans de sa vieillesse.

(*L* XVII, 32; *Pl* I, 800, modified)

The metaphor derives its vigour from its realistic precision
which, although exact to the extent of being technical, carries
grim implications with every word (thus: 'cassé mortepaye' to
designate a retired soldier, 'pendu ses armes au rateau', etc.);
the strongest effect being produced by the bold use of 'enrouille' both literally and metaphorically.

Ronsard's later poetry

Together with the misery of old age another aspect of reality is bound to appear in the foreground of his poetic vision: death. Not that it has not always been present in his works; but on the whole it was viewed as one of those general truths about the human condition. In the *Hymne de la mort*, published in 1555, death was a powerful, benevolent goddess, a 'Mere amiable', remote enough to be praised with serenity. Or else, if the poet tried to imagine death, no longer as a philosophical topic but as a personal experience, the nearest he could go was to picture it as a sleep:

> Quand je dors je ne sens rien
> Je ne sens ne mal ne bien . . .
> J'ai perdu le souvenir
> Du passé, de l'advenir,
> Je ne suis que vaine masse
> De bronze en homme gravé,
> Ou quelque terme eslevé
> Pour parade en une place. . . .
> Voyez donc que je seray
> Quand mort je reposeray
> Au fond de la tombe noire!
>
> (*L* VII, 283–4; *Pl* I, 526)

In this ode published in 1556 there is no great impression of personal involvement. The calculated simplicity of tone might suggest an immediate, almost naïve concern for the problem of death; but the negative attitude, given more comforting solidity by comparison with heavy objects of bronze or stone, and even the very simplification of outlook, remove the theme from the field of actual experience.

In the later poetry the philosophical commonplaces which are closely linked with the idea of death – the ephemeral quality of life, the fragility of human grandeur, the uncertainty of everything – reappear and with a stronger power of impact. They are not developed in a leisured and lengthy way as a lofty theme for sober meditation. Sometimes they are no more than a whisper reminding the reader at the end of the *Tombeau de Marguerite de France* that the fortune of the great is nothing but 'Un vent, un songe, un rien', but the three little words, more powerfully than the plain statement which comes a little before,

> Je diray que des Grands la vie est incertaine,
> (*L* XVII, 83; *Pl* II, 491)

shatter the magnificent illusion of immortality so carefully built up in the rest of the poem.

In the *Tombeau de Charles IX*, while the poet extols the virtues of the king, places him among the stars above and comforts the queen, a sinister and mocking echo of Lucretius predicts the annihilation of everything, including heaven:

> C'est qu'à la fin la mort toutes choses emmeine:
> Et que mesme le ciel, qui fait mourir les Rois,
> Et perir un chacun, perira quelquefois.
> (*L* XVII, 9; *Pl* II, 478)

This, however, is looking far into the future. The poet's own death, on the other hand, almost belongs to the present. What is surprising is to see Ronsard, when he treats the subject of his own death, trying to achieve, up to the very end, a satisfactory balance between the gruesome reality and the art which transcends it. The experience of physical suffering and impending death does not lend itself to the easy simplification we found in the ode of 1556. *Les Derniers Vers* show constant oscillations between fear, resignation, cries of pain, hope and regrets.

At times, between the actual glance of the poet at his wasted body and the poetic expression there is no more than a reminiscence of Petrarch and the alliteration which stresses the ruthless chiselling of the skeleton:

> Je n'ay plus que les os, un Schelette je semble,
> Decharné, denervé, demusclé, depoulpé,
> (*L* XVIII, 176; *Pl* II, 634)

and in the fourth line of the same sonnet:

Ronsard's later poetry

Je n'ose voir mes bras que de peur je ne tremble.

– a bare, pitiful statement – poetic distance vanishes altogether.

Yet Ronsard is still capable of placing between death and himself the graceful veil of the touching epitaph *A son ame* where the use of diminutives and the delicate flavour of classical tradition give to a gentle feeling of selfpity an impalpable lightness:

> Amelette Ronsardelette,
> Mignonnelette doucelette,
> Treschere hostesse de mon corps,
> Tu descens là bas foiblelette,
> Pasle, maigrelette, seulette,
> Dans le froid Royaume des mors . . .
>
> (*L* XVIII, 182; *Pl* II, 637)

The most successful perhaps of these last poems is the following sonnet:

> Il faut laisser maisons et vergers et Jardins,
> Vaisselles et vaisseaux que l'artisan burine,
> Et chanter son obseque en la façon du Cygne,
> Qui chante son trespas sur les bors Mæandrins.
> C'est fait j'ay devidé le cours de mes destins,
> J'ay vescu j'ay rendu mon nom assez insigne,
> Ma plume vole au ciel pour estre quelque signe
> Loin des appas mondains qui trompent les plus fins.
> Heureux qui ne fut onc, plus heureux qui retourne
> En rien comme il estoit, plus heureux qui sejourne
> D'homme fait nouvel ange aupres de Jesuchrist,
> Laissant pourrir ça bas sa despouille de boüe,
> Dont le sort, la fortune, et le destin se joüe
> Franc des liens du corps pour n'estre qu'un esprit.
>
> (*L* XVIII, 180–1; *Pl* II, 637)

What one notices immediately is the pattern of a progression which goes from regret for earthly possessions to the final triumph of the spirit. The ascending pattern is evident

[317]

also in the first tercet where a ternary movement upwards translates the passage from the most negative attitude to death to the most positive.

But this unifying structure does not oversimplify the complexity of attitudes to be found here, and the attitudes may well appear conflicting ones. In spite of the scornful reference to 'despouille de boüe', destined to rot, the regret for the material world is not a mean form of greed but reveals in the choice of the objects mentioned – 'Vaisselles et vaisseaux que l'artisan burine' – the tenacious adoration for artistic perfection. The poem is both Christian and pagan, religious and worldly. The clash between the pride of the poet and the humility of the Christian remains a clash. Ronsard does not really choose between the melodious swan and the newborn angel. Nor are we convinced that the power of Jesus Christ is necessarily stronger than that of 'sort', 'fortune' and 'destin', those blind deities whom Ronsard has sung all his life.

One marvels at the conciseness with which the poet has expressed so many facets of his personality within the short space of a sonnet: his love of nature and art, his belief in astrology, his dislike of the artificiality of the court, his interest in philosophical doctrines, his pride as a great poet and his Christian faith. This sonnet is also a very good illustration of Ronsard's superb technique in combining movement and solidity – an aspect of his art which, as the first section of this chapter has shown, was to remain with him to the end of his poetic career.

But perhaps the greatest beauty of this sonnet is to give a harmonious structure to the contradictions of a divided self. Here the distance between the subject and the poem reaches exquisite precision: the sonnet is poised exactly half way between the reality of the poet's mortal condition and the double immortality he claims.

Epilogue:
a sonnet by Ronsard

R. A. SAYCE

Si j'estois Jupiter, Marie, vous seriez
Mon espouse Junon; si j'estois Roy des ondes,
Vous seriez ma Tethys, Royne des eaux profondes,
Et pour vostre maison les ondes vous auriez.
  Si la terre estoit mienne, avec moy vous tiendriez
L'empire sous vos mains, dame des terres rondes,
Et dessus un beau coche, en belles tresses blondes,
Par le peuple en honneur Deesse vous iriez.
  Mais je ne suis pas Dieu, et si ne le puis estre.
Le Ciel pour vous servir seulement m'a fait naistre,
De vous seule je prens mon sort aventureux.
  Vous estes tout mon bien, mon mal, et ma fortune.
S'il vous plaist de m'aimer, je deviendray Neptune,
Tout Jupiter, tout Roy, tout riche et tout heureux.

(Pl I, 149–50)

This is from the *Amours de Marie* in the 1584 edition and appears to fit in perfectly with the sonnets addressed to the country girl of Anjou. At its first publication, however, in the *Second Livre des meslanges* of 1559, it looked very different:

Si j'estois Jupiter, Sinope, vous seriez
Mon espouse Junon: si j'estois Roy des ondes,
Vous seriez ma Thetys, Royne des eaux profondes,
Et pour vostre maison la grand mer vous auriez:

Ronsard the poet

Si la terre estoit mienne, avec móy vous tiendriez
L'empire sous vos mains, dame des terres rondes,
Et de sur une coche, en belles tresses blondes,
Par le peuple en honneur, Déesse, vous iriez.
    Mais je ne le suis pas, et puis vous ennuyez
D'aymer les bonnets rons, gras troupeau de l'Eglise.
Ah! vous ne sçavez pas l'honneur que vous fuiez,
    Ny les biens qui cachez dedans ce bonnet sont.
Si l'amour dans le monde a sa demeure prise,
Il ne la prit jamais que dans un bonnet rond.

(*L* X, 93–4)

Instead of Marie the recipient is Sinope, a Greek or Greek-sounding name; instead of the apotheosis of the poet and his mistress, fully worked out in the unified sonnet of the later version, the poem ends in a piece of special pleading on behalf of the 'round bonnets', clerics in minor orders like Ronsard himself; instead of a grand mythological scene we have a series of rather disorganized complaints. The difference is reflected in the rhyme schemes: in 1559 *abbaabbacdcede*, in the later version, more symmetrically rounded, *abbaabbaccdeed*. In 1560 the sestet is changed to read:

Mais je ne le suis pas, et si ne le puis estre.
Pour telles dignitez le ciel ne m'a fait naistre:
Mais je voudrois avoir changé de bonnet rond,
    Et vous avoir chez moy pour ma chere espousée:
Tout ainsi que la nege au chaut soleil se fond,
Je me fondrois en vous d'une douce rousée.

Again the rhyme scheme is different (*abbaabbaccdede*), more symmetrical than the first version, less organically satisfying than the final one (in which, it should be noted, the rhyme 'estre'/'naistre' is retained); the narrowly personal note persists in the poet's wish to abandon his round bonnet in order to marry his mistress but the poem now ends in a magnificent erotic image which harmonizes with the reference to Jupiter and recalls Ronsard's numerous allusions to Jupiter's amorous metamorphoses. Finally, the posthumous edition of 1587, though there is no such major upheaval, brings some further, and not unimportant, alterations:

(line 1)   Si j'estois Jupiter, Maistresse, vous seriez

(lines 4–6) Et pour vostre palais les ondes vous auriez:
             Si le Monde estoit mien, avec moy vous tiendriez
             L'empire de la terre aux mammelles fecondes.

This recital of the history of the text at once points to a serious theoretical difficulty in any critical approach to Ronsard: where and what is the poem? The present case is more complicated than most but not really exceptional. Excluding the minor variants (not all of which have been listed) it seems that we have here three poems rather than one:[1] the different conclusions alter the balance of the whole poem, and retrospectively even the sense of the octet, which itself remains fairly constant. On the other hand, it can equally be argued that all three are stages of a single poem, which can be observed in its living growth and evolution. The three versions are too closely connected to be treated entirely as separate entities: in particular the first half of line 9 occupies a crucial position as the point at which the three versions of the sestet are grafted onto the stem of the octet (the problem is not unlike that which confronts the reader of Montaigne). In what follows an attempt will be made to maintain a balance between the static and the dynamic view of the sonnet. The 1584 version (which seems to me on the whole the best) will be treated as a single unity, but illumination will also be sought in comparisons with the other versions.[2]

[1] Cf. Grahame Castor: 'The revisions can sometimes so alter the overall meaning of a poem that the result is in effect a different poem' ('Ronsard's variants', *Modern Language Review,* 59 (1964), p. 387).

[2] F. Desonay (*Ronsard poète de l'amour,* volume II, p. 161) argues convincingly that the recasting of the sestet is due to political motives: in the climate of the wars of religion it would have been a gift to Protestant propaganda to leave in the 'round bonnets' with their rich benefices and availability for love. But this is not poetically relevant: the question for us is what Ronsard did with the poem rather than what made him do it.

Ronsard the poet

The poem is built on a series of interlocking structures, syntactic and semantic as well as metrical and phonetic. These structures are sometimes convergent, sometimes contrapuntal: to separate them inevitably violates the unity of the final sonnet but for analysis it is necessary to do so. Perhaps the most immediately obvious feature is the handling of the persons. In discussing a novel, consideration of the person (first, second or third) is a matter of routine. In lyric poetry it is at least equally important, though less universally studied. Here the persons are *I* and *you*. This may seem automatically true of a love poem but in fact many variations are possible. The poet may be concerned entirely with his own feelings as in 'Les villes et les bourgs me sont si odieux' (*L* VII, 258; *Pl* I, 132). He may address the loved one exclusively with no reference to himself, so that all the attention is concentrated on her, though of course the relationship is implied in the use of the second person, as in 'Marie, vous avés la joue aussi vermeille' (*L* VII, 126; *Pl* I, 116). [1] He may speak of her in the third person:

> When as in silks my *Julia* goes,
> Then, then (me thinks) how sweetly flowes . . .

or 'Quand au matin ma Deesse s'abille' (*L* IV, 42; *Pl* I, 19). Here the effect is of objectification or at least of distancing, cool or regretful detachment rather than passionate involvement. In our poem what is striking is the interaction, the changing emphasis on first or second person, the shifting relations of co-ordination and subordination between them. Marie dominates the octet: it is her apotheosis and the poet is subordinate, both syntactically and imaginatively, though her elevation depends on his and there is a point of equality ('avec moy vous tiendriez'). In the first tercet we move from *you* to *I* as the subject but the second line stresses the subservience of the poet, in syntax as in fact. The second tercet combines the two persons but in the last two lines it is Marie who occupies the subordinate position in the conditional clause and the sonnet

[1] Cf. the remarks on direct address in the *Sonets pour Helene,* above, chapter 2, p. 119.

Epilogue: a sonnet by Ronsard

closes with the strongest affirmation of the poet's own triumph. Interaction is further emphasized by the possessives ('Mon espouse', 'ma Tethys', and the three in line 12), both protective and proprietary. Incidentally, the use of *vous*, rather than *tu* as in the Cassandre sonnets, may suggest greater formality. In fact I think the opposite is the case. *Tu* is the form of address for the gods and (by poetic convention) great ones. By calling Marie *vous* the poet treats her far more as an ordinary person.

The same movement is naturally apparent in the whole syntactic structure. The octet consists of three hypotheses or metamorphoses, pictures of what might be: the poet imagines himself in turn as Jupiter, Neptune and king of the earth, and in each case Marie would take on the attributes of his female companion. All this is worked out with powerful symmetry, and not only in the regular sequence of *si* clauses (Ronsard's characteristic anaphora). The use of four conditionals as rhyming words lays heavy stress on the hypothetical character of the metamorphoses but also, by the sonority of similar endings and the repetition of *vous,* turns them into something like affirmations: the note of triumph is already present. More subtly, in the first three lines, the name of a divinity is placed in the prominent position of the caesura. At the same time the structure is expansive as well as symmetrical: each hypothesis is considerably longer than the one that precedes it and contains more concrete detail. We can also observe in the conditionals the ascending order from the colourless 'seriez' and 'auriez' to the active 'tiendriez' and 'iriez'. The first line of the first tercet brings a change of tense (as well as of person) to the present indicative and the negative: at once the vision of the octet collapses as present reality is introduced. The poet is not a god and dreams are only dreams. However, the workings of the imagination are not quite the same as those of grammar. The vision may seem broken but it has not been destroyed, it remains fully and poetically realized in the mind.[1] And the

[1] Cf above, chapter 2, p. 91: 'the ideal and the unattainable have become totally real.'

negative in the first line of the first tercet is symmetrically balanced by a present positive in the first line of the second tercet ('Vous estes tout mon bien . . .'), which in turn leads to the last two lines and the final hypothesis, now set in the future. The desirable but impossible metamorphosis has become a certainty (subject to the one condition), the transformation of poet into god is nearly complete, and the vision is restored. The sequence of tenses has led us in a logical progression from the past (not perhaps a true past but the effect is made) through the present (together with the perfect of line 10) to the future, so that within the narrow compass of the sonnet the spread of time is extremely wide. Still more fundamental to the structure is the echo, at the close, of the three initial hypotheses now concentrated in one, with a decisive variation of tense and mood (in both the grammatical and the ordinary sense) and the reversal of the apodosis and protasis; condition has become fact and fact condition. The form of the poem is thus essentially a circle with person and syntactic structure at the end returning to the opening pattern. It is not, however, a closed circle since the movement of tenses runs through it, and beyond it into the future.[1]

The circular form receives further emphasis from the intricate pattern of repetitions, some of which have already been mentioned. These repetitions may be distant, like the *si* clause at the end, or near. It is clear that in the last two lines the repetition is semantic as well as syntactic: Neptune, Jupiter and king respond exactly to the three original hypotheses, then potential, now almost actual. It is here that study of the variants helps us to grasp the gradual process by which the ultimate perfection (at least in the sense of achievement of the circular form) is attained. In line 9 the substitution of 'Mais je ne suis pas Dieu' for the earlier 'Mais je ne le suis pas' not only replaces a weak word by a strong one but inserts in a key position a powerful link between the beginning of the sonnet and the end. 'Mais je ne le suis pas' is flat and doleful; 'Mais je ne suis pas Dieu' is proud even in negation, and of course it

[1] Cf. above, chapter 1, pp. 72–3.

Epilogue: a sonnet by Ronsard

chimes with the 'Deesse' of the preceding line. In the last line the 1578 edition reads:

> Tout Dieu, tout Jupiter, tout riche et tout heureux.

Apart from the fact that 'Dieu' merely summarizes Neptune and Jupiter, here only two out of the three original transformations are picked up: the fully circular movement is not yet realized.

In both versions the fourfold repetition of 'tout', echoing its first appearance in line 12, dominates the line and expresses even more forcibly than the words themselves the notions of richness and happiness (and certainty and confidence as well). This repetition depends partly for its effect on a less obvious echo of an earlier repetition, 'seulement' and 'seule' in lines 10 and 11. 'Seule' is exclusive, 'tout' inclusive, but both are absolutes.[1] The gradation is strongly marked: Marie expands to become the whole of the poet's universe and in the end he possesses only everything. The other repetitions have less structural importance but are none the less significant.

> si j'estois Roy des *ondes* . . .
> Et pour vostre maison les *ondes* vous auriez.

That this is deliberate can be seen from the alteration of the original 'la grand mer vous auriez'. It may be that 'grand mer' suggests an unwelcome pun on *grand'mère* but even without that it is, though magnificent, rather diffuse. The repetition, as well as suggesting the movement of the waves, locks the two lines together and with them the god and the goddess, Neptune and Thetis, the poet and Marie. Exactly the same process is visible (and this in itself constitutes a symmetrical repetition) in the second quatrain:

> Si la *terre* estoit mienne . . .
> L'empire sous vos mains, dame des *terres* rondes.

Here, as we have seen, the 1587 edition substitutes:

[1] Cf. above, chapter 7, pp. 301, 302.

Ronsard the poet

Si le Monde estoit mien . . .
L'empire de la terre aux mammelles fecondes.

In spite of the beauty of the last image, linking up with the mythological allusion of the following line, this does not seem to be an improvement, precisely because of the loss of the symmetrical repetition. Finally

Et dessus un beau coche, en belles tresses blondes

is also the result of a revision, from

Et de sur une coche . . .

The change was no doubt due to the change in the gender of 'coche', but this does not diminish the effect of the third repetition, enhanced by the variation of 'beau'/'belles', varying in gender, number, and form. The consonantal harmony also plays a part (*d* at the beginning and end, *b* three times, in the last two associated with *l*). All three repetitions, though the consequence of great and probably deliberate art, hardly accord with normal rhetorical patterns; they seem slipped in accidentally, with simulated naïveté, and so convey to the reader something of the astonishment which the country girl must experience as she finds herself the object of these unexpected transformations. More accurately perhaps, the astonishment is shared by poet, girl, and reader.

With repetition we may consider apposition and similar figures, marked particularly by the omission of the article. In

Vous seriez ma Tethys, Royne des eaux profondes,

we have another concealed and balancing repetition ('Roy'/ 'Royne') but this is not all. We have seen that 'ma Tethys' is proprietary, she is presented only in relation to him; as 'Royne', untrammelled by article or possessive, she is liberated to become the independent queen of the deep waters. Even more striking is

Par le peuple en honneur Deesse vous iriez.

Epilogue: a sonnet by Ronsard

'Deesse' without an article or other introduction isolates and elevates her (already visible in 'dessus') above the admiring and adoring multitude (themselves fixed by the article). The construction might be elliptical, with some such word as *comme* understood, but it seems more probably an almost familiar expression, suggesting that the triumphal procession is almost an everyday occurrence.[1] But the most extraordinary example appears in the opening line:

Si j'estois Jupiter, Marie, vous seriez . . .

There is nothing grammatically out of the way about this but the sudden and immediate collocation of the name of the god of gods and the simplest of French girl's names produces a violent impact: the god and the country girl and the gulf between them, bridged by the apotheosis of Marie, continue to dominate the poem. It is for this reason more than any other that the 1584 version seems to be superior. The earlier Sinope, an unfamiliar Greek name, lacks expressive character; the later 'Maistresse', though it fits in well enough with the first tercet, nearly destroys the contrast. (It hardly needs to be said that I am ignoring the biographical arguments about who Marie and Sinope really were and simply taking the picture of the country girl which emerges from the *Amours de Marie* as a whole.)

So far we have considered the syntax and structure of the poem, not its semantic content. It will be seen indeed that the two are inseparable: one is a function of the other and much of the substance has naturally figured in the discussion of structure. However, though the structure organizes the poem and gives it unity, it is still not the poem itself and cannot by itself explain the feeling aroused in us: we are still left with the flesh that clothes the skeleton. When we look at the octet from this point of view, we see that the three hypotheses now

[1] Laumonier's punctuation ('Par le peuple en honneur, Déesse, vous iriez') must be wrong: turning 'Déesse' into a vocative, it also makes the line commonplace.

Ronsard the poet

turn into three pictures, expanding like the clauses which carry them.

The first, with its double use of the colourless verb *être*, is limited to the names of Jupiter, Marie and Juno (with 'Mon espouse' which establishes the relationship and the fact of possession, all still more closely unified by the enjambment). But the names of Jupiter and Juno, the king and queen of heaven, are by themselves enough to evoke a sense of the whole universe, and with them, as we have seen, Marie is treated as an incongruous equal. The next episode takes us into a water world typical of Ronsard.[1] 'Roy des ondes' is an unremarkable periphrasis or antonomasia for Neptune, virtually a cliché, but it sets up an echo, to be completed two lines later. Marie's kingdom is not merely local, it extends over the whole surface of the waves, and beneath them as well in the marvellous 'Royne des eaux profondes', making the picture fully three-dimensional. The simplicity of 'maison' furnishes once more a vivid contrast with all this grandeur. In the 1587 'palais' the grandeur receives stronger emphasis but the contrast is lost: the poem becomes, to that extent, less moving.

The third picture again stresses universal sovereignty (again stressed by an enjambment symmetrical to that of the first quatrain), now expressed in terms of the roundness of the earth instead of the depth of the sea and so reflecting the circular form of the poem and Ronsard's identification of roundness with perfection.[2] The word 'dame' contributes to the notion of sovereignty and to the chain of words in the poem expressing it (['Maistresse'], 'Roy', 'Royne', ['palais'], 'empire', 'honneur', 'Deesse', 'riche');[3] but it also possesses a certain familiarity by reason of its wide range of uses in French, even wider at that period, and so emphasizes once more our astonishment at the simple girl transformed into an empress (and perhaps her astonishment as well). At this point, with the

[1] Cf., for example, Neptune as 'Roi de l'humide monde' (*L* II, 136; *Pl* I, 548); and above, chapter 1, pp. 18–19.
[2] Cf. above, chapter 1, p. 24.
[3] The words in square brackets occur only in the variants.

coach, the universality of the poem is suddenly and sharply localized, concentrated in a restricted though mobile space. 'Coche' was a neologism (first recorded in 1545 according to Bloch and Wartburg) and it seems at first sight surprising that it should be used here in preference to the noble *char,* the usual conveyance of the gods in the poetry of the Pléiade.[1] The reason must surely be that the coach, though already a luxurious enough vehicle to fit into the context, belonged none the less, unlike the chariot, to the everyday appurtenances of modern life: once again the divine is contrasted with the familiar. And although so far there has been no direct reference (this comes with 'Deesse'), the third picture is unmistakably mythological like the others. It is a triumph of Cybele (as the commentators explain) or more probably of Ceres: the 'belles tresses blondes' are Marie's hair but also, by an inescapable association, the ears of corn which served as the headdress of the goddess.[2] They are thus both literal and metaphorical, visual and abstract, the mantle and the enclosed truth. Exuberance and fertility are present by implication (explicitly stated, and therefore perhaps less cunningly effective, in the 'mammelles fecondes' of 1587); at the same time universality and the splendour of divinity are reduced to the dimensions of a rural harvest home. The whole

---

[1] Among many possible examples, in the *Hinne de Bacus*:

> Tu montas sur un char que deux lynces farouches
> Traynoient d'un col felon . . .
>
> (*L* VI, 182; *Pl* II, 277)

On the other hand *coche* is used in the *Sonets pour Helene*:

> Coche cent fois heureux, où ma belle Maistresse
> Et moy nous promenons . . .
>
> (*L* XVII, 226; *Pl* I, 235)

Here, it will be noted, the two lovers are together. Huguet (*Coche* 1) gives a number of examples of the word used instead of *char* in a mythological context: in nearly all, it seems, *coche* produces a less remote or dignified effect.

[2] Cf. Noël Le Comte (Natalis Comes or Natale Conti), *Mythologie* (Lyons, 1604), p. 494, with quotation from Ovid; also the *flava Ceres* 'yellow-haired Ceres', of the Roman poets.

picture offers a fine illustration of the quality which Marcel
Raymond discerns in the art of the Pléiade and the Fontainebleau school, 'la noblesse imprégnée de rusticité'.[1]

The content of the sestet is still more nearly coextensive with
the structure: change of person and tenses, future moving
forward beyond the limits of the poem, recall of the three
initial hypotheses, potential metamorphosis finally assured in
the affirmation of 'je deviendray'. However, the absolutes of the
final tercet deserve some further examination. The poet now
identifies himself completely with the gods and there can be
no doubt about the godlike aspects of Ronsard's poetry.[2]
Generosity, prodigality, Protean diversity of form and theme,
ubiquity in the amorous pursuit of mortals – these are the
characteristics of Jupiter as of Ronsard. More than anything in
the poem, 'tout riche' – richness raised to an absolute – sums
up his poetic character:

> On dit que le Printemps pompeux de sa richesse,
> Orgueilleux de ses fleurs, enflé de sa jeunesse . . .
>
> (L XVII, 191; Pl I, 213)

Although there is another and darker side, this is the note of
power, plenitude and 'exuberant self-confidence' (Dr Castor's
phrase) that runs through his whole work. Montaigne, with his
customary gift of succinct discrimination, already notices it
when in comparing Ronsard and Du Bellay he speaks of 'les
riches descriptions de l'un et les delicates inventions de
l'autre'.[3]

The trouble with stylistic analysis of this kind is that it
leads inevitably to a tautologous conclusion: the poem says
what it says. However, it may also help us to see that what it
says is more than the surface meaning of the words. In this

---

[1] *La Poésie française et le maniérisme* (Geneva, Droz; Paris, Minard, 1971),
p. 9.
[2] Cf. 'Je suis un demidieu . . .' (L VII, 313; Pl I, 161).
[3] *Œuvres complètes*, ed. Thibaudet and Rat (Paris, Gallimard: Bibliothèque
de la Pléiade, 1965), p. 170. On richness as dominant in Ronsard, cf.
above, chapter 2, *passim*.

Epilogue: a sonnet by Ronsard

case what emerges most plainly (and this applies to Ronsard's treatment of the sonnet form generally) is that the sense of richness is achieved within so brief a compass. The octet particularly embraces a vast expanse of time and space, generalized and localized; prodigality is matched and no doubt reinforced by compression. It is remarkable that in fourteen lines a vision of such far-reaching splendour can be constructed, demolished and rebuilt. In the longer poems, odes, hymns and elegies, Ronsard's exuberance and erudition have more room for play, but in a poem like this the mythological sweep, the pictorial depth, the circular form, the transforming imagination and the controlled expansion offer an epitome of his qualities raised to a higher pitch of intensity.

Select Bibliography

THE intention of this bibliography is to provide a wide range of possibilities for further reading within the field of Ronsard studies, while at the same time indicating the main lines of inquiry adopted by scholars in this field, particularly in more recent times. Since a complete Ronsard bibliography could not be envisaged, the line between inclusion and exclusion had to be finely drawn: in marginal cases – and some others – the editor followed his own preference.

The first three sections, comprising (i) editions of Ronsard's works, (ii) books and (iii) articles in which Ronsard is the principal focus of attention, are followed by a list of 'general studies' (iv), providing a wider context for the reading of his poetry.

Bibliographical references given by individual contributors which do not specifically concern Ronsard and which do not fall within the 'general studies' category are not included here.

ABBREVIATIONS

Titles of periodicals, etc., which occur only once in the bibliography are given in full.

BHR	*Bibliothèque d'humanisme et Renaissance*
CL	*Comparative Literature*
CNRS	Centre National de la Recherche Scientifique

Ronsard the poet

FS   *French Studies*
MLR   *Modern Language Review*
PMLA   *Publications of the Modern Language Association of America*
RR   *Romanic Review*
STFM   *Société des textes français modernes*
THR   *Travaux d'humanisme et Renaissance*
TLF   *Textes littéraires français*

*

*   *

*

(I) EDITIONS

Œuvres complètes, ed. P. Laumonier; edition completed by I. Silver and R. Lebègue, 18 volumes, Paris, Hachette, then Droz, then Didier (*STFM*), 1914–67. A further volume, containing indexes, etc., is announced.

This edition is unique in that it gives the text of the first edition of all of Ronsard's works, arranged in the chronological order of publication, and provides the variants found in subsequent editions as well as copious annotations. It should not be confused with an earlier edition produced by Laumonier (*Œuvres complètes*, 8 volumes, Paris, Lemerre, 1914–19), which is based on the text of the 1584 edition of Ronsard's complete works.

Œuvres complètes, ed. G. Cohen, 2 volumes, Paris, Gallimard (*Bibliothèque de la Pléiade*), 1950 (and subsequent reprintings).

This provides the text of the 1584 edition, the last to appear during Ronsard's lifetime; 'pièces retranchées', posthumous and supposititious works are included in an appendix. No variants are given.

Les Œuvres de Pierre de Ronsard. Texte de 1587, ed. I. Silver, 4 volumes in 8 tomes, Washington University Press; University of Chicago Press; Didier, Paris, 1966–70.

The first posthumous edition of Ronsard's complete works represents, arguably, the most authoritative 'definitive state'

Select Bibliography

of his much-corrected writings. No variants are given, but this edition (together with Cohen's) provides a useful counterpart to Laumonier's *variorum* text, both for a smooth reading of the poems in their later versions and for a clear view of their overall arrangement in 1584 and 1587.

Les Amours, ed. H. and C. Weber, Paris, Garnier, 1963.

A well-annotated edition, with variants, of all of Ronsard's love poetry, presented in a single volume at a reasonable price. It is based on the first edition of each collection. For the Hélène cycle, the *Sonnets pour Helene,* ed. M. Smith, Geneva, Droz (*TLF*), 1970, should also be consulted (text according to the 1587 version).

(II) BOOKS ON RONSARD

ARMSTRONG, E., *Ronsard and the Age of Gold,* Cambridge University Press, 1968.

BINET, C., *La Vie de Pierre de Ronsard de Claude Binet (1586),* ed. P. Laumonier, Paris, Hachette, 1910; Geneva, Slatkine, 1969.

CAMERON, A., *The Influence of Ariosto's Epic and Lyric on Ronsard and his Group*, Baltimore, Johns Hopkins University Press, 1930.

CHAMPION, P., *Ronsard et son temps*, Paris, Champion, 1925.

CHARBONNIER, F., *Pamphlets protestants contre Ronsard (1560–1577)*, Paris, Champion, 1923.

COHEN, G., *Ronsard, sa vie et son œuvre*, 5th ed., Paris, Gallimard, 1956.

CORNELIA, W. B., *The Classical Sources of the Nature References in Ronsard's Poetry*, New York, Columbia University Press, 1934.

DASSONVILLE, M., *Ronsard: étude historique et littéraire,* volume I: *Les Enfances Ronsard (1536–1545)*; volume II: *A la conquête de la toison d'or (1545–1550)*, Geneva, Droz, 1968 and 1970 (three volumes to follow).

DESGUINE, A., *Étude des 'Bacchanales ou le folastrissime voyage d'Hercueil fait l'an 1549' par Ronsard*, Geneva, Droz, 1953.

DESONAY, F., *Ronsard, poète de l'amour*, 3 volumes, Brussels, Gembloux J. Duculot, 1952–9.

Ronsard the poet

EXPERT, H., *La Fleur des musiciens de Ronsard,* Paris, Cité des Livres, 1923; New York, Broude Brothers, 1965.

FRANCHET, H., *Le Poète et son œuvre d'après Ronsard,* Paris, Champion, 1923.

FREY, D. E., *Le Genre élégiaque dans l'œuvre de Ronsard,* Liège, Thone, 1939.

GADOFFRE, G., *Ronsard par lui-même,* Paris, Éditions du Seuil, 1960.

GENDRE, A., *Ronsard poète de la conquête amoureuse,* Neuchâtel, La Baconnière, 1970.

GORDON, A. L., *Ronsard et la rhétorique,* Geneva, Droz (THR), 1970.

HALLOWELL, R. E., *Ronsard and the Conventional Roman Elegy,* Urbana, University of Illinois Press, 1954.

HUMISTON, C. C., *A Comparative Study of the Metrical Technique of Ronsard and Malherbe,* Berkeley and Los Angeles, University of California Press, 1941.

KATZ, R. A., *Ronsard's French Critics, 1585–1828,* Geneva, Droz (THR), 1966.

KLENGEL, A., *Pierre de Ronsards Hymnendichtung,* Leipzig, Vogel, 1931.

LAUMONIER, P., *Ronsard, poète lyrique,* Paris, Hachette, 1909.

—— *Tableau chronologique des œuvres de Ronsard, suivi de poésies non recueillies et d'une table alphabétique,* Paris, Hachette, 1911.

LEBÈGUE, R., *Ronsard,* 5th ed., Paris, Hatier (*Connaissance des lettres*), 1966.

NOLHAC, P. DE, *Ronsard et l'humanisme,* Paris, Champion, 1921.

PERDRIZET, P., *Ronsard et la réforme,* Paris, Fischbacher, 1902.

PY, A., *Ronsard,* Paris, Desclée De Brouwer (Les écrivains devant Dieu), 1972.

RAYMOND, M., *L'Influence de Ronsard sur la poésie française (1550–1585),* 2 volumes, Paris, Champion, 1927; reprinted in 1 volume, Geneva, Droz (THR), 1965.

SATTERTHWAITE, A. W., *Spenser, Ronsard and Du Bellay: a Renaissance comparison,* Princeton University Press, 1960.

SCHMIDT, A-M., *L'Hymne des daimons de Pierre de Ronsard,* Paris, Albin Michel, [1939].

Select Bibliography

SCHWEINITZ, M. DE, *Les Epitaphes de Ronsard*, Paris, Presses Universitaires de France, 1925.

SILVER, I., *The Pindaric Odes of Ronsard*, Paris [printed by Pierre André], 1937.

—— *Ronsard and the Hellenic Renaissance in France*, volume I: *Ronsard and the Greek Epic*, St Louis, Washington University Press, 1961 (two further volumes were announced when this work was published, but priority now seems to have been given to the four-volume work mentioned below).

—— *The Intellectual Evolution of Ronsard*, volume I: *The Formative Influences*, St Louis, Washington University Press, 1969 (three volumes to follow).

STONE, D., *Ronsard's Sonnet Cycles: a study in tone and vision*, New Haven and London, Yale University Press, 1966.

STORER, W. L., *Virgil and Ronsard*, Paris, Champion, 1923.

TERREAUX, L., *Ronsard correcteur de ses œuvres. Les variantes des Odes et des deux premiers livres des Amours*, Geneva, Droz, 1968.

THIBAULT, G., and PERCEAU, L., *Bibliographie des poésies de P. de Ronsard mises en musique au XVIe siècle*, Paris, Droz, 1941.

TIERSOT, J., *Ronsard et la musique de son temps*, Leipzig, Breitkopf & Härtel; Paris, Fischbacher, [1903?].

VIANEY, J., *Les Odes de Ronsard*, Paris, Sfelt (*Les Grands Événements littéraires*), 1946.

WILSON, D. B., *Ronsard, Poet of Nature*, Manchester University Press, 1961.

(III) ARTICLES ON RONSARD

Collections:

Cahiers de l'Association Internationale des Études Françaises, **22** (1970), première journée.

L'Esprit créateur, **10** (1970), No. 2.

La Revue musicale, 1 May 1924: *Ronsard et la musique*.

A number of articles on Ronsard are also to be found in the following collections, of which details are given in section (iv): *Humanism in France*; *Lumières de la Pléiade*; *Mélanges Henri Chamard*. Articles published in collections which are mentioned in the bibliography will not be listed separately below. Separate articles:

ADHÉMAR, J., Ronsard et l'école de Fontainebleau, *BHR*, **20** (1958), 344–8.

BENSIMON, M., Ronsard et la mort, *MLR*, **57** (1962), 183–94.

BROWN, F. S., Interrelations between the political ideas of Ronsard and Montaigne, *RR*, **56** (1965), 241–7.

BUSSON, H., Sur la philosophie de Ronsard, *Revue des cours et conférences,* **1** (1929–30), 32–48; 172–85.

CAMERON, K., Ronsard and book IV of the *Franciade, BHR*, **32** (1970), 395–406.

CARPENTER, N. C., Ronsard's *Préface sur la musique, Modern Language Notes,* **75** (1960), 126–33.

CASTOR, G., Ronsard's variants: 'Je vouldray bien richement jaunissant', *MLR*, **59** (1964), 387–90.

—— Imitation in Ronsard: 'O de Nepenthe . . .', *MLR*, **63** (1968), 332–9.

—— Ronsard: *Les Amours* – 'Quand en songeant ma follastre j'acolle', in *The Art of Criticism. Essays in French Literary Analysis,* ed. P. H. Nurse, Edinburgh University Press, 1969, 17–26.

—— The theme of illusion in Ronsard's *Sonets pour Helene* and in the variants of the 1552 *Amours, Forum for Modern Language Studies,* **7** (1971), 361–73.

CHADWICK, C., The composition of the *Sonnets pour Hélène, FS*, **8** (1954), 326–32.

CUISIAT, D., La lyre crossée. Un épisode de la vie de Ronsard (Anet et Fontainebleau, août 1556), *BHR*, **31** (1969), 467–80.

DAGENS, J., La théologie poétique au temps de Ronsard, in *Atti del Quinto Congresso Internazionale di Lingue e Letterature Moderne,* Florence, 1955, 147–53.

DASSONVILLE, M., Éléments pour une définition de l'hymne ronsardien, *BHR*, **24** (1962), 58–76.

—— Pour une interprétation nouvelle des *Amours* de Ronsard, *BHR*, **28** (1966), 241–70.

DAVIS, G., Colour in Ronsard's poetry, *MLR*, **40** (1945), 95–103.

Select Bibliography

DÉDÉYAN, C., Henri II, *La Franciade* et les *Hymnes* de 1555–1556, *BHR*, **9** (1947), 114–28.

FAISANT, C., Les relations de Ronsard et de Desportes, *BHR*, **28** (1966), 323–53.

FRANCHET, H., Erasme et Ronsard, *Revue de l'histoire littéraire de la France*, **39** (1932), 321–38.

FRANÇON, M., Ronsard panégyriste de la cour, *Convivium*, 1954, 556–64.

GADOFFRE, G., Ronsard et la pensée ficinienne, *Archives de philosophie* (January 1963), pp. 45–58.

—— Ronsard et le thème solaire, in *Le Soleil à la Renaissance. sciences et mythes* (colloque international, 1963), Brussels, Presses Universitaires de Bruxelles; Paris, Presses Universitaires de France, 1965, 501–18.

HORNIK, H., More on Ronsard's philosophy: the hymns and neoplatonism, *BHR*, **27** (1965), 435–43.

JOHNSON, W. M., and GRAHAM, V. E., Ronsard et la *Renommée* du Louvre, *BHR*, **30** (1968), 7–17.

KATZ, R. A., Ronsard and the theatre, *RR*, **57** (1966), 252–62.

LAPP, J. C., The potter and his clay: mythological imagery in Ronsard, *Yale French Studies*, **38** (1967), 89–108.

LEBÈGUE, R., Ronsard poète officiel, in *Studi in onore di V. Lugli e D. Valeri*, Venice, Neri Pozza, 1961, volume II, 573–87.

LONGNON, H., Les déboires de Ronsard à la cour. I: Les outrages de Melin de Saint-Gelais. II: Avanie à Hélène de Surgères, *BHR*, **12** (1950), 60–80.

MCFARLANE, I. D., Neo-Latin verse: some new discoveries, *MLR*, **54** (1959), 22–8.

MARGOLIN, J-C., L'*Hymne de l'or* et son ambiguïté, *BHR*, **28** (1966), 271–93.

MICHEL, J. G., Ronsard's *Victoire de François de Bourbon* – a reappraisal, *Studies in Philology*, **59** (1962), 97–110.

MORRISON, M., Ronsard and Catullus: the influence of the teaching of Marc-Antoine de Muret, *BHR*, **18** (1956), 240–74.

—— Ronsard and Desportes, *BHR*, **28** (1966), 294–322.

Ronsard the poet

NAÏS, H., A propos des corrections de Ronsard dans ses *Œuvres complètes*, BHR, **20** (1958), 405–20.

PELAN, M., Ronsard's *Amour d'automne, FS*, **7** (1953), 214–22.

QUAINTON, M., Some classical references, sources and identities in Ronsard's *Priere à la fortune, FS*, **21** (1967), 293–301.

—— Ronsard's philosophical and cosmological conceptions of time, *FS*, **23** (1969), 1–22.

RICHMOND, H. M., Rural lyricism: a Renaissance mutation of the pastoral, *CL*, **16** (1964), 193–210.

SANDMANN, M., '. . . ma douce fleur nouvelle' (Ronsard, *Chanson*), in *The French Renaissance and its Heritage. Essays presented to Alan M. Boase,* ed. D. R. Haggis and others, London, Methuen, 1968, 217–33.

SAULNIER, V-L., Autour du Colloque de Poissy: les avatars d'une chanson de Saint-Gelais à Ronsard et Théophile, *BHR*, **20** (1958), 44–78.

SAYCE, R. A., Ronsard and mannerism: the *Elegie à Janet, L'Esprit créateur*, **6** (1966), 234–47.

SILVER, I., Ronsard studies (1936–1950), *BHR*, **12** (1950), 332–64.

—— Ronsard studies (1951–1955), *BHR*, **22** (1960), 214–68.

—— Ronsard comparatist studies: achievements and perspectives, *CL*, **6** (1954), 148–73.

—— Pierre de Ronsard: panegyrist, pensioner and satirist of the French court, *RR*, **45** (1954), 89–108.

—— Ronsard's ethical thought, *BHR*, **24** (1962), 88–117; 339–74.

—— Ronsard's reflections on cosmogony and nature, *PMLA*, 79 (1964), 219–33.

—— Ronsard's reflections on the heavens and time, *PMLA*, 80 (1965), 344–64.

—— The qualities and conditions of the true poet according to Ronsard, in *Mélanges d'histoire littéraire, XVIe–XVIIe siècles, offerts à Raymond Lebègue*, Paris, Nizet, 1969, 83–90.

(*Note:* the articles listed above represent only a fraction of Silver's considerable output of studies on Ronsard: many of his earlier articles were absorbed into the material of the books

Select Bibliography

mentioned above, section (ii); the forthcoming volumes of *The Intellectual Evolution of Ronsard* will draw on many others.)

SMITH, M. C., Ronsard and Queen Elizabeth I, *BHR*, **29** (1967), 93–119.

SPITZER, L., Le *Bel Aubépin* de Ronsard: nouvel essai d'explication, *Le Français moderne*, **8** (1940), 223–36.

STEGMANN, A., L'inspiration platonicienne dans les *Hymnes* de Ronsard, *Revue des sciences humaines*, 1966, 193–210.

TROUSSON, R., Le mythe de Prométhée et de Pandore chez Ronsard, *Bulletin de l'Association Guillaume Budé*, 1961, 351–9.

—— Ronsard et la légende d'Hercule, *BHR*, **24** (1962), 77–87.

VON STACKELBERG, J., Ronsard und Aristoteles: zum Aufkommen der Wahrscheinlichkeitslehre in der französischen Dichtungstheorie der Renaissance, *BHR*, **25** (1963), 349–61.

WINTER, J. F., Visual diversity and spatial grandeur in Ronsard's *Ode à Michel de l'Hospital*, *Symposium*, **21** (1967), 331–7.

(IV) GENERAL STUDIES AND COLLECTIONS

BOURCIEZ, E., *Les Mœurs polies et la littérature de cour sous Henri II*, Paris, Hachette, 1886; Geneva, Slatkine, 1967.

CASTOR, G., *Pléiade Poetics: a study in sixteenth-century thought and terminology*, Cambridge University Press, 1964.

CHAMARD, H., *Histoire de la Pléiade*, 4 volumes, Paris, Didier, 1939–40.

CHARBONNIER, F., *La Poésie française et les guerres de religion, 1560–1574*, Paris, Bureau de la Revue des Œuvres Nouvelles, 1919; Geneva, Slatkine, 1969.

CIORANESCO, A., *L'Arioste en France, des origines à la fin du* XVIIIe *siècle*, 2 volumes, Paris, Presses Modernes, 1939.

CLEMENTS, R. J., *Critical Theory and Practice of the Pléiade*, Cambridge, Mass., Harvard University Press, 1942; New York, Octagon Books, 1970.

DASSONVILLE, M., La collaboration de la Pléiade à la *Dialectique* de P. de la Ramée, *BHR*, **25** (1963), 337–48.

DEMERSON, G., *La Mythologie classique dans l'œuvre lyrique de la 'Pléiade'*, Geneva, Droz (*THR*), 1972.

Ronsard the poet

FESTUGIÈRE, J., *La Philosophie de l'amour de Marsile Ficin et son influence sur la littérature française du* XVIe *siècle*, Paris, Vrin, 1941.

Les Fêtes de la Renaissance, ed. J. Jacquot, volume I, Paris, CNRS, 1956; vol. II: *Fêtes et cérémonies au temps de Charles Quint,* Paris, CNRS, 1960.

FORSTER, L., *The Icy Fire: five studies in European petrarchism,* Cambridge University Press, 1969.

HATZFELD, H., The role of mythology in poetry during the French Renaissance, *Modern Language Quarterly,* **13** (1952), 392–404.

HULUBEI, A., *L'Eglogue en France au* XVIe *siècle,* Paris, Droz, 1938.

Humanism in France at the End of the Middle Ages and in the Early Renaissance, ed. A. H. T. Levi, Manchester University Press, 1970.

HUTTON, J., *The Greek Anthology in France and in the Latin Writers of the Netherlands,* Ithaca, Cornell University Press, 1946.

JOUKOVSKY (JOUKOVSKY-MICHA), F., *La Gloire dans la poésie française et néolatine du* XVIe *siècle des rhétoriqueurs à Agrippa d'Aubigné,* Geneva, Droz (THR), 1969.

—— *Poésie et mythologie au* XVIe *siècle. Quelques mythes de l'inspiration chez les poètes de la Renaissance,* Paris, Nizet, 1969.

—— *Orphée et ses disciples dans la poésie française et néolatine du* XVIe *siècle,* Geneva, Droz, 1970.

—— La guerre des dieux et des géants chez les poètes français du XVIe siècle (1500–1585), *BHR,* **29** (1967), 55–92.

JOURDA, P., La Pléiade et les poètes antiques, in *Actes du Congrès de Lyon (1958) de l'Association Guillaume Budé,* Paris, Les Belles Lettres, 1960, 378–408.

JUNG, M-R., *Hercule dans la littérature française du* XVIe *siècle. De l'Hercule courtois à l'Hercule baroque,* Geneva, Droz (THR), 1966.

LEBÈGUE, R., *La Poésie française de 1560 à 1630,* 2 volumes, Paris, Société d'Enseignement Supérieur, 1951.

—— Horace en France pendant la Renaissance, *Humanisme et Renaissance,* **3** (1936), 141–64; 289–308; 384–419.

Lumières de la Pléiade (neuvième stage international d'études humanistes, Tours, 1965), Paris, Vrin, 1966.

Select Bibliography

Mélanges d'histoire littéraire de la Renaissance offerts à Henri Chamard, Paris, Nizet, 1951.

MERRILL, R. V., and CLEMENTS, R. J., *Platonism in French Renaissance Poetry,* New York University Press, 1957.

MOURGUES, O. DE, *Metaphysical, Baroque and Précieux Poetry,* Oxford University Press, 1953.

Musique et poésie au XVIe siècle, ed. J. Jacquot, Paris, CNRS, 1954.

NAÏS, H., *Les Animaux dans la poésie française de la Renaissance. Science: symbolique: poésie,* Paris, Didier, 1961.

PATTERSON, W. F., *Three Centuries of French Poetic Theory. A Critical History of the Chief Arts of Poetry in France (1328–1630),* 2 volumes, Ann Arbor, University of Michigan Press, 1935.

RAYMOND, M., *Baroque et Renaissance poétique,* Paris, Corti, 1955.

—— *La Poésie française et le maniérisme,* Geneva, Droz; Paris, Minard (TLF), 1971.

SCHMIDT, A-M., *La Poésie scientifique en France au seizième siècle,* Paris, Albin Michel, 1938.

SEZNEC, J., *The Survival of the Pagan Gods,* New York, Pantheon, 1953; Harper Torchbooks, 1961 (first published as *La Survivance des dieux antiques,* Warburg Institute, University of London, 1940).

VIANEY, J., *Le Pétrarquisme en France au XVIe siècle,* Montpellier, Coulet, 1909; Geneva, Slatkine, 1969.

WALKER, D. P., The *Prisca Theologia* in France, *Journal of the Warburg and Courtauld Institutes,* 17 (1954), 204–59.

WEBER, H., *La Création poétique au seizième siècle en France de Maurice Scève à Agrippa d'Aubigné,* 2 volumes, Paris, Nizet, 1956.

WILSON, D. B., *Descriptive Poetry in France from Blason to Baroque,* Manchester University Press, 1967.

YATES, F., *The French Academies of the Sixteenth Century,* Warburg Institute, University of London, 1947.

Chronological list of texts cited

The dates given here are those of the first published edition. Separate publications are indicated by the use of bold type. Roman numerals following principal titles refer to the relevant volume number in the Laumonier edition; Arabic numerals denote page numbers in the present volume. Titles within each separate publication are listed in the order in which they appear in Laumonier, with the exception of sequences of love poems, for which incipits are given in alphabetical order. In each case, as much information is given as seemed necessary to facilitate identification of the text: square brackets indicate a significant 1584 variant. However, not all changes have been indicated: for example, certain *elegies* appeared later as *discours*; in such cases, the indication of the incipit should avoid confusion. Certain titles have been abbreviated, and capitalization (in titles, not incipits) made consistent.

Asterisks indicate texts of particular importance, both in their own right and within the context of the present volume; no selection has been indicated for sonnet sequences since in these instances a handful of poems cannot be representative.

1549 Avantentrée du Roi treschrestien à Paris (I), 204n, 241

L'Hymne de France* (I), 58, 173n, 219, 220
Fantaisie à sa dame, 41

1550 Les Quatre Premiers Livres des odes . . . Ensemble son bocage (I–II)
Au lecteur: 'Si les hommes',* 166, 173, 206, 215, 218
Livre 1:
Au seigneur de Carnavalet,* 52, 220, 221
La Victoire de Gui de Chabot, 36
A Jouachim Du Bellai Angevin: 'Aujourdui je me vanterai', 171n
A Jan Martin, 203–4
A Joachim Du Bellai Angevin: 'Celui qui ne nous honore',* 198n

A sa lire: 'Lire dorée',* 206n, 230
Livre 2:
A René d'Oradour, 40
A sa guiterre, 161, 164, 230
A Cassandre: 'Ma petite columbelle', 214
A son lict, 201
Des peintures contenues dedans un tableau,* 25, 164, 165, 171, 175–6, 186
Livre 3:
A maistre Denis Lambin, 129
La Defloration de Lede,* 161, 164–5, 172, 201
A Mercure, 224
Livre 4:
De l'election de son sepulcre,* 35–6
A Gui Peccate, 36
Veu au somme, 58
Le Ravissement de Cephale,* 76, 160, 165, 328n
A sa Muse: 'Plus dur que fer',* 225

Chronological list

Au conte d'Alsinois: 'Bien que le reply de Sarte',* 64, 139n, 171n
Les Bacchanales ou le folastrissime voyage d'Hercueil,* 77

1553 Livret de folastries (V)
Premiere Folastrie, 130
Folastrie VIII: Le Nuage, ou l'yvrogne,* 46, 197
Dithyrambes,* 69, 70, 173n, 196

Les Amours . . . nouvellement augmentées . . . Plus quelques odes (V)
Sonnets:
  'Ha seigneur Dieu [Que de beautez]', 33
  'Plus mile fois [Plus que les Rois]', 233–5
  'Sur mes vint ans', 109n
Ode à Cassandre: 'Mignonne, allon voir',* 113, 287, 303

Le Cinqieme des odes . . . augmenté. Ensemble la harangue . . . (V)
Harangue que fit monseigneur le duc de Guise, 250
Elegie à M. A. de Muret, 146
A la fonteine Bélerie: 'Je veus, Muses aus beaux yeus', 229

1554 Le Bocage (VI)
Epitafe d'Albert, joüeur de luc du Roi, 232

1555 Les Meslanges[1] (VI)
A sa lyre: 'Naguiere chanter je voulois', 224
Elegie à Janet peintre du Roi: 'Pein moi, Janet',* 33, 312
Elegie du verre: 'Ceus que la Muse aimera [les Sœurs aimeront]',* 22–3, 54–5
L'Hinne de Bacus,* 70–1, 150n, 173n, 186, 193, 195, 198n, 329n
Ode à Christofle de Choiseul: 'Mon Choiseul, leve tes yeux', 64

Les Quatre Premiers Livres des odes (VII)
Livre 4: Epitaphe de Jan de La Peruse, 62

Continuation des amours (VII)
'Aurat, apres ta mort', 40
'Douce, belle, gentille [amoureuse]', 202
'Marie, vous avés la joue', 322
'Tu as beau, Jupiter', 202

Les Hymnes (VIII)
A tresillustre . . . Odet Cardinal de Chastillon (*dedicatory piece*), 256n
Hymne du . . . Roy de France Henry II,* 72–3, 204, 242, 243–4
Hymne de la justice,* 150, 151, 184n, 242, 245
Le Temple de messeigneurs le Connestable, et des Chastillons, 74–5, 245
Hymne de la philosophie,* 18, 58, 75, 146n, 151, 194, 195, 242, 245, 311n
Priere à la fortune, 245n, 256n
Les Daimons,* 46, 146, 151–2, 195–6
Hymne du ciel,* 24, 38–9, 144n, 146n, 152–3, 173n, 195, 228
Hymne des astres, 153, 195
Hymne de la mort,* 20, 39, 61–2, 143, 154, 195, 315
Hymne de l'or, 22, 154
Hercule chrestien,* 154–5, 185, 186, 242–3, 245
Epistre à Charles de Pisseleu: 'Avant que l'homme', 155
Epitaphe de Loyse de Mailly, 143n

1556 Nouvelle Continuation des amours (VII)
Sonnet: 'Les villes et les bourgs', 322
Chanson: 'Je ne veulx plus que chanter [Je veus chanter en ces vers]', 43
Ode: 'Quand je dors', 315, 316
L'Alouette, 30
[Elegie] à son livre: 'Mon fils, si tu sçavois',* 80, 101n, 130

Le Second Livre des hymnes (VIII)
Hymne de l'eternité,* 22, 37, 155, 195

---

[1] 'Achevé d'imprimer' 1554.

Chronological list

[1] On the dating of this collection, see *L* XII, v–viii.

Ronsard the poet

Chronological list

[1] MSS. of prose discourses delivered by Ronsard at the Palace Academy, date uncertain.

[2] Much of the love poetry which appeared for the first time in this edition was composed in the latter part of the reign of Charles IX (1570–4): see L XVII, Introduction, and notes to individual poems.

[1] Probably composed in 1573, at about the same time as *Ronsard au Roy Charles IX* (see above): for the evidence for this date, see *L* XVIII–ii, 299n.
[2] Presumably composed at about the same time as the *Ode au Roy Charles luy donnant un Leon Hebrieu* (published 1575, composed probably in 1573).
[3] Composed later than June 1584: see *L* XVIII–ii, 315n.
[4] MS., date uncertain: 1576? 1583? (see *L* XVIII–ii, 499n).

Index of names

Index

Index

Index of principal themes

Many of the entries represent thematic areas rather than precisely delimited themes; the synonyms provided in parenthesis are intended to be representative rather than exhaustive.

(I) GENERAL THEMES

abundance (fertility, plenitude, variety etc.; *see also* section (II), *copia*), 4, 19, **24–6**, 27, 33, 34, **38–9**, 48, 51, 56, 57, 60, 64, 65, 66, 72, 77, 78, **86–96** *passim*, 118, 157, **160–75** *passim*, 177, 178, 187–8, **191–2**, 194, 198, 199, 200, 204, 205, 206–7, 208, 225, 252, 272, 292–3, 299, 329, 330, 331

allegory (excluding allegorical personification, for which *see* section (II), personification), 6, 13, 40–1, 71, 83, 98, 138, 155, 165, **181–6**, 191, 196, 200, 202, 206, 207, 241, 242–3, 275, 277

classical influences (*see also* mythology, neoplatonism; and individual authors in index of names), 2, 16, 40–1, 48, 67, 68, 71, 78, 80, 84, 87, 92n, **93–4**, **95**, **109**, 116, 123, **127–31** *passim*, 139, 155, 159, **161**, 165–6, 166–7, **168–9**, 171, 175, 182, 192, 195, 202, 209, **212–16** *passim*, 218, 219, 225, 227, 229, 232, 233, 283, **306–7**, 310–11, 316, 317

cosmos (cosmology, the heavens etc.), 6, 13, 15, 24, 26, 39, 48, 86, 123, 124, 129, 131, 138, **139–41**, 145, 147, **151–4**, 173, 181, 184–5, 187, 189, **194–5**, 201, 204, 216, 228–9, 235–6, 253, 290, 291, **295–300**, 302, 311–12, 328

court (encomium, anti-aulic themes etc.), 5, 6, 10, 41, 49, 51, 52, 62, 65, 68, 70, 72–3, 74–5, 122, 130–1, 133, 134, 135, 137, 155, 156, 159, **162–4**, 165, 175, 176, 184, 189–90, 191, **203–5**, 211, 220, **230–8**, 239, **241–5**, 253, **255–7**, 260, 264, 273–4, **275–85**, 292, 303, **310–13**, 318

daimons, 41, 46, 48, 68, 69, 138, 146, 150, **151–2**, 153, **195–6**, 201

death, 8, 9, 34, 35–6, 37, 40, 48, 50, 51, **57–8**, 59, **61–2**, 63, 148, **154**, 158, 290, 301–2, 303, 311, **315–18**

dream, 4, 34, 36, 41, **43–5**, 53, 54, 55, 56, 63, 64, 69, 78, **91–5**, 98n, **115–18**, 151, 316, 323

fate (influence of stars, astrology etc.), 15, 44, 48, 56, 63, 71, 100, 153, 272, **298–300**, 318

golden age, **63**, 74, 75, 151, 204, 205, 216, 236, 252, 281

illusion (disillusionment), 5, 19, 23, **43–54** *passim*, 92, 94, **116**, 117–18, 120, 135, 156, 158, 160, 203–4, 205, 236, 255–7, 312, 316

imagination (fantasy) (as sixteenth-century concepts), 13, 16, 44, 45, 63, **144–6**, **147–8**, 152, 158, 177, 178, 181, **197–9**, 311

Index

inspiration (*fureur*, vatic conception of poet), 2, 5, 16, 48, 52, 69, 123, **124, 126**, 138, **140–9** *passim*, 155, **176–8**, 179, 181, 184, **185–6**, **187, 188**, 190, **191–2**, **193**, 194, **197–201**, 206, 213, 220–1, 244, 245, 248, 256, 260, 261, 265, 269, **271–2**, 274, 278, 294, 311

love (love poetry), 1–2, 4, 5, 9, 19, 21, 22, 27, **31–3**, **34–5**, 36, 37–8, 39, 41, 42, 43, 45, 49, 51, 56, 58, 61, 62, 64–5, 70, 72, **79–120**, 122, 124, 125, 126, **128–37**, 148, 155, 191, 201–2, 206n, 211–13, 214, 219, 221, 231–2, 233–6, 238, 241, 261, 283, 288–9, 289–90, 291, **300–2**, 303, 304, 306–7, 308–10, **319–31**

metamorphosis, 4, 34, 39, **40–3**, 46, 61, 64, 69, 70, **91**, **179–80**, 294, 313, 320–1, 323, 324, 330

movement, 18, 19, 20, **26–34**, 46, 47, 50, 61, 67, **114–15**, 173n, **288–302**, 307, 318, 325

music, 2, 4, 6–7, 23, 55, 71, 124, 133, 138, **139–41**, 143, 152, 164, 175, **209–39**, 278, 280, 281, 282, 283, 284

mythology, 2, 4, 6, 7, 8, 19, 21, 27, 33, 40, 41, 56, 63, **69–71**, 73, 90–1, 118, 121, 122, **138–58** *passim*, **159–208**, 209, **225–9**, 230, **243–5**, 250, 254, 259, 274–5, 276–7, 281, 282, 303, 305, 306, 308, 309, 313, **320–31** *passim*

nature (landscape, seasons, natural processes, nature personified etc.),[1] **17–23** *passim*, **26–36** *passim*, 42, 46–8, 50, 51, 57, 59, **63–6**, 85–7, 87–8, 100, 131–2, 157, 160, **173–4**, 176–80 *passim*, 187, 188, 191, 194, 195, 206, 225, 228, 280, **288–93** *passim*, 298, 299, **302–9** *passim*, 318, 329, 330

neoplatonism (*see also* allegory, inspiration), 4, 5, 13, 15, 16, 33, 49, 70, 79, 96–7, 107n, **121–58**, **182–4**, 187, 191, 199, 201, 283, 288–9

painting (and other visual arts; both literal and metaphorical references included), 6, 25, 26, 33, 64, 72, 74, 159, 161, **162–5**, 171, 173, 174, 175, **177–8**, 204n, 242, 244, 250, 252, 278, 312, 330

pastoral, 59, 62, 63, 65, 71, 72, 88, 127, 130–1, 161, 164, 173, 175, 176–7, 180, 191, 200, 202, 205, **221–4**, **279–82**

petrarchism, 4, 5, 14, 15, 34, 35, 40, 41, 49, 72, **79–120** *passim*, 128, 306, 309

poetic theory (*see also* allegory, imagination, inspiration), 9, 16, 20–1, 29, 65, 71, 123, **166–74** *passim*, 183, 193, 206, **215–17**, 238, 249, 258–9, 269n, 275, 279, 302–3, 304n

polemics and politics, 4, 7–8, 10, 131, 135, 147, 150, 156, 191, 233, 236, **241–85**, 321n

religion (Christian and biblical reference, theology etc.; *see also* wars of religion), 2, 6, 7–8, 10, 15, 26, 40, 44, 62, 63, 69, 70, 81, **123–7**, 134, **138–55** *passim*, **182–4**, 185, 186, 193, 194–5, 197, 208, 242–3, 253–4, **257–70** *passim*, 273, 274, 285, 318, 320, 321n

time (youth, old age, decay, etc.; immortality, eternity; past, present, future), 5, 7, 8, 16, 22, 24, 27, 35, 36, 37, 38–9, 42–3, 44, 49, 50, 51, 56, 57, 59, 64, 70, 73, 74, 77, 78, 99, **108–9**, 112, 115, 119, 147, 163–4, 175–6, 180, 181, 192, 195, 196, 198, **200–8** *passim*, 220, 228, 236, 244, 245, 277–8, 281, 288, 299, **300–2**, 303, 309–10, 312, **314–18**, 324, 330

wars of religion, 7, 57, 63, 65, 127, 131, 134–5, 147, 150, 156, 204–5, 230, 257, **261–9** *passim*, 273, 275, 278–9, 282–4, 321n

[1] On nature as a concept, see 124–7.

Ronsard the poet

[1] Imagery and types of image have been excluded from this list because the whole book revolves around the question of Ronsard's poetic imagination and the quantity of references would simply be confusing. However, in addition to themes already listed which are connected with imagery (abundance, allegory, cosmos, dream, golden age, metamorphosis, movement, mythology, nature, painting, pastoral, petrarchism, time), the reader will find detailed discussion of images and their use in chapter 1, *passim*; chapter 2, especially pp. 83–97; chapter 4, especially pp. 160–80; chapter 5, especially pp. 218–25; chapter 6, especially pp. 242–54; chapter 7, *passim*; and Epilogue, especially pp. 228–30.